RELATIONAL ARCHAEOLOGIES

Many of us accept as uncontroversial the belief that the world is comprised of detached and disparate products, all of which are reducible to certain substances. Of those things that are alive, we acknowledge that some have agency while others, such as humans, have more advanced qualities such as consciousness, reason, and intentionality. So deeply seated is this metaphysical belief, along with the related distinctions we draw between subject/object, mind/body, and nature/culture, that many of us tacitly assume past groups approached and apprehended the world in a similar fashion. *Relational Archaeologies* questions how such a view of human beings, 'other-than-human' creatures, and things affects our reconstruction of past beliefs and practices. It proceeds from the position that, in many cases, past societies understood their place in the world as positional rather than categorical, as persons bound up in reticular arrangements with similar and not-so-similar forms, regardless of their substantive qualities.

Relational Archaeologies explores this idea by emphasizing how humans, animals, and things come to exist by virtue of the dynamic and fluid processes of connection and transaction. In highlighting various counter-Modern notions of what it means 'to be' and how these can be teased apart using archaeological materials, contributors provide a range of approaches, from primarily theoretical/historicized treatments of the topic, to practical applications or case studies from the Americas, the UK, Europe, Asia, and Australia.

Christopher Watts is a SSHRC Postdoctoral Fellow at the University of Western Ontario in London, Canada, and a Research Associate at the Royal Ontario Museum in Toronto.

RELATIONAL ARCHAEOLOGIES

Humans, animals, things

Edited by
Christopher Watts

Routledge
Taylor & Francis Group

LONDON AND NEW YORK

First published 2013
by Routledge
2 Park Square, Milton Park, Abingdon, Oxon OX14 4RN

Simultaneously published in the USA and Canada
by Routledge
711 Third Avenue, New York, NY 10017

Routledge is an imprint of the Taylor & Francis Group, an informa business

British Library Cataloguing in Publication Data
A catalogue record for this book is available from the British Library

Library of Congress Cataloging in Publication Data
Relational archaeologies : humans, animals, things / edited by Christopher Watts.
pages. cm
Includes bibliographical references and index.
1. Archaeology--Philosophy. 2. Agent (Philosophy) 3. Ontology. 4. Relationism.
5. Human–animal relationships. 6. Human–plant relationships. 7. Material culture.
I. Watts, Christopher M., 1972- author, editor of compilation.
CC75.R455 2013
930.1--dc23
2012044453

ISBN: 978-0-415-52531-2 (hbk)
ISBN: 978-0-415-52532-9 (pbk)
ISBN: 978-0-203-55313-8 (ebk)

Typeset in Bembo
by Taylor and Francis Books

Printed and bound in Great Britain by
TJ International Ltd, Padstow, Cornwall

CONTENTS

LIST OF FIGURES

LIST OF TABLES

LIST OF CONTRIBUTORS

Vladimir I. Bazaliiskii is a Senior Researcher at Irkutsk State University in Russia. His scholarly interests include Middle Holocene mortuary practices in Eastern Siberia, Siberian Neolithic and Early Bronze Age foragers, human osteology, and mortuary archaeology.

Dušan Borić is Lecturer in Archaeology in the School of History, Archaeology and Religion at Cardiff University. His research interests include embodiment, social memory, foraging/farming change, and past cultural identities in European and Near Eastern early prehistory, particularly in the Balkans.

Kate Faccia is a Postdoctoral Fellow in the Division of Biological Anthropology at the University of Cambridge. Her research interests include osteoarchaeology, mortuary archaeology, skeletal biology, skeletal adaptation, and Northern foraging populations.

Vesa–Pekka Herva is an Assistant Professor in Heritage Studies at the University of Helsinki. His research interests are varied and range from the dynamics of Neolithization to the heritage of modern conflict. His recent research has focused on human–environment relations and cosmologies on the northeastern margins of early modern Europe.

Oliver J. T. Harris is Lecturer in Archaeology in the School of Archaeology and Ancient History at the University of Leicester. His research interests include Neolithic and Bronze Age Britain as well as issues surrounding the body, emotion, personhood, phenomenology, and the archaeology of communities.

Daniela Hofmann is a Researcher in the School of History, Archaeology and Religion at Cardiff University. Her academic interests lie in the Neolithic of

Central Europe, particularly the Linearbandkeramik and its successor cultures, along with issues of architecture, personhood, identity, and the body.

Tim Ingold is Professor of Social Anthropology at the University of Aberdeen. He has carried out ethnographic fieldwork in Lapland, and has written on environment, technology, and social organization in the circumpolar North, as well as on evolutionary theory, human-animal relations, language and tool use, environmental perception, and skilled practice. He is currently exploring issues on the interface between anthropology, archaeology, art, and architecture.

Angela R. Lieverse is an Associate Professor in the Department of Archaeology and Anthropology at the University of Saskatchewan. Her research interests include bioarchaeology, skeletal biology, paleopathology, dental anthropology, and human taphonomy among ancient hunter-gatherers of the circumpolar North (particularly Siberia and Hokkaido).

Robert J. Losey is an Associate Professor in the Department of Anthropology at the University of Alberta and a Research Associate at the Smithsonian Museum of Natural History. His scholarly interests include zooarchaeology, mortuary archaeology, human-animal relationships, fishing, and the archaeology of natural disasters within Northwest Coast and Siberian contexts.

Ian J. McNiven is Professor of Archaeology in the School of Geography and Environmental Science at Monash University. He specializes in Australian Aboriginal and Torres Strait Islander maritime societies and the spiritual and ritual dimensions of seascapes. His books include *The Social Archaeology of Australian Indigenous Societies* (2006) and *Appropriated Pasts: Indigenous Peoples and the Colonial Culture of Archaeology* (2005).

Barbara J. Mills is Professor and Director of the School of Anthropology at the University of Arizona as well as Curator of Archaeology at the Arizona State Museum. Her research interests include the archaeology of the American Southwest, materiality, social networks in archaeology, archaeologies of inequality (especially gender and colonialism), migration, identity, and heritage preservation.

Wendi Field Murray is a Doctoral Candidate in the School of Anthropology at the University of Arizona and a Research Archaeologist/Collections Manager for the State Historical Society of North Dakota. Her research currently focuses on coalescent processes and their effects on the historical and contemporary identities of Native American communities on the Missouri River. She has conducted ethnographic and archaeological fieldwork in New England, Alaska, the Northern Plains, and the Southwest.

Jonas M. Nordin is a Postdoctoral Researcher in Historical Archaeology at the National Historical Museum in Stockholm. He has worked on various issues in medieval archaeology and, in recent years, on processes of commodification and the use of history in early industrial societies. He is presently engaged in research concerning early modern colonialism and globalization.

Andrew Shapland is a Curator in the Department of Greece and Rome at the British Museum. His research interests revolve around the Greek Bronze Age and the role of material culture in human–animal relations. His PhD thesis examined animal depictions and animal remains in Bronze Age Crete.

Andrea Waters-Rist is an Assistant Professor of Osteoarchaeology in the Faculty of Archaeology at Leiden University. Her research interests include paleonutrition, paleopathology, and the dental anthropology of past populations from Siberia, Northwest Europe, and Central America.

Christopher Watts is a SSHRC Postdoctoral Fellow in the Department of Anthropology at the University of Western Ontario and a Research Associate at the Royal Ontario Museum. His research interests include the archaeology of Northeastern North America, particularly the Late Woodland Traditions of the lower Great Lakes, as well as issues in material culture studies, ceramic artifacts and technologies, human–animal relations, ecology, and archaeological theory.

Andrzej W. Weber is a Professor in the Department of Anthropology at the University of Alberta. His research interests are centered on the Holocene foragers of Northeast Asia, and he has completed thirteen years of fieldwork at hunter-gatherer habitation sites and cemeteries in the Cis-Baikal region of Eastern Siberia and two years of fieldwork on Rebun Island near Hokkaido, Japan.

Mary Weismantel is a Professor in the Department of Anthropology and Director of Gender and Sexuality Studies at Northwestern University. Her work in the Andean region of South America has covered topics ranging from food to adoption, and from contemporary popular culture to ancient ceramics. Her areas of expertise include Pre-Colombian art and materiality as well as race and sex.

Peter Whitridge is an Associate Professor in the Department of Archaeology at Memorial University of Newfoundland. His research interests include hunter-fisher-gatherer social and economic relations, the body, place and landscape, and the human-animal interface.

María Nieves Zedeño is Professor in the School of Anthropology and Co-Chair of the Bureau of Applied Research in Anthropology at the University of Arizona. Her recent work has focused on integrating archaeology, ethnohistory, and ethnography within an investigative framework oriented toward Indigenous land use history, territorial organization, and social cohesion in the North American Plains, Great Lakes, and Rocky Mountains.

ACKNOWLEDGMENTS

I wish to thank the various contributors to this book, all of whom worked diligently to produce such insightful work. Apart from contributions by Weismantel, McNiven, Herva and Nordin, Whitridge, and Ingold, versions of these papers were read in a session I organized at the 2012 Society for American Archaeology Meeting in Memphis entitled 'No (Hu)man Is an Island: Relational Ontologies in the Archaeological Past,' which also provided a forum for the exchange of ideas among the various participants. I am also grateful to Matthew Gibbons and Amy Davis-Poynter at Routledge for their editorial assistance, and to John Laford for permission to reproduce his work 'Circle Singers' on the cover. Finally, this volume was edited while I was supported by the Rebanks Postdoctoral Fellowship in New World Archaeology at the Royal Ontario Museum and, more recently, a Social Sciences and Humanities Research Council of Canada Postdoctoral Fellowship at the University of Western Ontario.

1

RELATIONAL ARCHAEOLOGIES: ROOTS AND ROUTES

Christopher Watts

Introduction

What would an understanding of the Andean past look like if stones were understood to disgrace or even destroy their human interlocutors? How might our sense of ancient wayfaring in the Canadian Arctic be altered by a 'zoocentric' perspective? Why was it considered necessary for Torres Strait Islanders to curate and construct intricate mounds of marine mammal bones? More broadly, how can we understand such practices and account for them in our research designs, field methods, and artifact analyses? These are just some of the questions posed by the contributors to this volume, all of whom advance a 'relational' understanding of past peoples and the animals, plants, and things with which their lives were entangled.

Defined here as a suite of approaches aimed at conflating the abstract and immutable dualities of modernist ontologies (e.g., nature and culture, self and other, subject and object, mind and body), relationality has been increasingly employed both as a conceptual device and heuristic technique by researchers across the social sciences and humanities. Such perspectives often highlight the transactions, translations, and transformations that are carried on between humans and non-humans, as opposed to the analysis of 'interaction effects' among pre-existing, self-contained entities. Generally speaking, this results in a concern with the relations themselves – the linkages rather than the nodes, the actions rather than the substances – in considering how various forms emerge and evolve together across space and through time. By tracing the contextual and contingent paths along which such forms come into being, as opposed to populating the categorical spaces of assorted dualist narratives, relational thinking shifts our analytical focus to the ways in which entities, thought of as processes rather than existents, become entwined. This is lucidly illustrated in the work of biologist Donna Haraway, whose cyborg theory (1985) and concepts of 'natureculture' and 'companion species'[1] (e.g., 2003, 2007) subvert traditional accounts of non-human animals and things as externalized entities with which we intermingle and of the 'social' contexts within which they are gathered. In their stead, Haraway offers a rich and nuanced recasting of the relationships which ultimately bring about ontic categories (e.g., humans and dogs). We, as humans, develop relationally with our 'partners' in the world through a process Haraway (2007:vii) refers to as "lively knotting."

A comparable metaphor is found in the recent work of Tim Ingold (e.g., 2007, 2011, this volume), where a process-oriented and thoroughly relational emphasis on 'meshworks' and entanglements is intended to capture the co-continuous flow of humans and non-humans along paths. This work builds upon Ingold's much celebrated collection of essays, *The Perception of the Environment* (2000), which sought to dismantle the "overriding academic division of labour between the disciplines that deal, on the one hand, with the human mind and its manifold linguistic, social and cultural products, and on the other, with the structures and composition of the material world" (Ingold 2000:1). Holding fast to such a dichotomy, Ingold argues, serves to cleave what is in fact a unified phenomenon. We do not simply traverse the world, confronting and abstracting objects of consciousness, but rather 'dwell' within it, open up to it, and incorporate it within ourselves as sensuous beings. Moreover, it is as whole bodies, rather than ethereal minds, that we develop perceptions, products, and life histories born of "specific dispositions and sensibilities that lead people to orient themselves in relation to their environment and to attend to its features" in particular ways (Ingold 2000:153). Accordingly, Ingold notes, meanings are never affixed to the world, but instead arise in a continuous and concordant manner alongside the other entities and features of the environment with which we are enfolded.

Ingold's anti-essentialist critique finds a receptive audience in the contributors to this volume, several of whom (i.e., Borić and Hofmann) explicitly engage with aspects of his work. But as these and the other authors make clear, there is also a burgeoning archaeological literature dealing more specifically with the biographical (e.g., Gosden and Marshall 1999) through agential or affective properties of things (e.g., Gosden 2005; Knappett 2005; Knappett and Malafouris [eds.] 2008; Olsen 2010; Webmoor 2007; Witmore 2007), and the ways in which they are relationally implicated in human designs. Likewise, drawing inspiration from Strathern's (1988) account of the Melanesian 'dividual,' work by Fowler (e.g., 2004) and others (e.g., Brück 2001; Conneller 2004; Jones 2005; Kirk 2006) has advanced the notion of a relational personhood in archaeology involving hybridized, distributed, or permeable bodies brought forth through a recurrent exchange with others and their products. To this we may add a heightened interest among archaeologists in assessing the ontological status of non-human entities such as animals and plants, and the extent to which they were embroiled in various 'animistic' ways of being with the world (see e.g., Alberti and Bray 2009; Brown and Walker 2008; cf. Bird-David 1999). That there is extramural appeal in moving past notions of the atomistic, Western self is also attested by contemporary developments in sociology (e.g., Crossley 2011; Pachucki and Breiger 2010) and psychology (e.g., Gergen 2009). And lest we think of these as rarefied pursuits, consider for a moment the transformative effects of relational social media platforms such as Facebook and Twitter, as well as the open-source movement in computer programming. In a larger sense, we might even see the ascendancy of topical interests in 'deep ecology' (e.g., Naess 1989), indigeneity, and animal rights as reflecting a disquiet with increasingly inward-looking ways of life. If that is true, it would not be the first time an archaeological movement has followed what Durkheim called the 'collective consciousness.'

In eschewing a belief in insular human beings set over against the world, and by instead tracing the material signatures of the manifold linking past entities together, the relational archaeologies described in this volume both incorporate and advance these themes. From the placement, articulation, and juxtaposition of human and non-human remains in various depositional contexts, to the dialogic, conductive, or animistic dimensions of architectural forms and environments, each contributor parses a wealth of archaeological data from a particular region and time period while obviating conventional analytic imperatives. The result is a view of humans, animals, and things as ontologically bound up in reticular arrangements with similar and not so similar forms, as well as new and uniquely archaeological ways of thinking about the world and how past peoples recognized their place within it. In the remainder of this introductory chapter, I spell out what I see as essential to such an understanding in archaeology, seeking to clarify points of articulation between a relational approach to the past and particular philosophical works, anthropological or sociological perspectives, and ethnographic accounts, before briefly summarizing the various contributions.

Humans

> The Western conception of the person as a bounded, unique, more or less integrated motivational and cognitive universe, a dynamic center of awareness, emotion, judgment, and action organized into a distinctive whole and set contrastively both against other such wholes and against its social and natural background is, however incorrigible it may seem to us, a rather peculiar idea within the context of the world's cultures.
>
> *(Geertz 1984:126)*

One of the more noteworthy yet nebulous features of Western modes of being concerns the distinction drawn between humans and non-humans. Intentionality, language, and rational thought, as well as the qualities noted in the above passage by Geertz, figure prominently in narratives of human evolution and the exclusivity with which the human condition is often defined. After all, we are taught that only humans are capable of knowing the world, abstractly and assuredly, through acts of consciousness. Such is the legacy of eighteenth-century Enlightenment thought, particularly Cartesian rationalism: it is the privileged, purified mind of the subject that recognizes objects and gives them meaning.

While Descartes' philosophy has greatly influenced the modern Western approach to knowledge production, various alternative conceptions informed by so-called 'continental' philosophy, non-Western 'indigenous' ontologies, and posthumanist or 'new materialist' thought (e.g., Bennett 2010; Coole and Frost [eds.] 2010; Ingold 2000, 2011), have sought to challenge some of its fundamental tenets. Among continental philosophers, Heidegger (e.g., 1962 [1927]) has argued that humans are not detached analysts of the world but rather concerned users of things. Owing to our familiarity with the places, creatures, and things with which we interact, the world is not 'out there' but rather part of our being, so much so in fact that it is impossible to disentangle the two. Moreover, as enmeshed in particular spatio-temporal contexts, our being-in-the-world means we encounter, experience, and understand things in specific, relational ways, within an elaborate field of possibilities. These include, for example, everyday items which are 'ready-to-hand' in contrast to objects of detached observation and contemplation (i.e., things which are 'present-at-hand'; see Heidegger 1962:98–99). His classic example is that of a hammer which is first and fundamentally known to us through our embodied engagement with it, as well as our understandings of its use and position within a web of other items such as lumber and nails. When it is used as intended, the hammer 'withdraws' from any explicit concern we might have with it. It is only when the hammer breaks that it becomes something to ponder in its uselessness.

Heidegger's concern with our practical understandings of the world, which implied that one could not tease apart the conscious and the corporeal in everyday modes of engagement, was recognized by Merleau-Ponty as a facet of post-Enlightenment thought in need of explication. To this end, in the *Phenomenology of Perception* (1962 [1945]), Merleau-Ponty advanced the theory of the *corps-sujet* or 'body subject' as a unified whole defined by the primacy of a perceptual rather than 'pure' consciousness. The world is always already understood as relational and meaningful because situations are experienced, first and foremost, not as atomized and idealized events instilled with meaning by the 'mind,' but rather as immediate and suffusive encounters that provide modalities for a bodily relationship with things that cannot be achieved by consciousness alone. This point is taken up by Mary Weismantel in her discussion of architectural features at Chavín de Huantar in Peru. Here, Weismantel's focus on the 'body/artifact interface' provides for a discussion of the kinaesthetic forms of engagement that must take place in order to view stones such as the Obelisk Tello and the Lanzón, processes which at times are frustrating, awkward, and incomplete.

But what is this corporeal form through which our relationships with the world become reified? Is it an inviolable and fixed container, as modern Western conventions would have it, the surfaces of which may be subject to a variety of 'cultural' modifications (e.g., through dress, cosmetics, prostheses, ornamentation, tattooing, etc.)? Following Strathern's (1988) performative account of Melanesian personhood and Csordas' (1990) call for a 'paradigm of embodiment,' (see also e.g., Butler 1993; Grosz 1994), many anthropologists and archaeologists have explicitly eschewed such biological conceptions, and have instead embraced a view of the body as a fabrication of the social relations that take effect among an assortment of human and non-human 'others.' Chief among the tenets associated with such a position is that the human body is a processual entity; it is continually made and remade through the exchange of human and non-human substances such as bodily fluids (e.g., Busby 1997; Weismantel 2004), foodstuffs, and medicines, as well as the incorporation of ornaments and the like. This theme is explored in contributions by Losey et al., McNiven, Hofmann, and Harris.

Crucially, it is also within such a view that the physicality of the body, rather than the ethereal properties of consciousness, can be regarded as the locus of difference between humans and animals. Considerable efforts have been devoted to advancing this topic within various strands of Amazonian (e.g., Descola 2005; Santos-Granero [ed.] 2009; Vilaça 2002, 2005; Viveiros de Castro 1998) and circumpolar (e.g., Willerslev 2004, 2007) anthropology, much of which turns on the idea that humans and animals share a consubstantial essence or 'soul,' but different corporeal forms. Viveiros de Castro (e.g., 1998, 2004) has discussed this idea according to what he calls 'perspectivism' or the ontological principle that "the point of view creates the subject" (1998:476–77; see also Figure 1.1). Among various Amazonian groups, Viveiros de Castro (1998:478) contends, one's perspective is given by the body one occupies, including its intentionality, dispositions, and capacities. As such, humans and (game) animals will see the world in different ways despite sharing the common essence of humanity (i.e., a spirit or soul), a theme which he refers to as 'multinaturalism.' Thus, what jaguars see as manioc beer, humans will see as blood. What tapirs regard as their large ceremonial house, we hold to be nothing more than a salt-lick.

Perspectival notions, which point to the ontological intersections and shared personhood of humans and animals, have long been noted among various indigenous groups by Ingold (e.g., 1988a, 2000:61–76) and are a subject common to the contributions of Borić, Losey et al., and McNiven. Among the Cree of Northeastern Canada, for example, Ingold (2000:48–52, 121–23) has described hunting practices as forming part of an ongoing interpersonal dialogue wherein animals must consent to be taken. Hunting here, as in other parts of the world, is based on principles of trust and regeneration; animals will not return to hunters who have mistreated them, a point which comes through in McNiven's discussion of dugong hunting rituals and Losey et al.'s interpretation of bear mortuary rites at Shamanka II. But it is also possible to see such notions as a facet of animism, as Descola (2005) does in his comprehensive taxonomy of ontologies. As discussed by both Borić and Shapland, Descola's classificatory scheme can be rendered as a two-way table (Figure 1.2) where a group's beliefs in the extent to which humans and non-humans share the same physical form and interior properties (e.g., conceptions of intentionality, subjectivity, reflexivity, etc.) come to define their way of being. These similarities and differences converge in four modalities. *Animism* sees humans and non-humans as possessing a shared interiority (e.g., spirit or soul) among a variety of outwardly different corporeal forms. *Totemism*, recast from conceptions put forward by Lévi-Strauss (e.g., 1964), sees groups of humans and non-humans as

FIGURE 1.1 Marcus Coates, *Goshawk* (1999). Produced by Grizedale Arts. Photography by Jet. In this 'self-portrait,' UK-based contemporary artist Marcus Coates, whose early work explored notions of animal embodiment and being–in–the–world, is secured to the upper reaches of a spruce tree in the Lake District so as to see the landscape from a goshawk's point of view. Courtesy of Kate MacGarry and Workplace Gallery, UK.

sharing a suite of essential features that sets them apart from all others. As the inverse of totemism, *analogism* recognizes distinctions along both axes (of physicality and interiority) which Descola equates with the ontologies of ancient Greece, China, and Medieval/Renaissance Europe. Lastly, as a hallmark of modernity, Descola identifies *naturalism* wherein biology forms the basis of life, but by virtue of 'interior' qualities, such as consciousness, reason, and intentionality (and their role in shaping culture), humans can be separated from everything else.

	Dissimilar in Physicality	Similar in Physicality
Similar in Interiority	Animism	Totemism
Dissimilar in Interiority	Analogism	Naturalism

FIGURE 1.2 Diagrammatic representation of the four ontological schemes given by the 'generative axes' of physicality and interiority (after Descola 2005:176).

While Viveiros de Castro has been criticized for his rather ahistorical and unre-flexive treatment of Amazonian ethnographic data (see e.g., Starn 2011:193), and Descola's ontological scheme can be singled out as oversimplified and generalized, their work nonetheless provides a useful counterpoint to the nature/culture and body/mind binaries of Western modernity. Rather than continuing to delineate a multicultural world projected onto a firmament of mononaturalism, as we do from the standpoint of naturalism, both Viveiros de Castro and Descola invite us to explore how non-humans can be variously bound up with or disconnected from humans in other, equally complex ontological frameworks. Such is the central pursuit of contributors to this volume. But while it is one thing to blur the dis-tinctions drawn between humans and animals by, for example, elevating the role of the body in perceiving the world and/or referring to such outward forms as indices of a common essence, few would agree that what it means to be a human is commensurate with what it means to be an animal.

Animals

> Animals are not lesser humans; they are other worlds.
>
> *(Barbara Noske 1989:xi)*

For some time now, and in quarters ranging from art and philosophy to linguistics and zoology, the question of 'animal being' has fascinated scholars. To what extent do animals make sense of the world, and does this approximate or overlap with human designs? For archaeologists working within what Descola would call a nat-uralist ontology, such an inquiry has rarely been attempted; animals are seen as economic resources or, following Lévi-Strauss (1964:89), as symbols that are 'good to think with.' This is understandable, given the discipline's alignment with matters of anthropological and historical interest, as well as the prevalent view that animals suffer from a poverty of intellectual and physical capabilities. Believing the language faculty to be absent in animals, Descartes, for one, suggested they were equally incapable of developing abstract concepts, possessing a soul, and feeling pain – qualities that made it fairly easy to draw the line between humanity and animality.

But just as this line is blurred in many indigenous ontological traditions, as indicated above, so too has it become increasingly obscure within various Western approaches to animal being. Noske's (e.g., 1997:133–57; see also Ingold 1988a, 1988b) review of recent ethological studies involving a host of mammals puts paid to the suggestion that language, conceptual thought, tool use, and altruism are all faculties unique to humanity. Ingold (this volume) takes this thinking a step further by arguing, somewhat in jest, that for those who would define humanity by properties such as intentionality and self-awareness, animals such as chimpanzees, dolphins, elephants, and perhaps rats may well be regarded as quasi-humans. And while the importance of such continuities remains controversial, a chorus of philosophers and other scholars has for some time now been challenging their broader ontological implications. Heidegger, for example, in defining what it means for humans to be "in-the-world" with other entities, took care to make an ontological distinction between humans, animals, and things. Indeed, he once remarked that while he thought humans were "world-forming," animals were "poor in world," while material objects were simply "worldless" (Heidegger 1995:177 [1983]). But in occupying a middle ground between the lofty, world-forming human and the lifeless existence of things, Heidegger (1995:260) struggled with the question of animal being. Were they too not immersed in a world replete with ready-to-hand entities? Furtively, he came to rest on an acknowledgment that while an animal may relate to its environment, what he called "the covert throng of a surrounding (*Umgebung*) into which [it is] linked" (Heidegger 1993:170), it does not have an understanding of *being*, which was given by a uniquely human capacity to access the world through a 'comportment' toward things. Animals, it seemed to Heidegger (1995:255), are poor in world because they are held hostage by behavior and instinct, and endlessly captivated by the 'encircling ring' (*Umring*) of their surroundings.

Heidegger's notion of an encircling ring is taken from the work of Jakob von Uexküll (e.g., 2010 [1934, 1940]) whose ideas have proven influential among continental philosophers (for summaries see e.g., Buchanan 2008; Calarco 2008; Oliver 2009), as well as semioticians such as Sebeok (e.g., 1972) and anthropologists such as Ingold (e.g., 2000:172–88). Grappling with the received wisdom of nineteenth-century biology and ethology, which painted animal life as inherently adaptive and mechanistic, respectively, von Uexküll pioneered a view of animal practices and environmental contexts as unified and meaningful. In furthering this notion, he employed the term *Umwelt(en)* or 'surrounding world(s),' which turned on the idea that the environment does not exist as an objective reality, but instead as an enmeshed suite of perceptual domains or 'appearance worlds' that come into being in and around various organisms. The *Umwelt* acts as a figurative limit within which particular things are disclosed to a specific organism in the course of its daily practices. The most oft-cited example of this comes from von Uexküll's description of the tick (*Ixodes rhitinis*). What we might recognize as significant features in our *Umwelt* – color and sound, for example – do not factor into the meaningful world of the blind and deaf tick. The tick, as von Uexküll (2010:44–46, 178–79) notes, is concerned only with the sensory perception of heat and sweat from a warm-blooded animal, to which it will ultimately attach itself, feed, lay its eggs, and die. These signs alone, which go unrecognized among other existents in different *Umwelten*, constitute the surrounding world of the tick.

Von Uexküll's belief that creatures differentially perceive, shape, and cohere with their surroundings also had a profound effect on Merleau-Ponty's later work (e.g., 1968 [1963], 2003 [1995]) wherein a primordial natural being was put forth to highlight the intertwining or 'chiasmic' relationships that exist between all living things. This is not to say that humanity and animality are ontologically comparable. They are rather comparative. Singularly human capacities for communication and art were recognized by Merleau-Ponty, but he regarded them as having emerged from a basal, perceptual form of being that nourishes and ties together all living things. Along these lines, and in contradistinction to Heidegger's view, *Umwelten* were used by Merleau-Ponty (2003:167–99) to argue that it is an animal's behavior, alongside the enmeshed activities of other forms, that serves to circumscribe its environment and thus co-construct its world. This is superbly illustrated in Whitridge's account of trail production and use in northern Labrador, Canada, where to tease apart the movements and intersections of humans and animals would be entirely unfeasible. To further illustrate this point, we might also turn to Lewis Henry Morgan's (1868) account of the American beaver (as discussed by Ingold [1988b]), whose engineering prowess in the construction of dams and lodges greatly affects the landscape and lifeways of other living things.

The theme to emerge here is one of empathy as opposed to exceptionalism in recognizing that both humans and animals relate to their surroundings and each other via various bodily modalities. Notably, this does not imply equivalence; these modalities vary in accordance with the perceptual apparatus of the organism and features of the world to which it is oriented. Here I am reminded of Thomas Nagel's (1974) essay entitled "What Is It Like to Be a Bat?" in which he broaches several fundamental questions of animal perception. Few would doubt that bats have experiences, he notes, just as all creatures do. But in instances where those experiences are given by embodied forms of perception unavailable to humans – echolocation in the case of bats, scent in the case of dogs – it cannot be said that animals exist in the same way as humans. In all instances, however, the relationship between perceiving existent and world goes beyond the mechanical. Returning to von Uexküll's description of the tick, for example, it is clear that this creature connects with a world as it climbs a blade of grass in search of light, discerns an approaching mammal by way of scent, and feeds by way of heat, oblivious to all else. For humans, of course, the world is much more expansive and the elements with which we can associate much more numerous, but underpinning and uniting both the worlds of ticks and humans (as with Nagel's bat and all other animals) are occasions for conjoinment. Von Uexküll (2010:187–88) characterized such relations using a musical metaphor: the tick enters into a contrapuntal 'duet' with each of the entities through which it is harmonically interdependent.

For Deleuze (e.g., 1988 [1970]; see also Deleuze and Guattari 1987 [1980]), this aspect of von Uexküll 's thought was vital to a definition of the animal based on its embodied capacities for connection or 'affects' rather than the biological characteristics that might serve to define it as an atomistic unit. "[Von Uexküll] will define [the tick] by three affects" writes Deleuze, referring to light, scent, and heat; "a world with only three affects, in the midst of all that goes on in the immense forest" (Deleuze 1988:124–25). Importantly, Deleuze argued that affects form the proper focus of ontological inquiry since they highlight the capabilities of bodies to "become" something else in proximity to other bodies. This idea was advanced by Deleuze and Guattari (1987:293) through a consideration of the 'rhizomatic' becoming that occurs between a wasp and an orchid where the former "becomes a liberated piece of the orchid's reproductive system" while the latter "becomes the object of an orgasm in the wasp, also liberated from its own reproduction." The resultant 'wasp-orchid' is a becoming that evades definition as a stable organism or detection within a subject-object binary, instead revealing itself temporarily and uniquely as a set of relations or complex of affects.

But Deleuze and Guattari (1987:262–63) would go further, however, in arguing that such becomings are not limited to the symbioses that can occur between disparate organisms but rather are immanent in and essential to the broader world. Echoing Heidegger (cf. Ingold 2011:115–25, this volume) they write "climate, wind, season, [and] hour are not of another nature than the things, animals, or people that populate them, follow them, sleep and awaken within them. This should be read without a pause: the animal-stalks-at-five-o'clock." Here, animal being, like that of humans, forms part of what Deleuze and Guattari (1987) would refer to as an 'assemblage' where the constituent parts cannot be disconnected from one another lest the very composition in question, fleeting as it may be, should change. That these ideas can be extended to the archaeological record and explored with reference to the diachronic 'flows' that take effect among people, animals, and things is fruitfully explored herein by both Hofmann and Harris, the latter of whom explicitly engages with these and other Deleuzo-Guattarrian concepts (by way of Manuel De Landa) in his investigation of British Neolithic and Bronze Age assemblages.

Reconstituting bodies as relational processes – as forms which are capable of affecting and being affected within delimited 'appearance worlds' or 'assemblages' – is fairly easy to conceptualize among humans, animals, and even plants, but what about things? Is it possible to focus on their 'affects' in a similar light, that is with reference to the techniques by which material culture modulates rather than accompanies the fluxes and flows of the world? In many ways, an interest in what things can 'do,' as opposed to what they are, has been taking place for some time now, in various guises, such that the relations which make up social identity are increasingly recognized as encompassing a wide range of non-human entities.

Things

> It is never we who affirm or deny something of a thing, but it is the thing
> itself that affirms or denies, in us, something of itself.
>
> *(Baruch Spinoza 1910:16:5)*

In archaeology, a concern with the symmetrical positioning of humans and non-human things can in many ways be traced to a shift in seeing artifacts as communicative devices (e.g., Hodder 1982; Wobst 1977), as opposed to the byproducts of various systemic processes and adaptive constraints. Taken up in large measure in the UK, and informed by a mix of French structuralism and post-structuralism, as well as Saussurean semiotics, it is perhaps no surprise that an early interest in examining the dynamic qualities of material culture was based on linguistic/textual models. Whether one was *Reading the Past* (Hodder 1986; see also Hodder 1989) or *Reading Material Culture* (Tilley [ed.] 1990; see also Tilley 1991), meaning was understood as inscribed in substances, according to certain grammatical rules or semiotic principles, the results of which could then be read or 'decoded.' And while the 'linguistic turn' is recognized as an important milestone in seeing artifacts for what they could do (see e.g., Olsen 2003:90; Thomas 2005:199), especially with regard to fluid, creative, and contingent processes by which encoded meaning was inter-preted, it soon became apparent that an appreciation of human-thing relations could not be gleaned from a strict adherence to linguistic or textual metaphors. Nor would such an understanding come from the emergent field of consumption studies in social anthropology (Miller 1987) and the ways in which consumer goods served as key constituents in identity formation and the production of meaning. Instead, from the mid-1990s, a brand of social theory inspired at turns by phenomenology (e.g., Bender [ed.] 1993; Gosden 1994; Thomas 1996; Tilley 1994; see also Brück 2005) and the structure-agency dialectics of Bourdieu (e.g., 1977) and Giddens (e.g., 1984) was used to attend to the manners in which landscapes and monuments shaped past human lifeways (see e.g., Barrett 1994; Bradley 1998). Now, far removed from a state of passive physicality and brute essentialism, artifacts and features were reconceptualized as extending the reach of human involvement in the world and contributing to the historical conditions in which people lived. Again, while for the most part a product of British archaeology, at least initially, calls for comparable approaches in various American quarters soon appeared (e.g., Hegmon 2003; Pauketat 2001).

But is this 'reach of human involvement,' considered in terms of independent purpose, intention, or volition, entirely dictated by humans? Just as a mise-en-scène involves the tangled arrangement of human and non-human elements on stage, could not the activities and experiences of everyday life result from collective endeavors? In real world situations, this sentiment has been explored to great effect by Bruno Latour (e.g., 1993) who has written about the ways in which mundane items such as seat belts, key fobs, and speed bumps conjoin with people and ulti-mately transform their daily activities. Latour and his colleagues (e.g., Callon 1986;

Law 1992) have also explored these ideas under the banner of Actor Network Theory (ANT) which affords an analytical parity to humans and non-humans by emphasizing the relational rather than dissociative character of being. Seeking to overcome several popular tropes of modernity, including distinctions drawn predominantly between nature/culture and subject/object, acting in the world (agency) is recast as a collectively shaped and hybridized process. Accordingly, agency does not issue from the active human subject, but rather is immanent in the vast heterogeneous networks which serve to unite people and things. Moreover, as agents (or 'actants' in the parlance of ANT) have no fixed ontological status, any interlocked component of a network can enlist the actions of any other element in its functioning; collectives of humans, animals, artifacts, texts, and even the weather can all be seen as in conversation.

While a number of archaeologists (e.g., Knappett 2008; Watts 2007, 2008; Whitridge 2004) have embraced ANT in their research designs, its uptake has waned in recent years. This may relate to various criticisms of the theory, as outlined for example by Knappett (e.g., 2008, 2011a), with regard to its under-conceptualized take on network dynamics, as well as by Ingold (2011:89–94), who playfully argues that the world and its products are inherently relational, in the first instance, and need not be joined up in ANT from a patchwork of analytically self-contained entities. Agency, Ingold asserts, is given by bodily skill, movement, and perception; things may help to facilitate agency, he notes, but are not in themselves agents. This contrasts with the conclusions reached by Alfred Gell (1998) in *Art and Agency*, another influential approach to human-thing relationships in archaeology (see e.g., Gosden 2005; Jones 2007; Osborne and Tanner [eds.] 2007). By advancing an anthropological framework for understanding 'art objects as persons,' as opposed to aesthetic works or communicative devices, Gell (1998:20–21) suggests that within the social contexts of production, circulation, and consumption, artworks serve as 'secondary' agents in referencing and amplifying the 'primary' forms of agency vested in their creators.

Whether an understanding of agency is more properly centered on the human or the network has, to some extent, been supplanted in recent years by a concern with the myriad and often provisional ways in which people and things become entangled through time. This theme is profitably examined here in chapters by Hofmann and Harris, as noted above, but also in contributions from Zedeño, Murray and Mills, and Herva and Nordin. At a more conceptual level, Hodder (2012) provides a lucid characterization of such relations. Cast in terms of dependence, he identifies human-human, human-thing, thing-human, and thing-thing entanglements, the last of which offers a foray into an ontology of material culture that has to date been rarely considered in archaeological circles (but see Olsen 2010). Ingold (e.g., 2007, 2011:67–75, this volume) has also sought to move us away from seeing the world as constellations of bounded entities, most recently through his writings on 'meshworks,' which provide a corrective to the somewhat ahistorical and systematic dimensions of network thinking in archaeology.[2] To Ingold, meshworks more effectively capture what is the nascent and positional character of human/non-human existence – an entwined field of relations made manifest by the ongoing movement and flow of people and things. It is along the lines of the meshwork that such entities travel and overlap, and by which we can glimpse the interwoven processes of growth that together make up the world. Whitridge (this volume) discusses this very phenomenon within the Nunatsiavut landscapes of northern Labrador in Canada, where human wayfaring 'maps onto' animal trails, and in so doing, serves to forefront the influence animals can have in how we encounter, experience, and ultimately know a place.

Relational archaeologies in practice

Collectively, these ideas can be seen to muddy the waters surrounding the 'social' by drawing other phenomena into our field of view. Now, quite apart from a world populated by knowing subjects (humans) and objects to be known (everything else), we have worlds filled with humans and/or non-humans and defined by the emergence and intersection of particular relationships. Within a relational archaeology, the contents of these worlds cannot be hived off and enclosed within analytical perimeters since to understand any one unit requires an appreciation of its relative positioning within a field of other entities and activities. And while methods are needed to characterize these relations, such as those described in the chapter by Zedeño, what the majority of contributors to this volume offer are opportunities to explore conceptually, and with reference to particular datasets, how such relational ways of life crystallize in the archaeological record.

We begin with a contribution from Mary Weismantel (Chapter 2) who seeks to reorient our approach to analyzing the architectural features of Chavín du Huantar in Peru. She notes that much of the extant literature pertaining to the site has understood its carved monoliths, including the famous Lanzón and Obelisk Tello, within a representational frame – as objects to be unilaterally instilled with meaning by the mind. Utilizing the work of Merleau-Ponty and W. J. T. Mitchell, as well as her own embodied experience of these monoliths, Weismantel argues that the stones seek to hinder, forestall, or facilitate certain kinds of engagement and perception, which at turns can be demanding, frustrating, and disquieting. This kinaesthetic awareness suggests that the site is more appropriately encountered than explained, and is illustrative of a Pre-Columbian ontology that is entirely at odds with modern Western sensibilities.

While Weismantel grapples with the demands of Chavín masonry, Dušan Borić (Chapter 3) tests the limits of Ingold's and Descola's thought vis-à-vis the depiction of animals at the site of Göbekli Tepe in Turkey. Here, too, we see a series of striking stone carvings that seem to defy conventional attempts at classification, especially in light of the site's early age (ca. 9000–7800 BC), its paucity of residential features, and the menagerie of animals portrayed, in some cases with menacing expressions. It is this phenomenon – more specifically, the presence of animals with bared teeth and predatory stances – to which Borić's attention is primarily directed. The evocative nature of the carvings, he argues, is suggestive of an 'animate theater' which, like Weismantel's interpretation of Chavín du Huantar, may have been a site of dialogue and danger.

In Chapters 4 and 5, Robert Losey et al. and Ian McNiven shift our attention from stone to bone in examining mortuary evidence for a shared human–animal kinship. For Losey et al., these relations are revealed through the presence of human and bear remains in graves at the Upper Paleolithic site of Shamanka II on Lake Baikal in Siberia. Weaving insights from Hallowell's work on bear ceremonialism with more recent Northern ethnographies and writings on the body, Losey et al. construct a potent argument for the ontological equivalence of humans and bears at Shamanka II. This argument is made all the more compelling by the care seen afforded to the mortuary treatment of bears at this special site, where various elements are nestled among the remains of their human counterparts. Similar mortuary contexts are described by McNiven in the Torres Strait region of northern Australia and southwest Papua New Guinea, where human, dugong, and turtle bones are found in close association. McNiven's focus, however, is on the role of the dead in hunting practices. Couched within an account of the "killing dialogue" that exists between hunters and prey, echoing Borić, McNiven combines detailed ethnographic observations and archaeological data to illuminate the affective and intimate role of human and animal remains in mediating the dugong hunt. But McNiven also takes seriously the more intangible aspects of this practice, including the rites through which Torres Strait Islanders embraced spiritual creators, dead prey, and dead humans, to more fully highlight the nature of relational ontologies in the region.

María Nieves Zedeño picks up on several of these themes in Chapter 6 wherein she explores the interlocutory aspects of Blackfoot communal bison hunting on the North American Great Plains. Zedeño's contribution has an entirely different flavor, however, seeking as it does to develop the more methodological aspects of a relational epistemology through a novel recasting of archaeological systematics. In advancing her approach, Zedeño cuts against the grain of conventional comparative analyses segregated by material 'types,' cultures, and practices by building bridges between what she calls "taxonomies of being." Here, scientific methods are brought into the service of a reflexive enquiry based on the agency, animacy, and association of materials. These ideas are explored with reference to the congeries of Plains bundles, including their regimens and myths, which aided in various Blackfoot hunting activities.

In Chapter 7, Wendi Field Murray and Barbara Mills examine the depositional practices of Chaco and Hohokam cultures in the US Southwest with an eye toward illuminating similarities and distinctions in their respective ways of memorializing. Evading the archaeological imperative to categorize and isolate studies by material, the authors demonstrate how a relational approach to the analysis of cached items provides an entré into the logics of indigenous personhood in the Southwest. By drawing our attention to the varied properties and biographies of caches, including, among other attributes, their size, content, treatment, and location, Murray and Mills speak to issues of group identity, animacy, and the extent to which ritual practices served to reinforce distinct "network topologies" linking humans, animals, and things together.

Daniela Hofmann's contribution (Chapter 8) affords another dimension to the analysis of identity categories and how they may have been understood in the past. As she notes in her examination of Linearbandkeramik (LBK) lifeways from central Europe between ca. 5300 and 4900 cal BC, the use of certain materials served to underscore twin concerns with transformation and fluidity. Drawing inspiration from Ingold's writings on entanglement (e.g., 2007), Hofmann contends that LBK ways of being were inherently unstable: bodies, like material culture, were understood to temporarily congeal within broader currents and processes of circulation. That these ways of being required constant maintenance and recasting suggests that the fixity of categories such as culture/nature, farmer/hunter and human/non-human may not have been recognized by LBK peoples. This, she asserts, can be seen in the wealth of site-specific data related to house construction and habitation, regimes of pottery and bodily decoration, and mortuary rituals.

Following Hofmann's focus on the relational aspects of past LBK ontologies, Oliver Harris (Chapter 9) invites us to consider community life in Neolithic and Bronze Age Britain without the threshing device of anthropocentrism. In thinking through the articulation of humans and non-humans, and how these configurations can change, Harris highlights the directional, affective, and multi-scalar aspects of 'relational communities' both conceptually and with reference to several archaeological case studies. After reviewing how notions of community life have been understood within various approaches to the past, Harris employs Manuel De Landa's assemblage theory, including its notions of heterogeneity, de/territorialization, and extensive vs. intensive relations in an effort to address the varied dimensions that gather together humans, animals, and landscapes across space and through time.

Harris' concern with long-term diachronic change, and its manifest mixing and melding of humans and non-humans into various relational forms, is resonant in Andrew Shapland's contribution (Chapter 10). Here, Shapland examines how alterations in trade and exchange activities during the Aegean Bronze Age (ca. 3200–1100 BC) can be assessed for their ontological effects, chiefly with regard to the emergence of elite collectives on Crete who manipulated the circulation of new materials, goods, and technologies as a means of differentiation. But Shapland, in working through Descola's model of analogism, is also concerned with the broader issue of how we think about the ontologies of hierarchical societies, where applications of animism or totemism can be seen as wanting and the naturalism of modernity is equally ill-suited to our accounts.

The intersections between social complexity and ontological forms are also explored by Vesa-Pekka Herva and Jonas Nordin in Chapter 11. In describing how the classical world was appropriated by planners, architects, and collectors in early modern Sweden, Herva and Nordin focus on the 'magical' or relational understandings of reality that accompanied such a move. From interests in runestones and cabinets of curiosities, to Gothic cults and the 'classicizing' of urban built environments, Herva and Nordin illuminate how such items and practices were intended to establish connections to a reality beyond the readily accessible physical environment. As they argue, however, it was these same practices that ultimately facilitated the emergence of a rational and mechanical view of the world.

In his framing of trail production and use in the remote reaches of northern Labrador, Canada, Peter Whitridge (Chapter 12) touches on similar themes as he explores the manners in which humans and non-human animals co-fashion the landscape. Delving into the palimpsest of routes travelled by precontact hunter-fisher-gatherers and their prey, Whitridge notes that humans often 'map onto' animal trails because they encompass the same contours, features, and conditions that we find desirous as we move from place to place. Paths were also instrumental in facilitating the complex settlement and subsistence activities that we have come to associate with the region, as well as its rich artistic and ontological traditions. It is with these things in mind that Whitridge encourages us to also consider the more experiential aspects of lifeways lived along trails.

The volume concludes with a short commentary from Tim Ingold (Chapter 13), who skillfully employs the metaphors of maze and labyrinth to explore competing approaches to a relational understanding of the world. Marked by tall buildings and branching passageways beset by advertising, Ingold equates the maze-like modern cityscape to the current state of postmodern thought in archaeology. Just as intentionality and agency serve to define the human navigator who must find a route through the maze, so have these qualities come to frame our understanding of the non-human objects and images beside which we pass. On the other hand, the unequivocal and non-branching path of the labyrinth, which foregrounds the attention rather than intention of the traveler, is for Ingold emblematic of life itself. The world of the labyrinth (or meshwork) is defined not by the myriad routes of embodied agents but by the interwoven paths of living, breathing beings.

In closing, it should be emphasized that the aim of this volume is not to present a new and consummate paradigm sated with methodological imperatives, but rather to highlight a nascent archaeological sensibility attuned to the ontological interplay between humans, animals, and things within particular environments. And while it can be said that this sensibility shuns classic humanist divides (e.g., culture and nature, human and animal, animate and inanimate), there is no one lens through which a relational understanding of past being and practices can be glimpsed, just as there is no one true past waiting to be discovered. Rather, as this collection of essays demonstrates, what we have is a suite of complementary conceptual frameworks and methods, each tailored to particular places, times, and peoples that might best be regarded as points along a continuum of relational understandings in archaeology. These might include, at one end, more established pursuits, such as making subjects out of objects, or extending the notion of selfhood to animals and things. At the other end, we might imagine more of an ontological confluence, where the concern is with illuminating common essences and ways of being among humans and non-humans, irrespective of things like reason and intentionality. Taken together, the contributions to this volume highlight the promise of such an approach and the plethora of possibilities that emerge within what may be defined very broadly as a relational archaeology.[3]

Notes

1 The concept of 'companion species,' which refers to a range of human and non-human animal relationships, is actually an old idea and one which is well documented by Serpell (1986). My thanks to Tim Ingold for pointing this out.
2 Knappett 2011a, which offers a multi-disciplinary and multi-scalar perspective on the networked interactions between people and things, is a notable exception (see also Knappett 2011b).
3 Portions of this chapter were written while I was the Rebanks Postdoctoral Fellow in New World Archaeology at the Royal Ontario Museum and, more recently, as a Social Sciences and Humanities Research Council of Canada Postdoctoral Fellow at the University of Western Ontario. I would like to thank Marcus Coates for permission to reproduce Figure 1.1, as well as Tim Ingold and Carl Knappett for their helpful comments on an earlier version of this chapter. Any shortcomings in this work, however, remain my own.

Bibliography

Alberti, Benjamin, and Tamara L. Bray (2009). Animating Archaeology: Of Subjects, Objects and Alternative Ontologies. *Cambridge Archaeological Journal* 19(3):337–43.

Barrett, John C. (1994). *Fragments from Antiquity*. Blackwell, Oxford.

Bender, Barbara (1993). Introduction. In *Landscape: Politics and Perspectives*, edited by Barbara Bender, pp. 1–17. Berg, Oxford.

Bennett, Jane (2010). *Vibrant Matter: A Political Ecology of Things*. Duke University Press, Durham, North Carolina.

Bird-David, Nurit (1999). Animism 'Revisited': Personhood, Environment, and Relational Epistemology. *Current Anthropology* 40(S):67–91.

Bourdieu, Pierre (1977). *Outline of a Theory of Practice*. Translated by Richard Nice. Cambridge University Press, Cambridge.

Bradley, Richard (1998). *The Significance of Monuments*. Routledge, London.

Brown, Linda A., and William H. Walker (2008). Prologue: Archaeology, Animism and Non-Human Agents. *Journal of Archaeological Method and Theory* 15(4):297–99.

Brück, Joanna (2001). Monuments, Power and Personhood in the British Neolithic. *Journal of the Royal Anthropological Institute* 7(4):649–67.

——(2005). Experiencing the Past? The Development of a Phenomenological Archaeology in British Prehistory. *Archaeological Dialogues* 12(1):45–72.

Buchanan, Brett (2008). *Onto-Ethologies: The Animal Environments of Uexküll, Heidegger, Merleau-Ponty, and Deleuze*. State University of New York Press, Albany.

Busby, Cecilia (1997). Permeable and Partible Persons: A Comparative Analysis of Gender and Body in South India and Melanesia. *Journal of the Royal Anthropological Institute* 3(2):261–78.

Butler, Judith (1993). *Bodies That Matter: On the Discursive Limits of 'Sex.'* Routledge, London.

Calarco, Matthew (2008). *Zoographies: The Question of the Animal from Heidegger to Derrida*. Columbia University Press, New York.

Callon, Michel (1986). Some Elements for a Sociology of Translation: Domestication of the Scallops and the Fishermen of St Brieuc Bay. In *Power, Action and Belief: A New Sociology of Knowledge?*, edited by John Law, pp. 196–223. Routledge and Kegan Paul, London.

Coole, Diana, and Samantha Frost (editors) (2010). *New Materialisms: Ontology, Agency, and Politics*. Duke University Press, Durham, North Carolina.

Conneller, Chantal (2004). Becoming Deer: Corporeal Transformations at Star Carr. *Archaeological Dialogues* 11(1):37–56.

Crossley, Nick (2011). *Towards Relational Sociology*. Routledge, New York.

Csordas, Thomas J. (1990). Embodiment as a Paradigm for Anthropology. *Ethos* 18(1):5–47.

Deleuze, Gilles (1988) [1970] *Spinoza: Practical Philosophy*. Translated by Robert Hurley. City Lights Books, San Francisco.

Deleuze, Gilles, and Félix Guattari (1987) [1980] *A Thousand Plateaus: Capitalism and Schizophrenia*. Translated by Brian Massumi. University of Minnesota Press, Minneapolis.

Descola, Philippe (2005). *Par-Delà Nature et Culture*. Éditions Gallimard, Paris.

Fowler, Chris (2004). *The Archaeology of Personhood: An Anthropological Approach*. Routledge, New York.

Geertz, Clifford (1984). 'From the Native's Point of View': On the Nature of Anthropological Understanding. In *Culture Theory: Essays on Mind, Self, and Emotion*, edited by Richard A. Shweder and Robert LeVine, pp. 123–36. Cambridge University Press, Cambridge.

Gell, Alfred (1998). *Art and Agency: An Anthropological Theory*. Clarendon Press, Oxford.

Gergen, Kenneth J. (2009). *Relational Being: Beyond Self and Community*. Oxford University Press, New York.

Giddens, Anthony (1984). *The Constitution of Society: Outline of the Theory of Structuration*. Polity Press, Cambridge.

Gosden, Chris (1994). *Social Being and Time*. Blackwell, Oxford.

——(2005). What Do Objects Want? *Journal of Archaeological Method and Theory* 12(3):193–211.

Gosden, Chris, and Yvonne Marshall (1999). The Cultural Biography of Objects. *World Archaeology* 31(2):169–78.

Grosz, Elizabeth (1994). *Volatile Bodies: Toward a Corporeal Feminism*. Indiana University Press, Bloomington.

Haraway, Donna (1985). Manifesto for Cyborgs: Science, Technology, and Socialist Feminism in the 1980s. *Socialist Review* 80:65–108.

——(2003). *The Companion Species Manifesto: Dogs, People, and Significant Otherness*. Prickly Paradigm Press, Chicago.

——(2007). *When Species Meet*. University of Minnesota Press, Minneapolis.

Hegmon, Michelle (2003). Setting Theoretical Egos Aside: Issues and Theory in North American Archaeology. *American Antiquity* 68(2):213–43.

Heidegger, Martin (1962) [1927] *Being and Time*. Translated by John Macquarrie and Edward Robinson. Harper and Row, New York.

——(1993). *Basic Writings*. Edited by David Farrell Krell. HarperCollins, New York.

——(1995) [1983]. *The Fundamental Concepts of Metaphysics: World, Finitude, Solitude*. Translated by William McNeill and Nicholas Walker. Indiana University Press, Bloomington.

Hodder, Ian (1982). *Symbols in Action: Ethnoarchaeological Studies of Material Culture*. Cambridge University Press, Cambridge.

——(1986). *Reading the Past: Current Approaches to Interpretation in Archaeology*. Cambridge University Press, Cambridge.

——(1989). This Is Not an Article about Material Culture as Text. *Journal of Anthropological Archaeology* 8(3):250–69.

——(2012). *Entangled: An Archaeology of the Relationships between Humans and Things*. Wiley-Blackwell, Chichester, U.K.

Ingold, Tim (1988a). Introduction. In *What Is an Animal?*, edited by Tim Ingold, pp. 1–16. Unwin Hyman, London.

——(1988b). The Animal and the Study of Humanity. In *What Is an Animal?*, edited by Tim Ingold, pp. 84–99. Unwin Hyman, London.

——(2000). *The Perception of the Environment: Essays in Livelihood, Dwelling and Skill*. Routledge, London.

——(2007). *Lines: A Brief History*. Routledge, London.

——(2011). *Being Alive: Essays on Movement, Knowledge and Description*. Routledge, London.

Jones, Andrew (2005). Lives in Fragments?: Personhood and the European Neolithic. *Journal of Social Archaeology* 5(2):193–217.

——(2007). *Memory and Material Culture*. Cambridge University Press, Cambridge.

Kirk, Trevor (2006). Materiality, Personhood and Monumentality in Early Neolithic Britain. *Cambridge Archaeological Journal* 16(3):333–47.

Knappett, Carl (2005). *Thinking Through Material Culture: An Interdisciplinary Perspective*. University of Pennsylvania Press, Philadelphia.

——(2008). The Neglected Networks of Material Agency: Artifacts, Pictures and Texts. In *Material Agency: Towards a Non-Anthropocentric Approach*, edited by Carl Knappett and Lambros Malafouris, pp. 139–56. Springer, New York.

——(2011a). *An Archaeology of Interaction: Network Perspectives on Material Culture and Society*. Oxford University Press, Oxford.

——(2011b). Networks of Objects, Meshworks of Things. In *Redrawing Anthropology: Materials, Movements, Lines*, edited by Tim Ingold, pp. 45–64. Ashgate, Burlington, Vermont.

Knappett, Carl, and Lambros Malafouris (editors) (2008). *Material Agency: Toward a Non-Anthropocentric Approach*. Springer, New York.

Latour, Bruno (1993). *We Have Never Been Modern*. Translated by Catherine Porter. Harvard University Press, Cambridge, Massachusetts.

Law, John (1992). Notes on the Theory of the Actor Network: Ordering, Strategy and Heterogeneity. *Systems Practice* 5:379–93.

Lévi-Strauss, Claude (1964). *Totemism*. Translated by Rodney Needham. Merlin, London.

Merleau-Ponty, Maurice (1962) [1945]. *Phenomenology of Perception*. Translated by Colin Smith. Routledge and Kegan Paul, London.

——(1968) [1963]. *The Visible and the Invisible*. Translated by Alphonso Lingis. Northwestern University Press, Evanston, Illinois.

——(2003) [1995]. *Nature: Course Notes from the Collège de France*. Translated by Robert Vallier. Northwestern University Press, Evanston, Illinois.

Miller, Daniel (1987). *Material Culture and Mass Consumption*. Basil Blackwell, Oxford.

Morgan, Lewis Henry (1868). *The American Beaver and His Works*. J. B. Lippincott and Company, Philadelphia.

Nagel, Thomas (1974). What Is It Like to Be a Bat? *Philosophical Review* 83(4):435–50.

Naess, Arne (1989). *Ecology, Community and Lifestyle*. Translated and edited by David Rothenberg. Cambridge University Press, Cambridge.

Noske, Barbara (1989). *Humans and Other Animals: Beyond the Boundaries of Anthropology*. Pluto, London.

——(1997). *Beyond Boundaries: Humans and Animals*. Black Rose, Montreal.

Oliver, Kelly (2009). *Animal Lessons: How They Teach Us to Be Human*. Columbia University Press, New York.

Olsen, Bjørnar (2003). Material Culture after Text: Re-Membering Things. *Norwegian Archaeological Review* 36(2):87–104.

——(2010). *In Defense of Things: Archaeology and the Ontology of Objects*. AltaMira, Lanham, Maryland.

Osborne, Robin, and Jeremy Tanner (editors) (2007). *Art's Agency and Art History*. Blackwell, Oxford.

Pachucki, Mark A., and Ronald L. Breiger (2010). Cultural Holes: Beyond Relationality in Social Networks and Culture. *Annual Review of Sociology* 36:205–24.

Pauketat, Timothy (2001). Practice and History in Archaeology. *Anthropological Theory* 1(1):73–98.

Santos-Granero, Fernando (editor) (2009). *The Occult Life of Things: Native Amazonian Theories of Materiality and Personhood*. University of Arizona Press, Tucson.

Sebeok, Thomas (1972). *Perspectives in Zoosemiotics*. Mouton de Gruyter, The Hague.

Serpell, James (1986). *In the Company of Animals: A Study of Human-Animal Relationships*. Basil Blackwell, Oxford.

Spinoza, Baruch (1910). *Short Treatise on God, Man, and His Well-Being*. Translated and edited by A. Wolf. Adam and Charles Black, London.

Starn, Orin (2011). Here Come the Anthros (Again): The Strange Marriage of Anthropology and Native America. *Cultural Anthropology* 26(2):179–204.

Strathern, Marilyn (1988). *The Gender of the Gift: Problems with Women and Problems with Society in Melanesia*. University of California Press, Berkeley.

Thomas, Julian (1996). *Time, Culture and Identity: An Interpretive Archaeology*. Routledge, London.

——(2005). Comments VIII: Between 'Material Qualities' and 'Materiality'. *Archaeometry* 47(1):198–201.

Tilley, Christopher (1991). *The Art of Ambiguity: Material Culture and Text*. Routledge, London.

——(1994). *A Phenomenology of Landscape: Places, Paths and Monuments*. Berg, Oxford.

Tilley, Christopher (editor) (1990). *Reading Material Culture*. Blackwell, Oxford.

Uexküll, Jakob von (2010) [1934, 1940] *A Foray into the Worlds of Animals and Humans with A Theory of Meaning*. Translated by Joseph D. O'Neil. University of Minnesota Press, Minneapolis.

Vilaça, Aparecida (2002). Making Kin out of Others in Amazonia. *Journal of the Royal Anthropological Institute* 8(2):347–65.

——(2005). Chronically Unstable Bodies: Reflections on Amazon Corporalities. *Journal of the Royal Anthropological Institute* 11(3):445–64.

Viveiros de Castro, Eduardo (1998). Cosmological Deixis and Amerindian Perspectivism. *Journal of the Royal Anthropological Institute* 4(3):469–88.

——(2004). Exchanging Perspectives: The Transformation of Objects into Subjects in Amerindian Ontologies. *Common Knowledge* 10(3):463–84.

Watts, Christopher M. (2007). From Purification to Mediation: Overcoming Artifactual 'Otherness' with and in Actor-Network Theory. *Journal of Iberian Archaeology* 9/10:39–54.

——(2008). *Pot/Potter Entanglements and Networks of Agency in Late Woodland Period (c. AD 900– 1300) Southwestern Ontario, Canada*. BAR International Series S1828. British Archaeological Reports, Oxford.

Webmoor, Timothy (2007). What about 'One More Turn after the Social' in Archaeological Reasoning? Taking Things Seriously. *World Archaeology* 39(4):547–62.

Weismantel, Mary (2004). Moche Sex Pots: Reproduction and Temporality in Ancient South America. *American Anthropologist* 106(3):495–505.

Whitridge, Peter (2004). Whales, Harpoons, and Other Actors: Actor-Network Theory and Hunter-Gatherer Archaeology. In *Hunters and Gatherers in Theory and Archaeology*, edited by George Crothers, pp. 445–74. Occasional Paper No. 31. Center for Archaeological Investigations, Southern Illinois University, Carbondale.

Willerslev, Rane (2004). Not Animal, Not *Not*-Animal: Hunting, Imitation and Empathetic Knowledge among the Siberian Yukaghirs. *Journal of the Royal Anthropological Institute* 10(3):629–52.

——(2007). *Soul Hunters: Hunting, Animism, and Personhood among the Siberian Yukaghirs*. University of California Press, Berkeley.

Witmore, Christopher L. (2007). Symmetrical Archaeology: Excerpts of a Manifesto. *World Archaeology* 39(4):546–62.

Wobst, H. Martin (1977). Stylistic Behavior and Information Exchange. In *For the Director: Research Essays in Honor of James B. Griffin*, edited by Charles E. Cleland, pp. 317–42. Academic Press, New York.

2

INHUMAN EYES: LOOKING AT CHAVÍN DE HUANTAR

Mary Weismantel

Materialist looking

Inhuman eyes confront anyone who looks at the monoliths from Chavín de Huantar, a temple complex in the Peruvian Andes that dates to approximately 1000–1300 BC, and has attracted pilgrims[1] from great distances for thousands of years. Those who came to the site and looked at the stones saw other eyes looking back; this interaction between humans, non-humans, and things is the subject of my study.

This paper is a manifesto for a new kind of archaeological writing about looking at artifacts. The existing literature on Pre-Columbian works of art[2] is almost exclusively iconographic; here, I want to invite researchers to think about ancient objects not just as texts, but also as things in the world. The materiality of these stones – their various shapes, their huge scale, their shallow engravings, and the hard, heavy substances that render them so immobile – is as significant as the images they bear. Previous studies of the Chavín stones have looked at them as representations of a deity, of the cosmos, or of an origin myth. These models are not wrong, but they do not capture the active, working life of the great stones. The monoliths were more than mirrors that reflected a cultural world: they were vital matter (Bennett 2010) in a social world where animals and things were interlocutors and sensory perception was a reciprocal, rather than a unilateral, activity. Material characteristics of the stones communicate aspects of this lost Pre-Columbian ontology, especially when read through ethnographic and ethnohistoric data from non-Western, non-modern societies.

The analysis I present here builds on the work of previous researchers, who have painstakingly unraveled the iconographic conventions that underlie Chavín art, and identified the flora and fauna depicted. Iconography is a necessary tool for interpreting Chavín's stones, which are covered with complex designs executed in a recondite style. It is an especially useful approach given the site's long post-occupation history, during which many of the monoliths were relocated and most contextual data was lost. But although the stones have been moved, they still exist; they only become dematerialized when scholars turn their backs on the three-dimensional sculptures in favor of two-dimensional copies (Weismantel 2012). Art historian Tom Cummins (2008:280–81) aptly characterizes this methodology as one that "dissociates the image from the object and space of which it is a part." My goal is to reverse that separation, and reintegrate iconographic analysis with a consideration of the stones themselves: their materiality and their spatial context, and especially the peculiar forms of interaction they demand of their viewers (Weismantel 2013, 2014).

I want to briefly address two potential objections. First, archaeological studies that espouse a phenomenological approach (e.g., Tilley 1994) have been criticized for ethnocentric and ahistorical assumptions (see e.g., Hall 2000:48–52; Smith 2003:62–63). As I demonstrate here, careful analysis of the body/artifact interface can produce the opposite result: a means to partially escape the inherent biases imposed upon us by our formal and informal training as modern Western observers (Watts, this volume; Weismantel 2011, 2012).

Secondly, in focusing on the bodily and sensory aspects of the stones, I appear to be abandoning the heady cosmological questions asked by twentieth-century researchers. Their approach had an implicit politics: to treat Pre-Columbian artifacts as sacred texts was to insist that the indigenous peoples of the Americas were as capable of complex abstract thought as Europeans (Weismantel 2014). But new developments in Western philosophy are changing the ideological terrain that made this argument necessary and compelling. Recently, a group of philosophers and other humanists known as the 'new materialists' (e.g., Bennett 2010; Coole and Frost [eds.] 2010; Promey 2014) have turned their attention away from the disembodied structures of language and thought. They emphatically reject the Enlightenment hierarchies that privileged cognition over emotion, abstract thought over concrete experience, and mind over body. By insisting that bodily and sensory forms of knowing are as significant as more abstract forms of cognition, their work opens the way for Pre-Columbianists like myself to move away from narrowly iconographic studies without abandoning an interest in ancient ways of thinking. Indeed, it is quite the opposite: close attention to the minutiae of bodily interaction between image, object, and perceiving body may ultimately give us greater insight into the most subtle and profound aspects of Pre-Columbian thought than could be attained by ignoring the materiality of the objects we study and the bodily practices of the people who made and used them.

There are related intellectual developments in other fields across the humanities and social sciences. These include Tim Ingold's materialist anthropology (e.g., 2000, 2011); the writings of art historian W. J. T. Mitchell (e.g., 1994, 2004) and literary theorist Bill Brown (e.g., 2001, 2003); posthumanist and animal studies (e.g., Braidotti 2002; Buchanan 2008; Calarco 2008; Haraway 2008); and a renewed interest in phenomenology among geographers (e.g., Llobera 2007). In this paper, I will rely in particular on Mitchell's 2004 book, which asks a provocative question:

What do pictures want? – a question we could also ask at Chavín. As works of art go, the monoliths seem exceptionally demanding: they bristle with aggressive animals and inflict difficult viewing experiences on those who come to look at them. Paraphrasing Mitchell, we can ask: what do these demanding stones want? Mitchell answers his own question as follows: "what pictures want, and what we have failed to give them, is an idea of visuality adequate to their ontology" (Mitchell 2004:47). In this article, I set out to provide the monoliths with just that: a theory adequate to their particular form of visuality, and to the particularly Pre-Columbian ontology that underlies that demand.

Mitchell's intellectual gambit is carefully constructed: he theorizes *as though* works of art have needs and desires that drive them to interact with humans. "I am concerned here," he says in setting out his project, "not so much to retrace the ground covered by semiotics, but to look at the peculiar tendency of images to absorb and be absorbed by human subjects in processes that look suspiciously like those of living things" (Mitchell 2004:5). Bracketing the question of whether things actually have agency, he points out that we act as though they do – producing the effect of agency, even while disguising its origins in human actors (see also Gell 1998). For twenty-first-century empirical researchers studying sacred objects that are several millennia old, this is a useful conceptual tool. There is little doubt that the ancient people who came to Chavín saw the stones as animate and personified; Mitchell enables us to do the same. "Pictures are something like life forms, driven by desires and appetites," writes Mitchell (2004:6); like him, I approach the stones as "something like life forms," not because I literally ascribe agency or cognitive and emotional capacities to them, but because that is how they were treated by the people who made them, and by those who traveled great distances to see them.

The stones and the site

The site of Chavín de Huantar is located in the north-central Andes of Peru at an altitude of 3,150 m asl. Its chronology is currently the topic of debate (Burger and Salazar 2008; Rick 2008; Rodriguez Kembel 2008), but it was certainly thriving between 1000 BC and 500 BC, and was occupied for many centuries during the Early Horizon (900–200 BC) and the preceding Initial Period (1800–1900 BC). The temple complex sits at the junction of two rivers, and comprises a tightly inter-connected set of monumental buildings, plazas, terraces, staircases, passages, and underground channels. It is best known for its elaborately carved monoliths, such as the Obelisk Tello, the Stela Raimundi, and the Yauya Stela, as well as for the network of stone-lined interior passageways or *galerías*, at the heart of which lies perhaps the most famous of the carved stones, a tall splinter of granite known as the Lanzón. The brilliant Peruvian archaeologist Julio C. Tello (1943; see also Burger 2009) was the first in a line of distinguished excavators to have worked at the site, including Wendell C. Bennett, Luis Lumbreras (1977, 1993), Richard Burger (1984, 1992), and John Rick (2005, 2008). Excavations are currently ongoing and will continue to transform our understanding of the temple compound.

New materialist philosophy is especially apropos for Chavín, a place where Enlightenment concepts have no purchase. The site was built and achieved fame long before the modern period, by people who were neither European nor Euro-American. They did not belong to the Mosaic (Judeo-Christian-Muslim) tradition; having no books, they were not a people 'of the Book'; nor did they believe that God had given them dominion over the animals. Although they were far from being egalitarian hunter-gatherers, they had not built a system of social inequality predicated on animal domestication (Ingold 2000:61–76). These two absences – of textual literacy and of subjugated animals – made room for a distinctive ontology and aesthetics, so different from our visual and cognitive conventions that we struggle to grasp it. It is the premise of this article that looking closely at the monoliths can help.

One source for hypotheses to bring to this non-Western world is the ethnographic and ethnohistoric record from Native South America, especially the Amazonian region, where Christianity and the modern nation-state have been the slowest to make inroads. There is strong iconographic evidence for this analogy in the Amazonian fauna and flora depicted on the Tello Obelisk and the frequent visual references to hallucinogens throughout Chavín art, which elicit comparisons to twentieth-century Amazonian shamanic practice (Burger 1992; Cordy-Collins 1977, 1980; Lathrap 1973; Roe 2008; Sharon 2000; Torres 2008; Urton 2008). As Roe suggests (2008:181–82), the influence of Native South American animist philosophy on Chavín art goes beyond the occasional iconographic reference. It is deeply integrated into the very principles that govern pictorial composition, just as Western ontologies shape the conventions of naturalistic art.

Of course, analogies based on twentieth-century ethnographies must be used with caution, given the great temporal distance involved; indigenous Amazonians today may be practicing Christians, Brazilian politicians, tour guides, or hotel maids. At most, Amazonia provides suggestive hypotheses about the ancient past, which must be rigorously tested against the archaeological record. Nevertheless, it is a region where the underlying ontological premises of Amerindian thought have been the subject of sustained, rigorous intellectual interrogation; this body of research provides an alternative to the modern Euro-American forms of thought that otherwise color our assumptions, and limit and distort our ability to see the ancient stones as they were once seen.

My focus in this paper is on the act of seeing. Empirical science teaches us to think of perception as an invariant physiological response to stimuli, but historians and cultural anthropologists turn instead to Marx's well-known dictum that the senses have a history. That is, that like other aspects of human life, such as eating and sex, sensory perception is a complex and multi-faceted phenomenon that is subject to enormous cultural variation (Berger 1980; Howes [ed.] 2005; Smith 2007). The archaeological record provides rich and abundant data about how past societies thought about perception – if we know how to look for it. Objects are constructed to engage our senses and our bodies in culturally sanctioned ways; archaeologists can therefore recover those cultural attitudes towards the senses and the body by analyzing the way that artifacts constrain, prevent, or enable specific forms of interaction and perception (Day [ed.] 2012). In the first part of this paper, I look at the temporality of seeing at Chavín, using ethnographic analogies from Amazonia; in the second part, I consider the spatiality of seeing, using archaeological data from the site itself.

Looking to know: temporality at Chavín

When I went to Peru to look at the Chavín monoliths, I received an immediate, first-hand lesson in how visual cultures differ. I had been intimately familiar with the published drawings of the stones since graduate school, and looked forward to seeing them in real life. But pleasurable anticipation soon changed to frustration: looking at the actual stones turned out to be surprisingly difficult, and involved an unsettling degree of bodily interaction. Over and over, I struggled to see details on their rocky surfaces – or even to make out the images at all. At different moments, I found myself standing on tiptoe in a Lima museum trying – and failing – to see the upper reaches of the Obelisk Tello (Figure 2.1); edging around the Lanzón, my back was pressed against the protruding walls, my body twisted awkwardly, and my head tilted upwards at odd angles; standing outside the temple, running my fingers along the hidden surfaces of the Black and White Portals, I wished, absurdly, that my head could fit into the tiny gap between the pillar and the wall.

I am not the only modern viewer to report frustration; the archaeological literature on Chavín is rife with complaints about "poor visibility" (see e.g., Ayres 1961; Rick 2005). For iconographers, this is just an obstacle to overcome; in a multidimensional analysis such as I propose here, however, the perceptual interface between human and artifact is itself an object of study (Weismantel 2012). The technologies we use today create accessible, instantaneous forms of visual presentation that implicitly reinforce the tenets of empiricism – an epistemology highly valued by modern archaeologists. The stones of Chavín, in contrast, create a kind of visuality that is slow, conscious, active, and interactive – qualities that enact key tenets of Native South American religious thought.

Seeing seeing

Slow seeing

One reason it takes a long time to see what is depicted on the monoliths is simply because the images are so complicated. In John Rowe's classic essay on Chavín style, he discusses a series of arcane visual conventions (1977 [1962]). In the hybrid human/feline/raptor figures on the Black and White Portals (Figure 2.2), for example, the interiors of the twin bodies brim with the metaphorical substitutions Rowe labeled 'kennings':[3] orifices are toothed mouths, the joints of the body are replaced by open-mouthed heads (from which the limbs emerge like tongues), spines are represented as long tooth-rows, and snakes take the place of appendages such as hair, feathers, or tassels. The imposing twin figures on the Obelisk Tello are

FIGURE 2.1 Obelisk Tello. Photo by James Q. Jacobs. Used with permission.

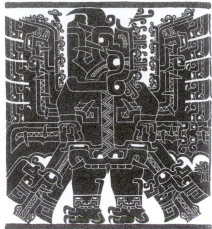

FIGURE 2.2 Roll-out drawings of the twin figures on the Black and White Portals, as originally published by John Rowe. Used with permission.

still more complex. Two giant caymans (*Melanosuchus niger*) are surrounded by smaller animals, plants, mollusks, and other creatures, while the faces, mouths, and limbs of other animals crowd *within* the caymans' bodies in a manner reminiscent of other Native American art styles, such as Nazca, Paracas, Northwest Coast, and Olmec.

This multiplicity of bodies makes it difficult to discern the primary figure. At first, a modern viewer presented with a line drawing of the Obelisk sees only a welter of detail and a confusion of limbs: it is hard to 'make out' what is depicted (Urton 2008:217–18). But these copies are far easier to read than the carvings on the stones themselves, where style and execution slow the viewing process still further. All the interesting detail, so clearly visible in line drawings, tends to vanish in real life, lost in the shiny surface of the Stela Raimundi or the low bas relief of the Obelisk Tello (Weismantel 2013, 2014). Where a Western sculptor might use deeper incisions or higher relief to limn the more important figures, the Chavín carvers employed a uniform execution that impedes rather than aids recognition (Doyon-Bernard 1997:27; Weismantel 2013).

Because these stylistic choices deliberately slow down the process of seeing, they call attention to perception as a physical act that takes place in time. Unlike realist painting or documentary photography, in which the moment of identifying the image is so immediate that we do not even notice it, Chavín delays the moment of recognition. This slowed temporality makes the viewer aware of the physical and cognitive effort involved, and thus creates conscious seeing: seeing that sees itself.

Conscious seeing

According to French philosopher Maurice Merleau-Ponty (2002 [1945]), all looking is active looking, but this property of sight is often invisible to us: we see what we are looking at, but not the looking itself. One thing that art can do, he says, is to bring the act of seeing into consciousness. Mitchell (2004:72) echoes this observation when he says that in some works of art, "seeing itself becomes visible and tangible." Historians of science have established that our modern experience of seeing as automatic and unremarkable is itself a cultural artifact, sanctioned by science and enabled by our books, laptop screens, and projectors. This is very different from the Chavín monoliths, which create a singularly self-aware form of seeing – but not an awareness that reinforces modernist hierarchies between the thinking mind and the sensate body. Euro-American academia exalts the mentally active, physically passive scholar, scientist, or priest who sits, reads, and thinks; Chavín religiosity demands an active body that absorbs knowledge kinetically.

Active seeing

When I encountered the great stones, I felt that the physical demands they made on me were unreasonable, even illegitimate – a reaction that reveals the deep impact of literacy on modern bodies and minds. The written page dictates a stationary way of looking that comes to seem natural, but that takes long, painful years of childhood bodily discipline to achieve. Non-literate peoples, free of this technological tyranny, often create works that make kinaesthetic demands; they may even perceive an unaccustomed form of movement as an especially pleasurable aspect of the encounter with a work of art. We are accustomed to sitting still, watching "moving pictures"; at Chavín, the stationary stones move *us*.

They do so partly through their scale and three-dimensionality, which make it impossible to see all of an image at once. Most of the monoliths are one-and-a-half to two times taller than a human being. This large size, combined with enormously complex imagery executed at a small scale in a difficult style, forces the viewer to move head, eyes, and even the entire body from one part of the design to another, taking it in bit by bit. In the process, the totality vanishes; to recapture it requires moving away again, and temporarily losing sight of the detail (Weismantel 2014).

This kind of seeing-in-motion is how we see more generally as we move about in the world: constant small, even imperceptible, movements of our head and eyes allow us to perceive figure and ground, foreground and background, and so to remain oriented and informed. Our vision is constantly oscillating between perspectives, but we process this information so quickly that we experience it as singular and momentary. Chavín pulls apart this fusion of perspectives, making us aware of the momentary disjunctures between close and distant, here and there, that are built into how we see. The viewer is thus made aware of seeing as action that takes place in time.

Elsewhere, I have described Chavín's visuality as incomplete and fragmentary (Weismantel 2013); alternatively, one might call it a more complete form of seeing than our own. We think of a photograph as an accurate visual representation, one that mimics human sight. But the instantaneous temporality of the camera, which captures a person or thing from a single perspective, is intrinsically partial and incomplete. In contrast, seeing at Chavín incorporates time, motion, subjectivity, and changes in perspective. Instead of a momentary glimpse of someone else, the visual forms of the monoliths impose the gradual acquisition of a diffuse and deeper knowledge of the body of the other.

Seeing as knowing

The stones require us to look at the same thing from more than one perspective. They do so through a variety of strategies, one of which is to wrap a two-dimensional image around a three-dimensional object. This forces the viewer into motion, and requires considerable cognitive dexterity. To study the imagery on the Obelisk Tello, for example, involves standing on one side, looking at the image before one's eyes while recalling the image on the other side, then moving to the other side and repeating the process in reverse (Weismantel 2013). The Stela Raimundi is carved on only one face, but its anatropic design requires similar mental and physical flexibility. Seen from one perspective, the image features a central figure; turn the image upside down, and the features on this figure's head dissolve, only to re-form into a different head facing the opposite direction. I demonstrate this to students by flipping an image projected on a screen; when confronted by the actual monolith, though, it was *my* body that had to move, and *my* head that turned upside down.[4]

The style of the carvings likewise offers contradictory perspectives on a single body: as in ancient Egypt, figures often display a frontal torso with legs and feet in profile. And as in Northwest Coast and other Native American art, X-ray depictions, split representations and the 'flayed-pelt convention' (Roe 2008:182) reveal alternating views of the interior and exterior of a body. These conventions appear to modern viewers to defy reality, but what they actually defy is time by delivering multiple perspectives simultaneously. In real life, these changing perspectives only become available over time, and through movement, as the bodily relationships between seer and seen change. The snapshot – a single glimpse of an unfamiliar entity – is no match for this long, intimate process of learning about another body over time, at different angles and distances, or even – as is suggested by glimpses of the skeleton or the flayed skin – both in death and in life.

What the stones do, in short, is create an experience that is akin to the experience of getting to know another living being: as Mitchell (2004:5) says of all pictures, they "absorb and [are] absorbed by human subjects" in processes that make them seem like "living things." In the animist[5] context of the Pre-Columbian Americas, the lifelike characteristics of sacred stones are no accident. Nor are the difficulties we experience when trying to look at them: their resistance and lack of passivity makes them into our equals and our interlocutors. The stones remove us from a Cartesian ontology in which things are inert and only humans have agency; instead, they demand that we engage in a lively visual dialogue with them – one that, like a conversation between two people, unfolds over time.

Perspectival seeing

The stones, then, engage us in seeing that is active and interactive. The mutuality of this kind of perception seems to enact an important precept of Native American ontological thought known as 'perspectivism.' As defined by Brazilian ethnologist Eduardo Viveiros de Castro (e.g., 1998), perspectivism asserts that reality is differently constituted for different kinds of beings.[6] In an animist world that does not privilege mind over matter, the goal of religious practice is to escape one's body, but not in order to achieve a transcendental, dematerialized vision. The goal is to enter into the bodily experience of other species – to see, as the Ye'kuana say, with 'anaconda eyes' (de Civrieux 1985:65–66, quoted in Viveiros de Castro 2012:31). This is how one gains wisdom: by experiencing the radical differences in perspective between humans and non-humans, whether other species, things, spirits, or the dead. It was to gain access to these differently embodied sensory paradigms that visitors came to Chavín de Huantar, where they could meet and learn to see the giant, animal-bodied stones.

The seer seen

Perspectivism is ultimately about reciprocity of vision: the seer seen. Mutual apprehension does more than allow us to know one another: it teaches us to see ourselves through others' eyes. For the great stones to fully embody this phenomenological precept, they too must appear to perceive their viewers. Indeed, the stones at the site feature an unsettling multiplicity of eyes, and draw the viewer's attention repeatedly to the organs of perception.

Non-western eyes

Merleau-Ponty notwithstanding, the dominant Western notion of vision is still a passive one: light travels to the eyes, which involuntarily receive visual information and transmit it to the brain through the optic nerve for processing. But outside the modern West, the eye has a far more muscular and exciting life.

In Melanesia in the 1920s, Malinowski (1929:140–42) recounts that when he asked the Trobrianders to name the sex organs, they immediately named the eyes. Despite his surprise, he found himself unable to counter their arguments: the eyes are the primary organs that control sex, they assured him, since arousal begins with looking. The other sex organs respond, and if that response is mutual, occurring both in the one who looks and in the one who sees that s/he is seen, then sexual intercourse may follow. Absent the initial ocular connection, however, neither arousal nor sexual activity occurs.

Sex does not play much of a role in Chavín art, but intimations of violence certainly do. This makes Mitchell more useful than Malinowski: he discusses aggressive works of modern art that appear to look back at the viewer, and mentions the Classical Greek notion of the 'eidolon'– an image that is the product of a strikingly aggressive eye, and an equally aggressive object. According to Mitchell (2004:352), the eidolon can be either "the projected template hurled outward by the probing, seeking eye, or the simulacrum of the seen object, cast off or 'propagated' by the object like a snake shedding its skin."

These cross-cultural instances of active and aggressive eyes bring a new perspective to the Chavín stones, where eyes play an important role. On the finely worked ashlar blocks that were once mounted on the temple's exterior, intricate carvings of multiple faces and bodies, repeating like a hall of mirrors or a hallucination, are rendered especially uncanny by the repetition of Chavín's characteristically round eyes.

On these blocks, and on other carved rocks such as the Stela Raimundi or Yauya Stela, the incised lines that convey the convoluted images of multiple bodies are shallow and uniform, barely scratching the flat surface of the rock: they could be described as skin-deep. But there is one striking exception, visible even from a distance, long before the rest of the design can be seen: pairs of deeper circular depressions, repeated at intervals along the stone. Come closer, and as the rest of the design becomes visible, these deep, perfect hemispheres are revealed to be body parts, repeated for each of the intertwined bodies within the image. They are always organs of perception: the eyes, the nostrils, and sometimes the interior of the mouth. Rendering these organs as uniquely three-dimensional forms in an otherwise two-dimensional plane makes them into penetrating/penetrated orifices that actively connect the inside of the body to the world outside.

Inhuman eyes

These round eyes are not human eyes; they belong to jaguars, caymans, and birds of prey. This is a far cry from Western monotheism, which holds that "God created Man in his own image." As heirs to the Western philosophical tradition, we have naturalized the belief that humans are uniquely conscious, thinking beings whose mental superiority allows us to exert our will over a world filled with inert matter and unthinking animals. But this belief is far from a universal, self-evident truth about what it means to be human, and to live with animals and things. The forms of perception embodied by the stones at Chavín indicate that in the eyes of their makers, animals and things possessed vitality, will, consciousness, and personhood.

Ethnographic analogy suggests that even in ordinary life, encounters with non-humans were vitally important and desirable experiences through which humans acquired wisdom, strength, and experience. These encounters were also, however, fraught with danger and unpredictability—still more so when the non-human inter-locutor was no ordinary being, but an extraordinary creature who could be found only in the unique setting of Chavín de Huantar. To encounter the great stones was not only to enter into their peculiar visual temporality; it was also to enter a very particular – and potentially dangerous – kind of space.

Looking to change: space at Chavín

The penetrating eyes on the monoliths gave Pre-Columbian viewers something they wanted: an intense perceptual exchange with non-human entities they knew to be animate and agentive, and possessed of great spiritual power. These exchanges were part of a journey that began with travel to the site and continued within it, as travelers encountered a series of carefully situated stones.

The temple and its surrounding plazas form a particular kind of place. It was a destination that one journeyed *to*. It was also a place one journeyed *within*, moving from plaza to plaza to temple, from exterior to interior, light to darkness, and ordinary to extraordinary perception. Each of the stones occupies a particular space within this journey, and each also constitutes its own place. The stones shape space as well as time. As Mitchell (2004:259) says, sculpture "wants to be a place, wants to offer us a space for thought and feeling." The monoliths create a place where human and non-human meet – not just as species come into contact in ordinary life, but in encounters with incredible hybrid animal/mineral/human creatures not to be found elsewhere. These creatures could create a space of learning, a space of transformation, or even Taussig's space of death (Taussig 1984) – what happened there depended on the capacity of their human interlocutors to face, absorb, and survive what they had to offer.

Piecing together the material and spatial evidence from those stones that are still *in situ*, from stylistic and physical comparison of all the stones, and from the overall spatial organization of the site, it is possible to discern striking differences between the stones and the kinds of encounters they created. Each stone creates its own kind of kinaesthetic looking, and in the process, each creates a different kind of place. Movement through the site took the viewer from distant seeing, to oscillating movement, to an overwhelming intimacy that few visitors may have been willing to risk.

Too far: the cornice stones

As visitors approached the largest building of the temple complex, they saw a façade crowned by cornices and rows of finely worked ashlar blocks. These stones featured the shallow, polished, low relief carvings of multiple faces, nostrils, mouths, and eyes described above – mounted so far above the ground that the designs must have been completely illegible.[7] Even if they were brightly painted, their mesmerizing designs would have been too far away to discern in any detail. Tantalizingly out of reach, these carvings make the visitor yearn to get closer – a desire that these stones arouse, but other stones will satisfy.

Oscillation: obelisk, pillar, and stela

Moving into the open areas of the temple complex, the visitor would have seen large monoliths with complex carved designs. Only the Black and White Portals are *in situ* today, and even they may have been moved during the lifetime of the site. It is probable, however, that at least some of the group of stones that includes the Stela Raimondi, Obelisk Tello, and others were erected in, on, or near the building exteriors, plazas, and staircases. These locations place the stones at ground level in an outdoor area where one could approach them – and also back away. Everything about them – their style, their dimensions, their complex iconography – suggests that they were designed to impel this kind of oscillating, interactive, dialogic viewing.

These are the stones that pull the viewer close to perceive the design, and then push them away to bring part or whole into focus; these are the pillars or prisms with wrapped images that the viewer circumnavigates in often futile efforts to see in their entirety[8] (Figure 2.3). These are also the stones with the complex iconography that previous scholars have compared to a text; they do indeed have a textual quality, but they seem less like books than kaleidoscopes. Impossible to get into focus all at once, and crammed with contradictory information, they create a space of kinaesthetic dialogue. The viewer interacts with one part of the stone; what s/he finds there raises a question that can only be answered by movement elsewhere, where another answer – and another question – is forthcoming, and so on. The imagery is not easy to assimilate into a coherent picture. A first encounter may reveal the taloned foot of an enormous bird of prey; subsequently, a human arm grasping a staff; next, the jaguar's round eye and nose. The viewer is free to

FIGURE 2.3 Unnamed lintel with repeating eyes. Photograph by the author.

move, and the stone creates the desire to move; it engages, provides partial answers – but also withholds information. The partial, fragmentary results of the encounter could be part of the message – or they could have provoked viewers to consult with others.

We can find hints of this experience in the sixteenth-century Spanish reports from another sacred site, the great coastal oracle of Pachacamac. These describe a series of approaches to various sacred precincts within the site, each of which required a specific regimen of fasting and ritual; adherents might spend days, weeks, or months in one single area, visiting and revisiting the sacred things that lived there (Pizarro 1970:123 [1533]; cited in Moore 1996). The complex carvings on these stones seem exactly suited to such slow, interactive viewing; one can imagine nights of long discussion with other visitors in which what was seen might be shared and compared, and the messages they contained absorbed until the supplicant felt s/he had grown stronger and wiser – ready either to return home, or to venture further within.

Although the social and material context is very different, there are resonances with modern-day religious practice. The Canelos Quichua of Amazonian Ecuador use long nights of dialogue about dreams and visions to gain access to the perspectives of the animals and the spirits. Men do so through ecstatic shamanic ritual; women potters sculpt ceramic effigies of their visions, making them visible and active in social life (Whitten 1976, 1985). This open space of dialogue and learning sounds appealing, but it is not the ultimate experience to be had at Chavín. At the heart of the temple complex is a singular monolith – one that few visitors may ever have seen, while others knew it only through whispers, myths, and stories.

Into the darkness: the circular plaza and the galerías

The external regions of large plazas, staircases, and buildings apparently date to later centuries, built to accommodate more visitors as Chavín's fame grew. Off slightly to one side is an older, smaller, inner complex (Burger 1992; Lumbreras 1977; Rowe 1977). This area is constructed to create a dramatic passage down into darkness through hidden tunnels, the galerías. From a large and public space, one enters a series of small and intimate rooms that accommodate only a few people at a time. The windowless galleries create an intense synaesthetic response. They induce disorientation, claustrophobia, and the unpleasant sensation of having entered into the bodily cavities or internal organs of a large, rocky beast. Elsewhere, Chavín stone masons created smooth, even surfaces; here, the rough, irregular rocks, equal in size and shape on all four sides, seem like an organic, fleshy substance transmuted into mineral.

This part of the site is structured as a conduit: one enters, moves through corridors, arrives, and departs. The sunken circular plaza is the launching pad: here, simple recurrent carvings of felines and humans march in procession toward the stairs that lead into the galerías, and ultimately to the Lanzón.[9] This message is reinforced architecturally by a stripe of colored stone down the middle of the plaza, a path leading visitors towards their goal.

Once visitors enter the galleries, they are in a performance space designed for special effects: auditory, visual, and kinetic. The tube-like galleries, with their dead ends, right-angle turns, and sudden changes in floor height, disorient and mystify. When the temple was fully functional, this spatial context must have intensified the effect of suddenly seeing an illuminated, costumed figure or hearing a chanting voice or the sound of a conch shell trumpet.[10] Add hallucinogens to this synaesthetic mix – an addition that is strongly hinted by exterior carvings showing people processing into the temple carrying hallucinogenic plants, as well as the conch shell trumpets – and the experience could have been unforgettable – and overwhelming.

Ongoing research into the galleries provides factual reinforcement for the seemingly fanciful notion of the temple as a sort of prehistoric 'Haunted House.' Internal features built into the galleries produce unexpected sensory impressions (Rick 2005). An elaborate system of ducts, shafts, and apertures introduces fresh air into the galleries and channels humidity out; the airiness of the galleries is welcome, but disconcerting, since its origins cannot be ascertained. The ducts also convey sounds produced in one chamber into other chambers, creating an unnerving impression of voices and whispers in an empty room. It has been suggested that some hidden channels might be responsible for the extraordinary roaring sounds audible within the underground galleries when rain falls on the ground outside (Burger 1992:143; Lumbreras 1977). Rick (2008) also postulates that polished hematite mirrors found at the site may have been used to refract light into the galleries through the shafts. This would have produced an extremely eerie, seemingly inexplicable visual sensation not unlike the auditory effects.

The overall experience is of a place outside of everyday experience. A recent technical study of the auditory characteristics of the galleries reinforces the archaeologists' impressions: the strange sonic characteristic of the galleries creates a "noncoherent energy density" that envelops and disorients the listener. "Such an auditory space is unusual in the natural world, and may augment the positional disorientation induced by the labyrinthine layout" (Abel et al. 2012:4172). At the end of the journey through these disorienting galleries, the traveler finally arrives at the place created by/for the most enigmatic monolith of them all: the Lanzón.

Final confrontation: the Lanzón

Coming to the Lanzón, we arrive at the heart of Chavín – and the place where complete and coherent vision is least possible. This granite prism may have begun life as a naturally occurring stone, worshipped long before the rest of Chavín de Huantar was built. In fact, the entire temple complex may have been gradually constructed around this originary holy place. According to this reconstruction, early in the site's history, worshippers erected a small stone chamber around the free-standing monolith, in keeping with highland religious tradition. Over the centuries, as the site grew in importance, successive generations continued building until they had completely entombed the stone and its network of surrounding galleries, turning the monolith into an underground deity (Rick 2008).

In pictures, the Lanzón is crude and somewhat unimpressive; in life, it is an object of great chthonic power. Even modern unbelievers speak of its "awe-inspiring quality ... [that] photographs and drawings fail to communicate" (Rowe 1977:9 [1962]). This effect originates in the striking architectural setting. The tall splinter of stone stands at the end of a claustrophobically small and windowless passageway within the underground *galerías*, trapped in a secret room that can barely hold its massive form.

Here, the viewer has no escape. From the gallery approaching it, the statue can be seen almost in its entirety; the closer one comes, however, the more incoherent and overwhelming it appears (Figure 2.4). The statue "exceeds the architectural space that envelops it" (Cummins 2008:287). Too big a statue in too small a space, it forces viewers into inescapable intimacy with an oppressively powerful figure.

FIGURE 2.4 The Lanzón. Photograph by the author.

More than twice as tall as any human being, the granite prism is difficult to see in its entirety; this problem is greatly exacerbated by the chamber's tight quarters and convoluted shape, which force viewers into such close proximity that the statue continually dissolves into fragments, offering only incoherent, partial views of body parts – clawed feet, naked spine,[11] human torso. Roll-outs of the figure reveal that incoherence and disorientation are built into its dimensions (Cummins 2008).

At the very end of the journey, then, one encounters a singular figure, not identifiable as any one species, yet unitary in appearance, unlike the composites found outside. Rather than a multivocalic text incorporating the perspectives of many different creatures, here there is a singular figure, carved in the round, that the viewer must face as one embodied creature to another. Here, there is no backing away, no gaining perspective, no ready escape: too close to see the entirety of the creature, one is left to look directly into the enormous, inhuman eye; the deep, active nostril; or the gigantic fanged mouth.

Few, indeed, would have been the travelers who entered this last, most sacred chamber. At Pachacamac, years of fasting and ritual preparation were necessary merely to approach the outermost wall of the innermost sanctum; until forced to by the Spanish, even powerful political leaders did not dare to enter the room. The entire site of Chavín de Huantar is constructed as a place of journey: the goal is to go, experience it, and return home, richer in perspective but still recognizably oneself. It is thus a materialization of the shamanic vision quest – a religious undertaking that the *galerías* and the Lanzón epitomize in its most extreme form. The vision quest is always hazardous: in the encounter with the spirits of the non-human, the student is always at risk of losing themselves and their own, human perspective. To gain significant knowledge, much less transformation, one must risk all by confronting an alien being – an encounter in which the weaker may be absorbed by the stronger.

At Chavín, the further one enters into the site, and the closer one comes to the monoliths, the more one experiences threats of violence, deathly force, and over-whelming inhuman power. But the stones embody other possibilities besides annihilation: an encounter with their exuberant imagery and perplexing physicality could also engender pleasure, stimulation, and growth. In exploring the temporality created by the stones, we discover a multiplicity of viewpoints, an inherent incoherence and a kinetic interactivity. These qualities suggest that playfulness, incredulity, and sheer delight should be included among the possible responses the stones might elicit. Even in the *galerías* and the innermost chamber, where the spatial experience is at its most challenging and claustrophobic, the kinaesthetic effects bring to mind modern entertainments such as the Haunted House, the horror movie, and the video game – a reminder that as humans, we willingly seek and create experiences that elicit the full gamut of emotional responses, dark as well as light.

Taking our cue from the stones, we might want to be similarly open-minded in our interpretive approach. Following Mitchell, we can let the picture show us what it wants, and especially how it wants us to look: slowly or quickly, partly or totally, kinaesthetically or synaesthetically. If we can overcome the deadened, anaesthetized responses that our own ontologies teach us, we may become more alive to the stones, just as they want to be alive to us. But as to whether the time and space that we find there will be those of learning, of transformation, of death, or just of momentary pleasure – in the end, the stones will leave that up to us.

Notes

1 Although Chavín has customarily been referred to as a 'pilgrimage site' based on descriptions by early Spanish chroniclers, archaeologists have recently become wary of this designation because of unexamined and possibly inappropriate connotations of the term 'pilgrimage,' that is, its association with state-level societies (Timothy Earle, personal communication 2012), or its suggestion of large numbers of ordinary people coming to the site (Earle, personal communication 2012; John Rick, personal communication 2011). I do not describe Chavín as a 'pilgrimage site' in this article, but I do occasionally use the word 'pilgrim' to describe travelers who came from afar in hopes of a transformative religious experience.

2 Many archaeologists shy away from using the word 'art' to describe Pre-Columbian artifacts, rightfully arguing that the modern category 'art' had no prehispanic equivalent. However, I use 'art' and 'artist' for the following reasons. First, the same could be said for any other word we might choose to use, including 'artifact.' Second, by using terms such as 'craft' or 'carving,' which in contemporary usage refer to things of lesser cultural value than 'art' or 'sculpture,' we build in unwarranted negative assumptions about the things we study; and third, art museums are full of things that were not originally conceived of as 'works of art' in the modern sense. This article is not written for a Pre-Columbian audience, but for a contemporary one, which can see Pre-Columbian sculpture, ceramics, textiles, and other artifacts are exhibited as 'art' in art museums, and recognizes them as such.

3 The comparison to textual analyses of metaphors used in ancient Nordic song is an awkward one; Urton 2008:220 criticizes Rowe on these grounds.

4 The stone was likely originally a lintel, on which the image would have been horizontal rather than vertical; in this case, one would turn one's body from side to side to make the anatropic transformation.

5 Amazonian religion has been variously described. I use the term 'animist' here, partly in response to the cogent criticisms of Klein et al. (2002) about the use of the term 'shamanism' in Pre-Columbian studies. For a recent debate on the most appropriate terminology, see Latour 2009.

6 I do not believe that all Native South Americans share exactly the set of beliefs Viveiros de Castro describes, but his discussion of perspectivism illuminates a general "Amerindian" ontology with a broad geographical and deep temporal reach, comparable to fundamental ontologies that might be described for other regions of the world such as Asia or Europe.

7 Soil surfaces in modern times and contradictory wall dimensions given in different publications prevent me from stating an exact height for these ashlar blocks' original positions. However, John Rick asserts confidently that many of them were cornices at the very top of exterior temple walls, above the normal human ability to see the carved images on their surfaces (Rick, personal communication 2005). Jerry Moore cites Lumbreras' figure of 12m above ground for the height of the Old Temple walls (Lumbreras 1977:2–3, cited in Moore 1996:51); the walls of the New Temple (Building A) are higher.

8 Regarding the particular challenges posed by the Black and White Portals, see Weismantel (2012, 2013, 2014).

9 See the excellent discussion of the spatial and iconographic relationship between the circular plaza and the Lanzón in Cummins (2008).

10 A cache of trumpets was found in a room off one of the galleries, apparently stored there and used in performances (Rick 2005).

11 This has variously been interpreted as a spine or a rope; comparison to the Sechín Alto carvings suggests the former interpretation may be the correct one.

Bibliography

Abel, J. S., J. W. Rick, P. P. Huang, M. A. Kolara, J. O. Smith, and J. M. Chowning (2008). "On the Acoustics of the Underground Galleries of Ancient Chavín de Huántar, Peru." Electronic document, https://ccrma.stanford.edu/groups/chavin/publications/Acoustics08. pdf, accessed July 15, 2012.

Ayres, Fred D. (1961). Rubbings from Chavin de Huantar, Peru. *American Antiquity* 27(2):239–45.

Bennett, Jane (2010). *Vibrant Matter: A Political Ecology of Things*. Duke University Press, Durham, North Carolina.

Berger, John (1980). *About Looking*. Pantheon Books, New York.

Braidotti, Rosi (2002). *Metamorphoses: Towards a Materialist Theory of Becoming*. Polity, Cambridge.

Brown, Bill (2001). Thing Theory. *Critical Inquiry* 28(1):1–22.

——(2003). *A Sense of Things: The Object Matter of American Literature*. University of Chicago Press, Chicago.

Buchanan, Brett (2008). *Onto-Ethologies:The Animal Environments of Uexküll, Heidegger, Merleau-Ponty, and Deleuze*. State University of New York Press, Albany.

Burger, Richard L. (1984). *The Prehistoric Occupation of Chavín de Huantar, Peru*. University of California Publications in Anthropology vol. 14. University of California Press, Berkeley.

——(1992). *Chavín and the Origins of Andean Civilization*. Thames and Hudson, New York.

——(2009). The Intellectual Legacy of Julio C. Tello. In *The Life and Writings of Julio C. Tello, America's First Indigenous Archaeologist*, edited by Richard L. Burger, pp. 65–89. University of Iowa Press, Iowa City.

Burger, Richard L., and Lucy C. Salazar (2008). The Manchay Culture and the Coastal Inspiration for Highland Chavín Civilization. In *Chavín: Art, Architecture, and Culture*, edited by William J. Conklin and Jeffrey Quilter, pp. 85–106. Cotsen Institute of Archaeology, University of California, Los Angeles.

Calarco, Matthew (2008). *Zoographies: The Question of the Animal from Heidegger to Derrida*. Columbia University Press, New York.

Coole, Diana, and Samantha Frost (editors) (2010). *New Materialisms: Ontology, Agency and Politics*. Duke University Press, Durham, North Carolina.

Cordy-Collins, Alana K. (1977). Chavín Art: Its Shamanic/Hallucinogenic Origins. In *Pre-Columbian Art History: Selected Readings*, edited by Alana Cordy-Collins and Jean Stern, pp. 353–62. Peek Publications, Palo Alto, California.

——(1980). An Artistic Record of the Chavín Hallucinatory Experience. *The Masterkey for Indian Lore and History* 54(3):84–93.

Cummins, Tom (2008). Felicitous Legacy of the Lanzón. In *Chavín: Art, Architecture, and Culture*, edited by William J. Conklin and Jeffrey Quilter, pp. 279–304. Cotsen Institute of Archaeology, University of California, Los Angeles.

Day, Jo (editor) (2012). *Making Sense of the Past: Towards a Sensory Archaeology*. Center for Archaeological Investigations, Southern Illinois University, Carbondale.

Doyon-Bernard, Suzette (1997). Jackson Pollock: A Twentieth-Century Shaman. *American Art* 11(3):8–31.

Gell, Alfred (1998). *Art and Agency: An Anthropological Theory*. Clarendon Press, Oxford.

Hall, Martin (2000). *Archaeology and the Modern World: Colonial Transcripts in South Africa and the Chesapeake*. Routledge, New York.

Haraway, Donna (2008). *When Species Meet*. University of Minnesota Press, Minneapolis.

Howes, David (editor) (2005). *Empires of the Senses: The Sensual Culture Reader*. Berg, Oxford.

Ingold, Tim (2000). *The Perception of the Environment: Essays on Livelihood, Dwelling and Skill*. Routledge, London.

——(2011). *Being Alive: Essays on Movement, Knowledge and Description*. Routledge, London.

Klein, Cecelia, Eulogio Guzmán, Elisa C. Mandell, and Maya Stanfield-Mazzi (2002). The Role of Shamanism in Mesoamerican Art: A Reassessment. *Current Anthropology* 43(3):383–419.

Lathrap, Donald W. (1973). Gifts of the Cayman: Some Thoughts on the Subsistence Basis of Chavín. In *Dumbarton Oaks Conference on Chavín*, edited by Elizabeth P. Benson, pp. 73–100. Dumbarton Oaks Research Library and Collection, Washington, D.C.

Latour, Bruno (2009). Perspectivism: 'Type' or 'Bomb'? *Anthropology Today* 25(2):1–2.

Llobera, Marcos (2007). Reconstructing Visual Landscapes. *World Archaeology* 39(1):51–69.

Lumbreras, Luis (1977). Excavaciones en el Templo Antiguo de Chavín (sector R): informe de la sexta campaña. *Ñawpa Pacha* 15:1–38.

——(1993). *Chavín de Huantar: Excavaciones en la Galería de las Ofrendas*. Verlag Philipp von Zabern, Mainz.

Malinowski, Bronislaw (1929). *The Sexual Life of Savages in Northwestern Melanesia*. Routledge and Kegan Paul, London.

Merleau-Ponty, Maurice (2002) [1945] *Phenomenology of Perception*. Translated by Colin Smith. Routledge, London.

Mitchell, W. J. T. (1994). *Picture Theory: Essays on Verbal and Visual Representation*. University of Chicago Press, Chicago.

——(2004). *What Do Pictures Want? The Lives and Loves of Images*. University of Chicago Press, Chicago.

Moore, Jerry (1996). *Architecture and Power in the Ancient Andes: The Archaeology of Public Buildings*. Cambridge University Press, Cambridge.

Promey, Sally (forthcoming 2014) Introduction. In *Sensational Religion: Sense and Contention in Material Practice*, edited by Sally Promey. Yale University Press, New Haven, Connecticut.

Rick, John W. (2005). The Evolution of Authority and Power at Chavín de Huántar, Peru. *Archaeological Papers of the American Anthropological Association* 14:71–89.

——(2008). Construction and Ritual in the Development of Authority at Chavín de Huantar. In *Chavín: Art, Architecture, and Culture*, edited by William J. Conklin and Jeffrey Quilter, pp. 3–34. Cotsen Institute of Archaeology, University of California, Los Angeles.

Rodriguez Kembel, Silvia (2008). The Architecture at the Monumental Center of Chavín de Huantar: Sequence, Transformations, and Chronology. In *Chavín: Art, Architecture, and Culture*, edited by William J. Conklin and Jeffrey Quilter, pp. 35–84. Cotsen Institute of Archaeology, University of California, Los Angeles.

Roe, Peter G. (2008). How to Build a Raptor: Why the Dumbarton Oaks 'Scaled Cayman' Callango Textile Is Really a Chavín Jaguaroid Harpy Eagle. In *Chavín: Art, Architecture, and Culture*, edited by William J. Conklin and Jeffrey Quilter, pp. 181–216. Cotsen Institute of Archaeology, University of California, Los Angeles.

Rowe, John H. (1977) [1962] Form and Meaning in Chavín Art. In *Peruvian Archaeology: Selected Readings*, edited by John H. Rowe and Dorothy Menzel, pp. 72–103. Peek Publications, Palo Alto, California.

Sharon, Douglas (2000). *Shamanism and the Sacred Cactus. Ethnoarchaeological Evidence for San Pedro Use in Northern Peru*. San Diego Museum Papers No. 37. San Diego Museum of Man, San Diego.

Smith, Adam T. (2003). *The Political Landscape: Constellations of Authority in Early Complex Polities*. University of California Press, Los Angeles.

Smith, Mark M. (2007). *Sensory History*. Berg, Oxford.

Taussig, Michael (1984). Culture of Terror—Space of Death. Roger Casement's Putumayo Report and the Explanation of Torture. *Comparative Studies in Society and History* 26(3):467–97.

Tello, Julio C. (1943). Discovery of the Chavín Culture in Peru. *American Antiquity* 9(1):135–60.

——(2009). *The Life and Writings of Julio C. Tello: America's First Indigenous Archaeologist*. Edited by Richard L. Burger. University of Iowa Press, Iowa City.

Tilley, Christopher (1994). *A Phenomenology of Landscape: Places, Paths and Monuments*. Berg, Oxford.

Torres, Constantino Manuel (2008). Chavín's Psychoactive Pharmacopoeia: The Iconographic Evidence. In *Chavín: Art, Architecture, and Culture*, edited by William J. Conklin and

Jeffrey Quilter, pp. 239–60. Cotsen Institute of Archaeology, University of California, Los Angeles.

Urton, Gary (2008). The Body of Meaning in Chavín Art. In *Chavín: Art, Architecture, and Culture*, edited by William J. Conklin and Jeffrey Quilter, pp. 217–38. Cotsen Institute of Archaeology, University of California, Los Angeles.

Viveiros de Castro, Eduardo (1998). Cosmological Deixis and Amerindian Perspectivism. *Journal of the Royal Anthropological Institute* 4(3):469–88.

——(2012). Immanence and Fear: Stranger-Events and Subjects in Amazonia. *Hau: Journal of Ethnographic Theory* 2(1):27–43.

Weismantel, Mary (2011). Obstinate Things. In *The Archaeology of Colonialism, Gender, and Sexuality*, edited by Barbara Voss and Eleanor Casella, pp. 303–22. Cambridge University Press, Cambridge.

——(2012). Coming to our Senses at Chavín de Huantar. In *Making Sense of the Past: Towards a Sensory Archaeology*, edited by Jo Day. Center for Archaeological Investigations, Southern Illinois University, Carbondale.

——(forthcoming 2013). Encounters with Dragons: The Stones of Chavín. *RES: Anthropology and Aesthetics*.

——(forthcoming 2014). Slippery and Slow: Chavín's Great Stones and Kinaesthetic Perception. In *Sensational Religion: Sense and Contention in Material Practice*, edited by Sally Promey. Yale University Press, New Haven, Connecticut.

Whitten, Norman E., Jr. (1976). *Sacha Runa*. University of Illinois Press, Urbana.

——(1985). *Sicuanga Runa: The Other Side of Development in Amazonian Ecuador.* University of Illinois Press, Urbana.

3

THEATER OF PREDATION: BENEATH THE SKIN OF GÖBEKLI TEPE IMAGES

Dušan Borić

Introduction

> Neither in their painting nor in their carving do people seek to reconstruct the material world they know, through their mundane subsistence pursuits of hunting and gathering, on a higher plane of cultural and symbolic meaning. Whether their primary concern be with the land or its non-human inhabitants, their purpose is not to represent but to reveal, to penetrate beneath the surface of things so as to reach deeper levels of knowledge and understanding. It is at these levels that meaning is to be found.
>
> *(Ingold 2000:130)*

Can the enclosures of Göbekli Tepe be seen as examples of the earliest recognized shrines, even temples, that completely exclude domestic functions? What was the social organization of the community that gathered their efforts to carve out large pillars, up to 7m tall, and occasionally to dress them with elaborate images of mainly wild and male animals? To what end was such a large labor pool mobilized? How big was the area around the site from which people were drawn in order to construct and/or visit this particular place? Was there a connection between broadly contemporaneous examples of intentional intensification in the use of wild plant resources across the area of the Fertile Crescent, eventually leading to their domestication, and aspects of life and ritual that surrounded what was going on at Göbekli Tepe during its earliest phases?

Over the past two decades, the excavator of Göbekli Tepe, Klaus Schmidt, has attempted to answer some if not most of these questions (e.g., Schmidt 2005, 2006, 2009, 2010). Very recently, however, other authors have also started questioning certain basic assumptions we have come to cherish about Göbekli Tepe, such as the site's role as a place for sacred ritual gatherings and the use of enclosures as shrines rather than houses (Banning 2011). But as many other scholars would agree (e.g., Belfer-Cohen and Goring-Morris 2011; Kuijt 2011; Verhoeven 2011), we may still be far from a comfortable place in answering many of these key questions. Despite years of hard work, significant surprises at this important site are still possible. This suggestion in particular refers to future excavations of the lowermost levels at the site, more refined absolute dating of its numerous features, and the opening of floors and stone benches, which potentially store numerous human remains. These inevitable future research efforts at Göbekli Tepe, and continuing work at other regional, broadly contemporaneous sites (Figure 3.1), should help to better inform future discussions about the site's place in a constellation of other sites, the nature of its use, and changes that affected it over the several phases represented by its stratigraphy.

While current evidence from Göbekli Tepe might be insufficient to address the changing nature of the site and the activities taking place therein, the rich repertoire of animal and other non-figurative depictions to be found carved onto large stone pillars and into sculptures using the same type of locally available stone,

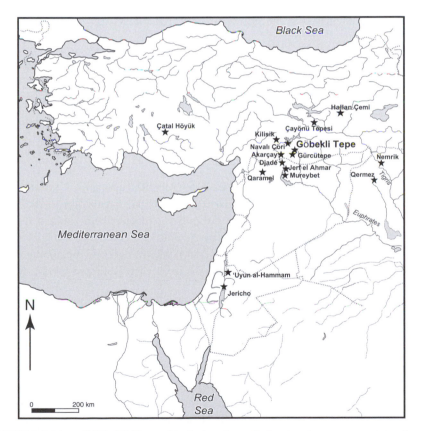

FIGURE 3.1 Map of Göbekli Tepe with the locations of related and contemporaneous sites in Upper Mesopotamia and the Near East.

invites us to attempt an analysis of this imagery. This striking imagery already has provoked interpretations by the site's excavator and his collaborators (e.g., Peters and Schmidt 2004; Schmidt 2005, 2006, 2009, 2010 and references therein) as well as other scholars (e.g., Hodder and Meskell 2010; Verhoeven 2002).

In this chapter, I contextualize the imagery from Göbekli Tepe, firstly within its local ecological and cultural milieu, and secondly in relation to discussions regarding depictions of animals among hunter-gatherer societies world-wide. The latter goal will explicitly be connected to recent discussions about different non-Western ontologies (e.g., Descola 1996, 2005; Viveiros de Castro 1998, 2004) that explore the usefulness of some recharged labels of older ethnographies, such as totemism and animism, and the currency that the notion of perspectivism has gained in recent years. This chapter takes as its main goal to understand whether the iconography and narrative structure of animal depictions at Göbekli Tepe, with similarities in the visual vocabulary seen in other broadly contemporaneous sites, can be read through a particular ontological key, and how we should best understand the function of such depictions. It is argued that this can be achieved even before deciding whether the site was a ceremonial center, and whether its exceptional features provide clues as to the site's assumed sacred nature.

The cultural and symbolic ecology of Pre-Pottery Neolithic Upper Mesopotamia

> … in Marx I found the fundamental idea that one cannot understand what is going on inside people's heads without connecting it to the conditions of their practical existence …
>
> *(Lévi-Strauss and Eribon 1991:108)*

It remains very difficult to fully contextualize Göbekli Tepe and its extraordinary features due to a lack of any substantial trace of human occupation in the wider region of Upper Mesopotamia prior to the earliest structures being built at the site. Current dating suggests that the earliest phase at Göbekli Tepe can probably be traced to the mid-10th millennium BC (Schmidt 2006), which marks the beginning of the Pre-Pottery Neolithic (PPN) period across the Levant (cf. Kuijt and Goring-Morris 2002).

The site is found on a large limestone ridge, some 800m asl, and consists of several large mounds; the location is somewhat unexpected as it is neither close to water nor arable land (Peters and Schmidt 2004; Schmidt 2001, 2003, 2006, 2009, 2010; Schmidt and Hauptmann 2003). To date, at least six semi-subterranean 'ritual' structures have been exposed (Figure 3.2), while geophysical survey has determined the existence of at least another 15 enclosures. The estimated number of enclosures is around 25. Documented 'ritual' structures contained numerous T-shaped pillars of different sizes. Over 45 of these pillars have been at least partially exposed with an estimate that the site may contain over 200 such pillars of different sizes. There are two main PPN phases distinguished at the site: the earliest

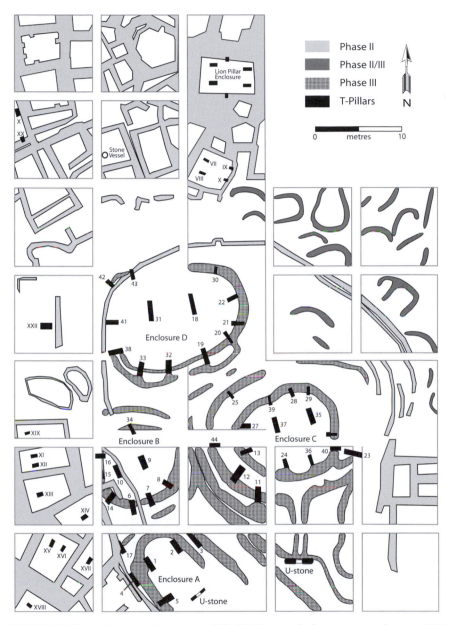

FIGURE 3.2 The main excavation area at Göbekli Tepe with features exposed up to 2009 (adapted after Schmidt 2009:Figure 3).

is represented by Layer III, attributed to the PPNA period, and dated to between 9100 and 8500 BC. This is followed by Layer II, assigned to the PPNB period, and dated to between 8700 and 8000 BC. At the moment, such dating remains confined to largely re-deposited materials from the backfilling of enclosures rather than primary deposits that may in the future yield more accurate and feature-specific chronological determinations.

While there are clear continuities between the two main phases in the use of T-pillars, the construction of enclosures, and the range of depicted images at the site, diachronic changes can also be detected. Such changes primarily relate to a reduction in the size of pillars from more than 5m in height (Layer III) to the 1.5m tall pillars found associated with Layer II. There is also a move from circular to rectangular enclosure plans. In Layer III circular enclosures, two large pillars were free-standing in the centers of the enclosures, while other pillars were partly encased by stone walls, with only the 'front' parts being visible, often with depictions of animals.

The shape of the T-pillars has been interpreted as anthropomorphic, and this interpretation is supported by engravings of human arms on the wide sides of some pillars, and of fingers on the narrow sides (Figure 3.3). The shape of these pillars, with large pronounced heads, has also been seen as phallic (Hodder and Meskell 2010:36). As well, many of these pillars are decorated with zoomorphic images,

FIGURE 3.3 T-pillar 18 with carvings of human arms, Enclosure D, one of the two central pillars at Göbekli Tepe (photograph by Irmgard Wagner, Deutsches Archäologisches Institut).

and to these animal depictions we can add the existence of a large number of limestone sculptures. Wolves, boars, dogs, aurochs, goitered gazelles, wild Asiatic asses, lions/leopards, hyenas, snakes, scorpions, spiders, and several species of birds, including vultures, are all portrayed. If such an anthropomorphic understanding of these pillars is accepted, carvings of animals would have thus been inscribed on, or in, human/ancestral bodies. Anthropomorphic elements, however, are also found, including a schematic human body shape (in one case headless), arms, fingers, and a giant phallus, as well as pictograms in the shape of the letter 'H' (Figure 3.3), which are sometimes associated with a belt feature. Regarding these T-pillars, it is not clear if the idea was to represent a stylized human body at the outset, or if this shape became anthropomorphized through the interpretive acts of carving human arms, fingers, and so on. Excepting the clear representation of a woman engraved, rather than sculpted, on a stone slab from the later phase (Layer II) of the rectangular-shaped 'lion pillar' enclosure (Schmidt 2006:Figure 10.4), the remaining depictions of animals, apart from birds, can be gendered as male.

Peters and Schmidt (2004) provide information on the number and kind of faunal remains found at the site between 1996 and 2001 (Figure 3.4a). Only wild fauna is documented at Göbekli Tepe, indicating intensive hunting in the environments surrounding the site. Based on the number of identified specimens (NISP), gazelle is by far the most represented food animal, followed by aurochs, equids, wild sheep, and wild boar. It has been estimated, however, that aurochs might have contributed close to 50 per cent of the diet. The number of fox remains is also relatively large, and their presence may suggest a possible economic and/or symbolic significance (see below).

If one compares the range and frequencies of animal remains with the range and frequencies of animals depicted on T-pillars or those carved in stone (Figure 3.4b), there are obvious differences between these cultural and symbolic ecologies (cf. Descola 1992, 1996). Gazelle, for example, is found in only one depiction, and while more frequently depicted than either gazelle or wild sheep, aurochs seem less important in this symbolic ecology than what their subsistence role suggests. On the other hand, one finds a large number of snake depictions, followed by fox, wild boar, cranes or ducks (?) and various larger, predatory animals such as lion/leopard, bear, wolf, and hyena. Comparable T-pillar forms or depictions are found at the PPNB sites of Nevalı Çori (Hauptmann 1993, 1999, 2002, 2007), Adiyaman-Kilisik (Hauptmann 2000; Hauptman and Schmidt 2007), downtown Urfa-Yeni Mahalle (Hauptmann 2003), Jerf el Ahmar (Stordeur 2000; Stordeur and Abbès 2002; Stordeur et al. 2000), and other sites in southeastern Anatolia (see Figure 3.1).

These examples suggest that a common set of iconographic rules might have stemmed from a shared symbolic ecology over a large area. There are also striking similarities between the depictions at Göbekli Tepe and certain contemporaneous sites in Upper Mesopotamia, and many parallels can be observed across southwest Asia over the several millennia that the PPNA and PPNB periods cover (cf. Hodder and Meskell 2010). It would be wise, however, to resist for the moment dehistoricizing the meanings established by particular communities that inhabited certain

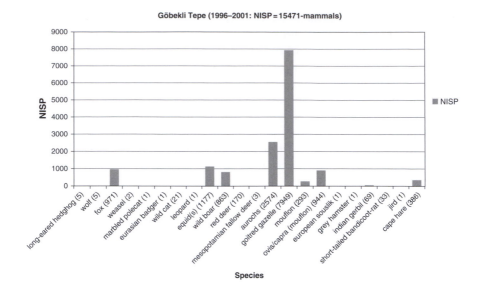

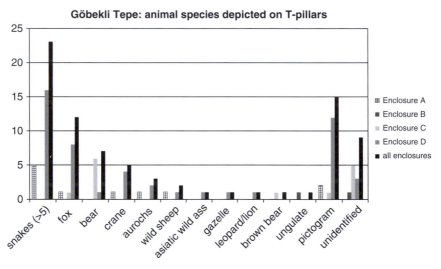

FIGURE 3.4 (a) Frequency of hunted animals at Göbekli Tepe; (b) frequency of depicted animals at Göbekli Tepe (appended after Peters and Schmidt 2004).

sites in the region by extrapolating some vague transhistorical similarities. Instead, a suggestion could be made that aspects of any symbolic ecology established at a particular site may differ significantly from other sites in the wider region, even when elements of the same cultural vocabulary or existing natural affordances are shared (cf. Descola 1996). Indeed, as Phillipe Descola (1992:124) points out, we should be reconstructing "localized systems of interrelations." Before I address the

underlying characteristics of the symbolic ecology of the community or communities that were using/inhabiting Göbekli Tepe, I turn to the wider theoretical
context of discussions regarding the transformation from hunting and gathering
to farming societies and the concomitant modes of relations that might have
characterized these differentiated past contexts.

Domestication as master narrative and other ontologies

The idea that the domestication process is part of a progressive move from 'nature'
to 'culture' has often been emphasized (e.g., Cauvin 2000; Hodder 2006, 2007;
Verhoeven 2002; Voigt 2000) and only rarely challenged (e.g., Boyd 2004). As the
foundation of modernist epistemology, it is often assumed that nature is given and
acted upon (e.g., mastered, tamed, etc.), whereas culture is something that becomes
an exclusive property of humans in an ever-progressive advance of rationality and
reason. In recent anthropological discourse, the abandonment of such a dualist
position and the adoption of a monist perspective has been, in large part, triggered
by both an internal questioning of Western metaphysics and epistemology (e.g.,
Latour 1993; cf. Descola 1996:82) and ethnographic fieldwork in non-Western
contexts where the nature-culture dichotomy in the conceptualization of the
world is meaningless (Descola and Pálsson 1996:7; see also Descola 2005). Rather
than assuming an abstract and absolute realm of nature or 'wilderness' from which a
particular culture or society is detached, these ethnographic cases indicate that the
definitions of 'culture' or 'nature' are always highly contextual and that 'wild-tame'
dimensions rarely work as a dichotomy (Hviding 1996; cf. Hodder 1990). And
while it is true that Lévi-Strauss used the nature-culture distinction for native
societies of the Americas, as Descola emphasizes, "the nature-culture distinction is
little more than a blanket label under which Lévi-Strauss has conveniently organized contrasted sets of sensible qualities which may be ethnographically relevant,
although Amerindians do not feel the necessity to subsume them, as we do, under
two different ontological domains" (1996:84).

Let us take the taxonomy of 'human' vs. 'non-human' bodies. The very
distinction that we draw between these labels may in itself appear problematic.
What lurks behind this difficulty in naming is the question of our own ontological
positioning, of what goes without saying in our universe when the concept of
human is contrasted with the concept of non-human: we equate human with
'culture' and non-human with 'nature.' Aparecida Vilaça (2005) stresses that being
human or non-human should not be considered in terms of *states* and *substances*
but rather in terms of *processes* and *relations* (cf. Descola and Pálsson 1996:12). In
such an ontological universe, the potential for transformation/metamorphosis is
acknowledged as an inherent capacity of all beings. To gain or preserve a particular
position along the human/non-human spectrum requires a constant negotiation
and construction of identity. For instance, Eduardo Viveiros de Castro quotes the
ethnographic example of Shokleng community myths, "that the original Shokleng,
after sculpting the future jaguars and tapirs in araucaria wood, gave these animals

their characteristic pelts by covering them with the diacritical marks pertaining to the clanic-ceremonial groups: spots for the jaguar, stripes for the tapir." In other words, continues Viveiros de Castro, "it is social organization that was 'out there,' and the jaguars and tapirs that were created or performed by it. The institutional fact created a brute fact" (2004:13). A similar inversion of our own conceptual categories can be found in the domain of relatedness and kinship – instead of sharing something in common as the main postulate for the existence of relations in our own society, Amerindian perspectivism would emphasize relations based on difference, seeing affinity as 'given' and consanguinity as constructed.

But where does this leave us? Is it possible to "challeng[e] universalistic models" while providing for a common discourse and "meaningful comparisons" (Descola and Pálsson 1996:16)? In his book *Par-delà nature et culture* (*Beyond Nature and Culture*), Descola (2005; see also Descola 1992, 1996) suggested schemes of praxis reflecting specific types of relations (between a finite number of elements) that each society establishes with its environment. By using the criteria of physicality, referring to the body, and interiority, which applies to self, personhood, and mind, Descola proposes a four-fold taxonomy of ontologies based on principles of identity and difference: animism, totemism, analogism, and naturalism (see also Watts, this volume; Shapland, this volume; Latour 2009). This typology is based on the varied relationships between humans and non-humans along the axes of interiority (mind and soul) and exteriority (body): (1) *totemism* sees the continuity between humans and non-humans both in terms of their bodies and souls; (2) *animism* sees humans and non-humans as having the same 'culture,' while differing according to their respective bodies; (3) *analogism* is equated with the Ancient Greek and Chinese worldviews where the discontinuity between humans and non-humans on both physicality and interiority axis can be demonstrated; and (4) *naturalism*, defines the current scientific Western ontology that sees continuity between humans and non-humans along the physicality axis, assuming the same biological basis of life, while discontinuity is postulated along the interiority axis in the assumption that what differentiates humans from other animals is the fact that the former have culture. One should note that Descola's four-fold typology of ontologies still allows that, along with a dominant ontology, in any given society, one may find residues of other ontologies, opportunistically surviving in heterogeneously composed assemblages. Descola (1992, 1996) also suggests that there can be several different ideologies or modes of relation present within these dominant ontologies (cf. Lloyd 2006), such as the ideologies of predation, reciprocity/exchange or protection. These different modes of relations can also be linked to particular types of social organization: totemic systems are more frequently found in segmentary societies with descent groups, while animism is more often present in cognatic societies (Descola 1996:88). I will return to some of these issues below with reference to the imagery from Göbekli Tepe.

This particular emphasis on distinctions between the bodies and souls of humans and non-humans as a way of providing clues about particular ontologies invites us to examine the imagery of Göbekli Tepe in the hopes of defining the ontological world of PPN communities in Upper Mesopotamia more closely. In the remainder of this chapter, I review a discussion by Tim Ingold (2000:111–31; cf. Descola 2010) of differences in depictions between what he identifies as totemic vs. animic hunter-gatherer contexts (for the preference in using the term 'animic' over 'animist,' see Descola 1992:125, n5). The suggestion that styles of depiction as human expression are cross-culturally indicative of underlying ontologies has most recently been explored further by Descola through the exhibition entitled "La Fabrique des Images" held in Musée Quai Branly in Paris (Descola 2010; cf. Descola 2006). After briefly reviewing aspects of totemic and animic depictions, an analysis of the iconography of Göbekli Tepe imagery follows.

Totemic and animic depictions among hunter-gatherers

In discussing animic and totemic cultural traditions of Aboriginal Australia and the circumpolar North, Ingold (2000) questions the common understanding of indigenous art and animal depictions, conventionally seen as symbolic representations of 'hunting magic' and asserts that these artworks should be understood as engaging with the plane of immanence, "probing more deeply into it and … discovering the significance that lies therein" (Ingold 2000:112). The artworks of both cultural traditions are thus not representational but serve to reveal this world of immanence, which the animal's gaze conceals (cf. Borić 2005). There are important differences between these different modes of depicting animals as defined by Ingold (2000) and Descola (2010).

Totemic depictions

In the totemic tradition of Aboriginal Australia, animals and humans share the same ancestral land. All living beings descend from the era of the 'Dreaming,' when the ancestral figures shaped the features of the land, impressing it through their movements and in this way shaping it. The relationship that all living beings have with the land can be described as *essential* – that is, these beings are *consubstantial* – and this is key to Ingold's definition of a 'totemic' context. When it comes to depicting animals and humans in Aboriginal Australia, one can often find images of kangaroos, some with the use of the so-called 'X-ray' style of painting, which shows the internal layout of organs and lines along which the body parts are partitioned during butchering. Describing examples of depictions from Western Arnhem Land, Ingold stresses the static, non-narrative portrayal of the animals, in this way conveying a message about the inanimate character of the depicted being. Ingold goes further to emphasize that the very body of the depicted kangaroo he describes can be seen as the ancestral, immobile landscape in its totality. Through this kind of painting, the ancestral presence is revealed to humans.

On the other hand, in the Kimberley region of northwestern Australia, one finds rock paintings in certain caves with the depiction of *Wandjina* figures, anthropomorphic ancestral beings with a halo-like band around their heads, large rounded eyes, and no other orifices. Such figures are often accompanied by similarly inanimate depictions of animal forms. According to Ingold (2000:121), these ancestral beings "did not picture themselves *on* the rock, they painted themselves *into* it" and thus, "[i]n the painting, they metamorphosed into their own depictions" since their "depiction is a mode of being." Similarly, in an essay about the iconography of artworks by the Walbiri of central Australia, Nancy Munn (1973:198) emphasizes that artworks can be seen as a process of revealing and opening up that which lies beneath the surface, and understood as efforts to 'pull out' an ancestral force from the immanent reality of Dreaming that lies beneath the surface of the earth.

Animic depictions

On the other hand, in the circumpolar North communities that Ingold discusses as an example of animic ontology, a vital force exists in human exchange with the animal world. Here, one emphasizes the importance of 'cooperation' between hunter and prey, since the meat that can be eaten comes only from the animal that "intentionally offers itself to the hunter" (Ingold 2000:121). In the animic system, hunting is the very activity that enables the flow of vital force between human and non-human beings. Human life "is here predicated on the mortality of animals" (Ingold 2000:114). If totemic ontologies are described as essential, with animal and human beings sharing the same ancestral substance, animic ontologies can be portrayed as *dialogical*. Worldly balance and human life are conditioned by a constant exchange between animals and humans. As well, body form is seen as permanently in flux: "[b]orne along in the current, beings meet, merge and split apart again, each taking with them something of the other" (Ingold 2000:113). What matters in this dialogue and exchange is taking up the point of view of the other, that is the 'relative positioning' of the two sides: "upon 'crossing over' to the animal side, a man will see his hosts as creatures like himself, while to the people back home he will now appear in animal form" (Ingold 2000:114; cf. Viveiros de Castro 1998). This ability to change perspectives is also credited to certain animals (e.g., bear; see Saladin D'Anglure 1994). But it is shamans in particular who can at will change their perspective and journey to the communities of animals in order to uncover the vital force and cure illness (cf. Willerslev 2007). In fact, a shaman in animic systems is seen as possessing a permanently unstable body, and is said to be "chronically ill" (cf. Vilaça 2005). On their journeys, shamans "negotiate with the spirit masters" the release of lost vital force: "[a]nimals of various kinds, known as his 'helpers', carry his inner being aloft on this journey, yet all the while his corporeal body remains where it stands" (Ingold 2000:115).

In examining the mode of depiction with regard to an animic system, Ingold uses an example of the Inuit of northern Québec. In the first narrative scene described by Ingold, a caribou encounters a hunter ready to send an arrow in his direction. In the described drawing, the caribou behaves suspiciously by holding a branch in its jaws and the hunter does not shoot. Yet, in another drawing coming

from the same cultural context, again the encounter between a hunter and a caribou is shown, but this time one sees the caribou with arrows that have penetrated
its body, while on the other side, the hunter who shot the arrows looks directly
at us and appears terrified. Moreover, the skin and fur of the wounded animal
are pulled back and the true face of an inner being is revealed with a dangerous
wolf-like snout and sharp, threatening teeth. The scene with the 'hoodless caribou,' shows a danger that may await the hunter if the animal does not give itself
up intentionally, that is when there is a violation of the subtle balance and vital
exchange between animals and humans. In such instances, killing the prey may
cause potential danger to the hunter and even lead to his own death in the
encounter with the animal's *real* face, that is, its inner being: " ... the possibility
of metamorphosis expresses the ... fear of no longer being able to differentiate
between the human and the animal, and, in particular, the fear of seeing the human
who lurks within the body of the animal one eats ... " (cf. Viveiros de Castro
1998:481).

In another instance, Ingold (2000) describes the intertwined worlds of animal
and human beings as reflected in the recorded ethnography of the Ojibwa of
central Canada. Here, the constitution of the human self is perpetually threatened
by the possibility of 'slipping' into the animal realm. For Ojibwa hunters and
trappers, the ability to metamorphose is left to very powerful persons, such as
sorcerers and shamans, and for most other humans it would mean death (Ingold
2000:93). Importantly, Ingold asserts that it would be misleading to view the process of metamorphosis among the Ojibwa only as a way of clothing or masking the
unchanged core of a being since this apparent surface is the actual body. Hence,
"[t]he metamorphosis is not a covering up, but an *opening up*, of the person to
the world" (Ingold 2000:94). For the Ojibwa, one's personhood and self are in
continuous movement – of becoming in relation with other humans and 'other-
than-human' beings. The concept of metamorphosis is seen as a way to bridge the
distance between one's self in becoming the 'other' through the faculty of empathy. Thus, Ojibwa animism (cf. Bird-David 1999; Descola 1992), or their notion of
animacy, enables metamorphosis into those classes of animal beings that are closest
to them, animals with whom these humans are genealogically related (Ingold
2000:106–9).

Degrees of danger and predatory moves: the meaning of bared teeth at Göbekli Tepe

So far in my discussion, following Ingold and Descola, I have challenged the
dominant mode of seeing Neolithic depictions abundantly found across southwest
Asia as abstract statements about symbolic and practical aspects of past societies from
the Western dualist perspective. Informed by the discussions of Ingold and Descola
regarding different styles of depictions in two different (ontological) systems, labeled
totemic and animic, it is now time to turn our attention to an interpretation of the
Göbekli Tepe animal imagery. The first question that comes to mind is whether

we can determine if the depictions at Göbekli Tepe come from the totemic or animic systems, according to the logic previously outlined.

The fact that many of the images depicted at Göbekli Tepe can be seen as having a narrative structure – even in the absence of hunting activities, the lack of an 'X-ray' style, and a sense of movement associated with the portrayal of animal forms – could perhaps be considered important clues about the animic, rather than totemic, logic behind the depictions. What is particularly striking here, however, is the similarity between the previously described depiction of a 'hoodless caribou,' which reveals a dangerous inner being underneath its skin by showing its teeth, and the depiction of a certain number of animals at Göbekli Tepe with similarly dangerous bared teeth. In my opinion, this formal similarity is not serendipitous and may point to an animic system behind the animal depictions at this site. But before making conclusions about certain cross-cultural invariants or universals in the use of particular corporeal affordances, such as using teeth of wild predator animals to indicate danger, let us take a closer look at the inner logic of such imagery and try to understand if this formal similarity in depicting certain animals with bared teeth can be seen as having the same underlying function as the caribou depicted by the Inuit.

On T-pillars at Göbekli Tepe, animals often shown with their teeth include wild boar (Figure 3.5), fox (Figure 3.6), lion or leopard, and hyena. Several other predatory animals such as wolves and bears (and a possible reptile) are likely depicted in sculptures found in the backfill of enclosures, attached to some of the T-pillars (e.g., the sculpture on Pillar 27 from Enclosure C [Schmidt 2009: Figure 3]), or as protrusions intentionally inserted in the stone walls of some enclosures. The animate character of these protrusions can also be related to T-pillars encased by stone walls (e.g., a canid and a bird depicted on Pillar 43 from Enclosure D [Schmidt 2009:Figure 8]) and these depictions may have been intended to create a dramatic, theatrical appearance of animals popping up 'alive' from another, parallel world or reality. As such, the stone walls of these structures may have been conceptualized in a similar way to the mudbrick walls of Çatalhöyük buildings: as membranes separating different worlds (cf. Lewis-Williams 2004:38). Associated depictions and sculptures can perhaps be interpreted as a way of releasing these animals or hybrid beings onto the surface that represented the interface between different realities.

That the main intention of depicting these animals in such a way was to underline strong, dangerous spirits lurking beneath the skin of the depicted animals is further strengthened by the display of enlarged canines and erect penises, as well as likely attack postures with raised heads and front legs in relation to the main body axis of a quadruped. Indeed, in certain instances where foxes are shown, we could even speculate that the raised posture of the body, as if the animal is standing on two legs, can possibly be connected with an attempt to mimic a human stance. If this interpretation is correct, it would further emphasize the underlying humanity of the depicted animals (cf. Sahlins 2008; Viveiros de Castro 1998). But before developing the theme of predation in relation to these images, let us dwell a bit longer on the choice of animals showing dangerous teeth (Table 3.1).

FIGURE 3.5 T-pillar 12 with the carvings of birds in a landscape (?), wild boar and fox, Enclosure C, Göbekli Tepe (photograph by Dieter Johannes, Deutsches Archäologisches Institut).

FIGURE 3.6 T-pillar 33, with the carving of a fox, Enclosure D, Göbekli Tepe (photograph by Irmgard Wagner, Deutsches Archäologisches Institut).

TABLE 3.1 Iconography, taxonomy, and categorization of Göbekli Tepe animal depictions based on the danger principle.

Dangerous, bared teeth, raised front legs and (attacking?) body posture	Dangerous (chthonic?), no teeth shown	With horn cores (danger?)	Not obviously dangerous (celestial?), upright posture
Fox	Scorpion	Aurochs	Duck
Wild boar	Snake	Goitered gazelle	Crane
Lion/leopard (?)	Spider	Wild sheep	Bird (?)
Reptiles (?)			Asiatic ass
Wolf (?)			Vulture
Unidentified canid			
Bear (?)			
Hyena			

While we might expect large predators (e.g., lion, brown bear, or wolf) to be portrayed with bared teeth, as well as potentially dangerous animals such as snakes, scorpions, and spiders,[1] it is curious that such a striking pattern of depiction is also found with animals such as fox and wild boar. Neither of these two animal species could be considered inherently dangerous (even though wild boar can present considerable danger if encountered by humans under particular conditions), and it might be that showing sharp, bared teeth in the depictions of both fox and wild boar (certainly not a characteristic of suids apart from their canines) is intended to remove any doubts about the character of the inner being that lurks beneath the skin. In this way, the potentially ambiguous position of fox and wild boar is laid bare and the message conveyed about both depicted animal species is consistent: these are wild, male, and dangerous beings. To judge by the meanings given to particular animals among the Inuit of the Canadian Arctic, the predatory character of certain species might have been mixed with the idea of scavenging, which may have been connected to various species of birds and perhaps also fox and wild boar (Saladin D'Anglure 1994:179). As mentioned before, a relatively high number of fox bones at the site gives us some idea about both the practical and symbolic uses of fox at Göbekli Tepe. The antiquity of beliefs related to fox and its importance in the wider regional context is supported by the recent discovery of fox bones associated with a human burial found at the Middle Epipalaeolithic site of 'Uyun al-Hammam in northern Jordan (Maher et al. 2011).

In contrast to the previous groups of animals, no bared teeth are shown in depictions of aurochs or several kinds of birds (likely cranes, ducks, and vultures). Yet, on several T-pillars, one finds a juxtaposition of these different groups of animals. Similar to aurochs, depictions of goitered gazelles, Asiatic wild ass, and wild sheep or mouflon also remain 'toothless.' As well, there is a recurrent practice of depicting aurochs by showing the skull with horn cores *en face* and never in profile. Here, we can only speculate as to whether the emphasis on showing auroch, gazelle, and wild sheep horn cores in this way might relate to the danger of this particular body part or to a host of other significations that might have surrounded horn cores in this cultural context (see Hodder and Meskell 2010 and references therein regarding the importance of horn cores from aurochs and other animals at Çatalhöyük).

Finally, the group of animals that is not in any obvious way implicated with predatory intentions is birds, such as cranes and ducks (Figure 3.5). In several instances, there are multiple depictions of their body form, as if to create an illusion of movement (a similar style of depiction is found in Upper Palaeolithic Franco-Cantabrian parietal art; see Lewis-Williams 2002 and Lewis-Williams and Pearce 2005 for an interpretation based on altered states of consciousness). It is probably no accident that only avian fauna is shown in this way. The ambulatory behavior of some birds, for example, such as crane or even duck, might have been understood as human-like (Russell and McGowan 2003), making them closer to humans in this classificatory universe or betraying their underlying humanity (cf. Lévi-Strauss 1966:204, 207).

In contrast to predatory, scavenging, and dangerous animals, birds might not have expressed any threat and, while this is speculative, may even have been understood as shamans under their feathers and skin. To emphasize this humanity, the bird depicted on Pillar 43, Enclosure D (Figure 3.7) at Göbekli Tepe also has incised neck ornamentation similar to the one depicted on the sculpture of the Urfa

FIGURE 3.7 An artistic reconstruction of construction works in enclosure D (Layer III) at Göbekli Tepe (drawing: John Gordon Swogger).

Man (cf. Hauptmann 2003). The depiction of the headless human riding this bird could perhaps be interpreted as a moment of shamanic transformation. Shamanistic journeys are often seen as temporary deaths of these individuals, and the perspective taken in this scene might have been from the point of view of the spirit world, or birds themselves, rather than that of ordinary life and the human world.

As we find many animal depictions at Göbekli Tepe which can be understood to display a predatory stance, we may ask in what types of ontological contexts would these intentions have been emphasized? In order to answer this question, we should return to the point stressed by Ingold when discussing the hunting scene in the circumpolar North, in which a wounded caribou reveals its predatory intentions towards the hunter:

> For not only does the hoodless caribou, its predatory intentions revealed, pose a direct threat to life and limb, but also the very sight of it casts a pall of uncertainty over [the hunter's] existential status as a human being. In short, the faces of animals are visible only to humans who have taken up the subject positions of the animals themselves, and who have therefore – in the eyes of other humans – actually *turned into* animals. Only shamans have the power to do this intentionally and with relative impunity.
>
> *(Ingold 2000:123)*

Following this passage, the imagery depicted at Göbekli Tepe on T-pillars and three-dimensional sculptures suggests an arena in which one is removed from the everyday conduct of the world. Here, it would seem, one encounters the parallel worlds of powerful animal communities, which are revealed by their release from T-pillars or by the intentional installations of dangerous animals that protrude from stone enclosure walls. Following the logic of an animic or perspectival system (cf. Latour 2009), the construction of such an animate theater might have presented considerable danger for those who were involved in such an undertaking (Figure 3.7). As Ingold (2000:126) notes, the act of carving, as opposed to painting, is closer to the animic system as "carving is not the wilful imposition of preconceived form on brute matter, but a process in which the carver is continually responsive to the intrinsic qualities of the material, to how it wants to be." It is again the dialogue with the very material being carved that might have enabled the release of vital force embodied in the animals depicted at Göbekli Tepe. Here, one is tempted to agree with Lewis-Williams and Pearce (2005) that the existence of ritual practitioners/specialists might have been a necessary condition for this type of social context. Such shamans may have mediated between what is perceived as everyday human existence and the perspectives taken up by the communities of depicted spirit animals. Such shamans may have been exactly those people whose hard labor went into the release of dangerous and predatory animals through the very acts of carving, suggesting horizontal, rather than vertical, shamanism in this context (cf. Hugh-Jones 1994).

So far, I have attempted to identify a grid of internal logic behind depictions of animal imagery at Göbekli Tepe with the help of ethnographic comparisons and the alignment of these artworks with animic or perspectival thought, rather than totemic ontological contexts. We still know little about the nature of activities that were taking place at Göbekli Tepe, partly due to the (likely intentional) demolition of certain sculptures and their deposition in secondary contexts, the intentional backfilling of enclosures by occupation refuse, and the still unexcavated lower levels and stone benches which may hide key pieces of evidence in this particular archaeological puzzle. It seems possible, however, to sketch a particular ontological system that might have perceived the human world as full of powerful beings, some with threatening, predatory powers. Such a world likely necessitated constant negotiations with humans and non-humans, as well as the living and the dead, for the retrieval of vital forces upon which the life of all beings is conditioned. One could also speculate that these animic or perspectival ontological systems might have brought together ethnically or culturally diverse communities that shared the same ontological outlook (Miracle and Borić 2008). It has been noted by Peters and Schmidt (2004:210) that a number of flint arrow points from different PPN regional traditions across Upper Mesopotamia (e.g., Aswad, el-Khiam, Helwan, Nemrik, and Nevalı Çori) are found at the site, suggesting to the authors that Göbekli Tepe may have served as a nodal point for supra-regional gatherings. Exploring each other's differences with predatory intentions of emulating and becoming the other might have been key elements of the general tendency for "transferability and intercultural validity" (Sherratt 1995:16–17) across the PPN world.

Conclusion

While I have attempted to give meanings to a range of depictions at Göbekli Tepe, it is clear that the spectrum of themes that these carvings reveal is far from singular. In other words, while depictions within totemic and animic systems have previously been discussed primarily in relation to the practice of hunting and relations between humans and animals established in such contexts, it becomes apparent that depictions at Göbekli Tepe can hardly be subsumed under the rubric of reflections on hunting. This extraordinary site suggests many other themes when it comes to the nature and range of its imagery: the question of metamorphosed anthropomorphic and schematized beings depicted on T-pillars, schematization in the depiction of bull heads in particular, the depiction of highly schematized carved symbols of unknown significance, such as H-signs positioned on particular parts of the T-pillar body, and the schematization of snakes in the creation of geometric non-figurative net-like patterns, among others. Moreover, one could argue that there is little obvious association between snakes, spiders, and scorpions on the one hand, and hunting on the other. And, there is no need for us to expect that the very activity of hunting was ever intended to be depicted here (or for that matter at the much later site of Çatalhöyük, where one indeed finds schematically depicted miniature human figures 'teasing' larger-than-life animals).

In accord with Ingold's and Descola's discussions of the nature, function, and meaning of depictions in animic and totemic contexts of hunter-gatherer societies, the portrayals at Göbekli Tepe do not show everyday aspects of hunting practices in relation to particular animals or provide statements about the human overpowering of the wild, as implied through the metanarratives of domestication so often evoked in archaeological interpretations of the Early Holocene symbolic ecology. Such narratives can only be read as our own impatient anticipations of the neatly assembled 'Neolithic packages' with domesticated plants and animals as key goodies. The depictions at Göbekli Tepe, rather, release the power of the predator and more ambiguously positioned animals. They might have come from a human desire and hunger for the vital force that particular animals harness beneath their volatile and changing skins. Surely, this release of vital force, power, and danger is hardly haphazard and, at Göbekli Tepe, it is not that only certain animals can be trusted and expected to release such powers, but it seems that the very choice of animals and their occasionally spatially structured depictions reveal the logic of their own, a particular classificatory system constructed through accumulation of 'wild thinking' (cf. Keck 2009) and by socializing particular animals and the powerful inner beings they embody. What seems to pervade in this particular ontological system is the notion of predation. At the same time, it is quite likely that the very existence of such a complex construction, with the concomitant mobilization of work that it entailed, represents a statement about socially complex ways of relating. And perhaps already at this historical moment it was becoming difficult to think about the multiplicity of existing relations among emerging singularities of the world without developing and resorting to modes of thinking involving analogical relations (*sensu* Descola). Yet, the question that has been posed before remains: was it an underlying animality or humanity that is being depicted here? Who is the hunter and who is hunted in this theater of predation?[2]

Notes

1 Apart from their dangerous character, perhaps this group of animals can be linked to the world below, that is, to the chthonic stratum of a tiered cosmos. For instance, in North American mythology, Spider has "a magical power he had received from the Thunders … . The Nighthawk (a goatsucker) stands halfway between the Thunders and, masters of the celestial world, and Spider, master of the terrestrial world: he bears the responsibility for the conflict between these powers" (Lévi-Strauss 1988:68).

2 I am grateful to Klaus Schmidt for his warm welcome to the site of Göbekli Tepe in the fall of 2008, his generous tour of the site, and images reproduced here. I would also like to acknowledge the support of the Cambridge-based, Leverhulme-funded programme "Changing Beliefs of the Human Body: Comparative Perspective," during which a field trip to the site and the exhibition in Karlsruhe, as well as some thinking and writing about Göbekli Tepe, took place. I am also grateful to Alasdair Whittle and Chris Watts for their comments on earlier drafts of the paper, and to Chris Watts for his meticulous editorial help.

Bibliography

Banning, Edward B. 2011. So Fair a House: Göbekli Tepe and the Identification of Temples in the Pre-Pottery Neolithic of the Near East. *Current Anthropology* 52(5):619–40.

Belfer-Cohen, Anna, and Nigel Goring-Morris 2011. Comment on So Fair a House: Göbekli Tepe and the Identification of Temples in the Pre-Pottery Neolithic of the Near East. *Current Anthropology* 52(5):642–43.

Bird-David, Nurit 1999. 'Animism' Revisited: Personhood, Environment, and Relational Epistemology. *Current Anthropology* 40(S):67–91.

Borić, Dušan 2005. Body Metamorphosis and Animality: Volatile Bodies and Boulder Artworks from Lepenski Vir. *Cambridge Archaeological Journal* 15(1):35–69.

Boyd, Brian 2004. Agency and Landscape: Abandoning the Nature/Culture Dichotomy in Interpretations of the Natufian. In *The Last Hunter-Gatherer Societies in the Near East*, edited by Christophe Delage, pp. 119–36. BAR International Series 1320. British Archaeological Reports, Oxford.

Cauvin, Jacques 2000. *The Birth of the Gods and the Origins of Agriculture*. Cambridge University Press, Cambridge.

Dietrich, Oliver 2011. Radiocarbon Dating the First Temples of Mankind. Comments on ^{14}C-dates from Göbekli Tepe. *Zeitschrift für Orient-Archäologie* 4:12-25.

Dietrich, Oliver, Manfred Heun, Jens Notroff, Klaus Schmidt, and Martin Zarnkow 2012. The Role of Cult and Feasting in the Emergence of Neolithic Communities. New Evidence from Göbekli Tepe, South-eastern Turkey. *Antiquity* 86:674-95.

Descola, Philippe 1992. Societies of Nature and the Nature of Society. In *Conceptualizing Society*, edited by Adam Kuper, pp. 107–26. Routledge, London.

——(1996). Constructing Natures: Symbolic Ecology and Social Practice. In *Nature and Society: Anthropological Perspectives*, edited by Philippe Descola and Gísli Pálsson, pp. 82–102. Routledge, London.

——(2005). *Par-delà Nature et Culture*. Éditions Gallimard, Paris.

——(2006). La Fabrique des Images. *Anthropologie et Sociétés* 30(3):167–82.

——(2010). *La Fabrique des Images*. Musée Quai Branly, Paris.

Descola, Philippe, and Gísli Pálsson 1996. Introduction. In *Nature and Society: Anthropological Perspectives*, edited by Philippe Descola and Gísli Pálsson, pp. 1–22. Routledge, London.

Hauptmann, Harald 1993. Ein Kultgebaude in Nevalı Çori. In *Between the Rivers and Over the Mountains: Archaeologica Anatolica et Mesopotamica Alba Palmieri Dedicata*, edited by Marcella Frangipane, Harald Hauptmann, Mario Liverani, Paulo Matthiae, and Machteld Mellink, pp. 37–69. University of Rome, Rome.

——(1999). The Urfa Region. In *Neolithic in Turkey: The Cradle of Civilization: New Discoveries*, edited by Mehmet Özdoğan and Nezih Başgelen, pp. 65–86. Arkeoloji ve Sanat Yayınları, Istanbul.

——(2000). Ein Frühneolitisches Kultbild aus Kommagene. In *Gottkönige am Euphrat – Neue Ausgrabungen und Forschungen in Kommagene*, edited by Jörg Wagner, pp. 5–9. Philipp von Zabern, Mainz.

——(2002). Upper Mesopotamia in its Regional Context during the Early Neolithic. In *The Neolithic of Central Anatolia*, edited by Frederick Gerard and Laurens Thissen, pp. 263–71. Ege Yayınları, Istanbul.

——(2003). Eine Frühneolitische Kultfigur aus Urfa. In *Köyden Kente: Yakindoğu'da ilk yerleşimler – From Village to Cities: Early Villages in the Near East*, edited by Mehmet Özdoğan, Harald Hauptmann, and Nezih Başgelen, pp. 623–36. Arkeoloji ve Sanat Yayınları, Istanbul.

——(2007). Nevalı Çori. In *Vor 12000 Jahren in Anatolien. Die ältesten Monumente der Menschheit (Gebundene Ausgabe)*, edited by Clemens Lichter, pp. 86–87. Badisches Landesmuseum, Karlsruhe.

Hauptmann, Harald, and Klauss Schmidt 2007. Anatolien vor 12000 Jahren: Die Skulpturen des Frühneolithikums. In *Vor 12000 Jahren in Anatolien. Die ältesten Monumente der Menschheit (Gebundene Ausgabe)*, edited by Clemens Lichter, pp. 67–82. Badisches Landesmuseum, Karlsruhe.

Hodder, Ian 1990. *The Domestication of Europe*. Basil Blackwell, Oxford.

——(2006). *The Leopard's Tale: Revealing the Mysteries of Çatalhöyük*. Thames and Hudson, London.

——(2007). Çatalhöyük in the Context of the Middle East Neolithic. *Annual Review of Anthropology* 36:105–20.

Hodder, Ian, and Lynn Meskell 2010. The Symbolism of Çatalhöyük in its Regional Context. In *Religion in the Emergence of Civilization: Çatalhöyük as a Case Study*, edited by Ian Hodder, pp. 32–72. Cambridge University Press, Cambridge.

Hugh-Jones, Stephen 1994. Shamans, Prophets, Priests, and Pastors. In *Shamanism, History, and the State*, edited by Nicholas Thomas and Caroline Humphrey, pp. 32–75. University of Michigan Press, Ann Arbor.

Hviding, Edvard 1996. Nature, Culture, Magic, Science: On Meta-language for Comparison in Cultural Ecology. In *Nature and Society: Anthropological Perspectives*, edited by Philippe Descola and Gísli Pálsson, pp. 165–84. Routledge, London.

Ingold, Tim 2000. *The Perception of the Environment: Essays in Livelihood, Dwelling and Skill.* Routledge, London.

Keck, Frédéric 2009. The Limits of Classification: Claude Lévi-Strauss and Mary Douglas. In *The Cambridge Companion to Lévi-Strauss*, edited by Boris Wiseman, pp. 139–55. Cambridge University Press, Cambridge.

Kuijt, Ian 2011. Comment on So Fair a House: Göbekli Tepe and the Identification of Temples in the Pre-Pottery Neolithic of the Near East. *Current Anthropology* 52(5):646–47.

Kuijt, Ian, and Nigel Goring-Morris 2002. Foraging, Farming, and Social Complexity in the Pre-Pottery Neolithic of the Southern Levant: A Review and Synthesis. *Journal of World Prehistory* 16:361–440.

Latour, Bruno 1993. *We Have Never Been Modern.* Harvester Wheatsheaf, New York.

——(2009). Perspectivism: 'Type' or 'Bomb'? *Anthropology Today* 24(2):1–2.

Lévi-Strauss, Claude 1966. *The Savage Mind.* University of Chicago Press, Chicago.

——(1988). *The Jealous Potter.* University of Chicago Press, Chicago.

Lévi-Strauss, Claude, and Didier Eribon 1991. *Conversations with Claude Lévi-Strauss.* University of Chicago Press, Chicago.

Lewis-Williams, David 2002. *The Mind in the Cave: Consciousness and the Origins of Art.* Thames and Hudson, London.

——(2004). Constructing a Cosmos: Architecture, Power and Domestication at Çatalhöyük. *Journal of Social Archaeology* 4(1):28–59.

Lewis-Williams, David, and David Pearce 2005. *Inside the Neolithic Mind.* Thames and Hudson, London.

Lloyd, Geoffrey 2006. Pint for the Cat. *The Times Literary Supplement* 17 March:22–23.

Maher, Lisa A., Jay T. Stock, Sarah Finney, James J. N. Heywood, Preston T. Miracle, and Edward B. Banning 2011. A Unique Human-Fox Burial from a Pre-Natufian Cemetery in the Levant (Jordan). *PLoS One* 6(1):e15815.

Miracle, Preston, and Dušan Borić 2008. Bodily Beliefs and Agricultural Beginnings in Western Asia: Animal-Human Hybridity Re-Examined. In *Past Bodies: Body-Centered Research in Archaeology*, edited by Dušan Borić and John Robb, pp. 101–13. Oxbow Books, Oxford.

Munn, Nancy 1973. The Spatial Presentation of Cosmic Order in Walbiri Iconography. In *Primitive Art and Society*, edited by Anthony Forge, pp. 193–220. Oxford University Press, London.

Peters, Joris, and Klaus Schmidt 2004. Animals in the Symbolic World of Pre-Pottery Neolithic Göbekli Tepe, South-eastern Turkey: A Preliminary Assessment. *Anthropozoologica* 39:179–218.

Russell, Nerissa, and Kevin J. McGowan 2003. Dance of the Cranes: Crane Symbolism at Çatalhöyük and Beyond. *Antiquity* 77(297):445–55.

Sahlins, Marshall 2008. *The Western Illusion of Human Nature: With Reflections on the Long History of Hierarchy, Equality, and the Sublimation of Anarchy in the West, and Comparative Notes on Other Conceptions of the Human Condition.* Prickly Paradigm, Chicago.

Saladin D'Anglure, Bernard 1994. Nanook, Super-male: Polar Bear in the Imaginary Space and Social Time of the Inuit of the Canadian Arctic. In *Signifying Animals: Human Meaning in the Natural World*, edited by Roy Willis, pp. 178–95. Routledge, London.

Schmidt, Klaus 2001. Göbekli Tepe, Southeastern Turkey. A Preliminary Report on the 1995–99 Excavations. *Paléorient* 26(1):45–54.

——(2003). 'Kraniche am See'. Bilder und Zeichen vom frühneolithischen Göbekli Tepe (Südosttürkei). In *Der Turmbau zu Babel. Ursprung und Vielfalt von Sprache und Schrift, Eine Ausstellung des Kunsthistorischen Museums Wien für die Europäische Kulturhauptstadt*, edited by Wilfried Seipel, pp. 23–29. Band IIIA, Graz.

——(2005). 'Ritual Centers' and the Neolithisation of Upper Mesopotamia. *Neo-Lithics* 2(5):13–21.

——(2006). *Sie bauten die ersten Tempel: Das rätselhafte Heiligtum der Steinzeitjäger: die archäologische Entdeckung am Göbekli Tepe*. Beck, Munich.

——(2009). Göbekli Tepe: Eine Beschreibung der wichtigsten Befunde erstellt nach den Arbeiten der Grabungsteams der Jahre 1995–2007. In *Erste Tempel – Frühe Siedlungen: 12000 Jahre Kunst und Kultur. Ausgrabungen und Forschungen zwischen Donau und Euphrat*, pp. 3–39. Isensee Verlag, Oldenburg.

——(2010). Göbekli Tepe: The Stone Age Sanctuaries. New Results of Ongoing Excavations with a Special Focus on Sculptures and High Reliefs. *Documenta Praehistorica* 27:239–56.

Schmidt, Klaus, and Harald Hauptmann 2003. Göbekli Tepe et Nevalı Çori. *Dossiers d'Archéologie* 281:60–67.

Sherratt, Andrew, 1995. Reviving the Grand Narrative: Archaeology and Long-term Change. *Journal of European Archaeology* 3(1):1–32.

Stordeur, Danielle 2000. New Discoveries in Architecture and Symbolism at Jerf el Ahmar (Syria), 1997–99. *Neo-Lithics* 1:1–4.

Stordeur, Danielle, and Frédéric Abbès 2002. Du PPNA au PPNB: Mise en lumière d'une phase de transition à Jerf el Ahmar (Syrie). *Bulletin de la Société Préhistorique Française* 99(3):563–95.

Stordeur, Danielle, Michel Brenet, Gérard Der Aprahamian, and Jean-Claude Roux 2000. Les bâtiments communautaires de Jerf el Ahmar et Mureybet horizon PPNA (Syrie). *Paléorient* 26(1):29–44.

Verhoeven, Marc 2002. Ritual and Ideology in the Pre-Pottery Neolithic B of the Levant and Southeast Anatolia. *Cambridge Archaeological Journal* 12:233–58.

——(2011). Comments on So Fair a House: Göbekli Tepe and the Identification of Temples in the Pre-Pottery Neolithic of the Near East. *Current Anthropology* 52(5):649–50.

Vilaça, Aparecida 2005. Chronically Unstable Bodies: Reflections on Amazonian Corporalities. *Journal of the Royal Anthropological Institute* 11:445–64.

Viveiros de Castro, Eduardo 1992. *From the Enemy's Point of View: Humanity and Divinity in an Amazonian Society*. University of Chicago Press, Chicago.

——(1998). Cosmological Deixis and Amerindian Perspectivism. *Journal of the Royal Anthropological Institute* 4:469–88.

——(2004). Perspectival Anthropology and the Method of Controlled Equivocation. *Tipití* 2(1):3–22.

Voigt, Mary M. 2000. Çatal Höyük in Context: Ritual at Early Neolithic Sites in Central and Eastern Turkey. In *Life in Neolithic Farming Communities: Social Organization, Identity, and Differentiation*, edited by Ian Kuijt, pp. 253–93. Kluwer Academic/Plenum Publishers, London.

Willerslev, Rane 2007. *Soul Hunters: Hunting, Animism and Personhood among the Siberian Yukaghirs*. University of California Press, Berkeley.

4

THE BEAR-ABLE LIKENESS OF BEING: URSINE REMAINS AT THE SHAMANKA II CEMETERY, LAKE BAIKAL, SIBERIA

Robert J. Losey, Vladimir I. Bazaliiskii, Angela R. Lieverse, Andrea Waters-Rist, Kate Faccia, and Andrzej W. Weber

Introduction

On the southwestern shore of Eastern Siberia's Lake Baikal is Shamanka II, one of northern Eurasia's most spectacular hunter-gatherer cemeteries (Figure 4.1). Shamanka has been subject to extensive excavations, the majority of which have been directed by Vladimir I. Bazaliiskii as part of the Baikal Archaeological Project. Work at the site from 2001–8 resulted in the discovery of 107 graves, yielding skeletal remains from a minimum of 165 human individuals.[1] Eleven of these individuals date to the Early Bronze Age (~5400–4000 cal BP), while the remaining 154 fall within the Early Neolithic period (~8000–7000 cal BP) and belong to Kitoi mortuary tradition. Importantly, the depositional environment at Shamanka has been highly conducive to the preservation of bone, antler, and teeth. This has allowed for the presence of the large human skeletal assemblage, but also has made possible the recovery of thousands of well-preserved faunal remains and osseous tools from the graves and surrounding sediments.

This paper discusses one set of animal remains widely distributed at Shamanka, namely, those of brown bears (*Ursus arctos*). Recovered from numerous Early Neolithic graves were bear teeth, head bones, and bacula (penis bones), and additional fragments of these same elements were present in the surrounding sediments. Typically, the bear head elements were found within the upper portions of grave pits and do not appear to have been buried concurrently with particular human bodies. The presence of these same elements in the sediments surrounding graves suggests that they were sometimes removed from the pits during episodes of grave reopening and reuse. Unlike the bear head elements, the bacula were often found directly on human skeletons or amongst other implements buried in bundles near bodies. Despite many decades of cemetery excavations in the Baikal area, the patterned treatment of bear parts at Shamanka is wholly distinct – few

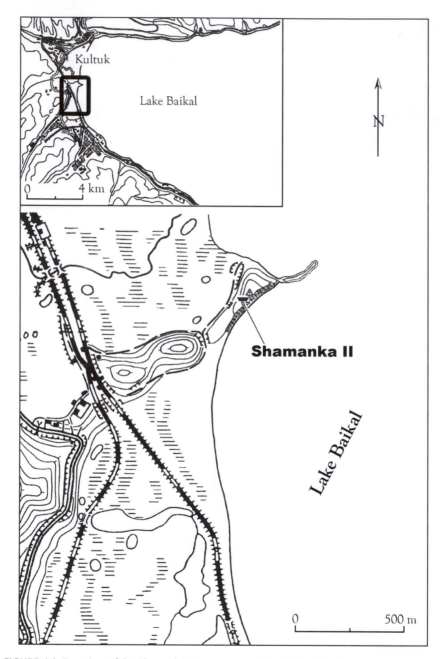

FIGURE 4.1 Location of the Shamanka II cemetery on Lake Baikal, Russia.

other individual human graves, let alone other cemeteries, have bear remains in them.

Animal remains from cemeteries in the Baikal area have seen little formal analysis or interpretation (but see Losey et al. 2011). Like many other regions of the globe, faunal remains from virtually all contexts here have been interpreted from implicitly 'modern western' perspectives (see Thomas 2004 for a review specific to archaeology), where animals are mindless food items, sources of tool materials, passive commodities, and status symbols that all are objects of cold calculations by their human counterparts. While these perspectives have proven informative and overwhelmingly dominate the discipline of zooarchaeology, the resulting portrayal of human engagements with the animal world is narrow and potentially misleading. Furthermore, these modern notions sharply contrast with ethnographic descriptions of human–animal relationships in indigenous societies throughout the North and elsewhere. Seizing upon this contrast, archaeologists working on many fronts have begun to employ interpretive perspectives that explore how peoples of the past understood their relationships with animals, and how these ways of knowing and interacting with fauna are evidenced in the material remains we study (see, among many others, Argent 2010; Conneller 2004; Losey 2010; Mannermaa 2008; McNiven 2010; McNiven and Feldman 2003; Sauvet et al. 2009).

Building upon this framework, we develop an explanation for the distinct treatments given to bear remains during the Early Neolithic at Shamanka. To accomplish this, we first examine in detail the archaeological context of the bear remains, including assessing how and with whom they were interred. Following this, we review the strong influence of Hallowell (1926, 1960) on understandings of bear ceremonialism in anthropology, and some questions that follow from his arguments are presented. We then review more recent ethnographic material on bears in Northern cosmologies and ontologies, paying particular attention to how persons (human or animal), bodies, souls, and bodily effects are understood and manipulated. We argue that bears were ontologically similar or equivalent to humans, having unique and powerful souls that cycled through the cosmos. Bears' deaths, like those of humans, were gradual processes, and their souls and the potencies of their bodies lingered on after what we would consider the time of death. Mortuary rites were held for the bears, in part to help them regenerate, but also as a means of showing them respect and to prevent their retaliation against the living. We suggest that these insights into bear burial practices at Shamanka also allow for new inferences to be made about the meanings behind human mortuary practices in the region.

Shamanka and its bears

Around 8,000 years ago, the Shamanka landscape began to be repeatedly used for a distinct set of activities, most of which involved rituals associated with the handling of the human dead. No evidence for contemporaneous residential sites has been found near this landform, suggesting that people placing their dead here first had to transport them some distance. Graves were found along the crest of a hill directly on the lakeshore, and down a gentle slope on its southwest side. The view from this place was (and is) spectacular – massive and imposing Lake Baikal, framed by forested mountains, stretches beyond the horizon to the northeast, while a thin finger of land extending from the base of the cemetery hill grasps out at the water.

This landform, known as Shamanka, is one of the most distinct areas of the lake's southwestern shoreline.

The cemetery was probably used for many centuries during the Early Neolithic (Weber et al. 2006), and this period witnessed the construction of at least 97 graves, many of which were dug down into the eroded and powdery white marble bedrock underlying the hill's upper soil horizons (Figure 4.2). Grave pits were typically elongated ovals capable of holding adult-sized bodies. Fifty-six of the graves contained remains of only one human each, while the remaining 41 held elements of multiple individuals. Early Neolithic males or probable males outnumber females and probable females by 69 to 36, with the remaining 48 individuals being unassigned to sex. Such sex ratios in cemeteries are not unusual and appear to be at least partially a product of male bodies being more readily identifiable than female ones (Weiss 1972). All age classes were buried at the cemetery, with at least 30 infants and children (0–12 years of age), 15 adolescents (12–20 years), and 108 adults (20+ years) being present.

FIGURE 4.2 Early Neolithic graves at Shamanka. Black ovals are graves with bear remains. Gray squares indicate the presence of bear remains in non-grave sediments.

Most of the anatomically intact human bodies from this period were found lying on their backs in the extended position. Other body positions also were present, including two prone, six flexed or semi-flexed, and five probable secondary burials in a variety of forms. By our count, however, as many as 60 of the Early Neolithic graves at Shamanka were revisited in antiquity, and the majority of individuals are represented by partially or wholly disarticulated skeletal remains, and some are evidenced only by isolated elements.

It appears that several processes were responsible for the disarticulated states of many of the Shamanka skeletons. First, single grave pits were repeatedly used for interments, and these acts of burial were perhaps months or even years apart. In some cases this resulted in bodies being deposited at different levels of a pit, with a later burial cutting into an earlier one, perhaps unintentionally. In other cases, bodies or body parts were clearly moved to one side or end of a grave to make space for a later burial. Moved body segments (e.g., arms, legs, etc.) were sometimes found articulated, indicating that acts of manipulation could involve bodies that were not fully skeletonized. We believe these patterns are signs that grave pits were marked in some way that allowed them to be easily relocated. The general paucity of overlapping Early Neolithic grave pits at the site (perhaps only five graves overlap others) also indicates that this was the case. Second, some graves were re-entered after an individual was interred and the body was handled or removed. This sometimes involved manipulating just the head, which when excavated was found out of anatomical position either beside the skeleton or inverted. In other cases, it appears graves were reopened and the head and other body portions (most often the upper body) were removed. Furthermore, many individuals are represented by only a few isolated bones, suggesting that either nearly whole bodies were buried here and later almost entirely moved or removed, or that people were transporting and burying only fragments or portions of skeletonized human remains. Some isolated human remains also were found scattered in the sediments around the graves, perhaps also the result of grave pit re-entry. These too may have entered graves unintentionally when the pits were refilled. Looting appears to be a very uncommon cause of grave disturbance, as re-entered graves still typically contained numerous artifacts. There appears to be little evidence for non-human entry of grave pits, except for a few cases of rodent burrowing.

Human remains at Shamanka were almost always found in association with other materials, including modified and unmodified faunal remains. Some items, such as marmot (*Marmota* spp.) incisors, red deer (*Cervus elaphus*) canines, and bone and shell beads, were found on bodies and almost certainly were parts of garments worn by the deceased. Other items, such as boar (*Sus scrofa*) canine pendants, antler harpoons, and insert-blade weapon heads appear to have been suspended on the body by means of cordage, or were simply placed loose on the head or chest during burial. Notably, most items with intact human skeletons were found in concentrations, often near or under the head, or at the feet. These included a vast array of items such as fish hooks, harpoons, adzes, points, needle cases, and antler spoons, as well as unmodified animal remains. These latter materials commonly included items such as teeth and head elements from sable (*Martes zibellina*), talons from birds of prey, and musk deer (*Moschus mochiferus*) canines, while rarer items include beaver (*Castor fiber*) incisors and mandibles, fox (*Vulpes vulpes*) and dog (*Canis familiaris*) teeth, and the osseous portions of bird beaks. Whole animal burials were limited to a dog in one grave and two possibly whole sables in two separate graves; human interments were present in all three graves containing these whole animal skeletons.

Thirty-five Early Neolithic and one Bronze Age grave contained the skeletal remains of brown bears (Table 4.1). We focus our discussion here on the Early Neolithic materials. With only two exceptions (a bear phalanx in grave 4 and a modified radius in grave 64), bear remains in grave pits are represented by elements of the head and bacula. All appear to be from adult animals (no juvenile dentition was present) and in several cases teeth are extensively worn, indicating that some bears were of advanced age. Of the head elements, only the heavily modified canine (a cutting implement) in grave 53 was found on or near a human body. Otherwise, head bones and teeth were in the upper and middle levels of grave pits and in no clear association with particular human bodies (Figure 4.3). When whole or nearly whole crania were recovered (as in graves 22 and 90), they were found inverted with their eye-sockets facing down. These two specimens also showed multiple cut marks, most likely from disarticulation and defleshing, and both had their brain cases opened while the bone was still fresh (Figure 4.4). All of the remaining crania were highly fragmented, perhaps from post-depositional erosion. Several of the mandibles and fragmented crania also have cut marks, signs of burning, and in one case gnawing marks. Nearly all maxillae and mandibles are missing teeth, and isolated teeth were recovered from a number of graves. In other words, it appears that at least some of the bear remains came from animals that were butchered and perhaps consumed, and many head elements appear to have been exposed, handled, and perhaps transported prior to being deposited.

The bear head elements show no clear association with particular human demographic groups or grave types. For example, bear elements are found in graves containing males, females, adults, and children, as well as in single and multiple interments, and in association with bodies in extended supine, flexed, and disarticulated positions. Some were in graves containing hundreds of artifacts (e.g., graves 15, 53, 56, 59, 112), while others were found in graves with little else in them other than the human skeleton (e.g., graves 24, 30, 47, 60, 88). The bear head elements were found in graves in all areas of the cemetery but are more common in the section near the cliff face on the crest of the hill. We also speculate that bear remains were once present in a greater percentage of the graves than is now apparent. Figure 4.2 shows the general locations of bear remains found outside of grave pits. Bear remains constitute the vast majority of the identified faunal remains recovered from these deposits, and like the remains in the graves themselves, are dominated by head elements (132 specimens) and bacula (five specimens; three phalanges and one femur also were present). These items too were found throughout the cemetery but are most dense in the hillcrest area, and we suspect

TABLE 4.1 Descriptions of graves at Shamanka with bear remains

Grave #	Bear elements	Location	Bear MNI	Element modifications	Human remains #	Age	Sex	Position/ Condition	Comments
4	Phalanx 3	In upper portion of grave pit	1		4–1	35–45	M	Human remains disturbed from overlying grave (#3); extended supine?	Healed mandibular fracture; element may derive from grave #3
8	R mandible with C only; undiff. molar	Mandible in upper portion of grave pit in charcoal patch and scatter of artifacts and human remains; molar found SW of grave pit in surrounding sediments	1	Two cutmarks on the lateral face of mandible body	8–1	35–40	M	Completely disarticulated	Molar identified by N.D. Ovodov
					8–2	20+	*	Mandible, radius, rib, and phalanx only	

TABLE 4.1 (Continued)

Grave #	Bear elements	Location	Bear MNI	Element modifications	Human remains #	Age	Sex	Position/ Condition	Comments
9	1 L and 1 R Fibula, 1 upper P4	At same level as intact portion of body with other artifacts, near where lower R femur would be	1	One fibula modified: one end ground to a sharp point	9–1	17–18	PM	Extended supine, but lower body disturbed except for L femur	Bronze Age grave; human has perimortem trauma to frontal, projectile wound on T12 vertebra
10	Upper R I1, undiff. molar fragments	In the sediments around grave 10 pit	1		10–1	25–35	M	Only lower legs articulated, appears to have been extended supine	
11	Three whole bacula, Lower R I1 and 2, upper R I3	Teeth in upper grave pit; bacula found in cluster of artifacts under feet of 11–2	3	All bacula are lightly worn or ground, base of one extensively ground	11–1	18–20	F	Completely disarticulated	Individuals buried sequentially
					11–2	30–40	M	Upper body disarticulated, lower body intact, extended supine	

TABLE 4.1 (Continued)

Grave #	Bear elements	Bear MNI	Element modifications	Human remains #	Age	Sex	Location	Position/ Condition	Comments
12	Fragmented braincase, upper L and R R2, lower M1, upper RC, L mandible with M2	1	Mandible is burnt and gnawed by carnivore	12–1	25–35	*	All in upper portion of grave pit, mandible in charcoal patch area with disarticulated human remains	Completely disarticulated	
14	Upper L I1 and 2, upper R I3, lower L I1, lower L P4, R premaxilla frag., R maxillary frag. with P2, temporal and palatine frag.	1		14–1	25–30	M	Found among angular marble rocks that may have formed paving on grave pit	Extended supine, beside and slightly overlaying 14–2	Simultaneous burials; healed depressed cranial fracture
				14–2	20–25	F		Extended supine	
15	Undiff. molars and canine	1		15–1	25–35	M	Mid-level in grave pit with some charcoal	Extended supine, on top of layer of artifacts that cover entire grave floor; head and cervical vertebrae articulated and found beside left arm	Teeth identified by N.D. Ovodov

TABLE 4.1 (Continued)

Grave #	Bear elements	Location	Element modifications	Human remains #	Age	Sex	Position/ Condition	Comments
16	Upper R I1, lower R M1, C crown fragment, post-canine crown fragments	Midlevel of grave pit with loose scatter of artifacts and disarticulated human remains		16–1	20–25	*	Disarticulated except for lower legs; possibly originally extended supine	
17	Lower L I1, I2, lower R and L I2, Lower R P4, R and L anterior partially fused mandible fragments, R anterior mandible frag., probable braincase frags.	In and around the upper grave pit		17–1	30–40	M	Simultaneously buried with 17–2, extended supine.	
				17–2	20–22	M	Extended supine, cranium not present	
18	Upper L I3, R mandible body frag.	In sediment just above grave pit		18–1	25–29	M	Extended supine, lower body articulated, upper body completely disarticulated and scattered through grave pit	Partially healed rib fracture

TABLE 4.1 (Continued)

Grave #	Bear elements	Location	Bear MNI	Element modifications	Human remains #	Age	Sex	Position/ Condition	Comments
20	R and L temporal, R M2 in maxillary frag. premaxilla, L palatine, braincase frags.	In upper middle level of grave pit with loose scatter of artifacts and disarticulated human remains			20-1	30-60	M	All individuals completely disarticulated	Healed depressed cranial fracture
					20-2	20-35	F		
					20-3	20-35	PF		
					20-4	20+	*		
					20-5	20+	*		
21	Three bacula, undiff. bear molar	Molar in upper portion of grave pit, bacula with cache of artifacts under 21-1 head/shoulders	3	One baculum has several cutmarks and incised lines, possibly to facilitate suspension from cord; other two lightly ground or worn	21-1	25-30	M	Extended supine	Bear molar identified by N.D. Ovodov
					21-2	25-30	M	Buried simultaneously with 21-3, lower in grave pit than 21-1; extended on left side	
					21-3	16-18	*	Extended on right side, with face oriented downward	

TABLE 4.1 (Continued)

Grave #	Bear elements	Location	Bear MNI	Element modifications	Human remains #	Age	Sex	Position/ Condition	Comments
22	One whole cranium with R P4, M1, M2, L P3, P4, M2, one whole bacula, one bacula fragment	Cranium upside-down in grave pit about 50 cm above human body; bacula fragment at same level of grave pit as cranium; whole bacula directly on chest of human skeleton	2	Cranium has cutmarks on ventral edge of foramen magnum, cut or scrape marks on R temporal process, large perimortem hole broken through L occipital and through to sphenoid area and ventral occipital; whole baculum appears worn	22–1	19–22	M	Extended supine	Bear teeth are extremely worn and cranium very large; human has healed cranial fracture

TABLE 4.1 (Continued)

Grave #	Bear elements	Location	Bear MNI	Element modifications	Human remains #	Age	Sex	Position/ Condition	Comments
23	Lower R M2, M3, upper M3 frag., L mandible body frag. with M2 and M3, L mandible with P4, M1, M2, M3	All but one fragment of mandible found in midlevel of grave pit in and around charcoal-rich patch and scattered human remains and artifacts; one refit mandible fragment found amongst articulated human remains at base of grave	2	Mandible body frag. is burnt in two areas, whole mandible has cutmarks on condyle and on lateral face of coronoid process	23–1	35–45	PM	At least three individuals were side by side and extended supine, but only legs or small portions of upper bodies intact; other two completely disarticulated and possibly later interments	
					23–2	20+	PF		
					23–3	20+	*		
					23–4	20+	*		
					23–5	20+	*		
24	Mandible body fragment	Found at the surface of the grave pit	1		24–1	25–35	M	Secondary burial, completely disarticulated, in a cluster on the legs of 24–2	
					24–2	12–15	*	Extended supine	

TABLE 4.1 (Continued)

Grave #	Bear elements	Location	Bear MNI	Element modifications	Human remains #	Age	Sex	Position/ Condition	Comments
25	Upper M3	Amongst highly disarticulated human remains and scatter of artifacts	1		25-1	20–22	F	All are jumbled and disarticulated	
					25-2	17–21	*		
					25-3	20+	PF	Left tibia only	
					25-4	6–12	*		
					25-5	20+	*		
28	Baculum	Near right shoulder in cluster of artifacts	1	Awl; extensively ground, one end sharply pointed	28-1	1.5–3	*	Extended supine	
30	Baculum distal frag.	In the upper portion of grave pit	1		30-1	35–50	M	Extended supine	Smaller than other bacula at site
45	One whole baculum, one distal frag.	Directly under the cranium	2	Whole specimen lightly worn or ground	45-1	25–45	M	Extended supine	
47	R mandible with C, P4, M2	Uppermost portion of grave pit	1		47-1	20–25	F		Healed depressed cranial fracture

TABLE 4.1 (Continued)

Grave #	Bear elements	Location	Bear MNI	Element modifications	Human remains #	Age	Sex	Position/ Condition	Comments
48	Lower R M3	Upper portion of grave pit with scatter of disarticulated human remains and tools	1		48–1	50+	M	Extended supine at base of grave pit	
					48–2	2–3	*	#s 48–2, 4, and 5 disarticulated in mid- and upper grave pit	
					48–4	20–35	*		
					48–5	20+	*		
49	Upper R I3, undiff. canine frag.	Canine in upper grave pit with loose scatter of human remains and artifacts; incisor at base of grave pit ~20 cm from feet of 49–1	1		49–1	17–20	PM	Prone, face down	Manual and pedal elements only
					49–2	20+	*	Scattered remains in the upper grave pit	
53	Undiff. canine	In a dense cluster of tools under and behind the head of 53–1	1	Lateral portion of tooth, interior face ground flat, lateral margins and tip very sharp	53–1	20–25	M	Extended supine, stacked on top of 53–2	
					53–2	50+	M	Extended supine, mandible, right shoulder, R foot slightly disturbed	

TABLE 4.1 (Continued)

Grave #	Bear elements	Location	Bear MNI	Element modifications	Human remains #	Age	Sex	Position/ Condition	Comments
55	Undiff. cranial fragment	In upper portion of grave pit in charcoal patch; a few scattered human remains also at this level	1		55–1	35–39	M	Jumbled, completely disarticulated	Bear remains identified by N.D. Ovodov
					55–2	5–7	*	Jumbled, completely disarticulated	
56	Upper L I1, I2, I3, P4, M1, fragmented L maxilla	Scattered throughout the mid-levels of grave pit	1		56–1	3–5	*	Probably extended supine, later entire upper body displaced	
					56–2	8–10	*	Disarticulated, only lower legs and one arm articulated	
59	Upper R M1, M2, undiff. canine and post-canine frags., L temporal and petrous, R temporal, R zygomatic, misc. burnt cranial frags.	All teeth and identifiable cranial elements in upper grave pit with scatter of tools, human remains, and charcoal patch.	1	All burnt	59–1	35–39	M	Extended supine	
					59–2	15–19	PF	Disarticulated and jumbled except for R lower arm and L lower leg; perhaps originally extended supine	
		Burnt cranial frags. near and directly on R knee of 59–1			59–3	20+	*	Vertebra, 1st metacarpal, and scapula only	
					59–4	20+	*	1st metacarpal only	

TABLE 4.1 (Continued)

Grave #	Bear elements	Location	Bear MNI	Element modifications	Human remains #	Age	Sex	Position/ Condition	Comments
60	Upper R M2	Directly on marble stone at the grave mid-level	1		60–1	50+	M	Extended supine, most of upper body disarticulated; simultaneous side-by-side burial with 60–2	
					60–2	40–44	F	Extended supine, most of upper body disarticulated	
62	Upper L M2, L zygomatic process of temporal	Temporal in upper grave pit in charcoal patch	1	Temporal has cutmark at mandibular fossa	62–1	35–45	PF	Individuals 1–2 appear to have been extended supine, later upper bodies completely disarticulated and jumbled	
					62–2	35–45	M		
					62–3	20+	PF		
					62–4	20+	PM		
					62–5	45–59	M		
					62–6	20+	*		L and R femora, burned
					62–7	20+	*		L femur, burned

TABLE 4.1 (Continued)

Grave #	Bear elements	Location	Bear MNI	Element modifications	Human remains #	Age	Sex	Position/Condition	Comments
64	Frontal, parietal crest frag., R temporal and petrous, possible radius	Cranial frags. at mid-level of grave pit in scatter of tools and human remains; radius in cluster of tools under head of 64-1	1	Small portion of parietal burnt; radius extensively ground, wedge or chisel	64-1 64-2	30-39 7-10	M *	Extended supine Completely disarticulated and jumbled	
71	Upper R I3	Upper portion of grave pit at same level as a few tools and human bones	1		71-1	35-45	*	All but lower legs completely disarticulated, jumbled. Possibly originally extended supine	
78	Two partial bacula, 1 canine crown frag.	Canine and one baculum in upper level of grave pit with charcoal patch, scattered artifacts; other baculum near base of grave with scattered artifacts and human bones	2		78-1	16-18	F	All completely disarticulated and jumbled	
					78-2	25-35	F		
					78-3	20-25	M		
					78-4	35-50	F		
					78-5	25-29	F	L and R ossa coxae only	
					78-6	20-24	M	L and R ossa coxae only	
					78-7	20-35	F	Sacrum only	

TABLE 4.1 (Continued)

Grave #	Bear elements	Location	Bear MNI	Element modifications	Human remains #	Age	Sex	Position/ Condition	Comments
86	Upper L and R C, R M2, L P4, L maxillary with M2, nasal, maxillary, parietal, and occipital frags., undiff. post-canine frag., lower L M1, L C, L mandibular body, L and R mandibular condyles	Upper and mid-levels of grave pit with scatter of tools, human remains, and charcoal patches	1		86-1	18–20	M	Disarticulated and jumbled	Bear M2s both extensively worn
					86-2	20+	*	Disarticulated and jumbled	
					86-3	?	*	Manual and pedal elements only	
88	Lower R C, M1, fragmented R mandible angle	Upper level of grave pit	1		88-1	6–8	*	Extended supine	

TABLE 4.1 (Continued)

Grave #	Bear elements	Location	Bear MNI	Element modifications	Human remains #	Age	Sex	Position/ Condition	Comments
90	One fragmented crania with R M2, L M1 and M2; cranium with most of the rostrum missing	Upper level of grave pit; whole braincase was upside-down	2	Braincase broken open through the basioccipital, cutmarks on left posterior face of L temporal process, just above foramen magnum, R occipital condyle	90–1	18–20	M	Flexed, supine	
112	Upper L M1, M2, R P4, M3, undiff. canine frag., R mandible body frag., sphenoid and temporal frag., two bacula	All cranial and mandible fragments and teeth found in and around grave in area disturbed by overlapping grave 111; both bacula in cluster of tools in L hip area	2	One baculum has a groove cut into it running lengthwise from base	112–1	25–35	M	Extended supine, upper body possibly disturbed and removed during digging of grave 111	

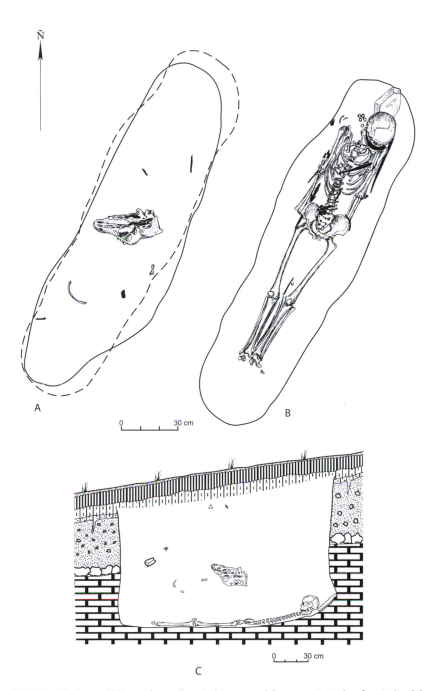

FIGURE 4.3 Grave #22 at Shamanka: a) the inverted bear crania and a few isolated human remains and artifacts found at midlevel in the grave; b) the skeleton of an adult male at the base of the grave pit. The black object lying diagonally on the chest is a bear baculum; c) profile view of grave #22.

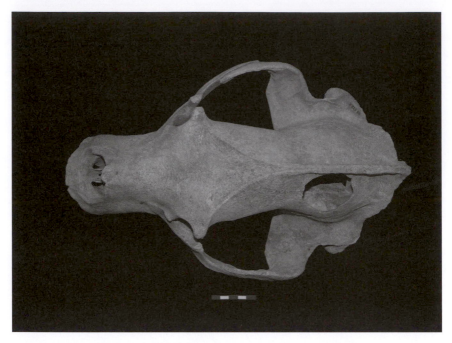

FIGURE 4.4 The whole bear cranium found in grave #22 at Shamanka.

they were removed from graves and left on the surface during episodes of reuse and revisiting. Three radiocarbon dates on bear canines from non-grave deposits at Shamanka indicate that these materials are contemporaneous with the graves themselves (Table 4.2).

In contrast to the pattern seen in the placement of bear head elements, the bacula were often found among concentrations of artifacts near human bodies, or directly on bodies. Eight graves yielded bacula, and six of these either contained only adult males, or the bacula in graves with individuals of both sexes were on or near the adult male bodies. The two exceptions are the baculum found under the shoulder of a 1.5- to 3-year-old child in grave 28, and the two bacula in grave 78, which contained the disarticulated and scattered remains of seven adult individuals of both sexes. The specimen in grave 28 was extensively ground at its distal end to form a sharp piercing implement (an awl) while nine other specimens show marks from light

TABLE 4.2 Radiocarbon dates on bear remains found in the sediments outside of human graves at Shamanka. Stable carbon and nitrogen isotope data also provided.

Sample #	Provenience	Uncalibratred age BP and error	D13C	D15N	Cn
OxA-21159	2006, P-1-27	6226 ± 36	16.22	6.0	3.3
OxA-21160	2006, P-1-34	6311 ± 33	16.35	5.9	3.3
OxA-21161	2002, P-III-10	6147 ± 35	16.74	6.4	3.3

grinding or use wear. One baculum in grave 21 was incised around its circumference, perhaps for facilitating suspension on a cord, and one from grave 112 was grooved lengthwise near its base for an unclear purpose. Recall also that five bacula were found in the sediments surrounding the graves, perhaps indicating that they too were removed from graves during episodes of grave reopening.

Bears and A. I. Hallowell

Arguably, the best known anthropologist to address the distinct treatments given to bears is A. Irving Hallowell, whose dissertation on bear ceremonialism was published in full in *American Anthropologist* in 1926. Hallowell's survey of ethnographic literature on bears had the stated goal of understanding "man's relation to the animals of his environment as he himself views it; that is to say, in its psychological aspect" (Hallowell 1926:3). In practice, his work was a trait list study in the Boasian fashion, singling out the characteristics of the treatment of these animals and trying to explain their geographical distribution (Darnell 1977). Hallowell's ultimate finding was that while there were many local variations in understandings and behaviors towards bears, many commonalities still could be found and these likely related to shared historical roots among peoples of the boreal region. In other words, bear 'veneration' was an ancient practice that had diffused throughout the northern hemisphere. Furthermore, Hallowell (1926:9–10, 19) noted many commonalities among northern cosmologies and ontologies, including notions such as animals having "the same sort of animating agency which man possesses," "magical or superhuman potencies," and "souls," and that "animals appear in the ancestral tree of man or become the eponyms of social units."

As Hallowell surmised from the ethnographic record, special attention to bear remains is both quite old and, even in antiquity, was widespread. The archaeological record has since revealed that bear remains were distinctly treated as early as the Upper Paleolithic in parts of Europe (Germonpré and Hämäläinen 2007), and during the Holocene similar practices spanned much of the Northern hemisphere (Berres et al. 2004; Heizer and Hewes 1940; Kosintsev 2000; Masuda et al. 2006; McLaren et al. 2005; Sato 2004a, 2004b, 2007; Shafer 2003:159; Zachrisson and Iregren 1974; Zaika et al. 2003). Despite dealing with a much more limited ethnographic dataset than the one available today, Hallowell's early ideas about Northern cosmologies and ontologies remain well supported (see below).

Hallowell was interested in human-animal relationships throughout his career, and returned to the topic of bears in a 1966 lecture given at Bryn Mawr College, now available as a paper on file at the American Philosophical Society. In it, he suggests that an obvious reexamination of bear ritual would involve

> looking at the attitudes towards, and treatment of, the bear in the framework of the world view of a people. In other words, how are the relations of man and animal conceived in general? How is this conceptualization expressed in relations with them, to hunting and its rituals, etc.? In this perspective the

bear, instead of being selected out for independent treatment, would fall into place in the total picture of the animal world and man's relation to it.

(Hallowell 1966:2)

He concludes that "man and animals instead of being separate categories of being are deeply rooted in a world of nature that is unified."

These perspectives are most fully developed in Hallowell's (1960) paper on Ojibwe world views, which has influenced a variety of scholars interested in the ontologies and cosmologies of foraging peoples (see Bird-David 1999; Fausto 2007; Ingold 1986, 2000; Tanner 1979; Willerslev 2007). Despite often working in areas far removed from the Ojibwe of eastern Canada, these latter authors describe ways of understanding and interacting with the surrounding world that closely parallel those described by Hallowell. In the article, he describes a world in which agency was potentially found in any number of objects and phenomena, and one in which personhood was not limited to humans. Bears and other animals clearly were among these 'other-than-human' persons, and in Hallowell's account they were ontologically equivalent to humans, having souls and social relations.

Taking Hallowell's assessments as informative about Northern cosmologies and ontologies allows us to pose a number of related questions, the proposed answers to which should provide insights on the treatments given to bear parts at Shamanka. For example, if humans and animals can be ontologically similar, what distinguishes humans from animals (and animals from one another), and what is the significance of these distinguishing features? Why are some animals more distinctly treated than others? In turn, it seems worth questioning how bodies, and their enduring parts such as the skeleton, were related to souls. Why is there such widespread, specialized care of skeletal remains from slain animals throughout the northern hemisphere? Furthermore, is death an instantaneous biological event, as it is commonly understood in the West, or more of a lingering process? Fortunately, to address these questions we now have a far more complex and thorough ethnographic dataset than was available to Hallowell during his dissertation work.

Cosmologies, ontologies, bodies, and death

Throughout much of the North, the cosmos was believed to consist of a series of tiers or levels, only one of which was regularly occupied by 'normal' living beings (Ingold 1986). All persons, human and otherwise, potentially possess enduring aspects of their being, which are often termed souls, spirits, or shadows in ethnographic literature (Hultkrantz 1953; Ingold 1986; Willerslev 2007). Typically, an individual can have several forms of souls, and at least one of these ideally moves to another tier of the cosmos after death. At some later point, this aspect of the person can recycle to the tier of the living to help form a new person. In such ontological systems, a person is a composite, made up in part by souls deriving from ancestors.

It has been argued that, while some animals in these systems were ontologically similar or identical to humans, it was the characteristics of their bodies, and the abilities and perspectives conferred to them by these bodies, which in part make them distinct beings (Viveiros de Castro 1998). These ideas are perhaps best evidenced in some Northern mythologies, where persons are capable of being separated into parts, and some of those parts could be given to another being (Ingold 2000:94). This being could wear the body parts, and that original person's unique abilities or ways of being in the world would transfer to the other being. In other words, like a gift, the body or its parts carried with it something of the giver, but what was given had more than social and political effects – it also had ontological or bodily ones (cf. Strathern 1988).

Conneller (2004) employed such ideas in her examination of the antler frontlets from the well-known site of Star Carr. These items appear to have been once worn on human heads, and Conneller refers to their effects on the body as "corporeal transformations." In other words, these animal body parts were active in their engagements with humans, and the human person was capable of being trans- formed or altered – in this case, 'becoming deer' – by wearing them. Ethnographic accounts also indicate that the handling and wearing of body parts, particularly of some recently deceased animals, was also potentially fraught with danger. This is because some beings' souls are aware of, and associated with, their bodies for some time after what we would consider the time of death, and some bodily effects are not necessarily positive ones. Notably, unlike humans, most animals in the North were understood not to have individual, unique souls but rather those that cycle back into a collective for that species (Ingold 1986:247; Jordan 2003:102; Paulson 1968:454; Vitebsky 2006:275). A select few animals, typically extremely powerful or intelligent ones, do retain individuality or uniqueness after death (and had uniqueness when living). Paulson (1968:452) and Ingold (1986:249) report that bears, walrus, and whales are the most common animals in the North to be endowed with such characteristics. These animals are particularly aware, easily offended, and also have perhaps the greatest capacity for retaliation against those who committed any transgressions toward them (cf. Willerslev 2007:130). Such differing ontological characteristics and capabilities of animals also seem to correlate with the power or potency of their bodily effects, a point we return to shortly.

These ideas underscore the need for understanding death as a complex process, rather than as an instantaneous biological moment. In Richard Nelson's film *The Life in the Bear* (1987), the narrator reports that for the Koyukon of Alaska, "death is never sudden." This brief but insightful statement gets at the notion that when the Koyukon kill an animal, they know that some aspect of it continues to be watchful for an indefinite time afterward, and its body remains potent for an extended time. It is clear in the film that hunters are careful in their actions and words to avoid offending bears, whether dead or alive (in our understanding). In fact, Nelson (1983:179) reports that there are as many, if not more, rules for appropriate behavior towards deceased bears' bodies than there are for living ones. He also refers to the act of killing a bear as being nearly murderous and eating it as almost cannibalistic (Nelson 1983:175) – this is clearly a being that is ontologically and physically like a human person (see also Willerslev 2007:78). Repercussions for offences towards these animals include lack of future luck in obtaining bears or other animals, or even mortal retaliation – vengeance – by another bear. In the film, after one bear has been killed, its eyes are carefully cut out so that it will not observe any transgressions the hunters may inadvertently make towards it. A feast on the bear's flesh is later held in a clean place in the forest, again to avoid offending the bear by consuming its body (and aspects of its life) in a contaminated place. Nonetheless, the Koyukon regularly hunted bears, which was considered a very prestigious and quintessentially male activity, and bear meat was highly regarded for its taste.

Many specific 'bear effects' also are noted in the ethnographic literature and are obtained by wearing, displaying, handling, or consuming parts of these animals' bodies. It seems these effects are not caused by souls, but by some other vital element present within the body. Nelson (1983:180) describes the Koyukon as knowing that "[b]ear skins retain their life, their extreme spiritual potency, for several years." Women in particular were prohibited from handling or even stepping over bear hides. Nelson also mentions that the flesh of bears remained alive and potent after death, and eating some body portions could be dangerous. For example, everyone was prohibited from eating meat from around the atlas vertebrae because it would cause one to move slowly – in the same slow manner in which a bear moves its head. Consuming bears' brains would cause a person to become angry, but they were still removed from the skull so that they would not rot inside (Nelson 1983:180). Bear bodies, even of long dead animals, were active and observant, not inert matter.

In parts of Siberia, bear heads, paws, and hides (sometimes as one unit) were used in acts of divination and to determine which deceased relative's soul resided within a bear's body; paws in particular were used as 'amulets' for various purposes, including protection from malicious spirits (Alekseenko 1968; Jordan 2003:103–4; Lot-Falck 1953; Shirokogoroff 1935:179). Vasil'ev (1948:87) mentions specifically that bear bacula were worn on the body by females to cure sterility and to ease the birthing process. Bear hides and sometimes teeth were also sworn upon (they were chewed, kissed, or even ingested) as evidence of truthfulness, and those swearing a false oath were doomed to punishment in the future by a bear (Alekseenko 1968:177). For some Khanty, bear crania and mandibles were kept on top of storehouses in visible locations during the lifetime of the bear hunter (Jordan 2003:123). These protected the household, but nonetheless the bear was believed to be able to revive from them, and the mouths of the displayed heads were wired shut to prevent a possible retaliatory attack. After the animals' hunter died, these displayed heads were buried or placed in lakes (Jordan 2003:123).

Distinct treatment of bear bones, not just fleshed bodies, is a common practice in the North, whether among groups such as the Ainu who hand-raised captured bear cubs and considered them deities, or groups like the Koyukon who primarily hunted adult bears in their winter dens. Hallowell (1926:146) notes that the bones most often shown special treatment were those of the head, but post-cranial remains were also often subject to special care. The head in particular is said to be the seat or container of the soul (Jordan 2003:115, 119–23; Lot-Falck 1953:214), a personification of the bear itself (Alekseenko 1968:190), and to have contained some other vital essence of the animal (Lot-Falck 1953:214). Notably, the specific ways in which bear heads (and other body parts) were treated, even within a single language group such as the Evenk, was highly variable, differing by place, clan, and time (Grøn 2005:24; Lavrillier 2007; see also Kulemzin et al. [2006:48] for variability among Finno-Ugric groups).

Rites involved in the handling of bear bodies are often closely related to those given to humans upon death. Nelson's film also shows a feast at which Koyukon males consume meat from several bears. The feast is in part held *for the bears*, though, and not just made on them. Nelson's (1983:181) ethnography, upon which the film is based, refers to this feasting as a "memorial potlatch" and a "funeral ritual" for the bears. Writing about the Evenk in Siberia, Vasilevich (1971:159) specifically mentions that bear heads were treated in the same manner as deceased human bodies (see also Lavrillier 2007; Shirokogoroff 1935:80). Grøn (2005:4), also writing on the Evenk, states clearly that bears, because they have three souls like humans (see Jordan 2003:217 for similar ideas among the Khanty), are buried in styles of graves otherwise used only for humans (and some hunting dogs). Finally, Paulson's (1968) survey of the handling of animal remains throughout northern Eurasia also directly links the specific treatments of bear bodies to patterns in human mortuary practices.

The nature of the relationship between bones, an animal's souls and bodily effects, and the care given to the bones is often unclear or was unstated by ethnographic informants. Paulson (1959, in Jordan 2003:101–2) has argued that the regenerating soul does not inhabit bones, but in some way remains associated with them. Instead, the bones retain a life matter or essence, which is perhaps similar to the life or potency remaining in bear hides and flesh, as described by Nelson's (1983) Koyukon informants (see also Lot-Falck 1953:211). Paulson (1959) also makes the case that care for the bones is meant to show the spirit or soul of the animal that the hunter was respectful of its remains, and that such treatments helped to ensure the animal's regeneration and prolong its post–mortem existence. It seems to us that souls or spirits of animals must be near to, and aware of, bones in order to take account of such treatments, and that the life matter contained in the skeleton, not just the soul, was clearly involved in regeneration. Furthermore, it seems the durability and physicality of the skeleton would be a very material reminder for both the hunter and the hunted of their interaction and as such would compel their relationship to last long after the killing and consumption of the body had ended.

Regardless, it is clear that in some cases damage to bones was damage to the soul or life matter and was both offensive to the animal and prevented it from reviving. To avoid this, bear bones were often placed on built platforms, deposited in water, buried, or hung in trees (Hallowell 1926; Paulson 1968). In some cases, damage to bear remains was done to retaliate against bears. The Ainu reportedly chopped in half the head of a bear that had killed a human and would then bury one half of it below the human body in a grave (Batchelor 1901:478). The other half might be left on the grave surface, or taken to the family of the human victim who would ensure that it would be "daily profaned." Both were done to keep the bear in a sort of "hell" (Batchelor 1901:478). Its crania broken and its parts separated, the bear was prevented from returning again to the living.

Finally, given that select animals and humans could be ontologically equivalent, it is not surprising that for some Siberian groups maintaining body integrity also was essential for the regeneration of *human* persons (Jordan 2003:220; Kulemzin et al. 2006:54–56). Furthermore, human souls, like those of bears, were dangerous and feared, and some elements of mortuary practices involved efforts by survivors to placate and distance themselves from these souls or spirits, which at a later point (at least for some) either departed or were sent to another tier of the cosmos (Chernetsov 1963; Jordan 2003:217; Kulemzin et al. 2006:65–70; Menovscikov 1968; Shirokogoroff 1935:208–17).

Conclusions: a likeness of being

In Northern ethnographies, bears appear to be the quintessential other-than-human person. While potentially all animals are ensouled, bears are more ontologically similar to humans than most others, having unique, individual souls. Bears also are potent, observant, and vengeful, but nonetheless were sought out, killed, and eaten. To ensure their regeneration and to placate their anger at being mistreated, bears were given mortuary rites on par with their human counterparts. This showed their observant souls that they were respected, but also made possible their regeneration. These rites were also a means of guiding or directing their souls to another tier of the cosmos from which they would return to form a new person. Their deaths, like those of humans, were not instantaneous moments but rather drawn out processes. Their bodily effects, like their souls, remained active after death. Consuming, wearing, or even handling them transformed the human person, and not always in desirable ways. In other words, people could be made and remade by engagements with bears and their bodies (and those of other animals), just as they could be made by interacting with other material things.

At Shamanka, bears appear to have received mortuary treatments more closely related to those of humans than at any other archaeological site we have seen described. Portions of their bodies, most often elements of their heads, were transported to this landform and deposited in graves that also contained human remains. Many of the head bones show cutmarks, indicating the bears were butchered and almost certainly consumed. Some show evidence of being exposed prior to burial, and this may indicate that they were first placed in trees or on platforms as occurs in modern settings. This would inhibit them from being defiled by other animals, allow them to gradually deteriorate, and would keep them visible and on the mind. Their later burial at Shamanka suggests the bears retained some awareness or potency long after death. Depositing them in graves at this special place, as humans did with their own dead, seems an ultimate means of showing deference, regard, and respect to their souls. Recall that the intact crania were found face down, as if those burying them did not want the bears to see who had carried out these acts, much like the Koyukon hunters who cut the eyes from bears they had killed.

Several human individuals at Shamanka were buried with bear bacula on or near their bodies. Unlike in the ethnographic literature cited above, the bacula here were mostly associated with adult males. As literal male reproductive tools with transformative power, these could have passed to the Shamanka males their generative potency or virility. They were "technologies of the self" (Foucault 1988), things that helped relationships emerge, both with animals and with other humans, and thus were elemental parts of people's identities. They were enveloped as part of the person when taken from the bear and handled, worn, and used on other things. Perhaps those carrying out the mortuary rites at Shamanka placed them in the grave as recognition that these items were important parts of the identity of the person who had died. Alternatively, these items were given as gifts by the living to the dead, an offering of their own self to one who was passing to another tier of the cosmos, and who would perhaps return in the future as a 'new' person.

The burial of bear heads and the inclusion of bear bacula in human burials does not seem to have occurred, either at such a scale or in this form, at any of the region's many other Middle Holocene cemeteries. While distinctive accumulations of bear head and foot elements have been documented at one other Neolithic habitation site on the Angara River near Bratsk (Ermolova 1978:45–46), nowhere else in the Baikal region have numerous bear head parts been found in multiple graves also containing human remains. This suggests a particular affinity, including kinship, between some people using the Shamanka landscape and bears. In other words, the bears perhaps were embodiments or incarnations of a specific ancestor or other kin (see Alekseenko 1968; Lot-Falck 1953; Petrov 1989; Vasilevich 1963 for Siberian ethnographic examples). Given the review of ethnographic understandings of bears presented earlier, it seems likely that other sites in the Baikal region may yet produce distinct accumulations of bear remains. Recall that historically specific treatment of bear remains often varied within a given linguistic community according to specific clan or tribal traditions. This suggests other ancient bear mortuary sites in the Baikal region may vary in form and may not only include burial in graves with humans.

Finally, it also seems reasonable to suggest that bears were sent or guided on their way through the cycle of ontological regeneration specifically from Shamanka, itself a distinct juncture point where land seemingly penetrates water through the projecting mini-peninsula at the base of the hill. If one allows for this as a possibility, and also accepts the notion that bears and humans were ontologically similar, then a reconsideration of the meanings behind the burial of *humans* at this and other burial places in the region is needed. If bear bodies and souls were potentially dangerous to the living and required dispatch or guidance so as to not harm, but rather to return as a future being, then perhaps humans' bodies and souls also needed such care. Virtually all recurrently used burial places (cemeteries) in Middle Holocene Cis-Baikal are located on shorelines overlooking bodies of water, sometimes at river confluences, but also on the coves and bays of Baikal itself – these are landscape juncture points, either between land and water, or between two flows of water. In cosmological systems where souls cycle between tiers of the cosmos, juncture points of this sort seem like very suitable places from which to send souls – they themselves are at major physical boundaries between 'worlds.' Unfortunately, there has been no consideration whatsoever of ontological and cosmological concepts and how they may have affected mortuary practices in the Baikal region during the Middle Holocene. Revised interpretive models clearly are needed here, and these should include humans who dwelt in worlds with meaning, where animals are more than mindless targets of human predation, and where landscapes are more than stages for foraging and human-centered political action.

Note

1 Isolated human skeletal elements were found in a number of graves. If we assume that these do not derive from individuals identified elsewhere in the cemetery, then at least another 25 individuals are represented.

Bibliography

Alekseenko, Evgeniia A. 1968. The Cult of the Bear among the Ket (Yenisei Ostyaks). In *Popular Beliefs and Folklore Traditions in Siberia*, edited by Vilmos Diószegi, pp. 175–91. Mouton and Co., The Hague, Netherlands.

Argent, Gala 2010. Do the Clothes Make the Horse? Relationality, Roles and Statuses in Iron Age Inner Asia. *World Archaeology* 42(2):157–74.

Batchelor, John 1901. *The Ainu and Their Folklore*. The Religious Tract Society, London.

Berres, Thomas E., David M. Stothers, and David Mather 2004. Bear Imagery and Ritual in Northeast North America: An Update and Assessment of A. Irving Hallowell's Work. *Midcontinental Journal of Archaeology* 29(1):5–42.

Bird-David, Nurit 1999. "Animism" Revisited: Personhood, Environment, and Relational Epistemology. *Current Anthropology* 40(S):67–91.

Chernetsov, Valeriy N. 1963. Concepts of the Soul among the Ob Ugrians. In *Studies in Siberian Shamanism*, edited by Henry N. Michael, pp. 3–45. University of Toronto Press, Toronto.

Conneller, Chantal 2004. Becoming Deer: Corporeal Transformations at Star Carr. *Archaeological Dialogues* 11(1):37–56.

Darnell, Regna 1977. Hallowell's "Bear Ceremonialism" and the Emergence of Boasian Anthropology. *Ethos* 5(1):13–30.

Ermolova, Natalia M. 1978. *Teriofauna Doliny Angary v Pozdnem Antropogene*. Nauka, Novosibirsk [in Russian].

Fausto, Carlos 2007. Feasting on People: Eating Animals and Humans in Amazonia. *Current Anthropology* 48(4):497–530.

Foucault, Michel 1988. *Technologies of the Self: A Seminar with Michel Foucault*. Edited by Luther H. Martin, Huck Gutman, and Patrick H. Hutton. University of Massachusetts Press, Amherst.

Germonpré, Mietje, and Riku Hämäläinen 2007. Fossil Bear Bones in the Eurasian Upper Paleolithic: The Possibility of a Proto Bear-Ceremonialism. *Arctic Anthropology* 44(2):1–30.

Grøn, Ole 2005. A Siberian Perspective on the North European Hamburgian Culture: A Study in Applied Hunter-Gatherer Ethnoarchaeology. *Before Farming* 1:1–29.

Hallowell, A. Irving 1926. Bear Ceremonialism in the Northern Hemisphere. *American Anthropologist* 28:1–175.

——(1960). Ojibwa Ontology, Behavior and World View. In *Culture in History: Essays in Honor of Paul Radin*, edited by Stanley Diamond, pp. 19–52. Columbia University Press, New York.

——(1966). Bear Ceremonialism in the Northern Hemisphere: Reexamined. Paper presented at American Association for the Advancement of Science 1966. Manuscript on file, American Philosophical Society, Philadelphia.

Heizer, Robert F., and Gordon W. Hewes 1940. Animal Ceremonialism in Central California in the Light of Archaeology. *American Anthropologist* 42(4):587–603.

Hultkrantz, Åke 1953. *Conceptions of the Soul among North American Indians.* Monograph Series No. 1. Ethnographical Museum of Sweden, Stockholm.

Ingold, Tim 1986. *The Appropriation of Nature.* Manchester University Press, Manchester.

——(2000). *The Perception of the Environment.* Routledge, London.

Jordan, Peter 2003. *Material Culture and Sacred Landscape: The Anthropology of the Siberian Khanty.* AltaMira, Walnut Creek, California.

Kosintsev, Pavel A. 2000. Chelovek i medved' v Golotsene Severnoi Evrazii (po arkheolozoologicheskim dannym) [Human and bear in the Holocene of Northern Eurasia (based on archaezoological data)]. In *Narody Sibiri: Istoriia i Kul'tura. Medved' v Drevnikh i Sovremennykh Kul'turakh Sibiri,* edited by I. N. Gemuev, N. A. Alekseev, and I. V. Oktiabr'skaia, pp. 4–9. Izdatel'stvo IAi'' SO RAN, Novosibirsk [in Russian].

Kulemzin, Vladislav M., Nadezhda V. Lukina, Timofei A. Moldanov, and Tatiana A. Moldanova 2006. *Khanty Mythology.* Akademiai Kiado, Budapest.

Lavrillier, Alexandra 2007. Comment les Évenks de Sibérie méridionale ont modifié le rituel sur le gibier tué. *Annales de la Fondation Fyssen* 22:112–21.

Losey, Robert J. 2010. Animism as a Means of Exploring Archaeological Fishing Structures on Willapa Bay, Washington, USA. *Cambridge Archaeological Journal* 20(1):17–32.

Losey, Robert J., Vladimir I. Bazaliiskii, Sandra Garvie-Lok, Mietje Germonpré, Jennifer A. Leonard, Andrew L. Allen, M. Anne Katzenberg, and Mikhail V. Sablin 2011. Canids as Persons: Early Neolithic Dog and Wolf Burials, Cis-Baikal, Siberia. *Journal of Anthropological Archaeology* 30(2):174–89.

Lot-Falck, Eveline 1953. *Les Rites de Chasse Chez les Peuples Sibériens.* Gallimard, Paris.

Mannermaa, Kristiina 2008. Birds and Burials at Ajvide (Gotland, Sweden) and Zvejnieki (Latvia) about 8000–3900 BP. *Journal of Anthropological Archaeology* 27(2):201–25.

Masuda, Ryuichi, Toshiyuki Tamura, and Osamu Takahashi 2006. Ancient DNA Analysis of Brown Bear Skulls from a Ritual Rock Shelter Site of the Ainu Culture at Bihue, Central Hokkaido, Japan. *Anthropological Science* 114:211–15.

McLaren, Duncan, Rebecca J. Wigen, Quentin Mackie, and Daryl W. Fedje 2005. Bear Hunting at the Pleistocene/Holocene Transition on the Northern Northwest Coast of North America. *Canadian Zooarchaeology* 22:3–29.

McNiven, Ian J. 2010. Navigating the Human-Animal Divide: Marine Mammal Hunters and Rituals of Sensory Allurement. *World Archaeology* 42(2):215–30.

McNiven, Ian J., and Ricky Feldman 2003. Ritually Orchestrated Seascapes: Hunting Magic and Dugong Bone Mounds in Torres Strait, NE Australia. *Cambridge Archaeological Journal* 13(2):169–94.

Menovscikov, Georgii A. 1968. Popular Conceptions, Religious Beliefs and Rites of the Asiatic Eskimoes. In *Popular Beliefs and Folklore Traditions in Siberia,* edited by Vilmos Diószegi, pp. 433–49. Mouton and Co., The Hague, Netherlands.

Nelson, Richard K. 1983. *Make Prayers to the Raven.* University of Chicago Press, Chicago.

——(1987). *The Life in the Bear: Make Prayers to the Raven.* Film produced by M. O. Badger and R. K. Nelson. University of Alaska, Fairbanks.

Paulson, Ivar 1959. Zur Aufbewahrung der Tierknocken im nördlichen Nordamerika. *MMVH* (Miscellanea Americana) 25:182–88 [in German].

——(1968). The Preservation of Animal Bones in the Hunting Rites of Some North-Eurasian Peoples. In *Popular Beliefs and Folklore Traditions in Siberia,* edited by Vilmos Diószegi, pp. 451–57. Mouton and Co., The Hague, Netherlands.

Petrov, Alexandr A. 1989. The Bear Taboo in Even Language and Folklore. *Études/Inuit/ Studies* 13:131–33.

Sato, Takehiro 2004a. Animal Ritual of the Okhotsk Culture: Spatial-temporal Characteristics. In *Collected Papers in Honor of Professor H. Utagawa's 60th Birthday: The Formation of Ainu Culture*, pp. 245–62. Hokkaido Shuppan Kikaku Center, Sapporo [in Japanese].

——(2004b). Bear-Sending Ceremony: Present Situation and Future Tasks of Archaeological Studies. In *Iomante of Bears and Owls: Ethnoarchaeology of the Ainu*, edited by Hiroshi Utagawa, pp. 91–110. Douseisha, Tokyo (in Japanese).

——(2007). Archaeology of Bear Sending Ceremony. *Sanshokuki* 712:5–7.

Sauvet, Georges, Robert Layton, Tilman Lenssen-Erz, Paul Tacon, and Andre Wlodarczyk 2009. Thinking with Animals in Upper Paleolithic Rock Art. *Cambridge Archaeological Journal* 19:319–36.

Shafer, Harry J. 2003. *Mimbres Archaeology at the NAN Ranch*. University of New Mexico Press, Albuquerque.

Shirokogoroff, Sergei M. 1935. *Psychomental Complex of the Tungus*. Routledge and Kegan Paul, London.

Strathern, Marilyn 1988. *The Gender of the Gift*. University of California Press, Berkeley.

Tanner, Adrian 1979. *Bringing Home Animals: Religious Ideology and Mode of Production of the Mistassini Cree Hunters*. St. Martin's Press, New York.

Thomas, Julian 2004. *Archaeology and Modernity*. Routledge, London.

Weber, Andrzej W., Roelf P. Beukens, Vladimir I. Bazaliiskii, Olga I. Goriunova, and Nikolai A. Savel'ev 2006. Radiocarbon Dates from Neolithic and Bronze Age Hunter-Gatherer Cemeteries in the Cis-Baikal Region of Siberia. *Radiocarbon* 48(1):127–66.

Weiss, Kenneth M. 1972. On the Systematic Bias in Skeletal Sexing. *American Journal of Physical Anthropology* 37:239–50.

Willerslev, Rane 2007. *Soul Hunters: Hunting, Animism, and Personhood among the Siberian Yukaghirs*. University of California Press, Berkeley.

Vasil'ev, Vladmir A. 1948. Medvezhii prazdnik [Bear Festival]. *Sovetskaia Etnografiia* 4:78–105 [in Russian].

Vasilevich, Glafira M. 1963. Early Concepts about the Universe among the Evenks (Materials). In *Studies in Siberian Shamanism*, edited by Henry N. Michael, pp. 46–83. University of Toronto Press, Toronto.

1971. O kul'te medvedia u Evenkov [About Evenk's bear cult]. In *Religioznye Predstavlenia i Obriady Narodov Sibiri v XIX – beginning of XX centuries*, pp. 150–69. Nauka, Leningrad [in Russian].

Vitebsky, Piers 2006. *The Reindeer People: Living with Animals and Spirits in Siberia*. Houghton Mifflin, Boston.

Viveiros de Castro, Eduardo 1998. Cosmological Deixis and Amerindian Perspectivism. *Journal of the Royal Anthropological Institute* 4(3):469–88.

Zachrisson, Inger, and Elisabeth Iregren 1974. *Lappish Bear Graves in Northern Sweden*. Early Norrland 5. KVHAA, Stockholm.

Zaika, Alexandra L., Nikolai D. Ovodov, Nikolai V. Martynovich, and Liudmila A. Orlova 2003. Sledy medvezh'ego kul'ta na Nizhei Angare (predvaritel'noe soobshchenie) [Traces of bear cult on the Lower Angara River (preliminary note)]. In *Problemy Arkheologii, Etnografii, Antropologii Sibiri i Sopredel'nykh Territorii*, Vol. IX, Part I, pp. 347–51. Isdatel'stvo Instituta Arkheologii i Etnografii SO RAN, Novosibirsk [in Russian].

5

BETWEEN THE LIVING AND THE DEAD: RELATIONAL ONTOLOGIES AND THE RITUAL DIMENSIONS OF DUGONG HUNTING ACROSS TORRES STRAIT

Ian J. McNiven

Introduction

In recent years, increasing archaeological attention has been given to the ontological dimensions of the human-animal divide through the metaphysical aspects of hunting (e.g., Hill 2011; McNiven 2010; Russell 2012). Anthropological theorizing informs us that the human-animal duality of Western thought is limited in scope for most of humanity and most of human history, where the human-animal divide was more commonly seen as ontologically fluid and permeable and understood in terms of overlapping personhood (e.g., Ingold 2000; Scott 1989; Tanner 1979). The fluidity of the human-animal divide is often most clearly expressed and negotiated through the dialectics of intense social engagements between hunters and prey. During these intense, spiritually-charged, and heightened sensorial engagements, the everyday qualities of human persons and animals as 'other-than-human' persons (Hallowell 1960) become unstable, such that the shared qualities of sentience and personhood and mutual understanding become all too apparent. In an illuminating paper, Hill (2011:408) makes the point that "key to understanding the role of animals in indigenous ontologies is relational thinking." Furthermore, "humans and other-than-human persons thus have no prediscursive existence; rather, they become themselves through experience, interaction and discourse. Identity and self are therefore constructs and must be perpetually constituted through social action" (Hill 2011:408). For Yukaghir hunters of Siberia for whom "all beings are constituted 'relationally': there would be no hunters without prey, just as there would be no living without souls of the dead, because a person only attains his identity by virtue of the relationship he has to his previous incarnation or the animal hunted" (Willerslev 2011:68). Thus, "human beings draw on animals to think about themselves" (Knight 2005:1), but also to ontologically situate and define themselves as one amongst many different types of sentient and social beings.

Such relational ontologies indicate that we only can begin to understand what it means to be human and animal from the situational and positional fluidity of the human-animal divide as revealed through human-animal inter-actions. For archaeologists, it is becoming clear that a fruitful avenue of research into this fluid and blurred divide is the ritual and spiritual dimensions of hunting and the role of material culture in ritually mediating a broad range of social engagements and intersubjective communications between hunters and prey, and the living and the dead. As archaeologists, we need to more closely examine the spiritual and ritual dimensions of hunting if we are to better understand what it meant to be a hunter in ancient societies. By exploring the materiality of the numinous world of hunters, we as archaeologists take a step closer to appreciating the complex and nuanced lives of ancient peoples. In short, these explorations focus our attention on the on-going decisions ancient peoples had to make in order to define, construct, and negotiate their everyday lives within a broader relational social matrix of blurred and fluid boundaries between human and non-human, animal and non-animal, sentient and non-sentient, animate and inanimate, agent and non-agent, alive and dead, and seen and unseen.

In a previous paper, I argued that the "killing dialogue" (Bradley 1997:9) between hunter and prey is often "ritually mediated by material culture that often incorporates animal body parts" (McNiven 2010:217). Yet it is clear that such a killing dialogue extends beyond the immediate social engagement of hunter and prey to include the broader community, which I argue also takes in the spiritual realm of the dead, both past prey and past humans (see Nadasdy 2007:29). Indeed, in some ethnographic contexts it appears that the social arena of hunting can be conceived of as a dialogical matrix between the living (hunter and prey) *and* the dead (prey and humans). Often dialogue between the living and the dead is mediated by the skeletal remains of dead prey and hunters, particularly skulls (McNiven and Feldman 2003; McNiven 2010). In many circumstances, these skulls were curated for on-going social engagement and had an ambiguous meta-physical status given that they inhabited a liminal realm. This liminal state reflected their curious status as both the remains of the dead and the embodiment of living spirits that could be socially engaged. The materiality of such skeletal remains often outlived the social context of their production, which presents archaeologists with a rare opportunity to access not only the ritual dimensions of past hunting practices, but also the broader spiritual context of such practices and perhaps even ancient relational ontologies. This chapter explores the four-way social relationship and dialogical matrix between hunters and prey, especially between hunters and the dead, focusing on ethnographic and archaeological information on the ritual dimensions of dugong hunting by Indigenous peoples of Torres Strait, northeast Australia. I preface this discussion with a theoretical overview of the ritual and spiritual dimensions of killing dialogue between hunters and prey to provide a hypothetical structure and heuristic for exploring relational ontologies in past hunting societies.

Hunters and prey

Over the past three decades, considerable theoretical attention has been directed towards the practice of hunting as an intimate social relationship between hunter and prey. An influential exploration of this relationship is the work of Ingold (1994), who argues that 'trust' is a fundamental dimension of a hunter's interaction with prey (cf. Armstrong Oma 2010; Knight 2005). Ingold (1994:12) suggests further that in contrast to a Western ontology, which sees hunting as a product of stealth, superiority, and technological might, Indigenous hunters see hunting success "as proof of amicable relations between the hunter and the animal that has willingly allowed itself to be taken." According to Ingold (2000:49–52), a revealing insight into how the Western "ontological dualism between society and nature" has little relevance in certain hunter societies is provided by Tanner (1979) and Scott's (1989) work with the Cree of Canada. For the Cree, conceptualizing the difference between a human and an animal is not based on an ontological division between human organism and non-human organism "but between one kind of organism-person and another" (Ingold 2000:50). According to Scott, the Cree see fundamental similarities between humans and animals and then contemplate differences. In contrast, a Western ontology sees a fundamental difference between humans and animals and then explores similarities, often through the lens of anthropomorphic metaphors (see Scott 1989:194–95). For Ingold, it is the ontological overlap and shared personhood of humans and animals that lies at the heart of the hunting process and understanding social engagements between hunters and prey. In this sense, "hunting itself comes to be regarded not as a technical manipulation of the natural world but as a kind of interpersonal dialogue, integral to the total process of social life wherein both human and animal persons are constituted with their particular identities and purposes" (Ingold 2000:49).

I agree with Ingold that simply seeing the social relationship between hunter and prey as a dimension of anthropomorphism presents an incomplete and, indeed, distorted picture of the ontological proximity of humans and animals (McNiven 2010). However, informed by Anderson's (2000) concept of "sentient ecology," I see the 'humanizing' of prey as "part of a broader ontology where the world is imbued with agency and intentionality" (McNiven 2010:218). Recognizing the humanness and sociality of prey is essential to all killing dialogues and meaningful social engagements between hunters and prey. Yet, as Morris (2000:21) reminds us, all hunters must equally engage in some form of "theriomorphic thinking" to enhance "a sympathetic relationship with the hunted animal." Hunters know they can socially engage with prey because they know that there exists a shared onto-logical space that provides the potential for dialogue and mutual understanding. In some cases, this understanding of ontological overlap is founded on a cosmological understanding that many animals represent transformed humans. For example, Black (1981:126) records that Aleuts conceptualize fur seals and sea otters as "transformed humans." Similarly, Feit (1973:116) notes that amongst the Waswanipi Cree, constructing the world such that animals are "like persons" vests causality in terms of the 'personal' and 'who did it,' as opposed to the 'mechanical or biological' and 'why.' Thus, as Hallowell (1960:43–44) points out, causal relationships between human and animals, hunters and prey, are about personal forces and social relationships.

Under normal circumstances, shared ontological space only presents the potential for meaningful dialogue to take place between hunter and prey. Killing dialogue requires an extra degree of intimacy between hunter and prey that can only be achieved situationally through ritual orchestration. As the dialogue is related to specific hunting events, the ontological overlap and corresponding intimate and mutually understandable dialogue is both situational and short-term. That hunters often enter into a liminal state during killing dialogue supports the view that the underlying ritually orchestrated ontological proximity is out-of-the-ordinary (see Willerslev 2001:47). "In many cases, intimate understanding of prey is part of a broader ontology and cosmogony that sees humans and certain animals as kin. That is, humans and animals cognitively, somatically, and spiritually overlap to the point that the human-animal divide is seen as fluid, permeable, and mutually intelligible" (McNiven 2010:218). While 'trust' is an important dimension of such relationships, a degree of coercion is usually involved as hunters employ hunting magic to lure, compel, charm, and even seduce prey to their death (Nadasdy 2007; Tanner 1979:176; cf. Ingold 2000:71).

It is my contention that the ritualized killing dialogue between hunters and prey also involves dead humans and dead prey as the act of killing is by definition a destabilizing and transformational act of transferring a non-human person from the realm of the living to the realm of the dead. The ontological proximity of humans and prey creates a situation where the killing of prey is ontologically ambiguous because it is killing a person, albeit a non-human person. Such spiritual and moral ambiguity calls for careful ritual intervention and spiritual control and management. The following ethnographic survey structures my conceptualization of ritualized killing dialogues in terms of those between hunters and the living (e.g., with prey and community members) and those between hunters and the spirit realm (e.g., with spiritual creators, dead prey, and dead humans). The aim of this survey is to emphasize the importance of the agency of the dead in ritualized hunting dialogues, as such a conceptualization provides enormous archaeological scope given the materiality of the dead, the long-term preservation of associated skeletal remains, and the structured and patterned deposition of such remains as material expressions of such dialogues.

Killing dialogue with the living

Hunter and prey

Perhaps the most obvious and direct form of killing dialogue is that between hunter and prey. In this form, hunters talk to prey prior to making a kill either to bring the prey closer, to appease the prey, and/or to apologize for the kill. For example, Hallowell (1926; see also Losey et al., this volume) documents a range of "speeches, songs, or addresses" made to bears prior to killing by hunters across sub-Arctic northern Eurasia and North America. In other cases, preparation for hunting involves communication between hunters and potential prey using complex ritual magic often mediated by amulets and charms made from the remains of previously hunted prey (see below). In other cases, prey may be immobilized or lured to hunters using various ritual incantations, medicines, gestures, etc.

In some cases, ritually-orchestrated proximity results in hunters closely assuming the identity of prey such that through their own behavior and sensory thought processes they control the prey's behavior. In this sense, communication between hunter and prey is sympathetic and instantaneous. Examples of such situational consubstantiation and sensorial confluence are found amongst the Yukaghir caribou and elk hunters of Siberia (Willerslev 2007), Central Yup'ik seal hunters of Alaska (Fienup-Riordan 1990) and /Xam Bushman antelope hunters of southern Africa (Guenther 1991:199). In the case of some Inuit groups of Alaska, a seal hunter could transform into a ("spirit helper") bird "in the eyes of the seals he sought," to which the seal could be "irresistibly drawn" (Fienup-Riordan 1990:27). Such an association between bird (hunter) and seal may account for Nunivak Inuit burial of seal skulls and long bones in association with small wooden carvings of birds that Lantis (1946:194) interpreted as mediating spirit helpers. These examples reveal that the shared personhood of hunters and prey was mutually comprehensible, such that hunters could see the animalness of themselves and the humanness of prey, and prey could see the humanness of themselves and the animalness of hunters (see Fienup-Riordan 1990:36; Willerslev 2011:51). Under such relational circumstances, "in outward manifestation neither animal nor human characteristics define categorical differences in the core of being" (Hallowell 1960:35).

Hunter and community members

Hunting societies invariably have a broad range of cultural practices between community members that can be considered part of the hunting process, given that they are aimed at enhancing hunting success. Such practices usually entail ritually-prescribed behaviors and gender-specific taboos prior to and during the hunt, and appropriate distribution of hunted animal products amongst community members after the hunt. For example, Scott (1989:203) notes that amongst the Weminji Cree goose hunters, "failure to contribute generously to the feast can be used to account for poor luck in hunting later on." Similarly amongst the Chisasibi Cree, respect for game to help ensure continued hunting success is assisted by appropriate elders distributing meat amongst the community (Berkes 2008:107). In most cases, these appropriate behaviors appear to relate mostly to showing respect to either the 'soul-spirit' or 'spirit-creator' of the prey to ensure future successful provisioning of prey and hunting success (see below). In many cases, hunting rituals involved specific practices between a hunter and his wife. For example, during a whale hunt by the Nuu'chah'nulth of Vancouver Island (Canada), a hunter's wife "would actually *become* the whale. If she remained completely still, the whale would be still" and easily harpooned (Jonaitis 1999:8–9; emphasis in original).

Killing dialogue with the spirits

Participants in the active social arena of hunting usually include more than hunter and prey. Ethnographic evidence reveals that amongst many hunting societies, the social process of hunting also involves engagement with the spiritual realm, encompassing spiritual creators, dead prey, and dead humans.

Hunter and spiritual creator

The best documented and understood dimension of hunting relates to respectful and propitiatory behavior by hunters towards spiritual creators/guardians that control the provisioning of prey. In some cases, dialogue begins prior to the hunt. For example, Mayan deer hunters in the Yucatan must provide maize offerings to the "guardian of deer … before hunting or else the hunter will miss his mark" (Brown and Emery 2008:311). Similarly, Khanty peoples of western Siberia deposit elk heads and vodka bottles, along with coins and cloth which have been "ritually smoked," at special places to propitiate the "forest spirit … who dispatches game to the hunter" (Jordan 2001:95, 101). Yukaghir hunters of Siberia seduce the "master-spirit" with sacrifices of items such as alcohol and tobacco into a fire to induce sexual desire towards the hunter such that elk prey ("the spirit's physical counterpart") will approach the hunter with lustful desire, whereupon it can be easily killed (Willerslev 2007:101). In many instances, communication between hunters and spiritual creators is mediated by shamans who possess special and unique powers to engage the spiritual realm (e.g., Jordan 2001:93; 2003:124–25, 137, 139, 141; Lewis-Williams 2001:21).

In many instances, such respectful behavior relates to formalized treatment of killed prey – both prior to butchering (i.e., intact carcasses) and after butchering (e.g., meat and bones). For example, Chisasibi Cree hunters place tobacco offerings into the mouth of a recently killed bear, thereby "thanking the Provider" (Berkes 2008:107). Such "drink giving" ceremonies are common amongst hunters of northern Eurasia (Hallowell 1926:84). The Chisasibi Cree know that wasteful use of hunted animals is disrespectful and will negatively impact future hunting success (Berkes 2008:107). Mayan deer hunters ensure their hunting dogs do not gnaw on deer bones to avoid retribution from the "animal guardian" (Brown and Emery 2008:312). More generally amongst hunters of Arctic/sub-Arctic Eurasia and North America, "[i]t is said that the bones of the bear, and often other game animals, must be kept out of the way of dogs. Should a dog gnaw or even touch them the 'spirit' or 'owner' of the animals will be offended and misfortune or poor luck in hunting will result" (Hallowell 1926:136).

Hunter and dead prey

Killing dialogue between hunters and prey relates to use of prey body parts and appropriate and respectful treatment of prey remains. As with rituals to appease spiritual creators/guardians, ritual practices aimed at appeasement of the spirits of dead prey involves respectful behavior towards the carcass to ensure the animal's renewal and future hunting success. Examples include the practice among various Inuit groups of providing seal carcasses with a drink of water and leaving seal skulls on ice packs near the kill site (Pelly 2001:60, 64, 66). In these instances, hunters and potential prey know whether or not appropriate and respectful treatment of past prey remains has taken place, knowledge which can determine hunting success. As such, the dialogue between hunter and prey is based on the mutual interpretation and understanding of each other's actions.

As with respecting spiritual creators/guardians, careful treatment of prey remains, especially bones, was critical in many hunting societies to appease animal spirits ("soul-spirits"), which was linked to prey regeneration and future hunting success. For example, amongst the Canadian Micmac, bones of beaver were "carefully preserved" and not thrown to dogs or into a fire or river "because the Indians fear lest the spirit of the bones ... would promptly carry the news to the other beavers, which would desert the country in order to escape the same misfortune" (Martin 1978:35–36).

Often, respectful treatment related to caching and curation of skeletal remains of prey in shrines, especially skulls, to allow regeneration/reincarnation of the animal's soul or spirit (for overviews of skull caches, see Hill 2011:416–20; McNiven and Feldman 2003:173–74; cf. Brown and Emery 2008). Ethnographic examples of such practices include Greenland Inuit seal hunters, who kept seal skulls outside of their homes (Pelly 2001:64, 66), and Gilyak seal hunters of Siberia, who place the "decorated heads of seals" in the sea (Child and Child 1993:34). Mayan hunters return bones to hunting shrines as "bones retain a latent agency that allows for the regeneration of species" (Brown and Emery 2008:313).

Hunting magic amulets and charms made from the remains of prey provide another form of object-mediated dialogue between hunters and prey. Of particular importance is the use of sensory organs of dead prey to help hunters communicate with, or at least control the behavior of, potential live prey (McNiven 2010; see also Tanner 1979:141–42). Examples include whales' eye charms by Chukchi whale hunters of Siberia (Bogoras 1907:408) and manatee ear bones by Rama manatee hunters of Nicaragua (Loveland 1976:74). Hill (2011:412–16) discusses examples of amulets from Arctic and sub-Arctic Alaska and northeast Asia made from bones and teeth of whale, walrus, and seal. To this list can be added scapula, and the divinatory practice of scapulimancy whose "explicit purpose is to receive communication from animals and the entities that control them" (Tanner 1979:132). Although the killing dialogue is primarily between hunter and prey, the role of previously killed prey whose remains form the hunting amulets reveals a complex, dialogical matrix between hunter, live prey, and dead prey. "The prehistoric use of amulets indicates that hunting success was onto-logically linked to animal agency" (Hill 2011:416). Thus, not only are hunters engaging with and responding to curated animal (prey) remains, but so too are potential prey.

Hunter and dead humans

Scattered evidence exists on communication between hunters and dead humans (usually hunters) related to the hunting process amongst northern Eurasian and North American hunters (e.g., Hallowell 1926). It is clear that dead people in some societies have agency in terms of enhancing hunting success. For example, amongst the Chisasibi Cree, "there was a respected old man who died on the point of a particular lake. He was buried there. When people went by his grave, they would make an offering to him. They rolled tobacco in tree bark and left it there. They were asking the old man to provide game for them in return for the tobacco" (Berkes 2008:107).

Aleuts were known to keep the mummified bodies of whale hunters and possibly powerful shamans in secret caves for the purposes of whale hunting magic. As part of the ritual preparations for a whale hunt, hunters would touch the mummies to gain special spiritual power. In addition, "fat or other tissues of corpses" were applied to the bodies of whale hunters and their kayak and hunting weapons. Upon returning to shore, whale hunters entered into a four-day period of isolation and "rejoined human society only after undergoing rites of purification" (Black 1981:129–30; see also Lantis 1946:229).

The Yuquot whalers' shrine on Vancouver Island of the Nuu'chah'nulth contained carved wooden figures of at least 88 humans and eight whales in association with 16 human skulls (Jonaitis 1999:3, 24). In the nineteenth century, the shrine was recorded as a place where chiefs (senior whale hunters) were buried, and where whale hunters (members of chiefly lineages) would visit to seek spiritual assistance to help ensure hunting success (Jonaitis 1999:5, 23–24). More generally, secret and sacred whaling shrines of the Nuu'chah'nulth "included figures of spirits and animals made of brush, masks, corpses, and skeletons" (Jonaitis 1999:9). In Nuu'-chah'nulth cosmology, "the dead have power to 'call' or attract various kinds of animals" which explains in part why whale hunters were known to steal human corpses to ritually assist with the hunt (Drucker 1951:165; Jonaitis 1999:199–200). Indeed, Drucker (1951:164) recorded that "The performance, for instance, of a certain ritual with a corpse invariably caused dead whales to drift ashore."

To further explore the agency of the dead in hunting practices, I turn to the Torres Strait region of northern Australia and southwest Papua New Guinea, where detailed ethnographic and archaeological information reveals the active and intimate role of humans and prey remains in the hunting of dugong (a marine mammal).

Torres Strait: agency of the dead

Torres Strait is located between the mainlands of northeast Australia and south central New Guinea. It is home to a range of Melanesian horticultural-hunting societies, ranging from maritime specialists living on numerous islands across the 150 km wide strait, to mainlanders of the Papua New Guinea coast who practice a

FIGURE 5.1 Ned Waria of Mabuyag, Torres Strait, holding a harpoon (*wap*) and demonstrating the use of a dugong hunting platform (*nath*) to Alfred Haddon, 1888. (Courtesy of Cambridge University Museum of Archaeology and Anthropology – P.1148. ACH1).

mixed marine-terrestrial economy (Beckett 1987; Haddon 1935; Landtman 1927). An important source of meat for peoples of the Torres Strait region is dugong and turtle hunted at sea with harpoons from dinghies. In the past, harpooning took place using canoes and, in the case of dugongs, from small platforms with tall posts set up over reefs supporting sea grass meadows (the preferred food of dugongs) (Figure 5.1). Archaeological evidence indicates that such hunting practices extend back at least 4,000 years (dugong) and 6,000 to 7,000 years (turtle) (Crouch et al. 2007; Wright 2011). The hunting of dugong by Torres Strait Islanders and their Kiwai neighbors on the adjacent mainland coast of Papua New Guinea involves considerable technical skill as well as extensive ritual practices (Landtman 1927:120–41). Indeed, a broad range of ritual practices involving incantations, taboos, shrines, and charms were used by Torres Strait Islanders and Kiwai people to attract dugongs to hunters (see McNiven and Feldman 2003 for a detailed overview). Landtman (1927:138) pointed out that hunting dugongs from stationary platforms required "many rigorous observances" as "it is the dugong which must be induced to go to" the hunter. The following discussion focuses on ritual connections between dugong hunters and the dead (humans and dugongs).

Hunting with dead humans

Ethnographic information reveals that hunters would consult the remains of recently dead humans to seek assistance in the hunting of dugongs and turtles. Such consultation took three forms: divination using skulls, consultation of grave sites, and use of charms with human remains. Human skull divination was commonly practiced across Torres Strait prior to Christian missionary influences of the late nineteenth century (Haddon 1904:251–2, 258–62, Plate XV.1; 1908:126–7, 266–9, Plate 28.2; 1935:78) (Figure 5.2). Mortuary ceremonies feature special rituals that formally transform spirits of the dead into ghosts (Beckett 1975:167). In ghost form, the dead are welcomed back into society, and the "skull is now the means of bringing the ghost back into relations with mortals" (Beckett 1975:180). Thus, in terms of the living communicating with the dead in Torres Strait Islander society, the "critical line … is not between the living and the dead, but between mortals and ghosts" (Beckett 1975:167). A rare early insight into the use of skulls to aid hunting is provided by Gill (1876:302) who noted that Torres Strait Islanders believe that "the spirits of their deceased friends aid them in chasing dugongs, turtle, etc." For this reason, portions of dugong are presented to the "skulls of parents and other relatives" to help in "securing their goodwill." Haddon provides further details:

> When a man intended to go out in his canoe in search of dugong or turtle, he prepared his bamboo tobacco pipe, *zub,* inhaled a big mouthful and puffed it into the mouth of the grinning skull of his father, which was hanging up in the house, and said: "This my last tobacco now, I give you smoke, you show me where dugong or turtle he stop." The smoke coming out from the skull whispered, "Whf, whf!" When at sea, the hunter and his friends, with open ears and every sense alert, would presently hear, a little to one side, a dugong faintly blowing, "Whf, whf!" Thus the father by means of the creature's breath was leading it by sound to the place where the hunters waited.
>
> *(Haddon 1935:78)*

The graves of renowned dugong hunters may be visited by dugong hunters to help bring hunting success. In the 1970s, Nietschmann and Nietschmann (1981:61) observed that some hunters on the island of Mabuyag would make a "visit to the graveyard to ask ancestors for luck" (Figure 5.3). Fitzpatrick-Nietschmann (1980:331, 344) argues that "skulls have been replaced by headstones" to mediate one-on-one dialogue with the dead. Amongst the Kiwai, "sometimes the spirit of some famous deceased harpooner is invoked [to increase hunting success] by saying, 'Boy belong you he go outside to-morrow, he take hand belong you, you no make him miss'" (Landtman 1927:131, 295–96). The association between ancestral powers and dugong hunting is represented in a Torres Strait Islander legend where a man named Sesere/Sessere introduced the hunting and eating of dugong to Torres Strait following advice provided by his dead parents through their skulls (Haddon 1904:40–44).

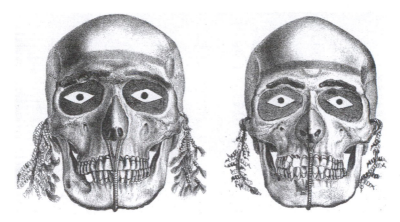

FIGURE 5.2 Torres Strait Islander skulls from the island of Naghi, Torres Strait, used for divination (from Thomas 1884: Plate 2).

FIGURE 5.3 Grave of Banasa (b. 1879, d. 1943), a renowned dugong hunter, Mabuyag Island Cemetery, Torres Strait (Photo: Ian J. McNiven).

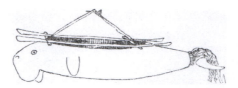

FIGURE 5.4 Carved wooden dugong hunting charm with two human leg bones (fibulae) attached (from Haddon 1901:Fig. 18). British Museum: 89+182.

Haddon collected a number of dugong hunting charms in the form of small carved wooden dugongs to which were attached selected leg bones of the sorcerer or magic man (*maidhalaig*) who carved the dugong. One such charm, collected from Mua in 1888, was subsequently attached to a dugong hunting platform on the nearby island of Mabuyag for Haddon's edification (Figures 5.1 and 5.4). This charm also had attached a tassel of sea grass (dugong food) and dugong fat. The addition of human leg bones was "to render the charm more effective" (Haddon 1901:153–54; see also Haddon 1904:338, Plate XVI.1; Moore 1984:49–50, 56).

Along with the remains of the dead helping to increase hunting success, such items could also be used in hunting sorcery to decrease hunting luck. For example, a "very malignant form of sorcery" amongst the Kiwai was "to fasten a small piece of the tongue of a man who had hanged himself into the harpooning rope of the enemy. The latter, when spearing a dugong, will get his head entangled in a loop of the rope ('he hang himself') and be drowned" (Landtman 1927:136). More treacherous is a man who wreaks havoc upon an entire community by attaching a dugong rib, along with "a small piece of the skull or some other bone of a human skeleton" to a tree trunk found floating in the sea to ensure that "there will be no more dugong in the sea" (Landtman 1927:136–37).

Amongst the Kiwai, association between the dead and dugong hunting was perhaps most clearly expressed through mortuary ceremonies, in particular the great *hóriómu* or *táera* ceremony which was performed annually in celebration of deaths over the past year (for details see Landtman 1927:327–49). Secondary burial was commonly practiced by the Kiwai and in some cases skulls would be kept by close relatives. After removal, the skull was taken back to a shrine in the village where a dance then took place with men holding their harpoons "in the same position as when spearing dugong or turtle" (Landtman 1927:260). "These harpoons are sure to bring a great catch" (Landtman 1927:262). The *hóriómu* ceremony involved men impersonating (embodying) ghosts of the dead and various other spiritual entities. Significantly, Landtman (1927:326) states that "one of the chief objects of the ceremony is to assist the people in the harpooning of dugong." An associated shrine included harpoon shafts belonging to different totemic clans, along with sea grass upon which dugongs feed and "a few dugong's teeth." Adjacent to the shrine were poles to build dugong hunting platforms. Those embodying a spirit of the dead at the ceremony "will afterwards be assisted by the real ghost when spearing dugong."

A similar association between death ceremonies and dugong rituals is found amongst Torres Strait Islanders. At the *kod* ceremonial site on the sacred islet of Pulu in the central western Strait, the local Goemulgal on the nearby residential island of Mabuyag held the annual *tai* or *markai* ceremony associated with transformation of the disembodied spirits of the dead (*mari*) into ghosts (*markai*) (for details see Haddon 1904:252–56; 1935:344). As with the closely related *hóriómu* ceremony of the Kiwai, *tai* ceremony involved dancers impersonating known dead individuals. *Markai* ghosts also hunt for dugongs and turtles across the waters of Torres Strait similar to their mortal counterparts. While not specifically mentioned as part of *tai* ceremonies, hunting rituals for turtle (and possibly dugong) using the carcasses of turtles and dugongs also took place at the *kod* (Haddon 1904:333–34; 1935:353–54). That a strong association existed between the *kod* and dugongs, however, is revealed by the three large dugong bone mounds that form parts of the site (McNiven et al. 2009).

Hunting with dead dugongs

In western Torres Strait, Haddon (1904:338) recorded hunting magic charms made from the "nose and anterior part of the face of a dead dugong," with the "larynx and trachea ... stuffed" with a range of plant products, including sea grass (dugong food) (see also Manas et al. 2008:390–91; Nietschmann 1977:9). On the island of Mua, a "small bag of [raw] dugong meat" can be placed in the front and back of a dinghy to "make the boat go straight to the dugong. The meat steered the dinghy straight to the dugong" (Manas et al. 2008:396). Kiwai hunters similarly used charms made from the skin of a dugong's "face, including the nostrils and the neck" and "the windpipe [which] is fastened at the mouth" and attached to a "bunch of magical herbs" (usually "sweet-smelling leaves") and a dugong mandible in order "to bring success to the harpooners" (Landtman 1927:128, 137).

Ethnographic insights into use of dugong body parts to aid hunting success have been enhanced considerably by archaeological research which reveals formalized discard of dugong bones and use of dugong ear bones as dugong hunting charms. Special treatment of dugong bones centered on the construction of dugong bone mounds containing the remains of hundreds and even thousands of dugongs. These mounds have been recorded on numerous islands across western and central Torres Strait and radiocarbon dated to the past 500 years (David et al. 2009; McNiven and Bedingfield 2008; McNiven and Feldman 2003; McNiven et al. 2009; Skelly et al. 2011). Ethnographic information on these mounds is scant, with Haddon (1912:131–32) stating simply that dugong skulls and bones were "massed in heaps ... for ceremonial purposes ... or merely to keep count of the number of animals caught in any one season." Dugong bone mounds contain mostly dugong rib and skull bones and evidence for the deliberate removal and arrangement of ear bones (tympano-periotic complex). Such deliberate removal and special arrangement of an organ associated with the acute hearing of dugongs (through which they primarily perceive the presence of hunters), coupled with recent ethnographic evidence for use of these 'radar' or 'wireless' bones to help establish dialogue between hunters and dugongs, have further supported McNiven and Feldman's (2003) hypothesis that these ear bones served as hunting magic charms (McNiven 2010; Skelly et al. 2011).

Kiwai hunters used to place the bones of dugong at a point called Ganalai as an "offering" to "three mythical beings called Nágimarkái, Kíbumarkái and Usáraba, who are said to be the 'bosses' of the dugong and turtle" (Landtman 1927:130). Hunters also "addressed" the three beings who were "asked to 'make him dugong cranky to-morrow, you shut him eye belong him, he come, me spear him, you bring him plenty dugong'" (Landtman 1927:131). On the same coastline, Gill (1876:232) mentioned a "huge pile of bones of the dugong" near to where the *hóriómu* ceremony was performed.

The dead combined

Ethnographic observations for the Torres Strait region reveal a close ritual association between the living (dugong hunters) and the dead (both humans and dugongs). At one level, this association reflects the cosmological reality that spirits of the dead form part of the daily social world of the living. Spirits of the dead were members of each community, and as such they could be engaged socially through verbal and non-verbal dialogue usually mediated by material culture that included remains of the dead. In the case of dugong hunting, the living (e.g., hunters) needed to invest in the dead (e.g., hunters of renown) through friendly engagement and reciprocity that often took the form of propitiation, offerings, and gifting. In return, the dead hopefully would enhance hunting success. I use the term 'hopefully' deliberately here as causality was not mechanical but social and relied upon the generosity of the dead to direct hunters to dugong and dugong to hunters. In this sense, hunters ritually orchestrated a killing dialogue between dead hunters and potential prey.

Yet the integration of dead dugongs (i.e., bones and fragments of soft tissue organs) into hunting practices speaks of a relational ontology where the blurred and fluid divide between humans and dugongs was ritually manipulated. This proximity was "founded upon an ontology of prey as kin and shared and permeable personhood" (McNiven 2010:225), such that, through ritual, a hunter could manipulate dugongs so that they would be socially and even sexually attracted to the hunter. This sexual attraction is exemplified well by the Kiwai whereupon ritual preparations for dugong hunting included associating the hunter's harpoon with his wife (e.g., his wife "anoints the harpoon-head with secretion from her vulva") such that the dugong (personifying the husband) would be attracted to the harpoon (personifying the wife) (Landtman 1927:128–29). Indeed sometimes, while a hunter is out hunting on the sea at night, his wife "lies down naked on her back at the door through which her husband has passed out, holding her feet widely apart, one at each doorpost. This causes the dugong to come" (Landtman 1927:138). The situational and short-term sexual consubstantiation that takes place for hunting is also found within numerous hunting societies of northern Eurasia and North America, and extends well beyond the mere metaphorical (see Losey et al., this volume; Nadasdy 2007; Tanner 1979; cf. Bird-David 1993:113–14).

The final act of consubstantiation took place at the death of humans. This complex process remains poorly documented and understood, but it involved in part the transformation of a human into a dugong at death. For example, it is known that Torres Strait Islanders, "when in the state of dying," will embody their totem and physically move as their totem would move as it were dying (Laade 1969:34). In the case of members of the dugong totemic clan, the dying person will move as a swimming dugong. Landtman (1927:293) recorded a story of men from Daru in northern Torres Strait who took the form of spirits with dugong bodies and human heads after being killed by Kiwai raiders. These spirits temporarily 'possessed' the body of an unconscious Daru man who survived the raid and taught him how to spear dugong. Amongst the Kiwai, "spirits of the dead … frequently appear in the shape of animals" (Landtman 1927:441; see also Haddon 1904:354).

After death, dugong skulls were recorded additions to some human graves in Torres Strait, suggesting strongly a post-mortem association between dead humans and dead dugongs (see Losey et al., this volume). For example, in 1791, Edwards recorded a site of the Kaurareg people on the island of Muralag in southwest Torres Strait consisting of "a heap of bones. There were amongst them two human skulls, the bones of some large animals [dugong], and some turtle-bones. They were heaped together in the form of a grave" (Hamilton 1793, cited in Haddon 1935:65). In 1844, Jukes (1847, I:149–50) recorded a similar "quite recent" mounded grave adorned with dugong skulls on Muralag (see also MacGillivray 1852, II:32; Moore 1979:153, 185, 217, 227, 240) (Figure 5.5). The Kaurareg

FIGURE 5.5 Grave decorated with marine shells, dugong ribs and skulls, and four wooden corner posts, Muralag, Torres Strait, 1844 (from Jukes 1847, I:149).

would also mark the place where a man dies with dugong and turtle bones (Moore 1979:219). Like many other groups in Torres Strait, the Kaurareg removed the head from the body prior to burial for use in divination (see above) (Moore 1979:217). Is it possible that the dugong and turtle skulls placed on graves were a symbolic replacement for the human skull? Aboriginal graves decorated with dugong bones have also been recorded on the adjacent mainland of northeast Australia (Rigsby and Chase 1998:207; Thomson 1934:254, Plate 31.2).

Conclusion

Ethnographic information on hunting societies ranging widely from the sub-Arctic boreal forests of Siberia to the tropical waters of Torres Strait reveals that the ritual dimensions of hunting are far more elaborate, complex, and time-consuming than the technological demands of making, maintaining, and using weapons. Yet, previous anthropological and archaeological studies on the ritual and spiritual dimensions of hunting have focused on the relationship between hunters and prey, and the role of spiritual providers, shamans, and material culture (e.g., amulets and hunting charms) in mediating such relationships. It has been a key aim of this paper to demonstrate that the social arena of hunting involves a complex, intersubjective dialogue between the living and the dead, both humans and prey. Paradoxically, through shared and permeable personhood between humans (hunters) and animals (prey), and the living (mortals) and the dead (spirits), fundamental differences between all four ontological categories of personhood could be blurred and even subsumed through special ritual performances. Such rituals were often complex and dangerous because manipulating and closing the divide between these four different ontological beings necessarily creates instability and liminality. Because this unstable state was dangerous, its creation was necessarily situational, short-term, and taken very seriously.

In many respects, the liminal status of hunting reflected the fundamental cosmological destabilization hunting creates through the transformation of prey from the realm of the living to the realm of the dead. Such destabilization is not a feature of all animals killed by humans, but only those with shared personhood due to ontological proximity. While no hunting societies formally undertake mortuary ceremonies for killed prey, considerable formality, ritualization, and respect is usually associated with treatment of prey food products (e.g., butchering and distribution of meat) and byproducts such as bones. In this formulation, the incorporation of dugong hunting rituals in the *hóriómu* death ceremony by Kiwai hunters is a likely acknowledgment of the ontological proximity of dugong death to human death. In this situation, such proximity is not only critical for understanding the complex rituals of dugong hunting and consubstantiation involving the sexual seduction between a hunter (cf. 'dugong') and his wife (cf. 'harpoon'), but equally important for demonstrating the fundamental ontological difference between humans and dugongs such that the act of dugong hunting is not the same as killing a human (e.g., murder).

Luckily for archaeologists, the complex social arena of hunting and its dialogical matrix involving humans and animals, the living and the dead, is often ritually mediated materially through bones (especially human and animal skulls), amulets, charms, etc. Understanding which dialogues are mediated by these items (e.g., hunters with the human dead, hunters with live prey) provides a window into the workings of the social arena of hunting and the nature of relational ontologies negotiated and ritually manipulated by hunters. Indeed, I argue that to understand this social arena requires not only a broad scale understanding of a society's hunting practices, but also of how they treat the remains of humans and animals. In parti-cular, the degree to which skeletal remains of humans and animals are deposited separately or together, and in what context such deposition takes place, speaks volumes of the ontological relationship between humans and animals. In terms of hunting rituals, the challenge is to identify how the dialogical matrix was estab-lished and mediated materially between participants in the social arena of hunting such that the ontological proximity and shared personhood of hunters and prey was temporarily destabilized and manipulated closer. Sensitivity to the theoretical notion of relational ontologies, and avenues of expression through practices such as hunting, can open archaeologists to new worlds of understanding how peoples of the past constructed and negotiated similarities and differences between what it meant to be human and animal, a human person versus a non-human person, and even alive versus dead.[1]

Notes

1 Thanks to Christopher Watts for the kind invitation to write this chapter. Helpful feedback on earlier drafts of this paper was kindly provided by Lynette Russell and Christopher Watts.

Bibliography

Armstrong Oma, Kristin 2010. Between Trust and Domination: Social Contracts between Humans and Animals. *World Archaeology* 42(2):175–87.

Anderson, David G. 2000. *Identity and Ecology in Arctic Siberia.* Oxford University Press, Oxford.

Beckett, Jeremy 1975. A Death in the Family: Some Torres Strait Ghost Stories. In *Australian Aboriginal Mythology*, edited by Lester R. Hiatt, pp. 163–82. Australian Institute of Aboriginal Studies, Canberra.

——(1987). *Torres Strait Islanders.* Cambridge University Press, Cambridge.

Berkes, Fikret 2008. *Sacred Ecology.* Routledge, New York.

Bird-David, Nurit 1993. Tribal Metaphorization of Human-Nature Relatedness. In *Environmentalism*, edited by Kay Milton, pp. 112–25. Routledge, London.

Black, Lydia T. 1981. The Nature of Evil: Of Whales and Sea Otters. In *Indians, Animals and the Fur Trade*, edited by Shepard Krech, III, pp. 109–53. University of Georgia Press, Athens.

Bogoras, Waldemar 1907. The Chukchee: Religion. *Memoirs of the American Museum of Natural History* 11(2).

Bradley, John J. 1997. "Li-anthawirriyarra, People of the Sea." Unpublished Ph.D. dissertation, Faculty of Arts, Northern Territory University, Darwin.

Brown, Linda A., and Kitty F. Emery 2008. Negotiations with the Animate Forest: Hunting Shrines in the Guatemalan Highlands. *Journal of Archaeological Method and Theory* 15:300–37.

Child, Alice B., and Irvin L. Child 1993. *Religion and Magic in the Life of Traditional Peoples*. Prentice Hall, New Jersey.

Crouch, Joe, Ian J. McNiven, Bruno David, Cassandra Rowe, and Marshall Weisler 2007. Berberass: Marine Resource Specialisation and Environmental Change in Torres Strait over the Past 4000 Years. *Archaeology in Oceania* 42:49–64.

David, Bruno, Ian J. McNiven, Joe Crouch, Mura Badulgal Corporation Committee, Robert Skelly, Bryce Barker, Kris Courtney, and Geoffrey Hewitt 2009. Koey Ngurtai: The Emergence of a Ritual Domain in Western Torres Strait. *Archaeology in Oceania* 44:1–17.

Drucker, Philip 1951. *The Northern and Central Nootkan Tribes*. Smithsonian Institution Bureau of American Ethnology Bulletin 144. United States Government Printing Office, Washington.

Feit, Harvey A. 1973. The Ethno-Ecology of the Waswanipi Cree; or How Hunters Can Manage Their Resources. In *Cultural Ecology*, edited by Bruce Cox, pp. 115–25. McClelland and Stewart, Toronto.

Fienup-Riordan, Ann 1990. The Bird and the Bladder: The Cosmology of Central Yup'ik Seal Hunting. *Etudes/Inuit/Studies* 14(1):23–38.

Fitzpatrick-Nietschmann, Judith 1980. "Another Way of Dying: The Social and Cultural Context of Death in a Melanesian Community, Torres Strait." Unpublished Ph.D. dissertation, Department of Anthropology, University of Michigan, Ann Arbor.

Gill, William W. 1876. *Life in the Southern Isles*. The Religious Tract Society, London.

Guenther, Mathias 1991. Animals in Bushman Thought, Myth and Art. In *Hunters and Gatherers, Volume II: Property, Power and Ideology*, edited by Tim Ingold, David Riches, and James Woodburn, pp. 192–211. Berg, New York.

Haddon, Alfred C. 1901. *Head-Hunters*. Methuen, London.

Haddon, Alfred C. (editor) 1904. *Reports of the Cambridge Anthropological Expedition to Torres Straits. Vol. V: Sociology, Magic and Religion of the Western Islanders*. Cambridge University Press, Cambridge.

——(1908). *Reports of the Cambridge Anthropological Expedition to Torres Straits. Vol. VI: Sociology, Magic and Religion of the Eastern Islanders*. Cambridge University Press, Cambridge.

——(1912). *Reports of the Cambridge Anthropological Expedition to Torres Straits. Vol. IV. Arts and Crafts*. Cambridge University Press, Cambridge.

——(1935). *Reports of the Cambridge Anthropological Expedition to Torres Straits. Vol. I. General Ethnography*. Cambridge University Press, Cambridge.

Hallowell, A. Irving 1926. Bear Ceremonialism in the Northern Hemisphere. *American Anthropologist* 28(1):1–175.

——(1960). Ojibwa Ontology, Behavior, and World View. In *Culture in History*, edited by Stanley Diamond, pp. 19–52. Columbia University Press, New York.

Hill, Erica 2011. Animals as Agents: Hunting Ritual and Relational Ontologies in Prehistoric Alaska and Chukotka. *Cambridge Archaeological Journal* 21(3):407–26.

Ingold, Tim 1994. From Trust to Domination: An Alternative History of Human-Animal Relations. In *Animals and Human Society*, edited by Aubrey Manning and James Serpell, pp. 1–22. Routledge, London.

——(2000). *The Perception of the Environment*. Routledge, London.

Jonaitis, Aldona 1999. *The Yuquot Whalers' Shrine*. University of Washington Press, Seattle.

Jordan, Peter 2001. The Materiality of Shamanism as a 'Worldview': Praxis, Artefacts and Landscape. In *The Archaeology of Shamanism*, edited by Neil S. Price, pp. 87–104. Routledge, London.

——(2003). *Material Culture and Sacred Landscape*. AltaMira, Walnut Creek, California.

Jukes, Joseph B. 1847. *Narrative of the Surveying Voyage of H.M.S. Fly*. 2 vols. T. and W. Boone, London.

Knight, John 2005. Introduction. In *Animals in Person: Cultural Perspectives on Human-Animal Intimacy*, edited by John Knight, pp. 1–13. Berg, Oxford.

Laade, Wolfgang 1969. Ethnographic Notes on the Murray Islanders, Torres Strait. *Zeitschrift für Ethnology* 94:33–46.

Landtman, Gunnar 1927. *The Kiwai Papuans of British New Guinea.* Macmillan and Co., London.

Lantis, Margaret 1946. The Social Culture of the Nunivak Eskimo. *Transactions of the American Philosophical Society* 35(3):153–323.

Lewis-Williams, J. David 2001. Southern African Shamanistic Rock Art in its Social and Cognitive Contexts. In *The Archaeology of Shamanism*, edited by Neil S. Price, pp. 17–39. Routledge, London.

Loveland, Franklin O. 1976. Tapirs and Manatees: Cosmological Categories and Social Process among Rama Indians of Eastern Nicaragua. In *Frontier Adaptations in Lower Central America*, edited by Mary W. Helms and Franklin O. Loveland, pp. 67–82. Institute for the Study of Human Issues, Philadelphia.

MacGillivray, John 1852. *Narrative of the Voyage of H.M.S. Rattlesnake.* 2 vols. T. and W. Boone, London.

Manas, John, Bruno David, Louise Manas, Jeremy Ash, and Anna Shnukal 2008. An Interview with Fr John Manas. *Memoirs of the Queensland Museum Cultural Heritage Series* 4(2):385–418.

Martin, Calvin 1978. *Keepers of the Game.* University of California Press, Berkeley.

McNiven, Ian J. 2010. Navigating the Human-Animal Divide: Marine Mammal Hunters and Rituals of Sensory Allurement. *World Archaeology* 42(2):215–30.

McNiven, Ian J., and Alice C. Bedingfield 2008. Past and Present Marine Mammal Hunting Rates and Abundances: Dugong (*Dugong dugon*) Evidence from Dabangai Bone Mound, Torres Strait. *Journal of Archaeological Science* 35:505–15.

McNiven, Ian J., and Ricky Feldman 2003. Ritually Orchestrated Seascapes: Bone Mounds and Dugong Hunting Magic in Torres Strait, NE Australia. *Cambridge Archaeological Journal* 13(2):169–94.

McNiven, Ian J., Bruno David, Goemulgau Kod, and Judith Fitzpatrick 2009. The Great *Kod* of Pulu: Mutual Historical Emergence of Ceremonial Sites and Social Groups in Torres Strait, NE Australia. *Cambridge Archaeological Journal* 19(3):291–317.

Moore, David R. 1979. *Islanders and Aborigines at Cape York.* Australian Institute of Aboriginal Studies, Canberra.

——(1984). *The Torres Strait Collections of A.C. Haddon.* British Museum Publications, London.

Morris, Brian 2000. *Animals and Ancestors.* Berg, Oxford.

Nadasdy, Paul 2007. The Gift in the Animal: The Ontology of Hunting and Human–Animal Sociality. *American Ethnologist* 34(1):25–43.

Nietschmann, Bernard 1977. Torres Strait Islander Hunters and Environment. Work-in-progress seminar, Department of Human Geography, Research School of Pacific Studies, Australian National University, Canberra.

Nietschmann, Bernard, and Judith Nietschmann 1981. Good Dugong, Bad Dugong; Bad Turtle, Good Turtle. *Natural History* 90(5):54–63, 86–87.

Pelly, David F. 2001. *Sacred Hunt.* University of Washington Press, Seattle.

Rigsby, Bruce, and Athol Chase 1998. The Sandbeach People and Dugong Hunters of Eastern Cape York Peninsula: Property in Land and Sea Country. In *Customary Marine Tenure in Australia*, edited by Nicholas Peterson and Bruce Rigsby, pp. 192–218. Oceania Monograph 48, University of Sydney, Sydney.

Russell, Nerissa 2012. *Social Zooarchaeology.* Cambridge University Press, Cambridge.

Scott, Colin 1989. Knowledge Construction among Cree Hunters: Metaphors and Literal Understanding. *Journal de la Société des Américanistes* 75:193–208.

Skelly, Robert, Bruno David, Ian J. McNiven, and Bryce Barker 2011. The Ritual Dugong Bone Mounds of Koey Ngurtai, Torres Strait, Australia: Investigating their Construction. *International Journal of Osteoarchaeology* 21:32–54.

Tanner, Adrian 1979. *Bringing Home Animals.* Institute of Social and Economic Research, Memorial University of Newfoundland, St. John's, Canada.

Thomas, Oldfield 1884. Part 1. The Collections from Melanesia. Mammalia. In *Report on the Zoological Collections Made in the Indo-Pacific Ocean during the Voyage of H.M.S. 'Alert' 1881–2*, pp. 5–10. Trustees of the British Museum, London.

Thomson, Donald F. 1934. The Dugong Hunters of Cape York. *Journal of the Royal Anthropological Institute of Great Britain and Ireland* 64:237–62.

Willerslev, Rane 2001. The Hunter as a Human 'Kind': Hunting and Shamanism among the Upper Kolyma Yukaghirs of Siberia. *North Atlantic Studies* 4(1/2):44–50.

——(2007). *Soul Hunters*. University of California Press, Berkeley.

——(2011). Seeing with Others Eyes: Hunting and 'Idle Talk' in the Landscape of the Siberian Iukagir. In *Landscape and Culture in Northern Eurasia*, edited by Peter Jordan, pp. 49–70. Left Coast Press, Walnut Creek, California.

Wright, Duncan 2011. Mid-Holocene Maritime Economy in the Western Torres Strait. *Archaeology in Oceania* 46:23–27.

6

METHODOLOGICAL AND ANALYTICAL CHALLENGES IN RELATIONAL ARCHAEOLOGIES: A VIEW FROM THE HUNTING GROUND

María Nieves Zedeño

Archaeologies that focus on the recovery of past relational views of the world – a world where such things as non-human agency and animacy played a key role in the formation of the material record – present unique methodological challenges, not the least of which is the development of systematics that link relevant theory and practice. Important strides have been recently made toward the development of relational archaeologies that are both firmly grounded in modern social theory and open to culturally diverse notions of nature, objects, and the social order (e.g., Alberti and Bray 2009; Brown and Emery 2008; Dobres and Robb 2000; Fogelin 2008; Ingold 2000, 2006; Knappett and Malafouris [eds.] 2008; Meskell 2004; Meskell [ed.] 2005; Miller 2005; Mills and Ferguson 2008; Mills and Walker 2008; Olsen 2010; Pauketat 2012; Preucel 2006; Tilley 1999; Walker 1995, 1999, 2008). The goal of this chapter is to contribute to this growing body of literature by outlining *relational systematics* as a framework for the analysis of archaeological objects and recovery contexts that is founded on principles of relational ontology.

My interest in developing such a framework is two-fold: first, 18 years of work with North American tribes of various ethnicities and with their incredibly rich archaeological and ethnographic records has convinced me that an explicitly analytical approach to relationality can help build intellectual bridges between different ontologies as well as do justice to the work and lives of people in the past (Carroll et al. 2004; Murray 2011; Stoffle et al. 2001; Zedeño 2000, 2008a, 2008b, 2009). And second, if relational archaeologies are to be embraced and refined by our students, then we have a duty to help them operationalize their research projects so that these may be properly evaluated for funding and job opportunities. The ideas presented here are pragmatic, messy, and tentative, but they nonetheless reinforce the assertion that relational archaeologies can create meaningful connections between past and present ontologies.

Why systematics?

In so far as one regards archaeology as a scientific discipline, or at the very least as a formal mode of inquiry that answers relevant questions about people in the past through the construction of logical arguments, replicable analyses, and explanations based on material remains, systematics is key to learning about sources of variation in archaeological things and beings, both past and present, as well as about the relationships among entities through time. I have combined biological and archaeological elements of this concept (Dunnell 1971; Schuh 2000) to highlight the notion that, if a new systematics is to be developed for relational approaches to the past, it must include objects and subjects in all their absolute, transitory, and fluid states of existence (Zedeño 2008a, 2008b, 2009). Relational systematics and its operational daughter, ontological (relational) taxonomy, are a most needed departure from the epistemological taxonomies that characterize conventional archaeological methods (e.g., Adams and Adams 2007; Ramenofsky and Steffen 1998) because they are flexible enough to accommodate the peculiarities and ambivalences of *taxonomies of being* (folk taxonomies, Berlin 1992) that characterize the vast majority of people's understandings of the world.

When confronted with taxonomies of being, which by definition are not the subject matter of Western science (Dunnell 1971), the analyst cannot help but note the limitations of conventional systematics. As Wildman and Neville (2000:220) ably put it, these limitations, and the sense of arbitrariness they provoke "derive from the fact that the theory furnishing the categories for comparison is too neat, too easily able to deflect objections, and thus too convenient, too invulnerable, too unresponsive to criticism, and too uninterested in correction and improvement." For one, as long as the taxonomic emphasis is on isolating artifact classes by similarity, as opposed to embracing the great diversity of objects in an environment, encapsulating the fluid nature of object-subject relations imprinted in archaeological assemblages will remain untenable. I have no doubt that by proposing the development of relational systematics, I am introducing yet another arbitrary means to order the material record of beings, things, and relations. A measure of external order is critical to maintaining a separation between the analyst and what is to be analyzed; nevertheless, because of its alignment with taxonomies of being, relational systematics can potentially approximate past ontologies closer than its conventional counterpart will ever do.

Questions and preoccupations

In the search for fresh perspectives about relational ontologies that may be relevant to the pursuit at hand, I have explored the writings of contemporary philosophers and theologians whose preoccupations with scientific method parallel those of a relational archaeology. The first common preoccupation deals with ontological difference and communication: *Is it possible to approach the substance of another ontology from the perspective of the analyst's own, and succeed at deriving concepts and guiding principles of* that *ontology?* In conventional systematics, the analyst (generally a person trained in Western scientific method) creates epistemological taxonomies that mirror his or her ontology. This is, indeed, a standard practice that responds to the need to communicate and compare ideas, data, and research results. Yet, because of the imposition of the analyst's ontology over the object of study, the possibility of uncovering ontological diversity dims during the actual process of classification, and rarely returns during reconstruction or interpretation.

The inadequacy of a Western ontology and scientific epistemology for grasping how different people see their place in the world has been richly discussed by Gell (1998), Dupré (1993), Latour (1993), Meskell (2004), and Viveiros de Castro (2004), among others, and this shortcoming has very deep philosophical roots. For example, in his "Analysis of the Constitution of Objects," J. K. Swindler (1991:xi-xii) notes that, "ever since Kant, it has come to appear that the notion of a shared ontology is not only desirable but essential to proper communication in philosophy and science." Epistemological taxonomies are very successful at splitting the record into formally equivalent, measurable, and describable categories, and at providing the foundation for reconstructing social and cultural trajectories (O'Brien and Lyman 2002; Ramenofsky and Steffen 1998). But because they respond to the assumptions of a shared ontology in Swindler's sense, these taxonomies miss or dismiss important evidence of the impact of ontologies on archaeological variation.

Swindler rightly points out that a shared ontology is neither necessary nor sufficient for communication, if communication is to be mediated by non-verbal interactions and inferential processes, that is, through physical reality (objects) and in our case, the material record. Overcoming the limitations of conventional systematics without compromising the transparency of the research process is a big challenge, because ontological variation that may shape the archaeological record encompasses concepts and categories of reality and nature, the organization of relations and causation, information transfer, notions of value and capital, and practice in all its forms (Abdoullaev 2008:41), that may be alien or irrelevant to the aims of Western science. Transparency in archaeological analysis may be preserved through the development of a relational discipline that encourages the construction of explicit theoretical and practical bridges between different ontologies.

The second common preoccupation concerns the analysis of relations: given the diversity of past notions about tangible and intangible components of the universe and its workings, *how can one systematically approach relationships among these components, specifically, the human body, nature, objects, intangible entities, and coded representations (verbal and non-verbal)?* The traditional spatio-temporal-formal framework of archaeology allows us to determine the origin and characteristics specific to an artifact, isolate its position in a particular context, and derive inferences about its role in specific realms of human activity and cognition. Through classification, artifact "types" or classes are constructed according to substance alone; relationships among formally dissimilar objects are viewed as mechanical, or external to the object itself. Unfortunately, this framework is narrowly designed to tackle only certain categories of reality and relations; thus, it does not thoroughly address the full range of causal dynamics that exist between the origin and position of any object relative to other entities and things.

Philosophers tell us that, since relations provide order to the world, they are consistently classifiable in terms of kind (what they connect), direction, materiality, and replicability (Abdoullaev 2008:126; Wildman 2010). Thus, once we acknowledge that inter-ontological communication is possible, a taxonomy that encompasses not only the substances of discrete things, but relationships among them, may be constructed. The key to this development may entail casting the net wide enough to incorporate as many relational components as is feasible, given the conditions of the archaeological record. I have tackled this seemingly daunting task through the study of hierarchies and heterarchies of complex or polythetic objects or sets, as in the case of ceremonial bundles and certain caches (Zedeño 2008b; see also Mills and Murray, this volume; Pauketat 2012).

The third common preoccupation deals with comparison. The comparative method is pervasive in formal education and academic research and, of course, constitutes one of the pillars of anthropological archaeology. Outstanding examples include Lewis Binford's (2001) *Constructing Frames of Reference*, Lawrence Keeley's (1996) *War Before Civilization*, and Robert Kelly's (2007) *Foraging Spectrum*, which is going into a third, reworked edition. These treatises, and especially Binford's, are geared toward archaeological theory-building from a global ethnographic foundation. So why should we mess with something as effective and venerable as the comparative method? Because controlled comparison, in all its past and present incarnations, is grounded in non-relational, epistemological systematics whose categories are ill-equipped to apprehend relationality, at least without some effort at expansion or modification.

But let me turn for a moment to philosophical concerns about the comparative method that may be relevant to the aims of relational archaeologies. One area where comparison has become an enduring source of debate is religion. The debate centers on whether religion is commensurable or not and, if it is, whether comparative inquiry can actually generate new data (Smith 1982; Wildman 2013). Part of the challenge lies in the development of categories that can provide strong data to buttress the theory underlying comparison; otherwise the theory collapses under the weight of faulty methods. For this reason, certain schools of theological thought either avoid comparison altogether, or engage with it as a form of metaphorical discourse rather than legitimate inquiry (Wildman and Neville 2000:215).

Archaeologists who reject the notion of a shared ontology may avoid controlled comparison as a data-producing task because the underlying taxonomy is too constraining and culturally biased. And yet, explicit categorical reference is essential for structuring research in an internally consistent and externally intelligible and replicable way that allows for comparison, and thus may produce new data and ideas. Comparative theologians Wildman and Neville (2000:227), leaning strongly on phenomenology and semiotics, propose a compromise: complex comparative categories that may be born of an intuitive awareness of similarity (or emic concepts derived from ethnography) can be given flexible structures that render them able not only to inspire, but also to correct, theories and topics. I suggest that such a compromise in archaeological systematics can lead to new and significant insights into archaeological inquiries that explicitly embrace relationality. Here I have taken into careful consideration these common concerns to refine and expand a relational taxonomy I have been working on for a few years now (Zedeño 2008a, 2008b, 2009).

Relational taxonomies: basic principles

Ontological taxonomies (taxonomies of being or folk taxonomies), which essentially exist to help people understand their place in the cosmos, are based on social and cultural perceptions and experiences of reality that, in turn, affect practice in all its tangible and intangible expressions. In the modern West, taxonomies derived from a shared ontology underlie formal education and thus largely fulfill this role. Elsewhere I have discussed taxonomic differences between this and relational ontologies (particularly Native American), so here I will briefly touch on the topic with some innovation.

As noted above, chief among the principles to be considered for the construction of relational taxonomies of archaeological objects are agency and animacy. There is a huge literature on agency in archaeology, one of the most recent contributions to which is Tim Pauketat's book, entitled *An Archaeology of the Cosmos* (2012). There are, too, variations in the usage of the terms "animacy" and "animism." I reject the term "animism" because of its reference to an old and narrow anthropological understanding of native religion, and so I simply draw the following distinction, derived from Brown and Walker (2008): *agency* denotes the power of objects to shape human behavior and influence change, whereas *animacy* literally refers to the possession of life-force or 'soul.' More broadly, animacy is a sociolinguistic concept that denotes the phenomenological manifestation of personhood, or the capacity of an object to express human-like abilities and engage in independent and purposeful action. As such, objects are not only causal agents, but also social entities capable of complex interactions (Gell 1998; Ingold 2000; Olsen 2010; Tilley 1999). It follows that social and cultural practices that are informed by these principles can influence the configuration of objects in activity contexts and discard behaviors (Walker 1995, 1999, 2008).

Due to both their intrinsic properties and interactions with other things and beings that shape their life histories, objects may have transitory identities as non-human persons – a term coined by Irving Hallowell back in the 1920s to refer to Algonquian understandings of animacy (Hallowell 1976; see also Black 1977). In Algonquian taxonomies, with which I am most familiar, objects are generally categorized according to their intrinsic substances – animate or inanimate – as well as to their transformative and communicative capabilities. In these taxonomies, the formal dimension of objects is subsumed under animate-inanimate states, the spatial dimension is conditioned by the actual or potential self-propelling and speaking powers of objects, and the temporal dimension is understood according to cause-and-effect transitions between animate and inanimate states within and between objects.

Reading archaeological contexts in search of evidence for animacy is difficult at best without the guiding parameters of *animateness,* or the necessary and sufficient conditions for animacy (Zedeño 2009:410). My ethnographic research leads me to suggest that there are, in fact, certain guiding principles for interpreting archaeological contexts and materials from a relational perspective, and that such a perspective can be systematized to aid in research, while preserving at least a few enduring expressions of past relational ontologies. In constructing a relational taxonomy, I have leaned heavily on origin stories, epic events, historical trajectories, ethnographic observations, ethnographic collections, and archaeological contexts, as well as on my research with Algonquian and Numic speakers. This data was used to determine the appropriate units of observation, dimensions, and scales that may best approximate the dynamic quality of native notions of agency, animacy, and causation.

Units of observation, dimensions, and analysis

The practical inspiration to explore a relational systematics derives from two sources: archaeological site and artifact assessments by Native Americans, and complex objects (bundles). Archaeological site and artifact assessments by descendants of past groups are no different than standard archaeological assessments of form and function, except that they reveal the unique ontological pathways taken by descendants to infer causation behind contextual associations in their own ancient sites, and to trace hierarchies and heterarchies of things and beings from the perspective of the material record (Zedeño 2008a). This exercise brings to bear all types of knowledge and practical experience well beyond the physical appearance of a site or object. Pathways are explicit and thus afford a view of relational ontology that enhances and complements classic ethnography. The study of complex objects or sets, particularly ceremonial bundles, provides a means to identify constant and variable relations among two or more objects. From a strictly material perspective, a bundle is composed of two or more items intentionally held together by wrapping so that they may influence one another and act in concert as needed in ritual activities (Wissler 1912:92). Bundles, however, are far more than collections of objects; they are regarded, in principle and in fact, as powerful persons – each with its own life history, personality, and position in society (Zedeño 2008b). Pauketat (2012) goes even further to propose that bundles are also metaphors for the cosmic order that guides human society. Thus, these object sets are strong analytical cases for deriving relational taxonomic principles that may in turn be applied to the study of relations among objects in heterogeneous contexts and assemblages with less clear boundaries and associations than bundles.

I started out by classifying every object in a series of Blackfoot pipe bundles, whose contents have been described in detail by McClintock (1992) and Wissler (1912) and illustrated by Scriver (1991), by their formal properties and observable modifications. Then, from the narratives of origin and descriptions of liturgical sequences recorded ethnographically, I determined the history behind each object and its interactive role in the pipe bundle. I then arranged the data along two parsimonious dimensions: *origin* and *position*. Origin refers to animating properties that are intrinsic to an object versus those that are acquired through time. Intrinsically animate objects are in a *pure state* whereas biographical objects have mutable or *changed states* because their potential for animacy may be modified temporarily or permanently due to interaction with other objects, entities, and contexts. Position, on the other hand, refers to the role an object plays in a set: *fixed* objects are those essential to the set; they may materialize a kind of interaction (e.g., consecration, divination, or communication), indicate direction, point to a specific geography, or guide the order of components in a set. In contrast, *flexible* objects are circumstantial or accessory to the set. Flexible objects generally denote singular trajectories as bundle ownership changes through time and things may be added to, or subtracted from, it. For example, in a pipe bundle, bowl and stem are fixed, whereas objects affixed to the stem, such as feathers and fur strips, vary from pipe bundle to pipe bundle and thus may be classified as flexible. Fixed objects are not simply functional, but reflect the rationale behind the bundle, usually representing the supernatural origin story of the bundle itself, deities and spirits involved in its transfer to humans, and requisite liturgical sequences. Importantly, a single kind of object can assume different positions depending on its particular interacting role in each object set. For example, an arrowhead may be accessory to a pipe bundle, but it becomes fixed in a hunting kit.

When I combined my own ethnographic observations with older narrative descriptions and artifact collections, I was able to define *animateness*, or the necessary and sufficient conditions for determining an object's intrinsic or potential animacy, which could in turn be used comparatively across temporal, spatial, and cultural contexts. These animic categories were, namely: (a) objects that have an inherently animate substance such as red paint, crystals, fossils, copper, and certain rocks; (b) objects that embody the soul of living beings such as animal parts, human scalp locks, skulls, and phalanges found in non-funerary contexts, and their likenesses; (c) objects that enhance communication, such as tobacco seeds, pipes and pipestone, and parts of plants used for chewing, smoking, smudging, or visions; and (d) certain objects of European origin, such as horses, guns, and kettles (Zedeño 2009:416). Plants are a counterintuitive category; although technically living beings, they are not always intrinsically animate as an animal would be (Quinn 2001). To this list I added relational conditions for animacy such as: (a) the spatial association between intrinsically animate objects and any other objects; (b) the spatial association between any object and certain animate landforms, such as caves, river rapids, springs, lakes, mountaintops, and prominent rock formations, rock crevices, and erratic boulders; and (c) use in activities or contexts aimed at managing and transferring power.

From these conditions, the concept of *index object* was outlined as a plausible analytical unit for building a relational taxonomy. An index object is a distinctive kind of natural object or artifact that can modify or altogether alter the properties of any object, human, or place that becomes associated with it. An *index place* would have the same effect on objects and humans. When two or more index objects are put together in a bundle or deposited in an index place, for example, the combined life-force becomes a portal that humans may tap to become powerful or to transfer animating power to other humans and things; Numic painted caves and glyphs next to natural springs are examples in point (Carroll et al. 2004). Finally, index objects also have the potential for animating seemingly 'ordinary' contexts, such as houses and buildings, as Barbara Mills and Wendi Murray explain in this volume (see also Walker 1999).

Once the basic conditions of animateness were laid out, I tested various ways in which one could classify the contents of complex objects by the origin (intrinsic or biographical) and position (fixed or flexible) of each object in a set. I started out with a paradigmatic classification applied to a ceremonial bundle (Zedeño 2008b) and then to a hunting kit (Zedeño 2009). After some refitting, it became obvious that paradigmatic classes, which are mutually exclusive by definition, are counter-productive in a relational taxonomy; nevertheless, so long as objects are not pigeonholed into one or another class, the two dimensions are incredibly useful for teasing out the range of exclusive, inclusive, and conditional relationships among objects in a set. Then I turned to drawing a non-exclusive, relational classification. The first classification strategy focuses on an index object and is based on progressive contextualization of all its possible relations with other objects and contexts. This classification, which may be represented in various ways, is useful for identifying the scales of interaction, from single object sets to the entire social order. For example, in my experiments I looked at red paint (a near-universal index object) heuristically to illustrate how position may be used to map relations through which animating power may be transferred from index objects to ordinary people, places, and things, both past and present (Zedeño 2009). In another case study, Murray (2011) focused on the eagle as an index object, to define the complex of eagles' roles and interactions in all realms of the Mandan-Hidatsa social order. I also applied this approach successfully to characterize the role of elk in the evolution of modern Blackfeet[1] hunting practices (Zedeño 2013).

The comparison of two or more complex objects requires a different, non-exclusive classificatory approach. A useful comparative classification is based on Cantor set theory and may be illustrated in Venn diagrams, which have been used by ethnobiologists since the 1970s to sort out taxonomies (e.g., Kenny and Parker 2004; King 1972), and are popular in contemporary philosophy and comparative theology (e.g., Abdoullaev 2008; Wildman 2013). At its simplest, this approach helps to identify complex object combinations and intersections. In straightforward cases, Cantor notation or Venn diagrams may seem like an amusing, but unnecessary or even reductive, step, until one encounters five or six sets, containing a dozen or more objects, some of which are fixed in one or two sets but not in others, and so on. Here, the appropriate representation helps to distinguish index objects from situational or biographical objects, to understand the position of similar objects in different sets, and in a broader scale, to extract also the kinds of interactions in which object sets may engage in different contexts. For the purpose of illustrating the importance of non-anthropocentric, structurally flexible systematics that may capture the nuances of a people's relational ontology, I will focus on objects associated with communal bison hunting among the Blackfoot.

Blackfoot bison hunting

Classical archaeological approaches to the material record of big game hunters are deceivingly simple; they begin with bones and stones (archaeology's bread and butter) and expand to incorporate all scales of natural phenomena, from micro-scopic organisms that record climate change to extraterrestrial bodies hitting the earth and causing all kinds of trouble. Humans are, of course, important, but their ways of relating to things are generally less amenable to analysis than their dietary habits or the products of their labor. Landscape looms large in big-game-hunter studies (think Clovis folk leap-frogging from stone quarry to stone quarry across the North American Plains) but the cultural wealth of human-nature relations has been often subsumed within the narrow analytical view of hunting as an activity that occurs as part of a definite (and rather constraining) set of natural and cultural parameters. And yet, history and ethnography inform us that big-game hunting is a worldview so old and so profound that it has defined the trajectory of human relationships with nature and the cosmos. While we may never fully understand the true complexities of this trajectory, we can begin, humbly, by looking at hunting as a network of interactions among people, prey, place, and a number of natural forces and intangible entities. Outside this web, deceivingly simple and elegant acts such as driving bison over a cliff may not have succeeded at all. Let us take this very act as the starting point for discussing the challenges and potentials of a relational archaeology.

Briefly, native hunting of American bison has a 10,000-year history; in the northwest Plains, conditions for the development of large-scale communal bison hunting existed since the Archaic period but crystallized about 2,000 years ago with the adoption of the bow and arrow and the production of storable and transportable meat by-products (Reeves 1990). The rise of a complex and specialized organization dates to the last 1,000 years or less (Zedeño et al. 2013). The footprint of com-munal bison hunting is the driveline system: a funnel laid out with hundreds of rock piles aligned a few feet from one another, connecting a bison gathering basin to a cliff or a pound. A group of hunters would incite a herd to move inside the funnel creating a stampede that would end in dozens to hundreds of animals plunging to their deaths. This system was literally a killing machine that could render untold numbers of bison in a single episode. Below the cliff, a corral was built to contain dead and dying animals and to butcher them. Butchered cuts were then taken to an adjacent task camp for further processing (Verbicky-Todd 1984). Time and again, these acts would be repeated with increasing frequency and intensity, each hunt reproducing the preceding one and, simultaneously, creating new conditions for future hunts. This much has been dissected and explained archaeologically, and very well at that (e.g., Brink 2008; Frison 2004; Peck 2004).

At some point in their cultural trajectory, perhaps in connection with the arrival of the Mississippian-like Mandan to the Middle Missouri River after AD 1000 or even earlier (Brink and Dawe 1989:297–302; Walde 2006), the ancestral Blackfoot developed a socio-ritual complex centered on bison hunting that involved the assembly, use, and formal transfer of ceremonial bundles among community members (Lokensgard 2001; Wissler 1912). Within a short period of time, this complex would become a socio-political, regulatory system controlled by esoteric societies of exclusive and expensive membership. These societies were not only in place, but already evolving, toward the end of the eighteenth century when Hudson's Bay Company traders first observed and recorded their existence. The system expanded during the Colonial and early American periods, and persisted in the Reservation period despite the travails of bison near-extinction, religious persecution, acculturation, and sociopolitical change. Today, owing to repatriation of bundles and associated artifacts, the system has been revitalized and is once again thriving, albeit in a transformed social and ecological environment.

While archaeology clearly shows the temporal and spatial breadth of large-scale communal bison hunting, history and ethnography reveal that this venerable bone-and-stone record has far more interrelated parts than conventional archaeology, which has focused overwhelmingly on kill sites and stone tool technology, may uncover. A cursory review of major sources of information about the relational ontology of Blackfoot bison hunting reveals myriad actors, contexts, and multi-scalar sequences of events that go far beyond the actual killing episode. The Blackfoot hunting complex may be divided into segments that speak of increasing human agency in a world populated and largely controlled by non-human persons. For example, 'the water bull,' (bison) like other primordial game animals, rose from a lake after the second flood of the world (Zedeño et al. 2008:124). The primary architectural elements of bison hunting, namely the driveline systems, are of divine origin and date to pre-human times (Bullchild 2005). Thunder kept bison as 'his horses,' which he gifted to a man to atone for stealing the man's wife. Likewise, hunting weapons came from the Napi and the star people. Ecological knowledge about bison hunting came from the wolf (Barsh and Marlor 2003), whereas the skills to overpower bison and reverse its cannibalistic tendencies were given to them by Old Man Napi. Solving the politics of sharing food and property, on the other hand, were learned from the culture-hero Kutoyis, a demigod who was born of bison blood and came to the human world to slay the people's enemies (Grinnell 1962). The ethnogenesis of the Blackfoot-speaking groups (Peigan, Blood, and Blackfoot proper) is also closely connected with hunters' ability to find a certain magical root that helped them pursue and kill bison (Zedeño et al. 2008:125).

Ritual protocols to drive bison herds to their deaths came from a woman who discovered the magical *Iniskim*, an ammonite fossil that looks like bison; the woman transferred her dream knowledge to her husband, the founder of the Buffalo Catchers Society (Duvall 1908:121). In time, the Blackfoot obtained more power over bison, which was exercised through the calling rituals of the Beaver Bundle, the altars of the black and yellow buffalo tipis, and the rites of the Buffalo Catchers Society and the *Motoki* or Buffalo Women Society, which owned the ritual knowledge of the communal bison drive and corral construction, respectively. Thus, the activities that propitiated the bison hunt involved a nested series of powerful objects, bundles, and painted tipis that were controlled by esoteric societies and individuals with knowledge and power. The social sanctions and liturgical order linked to each powerful object, in turn, derived from their supernatural origin and the human–deity communications that materialized in what I call index and complex objects.

Index objects and complex relations

Intricate as it is, the materiality of Blackfoot ontology associated with the bison hunt rests on a handful of index objects and their ability to communicate with, or transform things around them: red paint, Iniskim, a certain root, and tobacco. Each object came with its own myth, natural and supernatural associations, and unique protocols that required daily attention year-round. But nonetheless, all are complementary and interactive. Red paint is consecratory and also protects, heals, and animates everything it touches; Iniskim have magical properties associated with speed, attraction, and divination (Duvall 1908:381); a certain root transforms spoken words and songs into holy language (Hanks and Hanks 1938); and tobacco helps people communicate with God and other entities. Through these objects, people engage with just about everything else in the world and the heavens in order to maintain and reproduce the Blackfoot universe. Bundles, and the Beaver Bundle in particular, are the tangible representations of this relational world.

The Beaver Bundle represents the natural world, thus it contains animals associated with water, land, and air in addition to the four index objects and other things associated with the liturgical sequence of the bundle opening ceremony (McClintock 1992). The bundle songs further connect the mountains to the prairie. The pipe and red paint are part of the supernatural origin of the bundle. During each opening ceremony, the female bundle owner anoints each ceremony participant with red paint; all objects in the bundle are also anointed to renew their holy condition and create a protective network among people and things. The sacred tobacco seeds and the Iniskim, on the other hand, came to the Beaver Bundle later in its trajectory and through the visions of individual men and women. Eventually they became institutionalized in the liturgical order of the bundle itself and associated ceremonies, notably bison calling and sacred tobacco planting (Duvall 1908–11). The designs on the black and yellow buffalo painted tipis, which were also acquired through individual visions, are associated with underwater animals and water bodies; they brought to the people the knowledge of how to trap bison at river crossings, especially in winter. The tipi owners originally kept an altar that included representations of the sun, moon, and star deities, the Iniskim, and a pipe. The tipis were also connected with the now extinct

Buffalo Catchers Society. The contemporary bundle that accompanies the Black Buffalo Tipi contains over 200 Iniskim accumulated over centuries.

While the archaeological record of communal bison hunting is made of 99 percent bone and stone, occasionally that elusive 1 percent presents itself in the form of red pigment or a red-painted artifact, a stone pipe, a certain root, or perhaps an ammonite fossil, all of which provide a tiny glimpse of the powerful relational engine that Blackfoot hunters greased and primed year-round in order to live well and be prosperous.

Towards a taxonomy of bison-hunter relations

Two approaches may be used to systematically classify objects as relational agents/ persons; both proceed from the concept of index object and the dimensions of origin and position of different objects in a set. Index objects provide a means to unpack hierarchical relations that are driven by relational distance between an index object and anything else around it (Zedeño 2009:figs. 2–4). Origin and position of any object, on the other hand, reveal heterarchies within and between object sets. Index objects may play multiple roles in different sets, being fixed or flexible in different circumstances, and either interacting with other index and ordinary objects or exclusively with their human owners. Classification may proceed by focusing on a set, then teasing out relations among component objects, or may be accomplished by singling out a specific object of interest, then progressively con-textualizing it. The former procedure is appropriate for understanding relational principles that remain constant across different object sets as well as unique varia-tions. The latter is particularly useful for evaluating the scale of the network within which single objects interact. Progressive contextualization also works quite well for cross-cultural comparison of relational properties based on a common object. To illustrate the first approach, I have listed in Table 6.1 the contents of several complex objects associated with bison calling rituals and the hunt. The list of Beaver Bundle items is short, but typical of a bundle that would contain animate and inanimate, fixed and flexible items. When two related object lists are added, the index objects become evident across all sets. Fixed items can be easily dis-tinguished from flexible items, although to fully illustrate position and explain its significance, the comparison would have to be made across similar items, like two or more Beaver Bundles.

Figure 6.1 illustrates simply the progressive contextualization approach that focuses on Iniskim. As an index object, Iniskim stands alone for its own animate power. It also engages in simple intersections with other objects. An individual who has found an Iniskim will have it painted in red by a Beaver Bundle owner to make it holy. He or she may carry it alone as an amulet usually decorated with leather and beads (Scriver 1991:178); painted Iniskim may be gifted for protection and good luck. Iniskim power to bring speed to its owner, which in turn comes from the wind, was sought after by warriors who kept them in their war bundles (Duvall 1910). This index object also may be found in certain healing bundles

TABLE 6.1 Complex object sets used in the Blackfoot bison calling rituals (from Duvall 1904–11; Scriver 1991).

BEAVER BUNDLE	TOBACCO PLANTING	BLACK & YELLOW TIPI
Covering (blanket, hide)		Tipi cover and poles
Water pipe and stem	Pipe bundles	Pipe and stem
Forked sticks for smudging	Sticks for burning the field	Forked stick for smudging
Red paint	Red paint	Black, red, yellow paint
Rattles	Rattles	
Root	Root	
Drums	Drums	
Iniskim bundle	Iniskim bundle	Iniskim bundle
Beaver skins	Beaver skin	Underwater animals (in story)
Otter skins	Otter skin	
Loon skins		
Mussel shell		
Beaver-chewed sticks		
Raven feathers, skins		
Buffalo tail, hooves		
Lynx tail		
Scalp locks		
Beads, elk teeth		
Badger skin		
Eagle feather, fan		
Swan skin, head		
Sweetgrass braids		
Ceremonial clothing		
	Hide bowl for seed mix	
	Dung of fast animals	
Pouch with tobacco seeds	Serviceberries	Tobacco mix for smoking
	All night smoke banners	Smudging plant
	Tobacco People sticks	

where its divinatory power would be useful to the healer. Scriver (1991:179) lists the following contents for one such bundle:

wrapping or container
three bags of 'holy paint'
Iniskim
sucking tubes made of eagle wing bone
piece of fungus
brass bells
sharp flint knife for making incisions
stone with hole
bag containing summer weasel pelt hair amulet
strip of otter fur

small key
metal disk with seven holes representing the moon and seven stars (Pleiades)
small dish
piece of argillite (the preferred stone tool material used by women)

Clearly there are index, fixed, and flexible objects in this bag, and many of these would likely tell the story of how the healer acquired his or her powers through time. The eagle bone sucking tubes, for example, suggest that the healer obtained his or her power from an eagle, as this is the main instrument of illness extraction. The Iniskim bundle, on the other hand, fulfills far more complex intersections with the Beaver Bundle, sacred tobacco planting ceremony, and black and yellow buffalo painted tipis. These intersections, which are laid out in Table 6.1, explicitly refer to the Iniskim role in buffalo calling rites. Incorporating other Upper Missouri River groups who, likewise, used this index object in various ways (Peck 2002), these items could be further contextualized through controlled comparison using the dimensions of origin and position, the index object concept, and the necessary and sufficient conditions for animateness. This exercise, in turn, may uncover meaningful intersections in various relational ontologies.

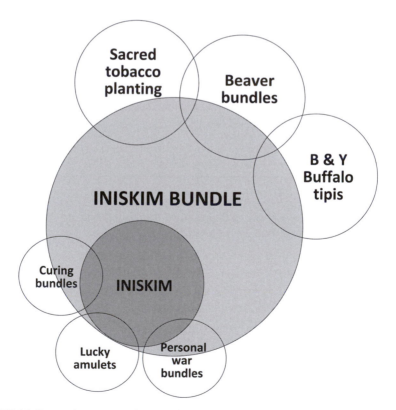

FIGURE 6.1 Progressive contextualization of Iniskim in simple and complex intersections.

Concluding thoughts

In short, a flexible but replicable relational taxonomy that centers on object–subject transitions by observing and analyzing complex objects and heterogeneous assemblages as 'more than the sum of its parts' can furnish a systematic vehicle for formally inquiring into past human/non–human relationships. I would not have embarked on experiments with relational taxonomy had I not been convinced that it is essential to bring life to the bleakest of archaeological records. Such a taxonomy has the potential for moving archaeological systematics beyond the time-space-form framework and into ambivalent and transitory, but very human, relational ontologies. Ethnographic and historical documents have paved the road for overcoming a few challenges in the archaeology of relations, but even without these important resources, proper systematics is needed to balance metaphorical discourse with explicit inquiry. Archaeologies of relations must structure research in an internally consistent, and externally intelligible and replicable way that allows for comparison and the generation of new data and ideas. My experiment is intended to inspire discussion, and I hope it will be challenged so that we may all contribute to a mature and productive practice of relational archaeology.

Note

1 The term Blackfeet is exclusively used in reference to the Blackfeet Tribe of Montana. In this text, the term Blackfoot refers to the ethnic and linguistic group and its cultural manifestation.

Bibliography

Abdoullaev, Azamat 2008. *Reality, Universal Ontology, and Knowledge Systems*. IGI Publishing, Hershey, New York.

Adams, William Y., and Ernest W. Adams 2007. *Archaeological Typology and Practical Reality: A Dialectical Approach to Artifact Classification and Sorting*. Cambridge University Press, Cambridge.

Alberti, Benjamin, and Tamara L. Bray 2009. Animating Archaeology: Of Subjects, Objects, and Alternative Ontologies. *Cambridge Archaeological Journal* 19(3):337–43.

Barsh, Russel L., and Chantelle Marlor 2003. Driving Bison and Blackfoot Science. *Human Ecology* 31(4):571–93.

Berlin, Brent 1992. *Ethnobiological Classification: Principles for the Categorization of Plants and Animals in Traditional Societies*. University of Princeton Press, Princeton, New Jersey.

Binford, Lewis R. 2001. *Constructing Frames of Reference: An Analytical Method for Archaeological Theory Building Using Hunter-Gatherer and Environmental Data Sets*. University of California Press, Berkeley.

Black, Mary B. 1977. Ojibwa Power Belief System. In *The Anthropology of Power: Ethnographic Studies from Asia, Oceania, and the New World*, edited by Raymond D. Fogelson and Richard N. Adams, pp. 141–51. Academic Press, New York.

Brink, Jack W. 2008. *Imagining Head-Smashed-In: Aboriginal Buffalo Hunting on the Northern Plains*. Athabasca University Press, Edmonton.

Brink, Jack W., and Robert Dawe 1989. "Final Report of the 1985 and 1986 Field Season at Head-Smashed-In Buffalo Jump." Manuscript Series No. 16. Archaeological Survey of Alberta, Edmonton.

Brown, Linda A., and Kitty F. Emery 2008. Negotiations with the Animate Forest: Hunting Shrines in the Guatemalan Highlands. *Journal of Archaeological Method and Theory* 15:300–338.

Brown, Linda A., and William H. Walker 2008. Prologue: Archaeology, Animism and Non-Human Agents. *Journal of Archaeological Method and Theory* 15:297–99.

Bullchild, Percy 2005. *The Sun Came Down: The History of the World as My Blackfeet Elders Told It*. University of Nebraska Press, Lincoln.

Carroll, Alex K., María Nieves Zedeño, and Richard W. Stoffle 2004. Landscapes of the Ghost Dance: A Cartography of Numic Ritual. *Journal of Archaeological Method and Theory* 11:127–55.

Dobres, Marcia-Anne, and John Robb 2000. Agency in Archaeology: Paradigm or Platitude? In *Agency in Archaeology*, edited by Marcia-Anne Dobres and John Robb, pp. 3–17. Routledge, London.

Dunnell, Robert 1971. *Systematics in Prehistory*. McMillan, New York.

Duvall, D. C. 1904–11. *Papers (Vol. 1)*. Typed manuscripts. New York: American Museum of Natural History.

Dupré, John 1993. *The Disorder of Things*. Harvard University Press, Cambridge, Massachusetts.

Fogelin, Lars 2008. Methods for the Archaeology of Religion. In *Religion, Archaeology, and the Material World*, edited by Lars Fogelin, pp. 1–14. Occasional Paper No. 36. Center for Archaeological Investigations, Southern Illinois University, Carbondale.

Frison, George C. 2004. *Survival by Hunting: Prehistoric Animal Predators and Animal Prey*. University of California Press, Berkeley.

Gell, Alfred 1998. *Art and Agency: An Anthropological Theory*. Clarendon Press, Oxford.

Grinnell, George B. 1962. *Blackfoot Lodge Tales: The Story of a Prairie People*. University of Nebraska Press, Lincoln.

Hallowell, A. Irving 1976. Ojibwa Ontology, Behavior, and Worldview. In *Contributions to Anthropology: Selected Papers of A. Irving Hallowell*, edited by Raymond D. Fogelson, pp. 357–90. University of Chicago Press, Chicago.

——(1992). *The Ojibwa of Berens River, Manitoba: Ethnography into History*. Harcourt Brace Jovanovich, Fort Worth, Texas.

Hanks, Lucien, and Jane Hanks 1938. *Blackfoot Papers. Correspondence and Field Notes*. Manuscript on file, Glenbow Museum, Calgary, Alberta.

Ingold, Tim 2000. *The Perception of the Environment: Essays in Livelihood, Dwelling and Skill*. Routledge, London.

——(2006). Rethinking the Animate, Re-animating Thought. *Ethnos* 71(1):9–20.

Keeley, Lawrence 1996. *War Before Civilization*. Oxford University Press, New York.

Kelly, Robert L. 2007. *The Foraging Spectrum: Diversity in Hunter-Gatherer Lifeways*. Smithsonian Institution Press, Washington, D.C.

Kenny, Mary B., and William H. Parker 2004. Ojibway Plant Taxonomy at Lac Seul First Nation, Ontario, Canada. *Journal of Ethnobiology* 24(1):75–91.

King, J. 1972. Set Theory Models: An Approach to Taxonomic and Locational Relationships. In *Models in Archaeology*, edited by David Clarke, pp. 735–55. Methuen, London.

Knappett, Carl, and Lambros Malafouris (editors) 2008. *Material Agency: Towards a Non-Anthropocentric Approach*. Springer, New York.

Latour, Bruno 1993. *We Have Never Been Modern*. Translated by C. Porter. Harvard University Press, Cambridge, Massachusetts.

Lokensgard, Kenneth 2001. "Gift and Commodity: Sociocultural Economies, Indigenous Religions, and Academic Exchange Practices." Unpublished Ph.D. dissertation, Department of Anthropology, Syracuse University, New York.

McClintock, Walter 1992. *The Old North Trail: Life, Legends and Religion of the Blackfeet Indians*. University of Nebraska Press, Lincoln.

Meskell, Lynn 2004. *Object Worlds in Ancient Egypt: Material Biographies Past and Present*. Berg, London.

Meskell, Lynn (editor) 2005. *Archaeologies of Materiality*. Blackwell, Malden, Massachusetts.

Miller, Daniel 2005. Materiality: An Introduction. In *Materiality*, edited by Daniel Miller, pp. 1–50. Duke University Press, Durham, North Carolina.

Mills, Barbara J., and T. J. Ferguson 2008. Animate Objects: Shell Trumpets and Ritual Networks in the Greater Southwest. *Journal of Archaeological Method and Theory* 15:338–61.

Mills, Barbara J., and William H. Walker 2008. Introduction: Memory, Materiality, and Depositional Practice. In *Memory Work: Archaeologies of Material Practices*, edited by Barbara J. Mills and William H. Walker, pp. 3–23. School for Advanced Research Press, Santa Fe, New Mexico.

Murray, Wendi F. 2011. Feathers, Fasting, and the Eagle Complex: A Contemporary Analysis of the Eagle as a Cultural Resource in the Northern Plains. *Plains Anthropologist* 56 (218):143–53.

O'Brien, Michael J., and R. Lee Lyman 2002. The Epistemological Nature of Archaeological Units. *Archaeological Theory* 2:37–56.

Olsen, Bjørnar 2010. *In Defense of Things: Archaeology and the Ontology of Objects*. AltaMira, Lanham, Maryland.

Pauketat, Tim 2012. *An Archaeology of the Cosmos: Rethinking Agency and Religion in Ancient America*. Routledge, London.

Peck, Trevor R. 2002. Archaeologically Recovered Ammonites: Evidence for Long-Term Continuity in Nitsitapii Ritual. *Plains Anthropologist* 47(181):147–64.

——(2004). "Bison Ethology and Native Settlement Patterns During the Old Women's Phase on the Northwestern Plains." BAR International Series 1278. British Archaeological Reports, Oxford.

Preucel, Robert W. 2006. *Archaeological Semiotics*. Blackwell, Oxford.

Quinn, Conor 2001. A Preliminary Survey of Animacy Categories in Penobscot. In *Papers of the 32nd Algonquian Conference*, edited by John D. Nicholson, pp. 395–426. University of Manitoba, Winnipeg.

Ramenofsky, Ann, and Anastasia Steffen 1998. Units as Tools of Measurement. In *Unit Issues in Archaeology: Measuring Time, Space, and Material*, edited by Ann Ramenofsky and Anastasia Steffen, pp. 1–18. University of Utah Press, Salt Lake City.

Reeves, Brian O. K. 1990. Communal Bison Hunters of the Northern Plains. In *Hunters of the Recent Past*, edited by Leslie B. Davis and Brian O. K. Reeves, pp. 168–94. Unwin Hyman, London.

Schuh, Randal T. 2000. *Biological Systematics: Principles and Applications*. Cornell University Press, Ithaca, New York.

Scriver, Bob 1991. *Blackfeet: Artists of the Northern Plains: The Scriver Collection of Blackfeet Indian Artifacts and Related Objects, 1894–1990*. Lowell Press, Kansas City, Missouri.

Smith, Jonathan Z. 1982. In Comparison a Magic Dwells. In *Imagining Religion: From Babylon to Jonestown*, edited by Jonathan Z. Smith, pp. 19–35. University of Chicago Press, Chicago.

Stoffle, Richard W., María Nieves Zedeño, and David B. Halmo (editors) 2001. *American Indians and the Nevada Test Site: A Decade of Research and Consultation*. U. S. Government Printing Office, Washington, D.C.

Swindler, J. K. 1991. *Weaving: An Analysis of the Constitution of Objects*. Rowman and Littlefield, Savage, Maryland.

Tilley, Christopher 1999. *Metaphor and Material Culture*. Blackwell, Malden, Maryland.

Verbicky-Todd, Eleanor 1984. Communal Buffalo Hunting among the Plains Indians: An Ethnographic and Historic Review. *Occasional Paper No. 24*. Archaeological Survey of Alberta, Edmonton.

Viveiros de Castro, Eduardo 2004. Exchanging Perspectives: The Transformation of Objects into Subjects in Amerindian Ontologies. *Common Knowledge* 10(3):463–84.

Walde, Dale 2006. Sedentism and Pre-contact Tribal Organization on the Northern Plains: Colonial Imposition or Indigenous Development? *World Archaeology* 38(2):291–310.

Walker, William H. 1995. Ceremonial Trash? In *Expanding Archaeology*, edited by James M. Skibo, William H. Walker, and Axel E. Nielsen, pp. 67–79. University of Utah Press, Salt Lake City.

——(1999). Ritual, Life Histories, and the Afterlives of People and Things. *Journal of the Southwest* 41(3):383–405.

——(2008). Practice and Nonhuman Social Actors: The Afterlife Histories of Witches and Dogs in the American Southwest. In *Memory Work: Archaeologies of Material Practices*, edited by Barbara J. Mills and William H. Walker, pp. 137–58. School for Advanced Research Press, Santa Fe, New Mexico.

Wildman, Wesley J. 2010. An Introduction to Relational Ontology. In *The Trinity and an Entangled World: Relationality in Physical Science and Theology*, edited by John Polkinghorne, pp. 55–73. Eerdmans, Grand Rapids, Michigan.

——(2013). Comparative Natural Theology. In *The Oxford Handbook of Natural Theology*, edited by Russell Manning, John Hedley Brooke, and Fraser Watts. Oxford University Press, Oxford.

Wildman, Wesley J., and Robert C. Neville 2000. How Our Approach to Comparison Relates to Others. In *Ultimate Realities*, edited by Robert C. Neville, pp. 211–36. State University of New York Press, Albany.

Wissler, Clark 1912. *Ceremonial Bundles of the Blackfoot Indians.* Anthropological Papers Vol. VII, Pt. 2. American Museum of Natural History, New York.

Zedeño, María Nieves 2000. On What People Make of Places – A Behavioral Cartography. In *Social Theory in Archaeology*, edited by Michael B. Schiffer, pp. 97–111. University of Utah Press, Salt Lake City.

——(2008a). Traditional Knowledge, Ritual Behavior, and Contemporary Interpretation of the Archaeological Record. *In Belief in the Past*, edited by Kelley Hays–Gilpin and David S. Whitley, pp. 259–74. Left Coast Press, Walnut Creek, California.

——(2008b). Bundled Worlds: The Roles and Interactions of Complex Objects from the North American Plains. *Journal of Archaeological Method and Theory* 15:362–78.

——(2009). Animating by Association: Index Objects and Relational Taxonomies. *Cambridge Archaeological Journal* 19(3):407–17.

——(2013). To Become a Mountain Hunter: Flexible Core Values and Subsistence Hunting Among Reservation-era Blackfeet. In *The Archaeology and Historical Ecology of Small-Scale Economies*, edited by Victor D. Thompson and J. Waggoner, pp. 141–63. University of Florida Press, Gainesville.

Zedeño, María Nieves, John R. Murray, Wendi F. Murray, and Samrat Miller 2008. *Blackfeet Sacred Land Recovery Project.* Final Report for the Indian Land Tenure Foundation. Bureau of Applied Research in Anthropology, University of Arizona, Tucson.

Zedeño, María Nieves, Jesse A. Ballenger, and John R. Murray 2013. Landscape Engineering and Organizational Complexity Among Late Prehistoric Bison Hunters of the Northwestern Plains. *Current Anthropology.* In press.

7

IDENTITY COMMUNITIES AND MEMORY PRACTICES: RELATIONAL LOGICS IN THE US SOUTHWEST

Wendi Field Murray and Barbara J. Mills

Identity and materiality

The methodological challenges of locating identity in the archaeological record have been well-documented, particularly as the concept of "culture" in archaeological discourse has evolved from a static set of spatially-defined traits to a collective of interactive, overlapping, and intersecting identities that operate at multiple social scales (e.g., Strathern 1988). From this perspective, social actors belong to multiple identity groups at any given time. Their sense of belonging within an identity group is anchored to shared perceptions and ontologies, which are (to archaeology's advantage) expressed through shared cultural practices as people engage with the material world (Casella and Fowler 2005:2, 7). Thus, elucidating these "communities of practice" (Wenger 1998) in the archaeological record is central to identifying and understanding the meaningful social boundaries and relations integral to social reproduction in the past.

Concomitant with theoretical developments in the archaeology of identity has been the increased participation of indigenous communities in archaeological research, and the incorporation of indigenous concepts and perspectives in research frameworks (e.g., Bernardini 2005; Ferguson and Colwell-Chanthaphonh 2006; Jackson and Smith 2005). This dialogue has problematized that which archaeologists have always taken for granted – the material world (Olsen 2003, 2010; Preucel and Meskell 2004:13). Specifically, it has highlighted the subjectivity of the material world in indigenous worldviews – the capacity of objects, spaces, and landscapes to possess personhood and engage in relationships with other beings and things (Brück 2006; Fowler 2001, 2004; Gillespie 2001; Salmón 2000; Viveiros de Castro 2004). People in the past did not interact with an inanimate world, which should fundamentally change how we approach the archaeological record. By liberating the material we study from modernist assumptions about its objectivity, the social world suddenly becomes more crowded, and people's engagement with things becomes socially and historically consequential (Latour 2005). This has important methodological implications; patterns in depositional practices, which embody the taxonomies of being and social relations that constitute a given community, provide access to what Catherine Bell (1992) calls "indigenous distinctions" – produced and practiced by people in the past, rather than archaeologists' superpositioning of preconceived identity categories.

In this paper we use the term *identity communities* to refer not to communities in the traditional sense as settlements, but instead to the networks of social relationships (Yaeger 2000). From this perspective, an individual's personhood is not a static amalgamation of distinct attributes, but rather a fluid product of his or her membership in different learning and practice communities, and of the connections between them. Given that an individual belongs to, or engages with, myriad different groups at a given time, our approach recognizes the multifaceted nature of identity, and that there are overlapping or intersecting communities of practice (e.g., Lave and Wenger 1991). In the present study, we look beyond the "special object" status of cached artifacts to their situatedness within these communities of practice. We argue that in certain contexts, caching was a means of infusing objects and spaces with agency; thus an object's inclusion in a ritual cache communicates its engagement in social relations between people, spaces, and other objects (Groleau 2009:398–99; Ingold 2006; Weiner 1992). As a community of related agents, caches embody structured object associations that were guided by the culturally specific logics of their creators (Zedeño 2008). In this paper, we investigate and compare ritual caches in Chaco and Hohokam sites, focusing on how patterns in depositional practices can elucidate the identity communities that created them and the distinct ontologies that guided their engagement with the material world.

Theorizing identity communities

Our use of identity communities aligns with a number of recent anthropological and archaeological studies that focus on depositional practices, such as Brück's (2004) re-interpretation of Early Bronze Age burials in Western Europe. As she notes, objects placed with a person were not a reflection of the status of the individual, but they rather revealed the relational construction of that person's identity (see also Cerezo-Román, forthcoming). Similarly, Owoc's (2005:276) work in Bronze Age Britain demonstrates how shared practices in certain contexts embodied the "rules of engagement" between humans and their material environments. These rules were derived from a shared sense of belonging in the world, and they were therefore integral to the formation of identity communities. These approaches offer a multifaceted interpretation of people's place in the world – a place that prioritizes an individual's situatedness in social networks over his or her geographic location or social position (Hoskins 1998; Strathern 1988, 1993). As Brück (2004:312) points out, such an approach requires a view of action as constrained and enabled by one's connectivities with other people. In this sense, agency is not *what* an individual can do, but *how* a person participates in a multitude of intersecting social relations. Relations are not only those that exist contemporaneously, but also those that connect people over time through genealogies of material practices (see e.g., Gillespie 2008; Joyce 2008; Mills 2008; Pollard 2008; Stahl 2008).

In this paper we extend Brück's and Owoc's relational approach to non-burial assemblages – specifically caches. We define caches as clusters of objects that were intentionally placed in contexts that were not directly associated with human burials, but which were treated differently from domestic refuse (Walker 1995). These clusters of objects have also been called "placed" or "structured" deposits because of their unique pathways of discard (Lucero 2003:526; Pollard 2008) and the particularity of their placement in space (Bradley 2000:49; Maxwell 1996:38; Richards and Thomas 1984). Such an approach takes as a beginning point that religious practices are "marked" (Keane 2010), which allows us to use structured deposition as a means of getting at indigenous aesthetics (Pollard 2001) and to distinguish practices with different genealogies.

We view the contents and locations of these intentionally deposited objects as evidence for the varied ways in which people participated in identity communities through the massing together of objects with different biographies. These caches of objects are products of communities of ritual practice that can be thought of in terms of network topologies – that is, as stemming from the structure of networks constructed by the relationships between people, places, and objects. The structure of caches produced through religious ritual lends insight into a particular community's shared perceptions about the order of the world and the relationships that comprise and sustain it. But we also recognize that there may be some shared aesthetics among the case studies that we write about in this chapter, particularly since they come from the same geographic area – we return to this interesting paradox. Though there are relational ontologies that are quite distinctive between cultural groups, many of the materials that people engaged with were the same, and those materials must have held similar, if not the same, importance across Southwestern societies through both their shared historical relationships and their intrinsic properties. Recognizing the multiple contributions of identities, material properties, and historical relations to relational ontologies is one of the challenges in interpretations of materiality (e.g., Ingold 2007).

We now turn to the rich record of "marked" practices of deposition from the Greater Southwest to look at different logics of depositional practices in the Chaco and Hohokam areas – contemporaneous and iconic archaeological regions that have been subject to extensive excavations. We compare cache deposits in these two areas to illustrate how differences in the scale and secrecy of ritual perfor- mances, geographies of social networks, and the meanings and temporality of ritual were expressed through the actions of individuals who belonged to different communities of practice. The deposits from each of these areas were made following different logics and based on varying indexical properties that structured where objects were placed, their associations, and their treatment at the time of deposition. Although we focus on the final deposition of these objects, ultimately these logics were part of memory work (Mills and Walker 2008) created within communities of practice of different social scales and duration.

The setting: Chaco and Hohokam

Several large regional traditions have been identified in the prehispanic North American Southwest including Chaco, Hohokam, and Casas Grandes. Casas Grandes is latest, but Chaco, in the Ancestral Pueblo area in the north, and Hohokam, in the basin and range country in the south, were roughly contemporaneous between the ninth and twelfth centuries AD (Figure 7.1). Chaco Canyon, on the Colorado Plateau, was at the center of a wide distribution of Great Houses linked by similarities in ceramics, large and small scale ritual architecture, and a discontinuous set of

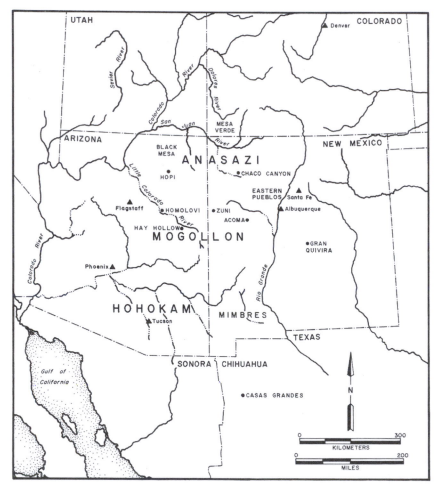

FIGURE 7.1 Location of Chaco and Hohokam areas in the North American Southwest. Courtesy of Crow Canyon Archaeological Center.

"roads," many of which are now interpreted as ritual pathways. Most archaeologists working in the area recognize that there was social hierarchy at Chaco, which grew out of a complex series of interactions as households with diverse social backgrounds moved into Chaco Canyon joining an already resident community (Van Dyke 2007).

The Hohokam region includes a number of river valleys within the basin and range country of the southern Southwest. The Hohokam Preclassic period was characterized by large sedentary farming villages, elaborate water management systems, pit structures that surround central plazas, complex mortuary rituals, and a paddle and anvil ceramic technology with distinctive red-on-buff decoration. Pit structures were arranged in courtyard groups, which collectively comprised larger villages. During the period contemporaneous with Chaco, these villages contained extensive public spaces including plazas, ballcourts, and capped mounds. Later, during the Classic Hohokam period, large above-ground adobe rooms and compounds were constructed with platform mounds replacing ballcourts as public architecture, but here we focus on Preclassic sites, primarily dating to the Colonial (ca. 700–900 AD) and Sedentary (ca. 900–1150 AD) periods within the Phoenix area chronology. These periods are marked by evidence of increasing sociopolitical complexity in the form of religious practice (e.g., Mesoamerican ball game), intensification of long-distance trade suggesting ties to Mesoamerica, and the construction of integrative ritual architecture. In the Salt and Gila drainages, large settlements like Snaketown were tethered to the largest prehispanic New World irrigation network north of Peru.

Both the Chaco and Hohokam areas saw major excavations beginning in the late nineteenth century, particularly at the sites of Pueblo Bonito in Chaco Canyon and Snaketown along the Gila River (Gladwin et al. 1937; Haury 1976; Judd 1954, 1964; Pepper 1920). These excavations produced spectacular quantities of materials from caches, many of which have never been fully inventoried or analyzed, particularly in light of recent theories that highlight the interconnectedness of materiality and identity. Because the interpretation of the materiality of objects is often context-specific, we pay special attention to the locations, content, and relational qualities of caches in both of these cultural areas.

Cache locations and performative visibility

First we address the spatial contexts of caches to understand where they were deposited and their performative visibility. Mills' (2008) recent investigation of Chacoan caches at Pueblo Bonito demonstrates that the strategic placement of particular objects or sets of objects in round rooms used for religious ritual, called kivas, occurred at multiple scales, and was integral to processes of remembering and forgetting. Discernible patterns in cache placement, such as in the niches or floor boxes of round rooms, suggest that caching was an important component of structure dedication and termination rituals. The act of memorializing these structures was a social process that linked people through space and time; it was thus a means for different social groups, who had distinct relationships with different kinds of ritual structures, to "inscribe" their memories in powerful spaces and moments.

The variability evident in the placement and content of Chacoan caches speaks to the multiple identity communities involved in the performance of memory work at various scales of participation and visibility. Whether small kivas or great kivas, round rooms were treated differently than the square rooms in the pueblo, and even kivas of different sizes show some important distinctions. Objects were placed in the niches of larger kivas, and in cavities hollowed out of architectural wood embedded within the pilasters of kivas that served as foundations for crib-bed-style log roofs (also called court kivas and room block kivas). The variation in the size of round rooms might suggest that the viewing of cached objects also varied in social scale. However, a few religious specialists may have placed the objects in niches in the larger structures when these buildings were relatively empty. Nonetheless, the placement of strings of jet and shell in ten caches within the niches of Great Kiva II at Chetro Ketl (Hewett 1936) must have involved many hands in their procurement, production, and deposition – high visibility at one end of the spectrum.

Other cache deposits at Chaco are found in the square rooms of the pueblo. These deposits are in or near the oldest rooms in the structure, which also contain the pueblo's burials. Interestingly, many of these caches do not appear to be directly associated with specific burials. Instead, they are found in sealed floor cavities, benches, floors, or the layers of fill of rooms near burials or associated with secondary burials (Akins 2003). The clustering of artifact locations in the oldest areas of the site corresponding to these burial clusters has been suggested as evidence for memory practices associated with the honoring of founding families (Mills 2008), whose statuses were reinforced through the transfer of property and religious knowledge within a "house society" (Heitman and Plog 2005). The placement of objects in square rooms would have been socially restricted; many of these rooms were only accessible by going through other rooms, which provided some control over who was able to place items in the rooms (e.g., Hillier and Hanson 1984). This suggests that caching was a controlled activity, practiced by select individuals who had the authority to enter and engage with particular spaces and memories.

By contrast, most Hohokam caches were not found in ritual architecture such as ballcourts and capped mounds, but rather interred in trash-filled pit structures (Haury 1976:175) or in open spaces situated between courtyard groups. At the large Preclassic period Grewe Site, Woodward (1931) describes an "offertory area" that contained multiple caches. The caches were laid on surfaces that may have been former pit structure floors, but the structures had been cleared. When caches were placed in filled pit structures, later structures may have been superimposed, sealing the earlier deposits. As with the Chaco caches in square rooms, many of the Hohokam caches are in structures that form spatial clusters occupied for long periods of time, marking the locations of long-term residential occupations at the site. Their visibility, however, would have been much higher than those at Chaco since the objects were placed in rooms after their roofs had been removed.

The prevalence of caches found in religious spaces at Chaco thus contrasts sharply with the placement of Hohokam caches, which tend to be more spatially restricted to residential structures. As Chacoan ritual architecture was used by crosscutting sodalities, caches were likely deposited by individuals who were members of identity communities associated with the construction, use, and termination of these structures. This raises interesting questions about the lack of caches in Hohokam ritual spaces, particularly because ballcourts and canal systems must have been important organizing elements or integrative mechanisms in Hohokam society. But we note that even though pit structures would seem to be domestic in use, the very process of marking these structures through deposition would have imbued them with symbolic importance, albeit in a more socially restricted way than at Chaco.

Cache temporality

The temporality of cache accumulation is also much different between the two areas. Many of the Chaco caches in pueblo (square) rooms appear to be accumulations over long periods of time, as long as three centuries in the case of the north cluster of rooms at Pueblo Bonito. At least some of these cache locations are former ritual storerooms where objects cared for by specific families were used, returned to storage, and then ritually retired as inalienable possessions too dangerous to discard in any other context (Mills 2004; Vivian et al. 1978). Repeated access to these rooms resulted in a complex depositional history, yielding layers of deposition between artifact clusters. Rooms at Pueblo Bonito were filled over long periods, but many remained accessible even if rooms were built over them.

Objects within individual Hohokam caches appear to have been deposited over a shorter period of time, perhaps representing a single event – a pit was dug, the contents placed inside and then covered with dirt. A pit structure was built over at least one cache at Snaketown without disturbing the contents, indicating that it was covered, perhaps remembered, but not intruded upon. This does not rule out the possibility that the objects deposited in Hohokam caches were accumulated over long periods of time prior to their burial. Before they were deposited, the items were brought together, perhaps over the lifetime of an individual or a particular family unit. For example, some of the Hohokam caches have dozens of redundant objects, such as censers, which were deposited all together (Figure 7.2).

Even though Hohokam caches appear to be placed at one time, they did accumulate over time in particular parts of settlements. Some families persisted over long periods of time, which is especially evident for the Preclassic period pit structures superimposed on top of each other such as at the Grewe Site (Craig 2007) or Snaketown (Gladwin et al. 1937; Haury 1976). These long-occupied areas of individual settlements were persistent places, with caches more discretely located within individual structures. The "offertory area" described for the earliest excavations at Grewe (Woodward 1931) was an area where repeated deposition took place.

In both the Chaco and Hohokam cases, the long-term accumulation of materials was part of the "memory work" (Mills and Walker 2008) of societies in each

FIGURE 7.2 Snaketown Cache 1:10G, a cache of Hohokam censers. From *The Hohokam: Desert Farmers and Craftsmen* by Emil W. Haury, Figure 11.15. © 1976 The Arizona Board of Regents. Reprinted by permission of the University of Arizona Press.

respective area. This is evinced by the repeated deposition in certain areas of sites, and the placement of caches in or on top of former residential areas. Pueblo Bonito in the Chaco area and sites such as Grewe and Snaketown in the Hohokam area are among the longest-lived sites for their respective regions. The repeated placement of highly valued objects established and reaffirmed relations between the ancestors and their descendants.

The content and relational qualities of the caches

There are many interesting parallels and contrasts in the geography of relationships expressed through cache contents between the two culture areas. One parallel is that both Chaco and Hohokam caches included objects from a number of sources, ranging from those acquired locally, to those obtained from more distant regions. The most distant items documented are those that came from West Mexico, including pyrite mirrors and copper bells (e.g., McGuire and Villalpando 2007: Figure 7.6; Vargas 1995), tropical birds (Hill 2000), and cacao, which may have been associated with cylinder jars cached at Chaco (Crown and Hurst 2009). Shell from the Sea of Cortez and the Pacific Coast are prominent at sites in both areas, but particularly in the Hohokam area. These objects have some intrinsic properties such as bright colors, shininess, and distinctive aural properties (in the case of shell trumpets) that likely made them desirable. But as Ingold (2007:14) points out, these materials do not have "fixed" or "essential" properties. Instead, they need to be thought about within their relational contexts and as they were "practically experienced." The association of objects from areas well outside the Southwest must have added to their value through the practices of acquiring them (Helms 1988; Nelson 2006). The social networks that people and items passed through on the way to their final destinations created relationships or chains linking people across broad areas. The use of pyrite mirrors, shell trumpets, and cacao was probably limited to a few individuals in each settlement. What is not known is whether individuals made the long distance journey specifically to acquire finished products, or whether objects were transfered through networks of individuals, perhaps those who were religious specialists. The transmission of objects, the knowledge of how to use them, and how and where to discard such things connected these individuals over broad areas and added to their significance.

Intermediate in distance were many of the minerals used as pigments and ornaments including jet, argillite, and turquoise. Turquoise was especially important at Chaco, and it is rare for any cache to not include this material (Figure 7.3). Locally acquired materials were also made into objects deposited in caches, including ground and chipped stone tools, ceramics, and a variety of perishables including baskets, sandals, and wooden items. Importantly, objects deposited in caches were not all artifactual – many other "natural" forms were included such as fossils, crystals, seeds, and animal

FIGURE 7.3 Small set of objects placed in a pilaster niche at Pueblo Bonito, Room 161, Log 5 (Hyde Expedition), AMNH #H16184. Photo by Barbara Mills.

and insect parts. A higher quantity of perishable objects may have been recovered from Chaco, but this is probably a taphonomic product since, as noted earlier, they were placed in sealed contexts within buildings such as niches and storage rooms. Nevertheless, the inclusion of unmodified objects in ritual caches is provocative, suggesting that categories of objects commonly considered by archaeologists to be quotidian or "mundane" figured prominently in the relational ontologies of human communities in the past.

Although many identical materials were used and deposited by both groups, the associations of objects were quite different in each region. Shell was one of the most common artifact classes found in Chaco caches. Whole shell "trumpets" (mostly *Strombus* sp. and *Murex* sp.) from the Sea of Cortez were placed in the cavities of a court kiva and deposited in ritual storerooms. One of these rooms at Pueblo Bonito (Room 38) contained four conch trumpets or trumpet fragments along with "native copper, pipes, turquoise ornaments, bird fetishes, grinding slabs, fossils, pigments, 14 parrot skulls, whole vessels with parrot bones, painted and unpainted wood, and dozens of fragments of ground stone" (Mills and Ferguson 2008:346). The most common forms of objects in caches within ritual structures at Chaco were, however, shell and turquoise beads. As Mills (2008) has argued, the common use of ornaments in ritual structures was part of a metaphor for the house as a living entity. Ritual structures were treated as living spaces, like a person, and ornaments placed in architectural cavities were used to "dress" the house. The attribution of personhood to these ritual structures suggests that caching behavior at Chaco constituted an important and consequential social interaction between the identity community and the structure itself.

Hohokam caches also have a reference to persons through the deposition of ornaments, many of which were again made of shell. One of the most ubiquitous ornaments in the Hohokam area generally is the *Glycymeris* shell bracelet. Several of these were found at the base of one cache deposit. These bracelets were made by specialized producers and are considered one of the strongest symbols of a region-wide Hohokam identity (Cerezo-Román and Wallace 2008).

Animals are present in caches in both the Chaco and Hohokam areas, either as complete or incomplete specimens. The structures of the deposits, however, communicate different relational properties. Turkeys are absent, and macaws and parrots are rare in the Hohokam area – especially for the Preclassic period, though all have been recovered from Chaco sites (Hill 2000). Bear claws and digital bones, mountain lion claws, and canine claws and digital bones were found in a highly diverse cache from Kiva Q at Pueblo Bonito (Judd 1954; Mills 2008) that also contained dozens of other materials including fossils, shells, turquoise, bifaces, seeds, fibers, insects, crystals, ground stone items, and potsherds. In the Hohokam area, piles of mountain sheep horn cores and deer antlers have been found in "offertory" areas, such as at Grewe (Mills et al., forthcoming; Woodward 1931). Woodward (1931:14) describes the association of these with stone palettes, mirror bases, bone tools, and projectile points. Ceramic vessels were also intentionally broken and carefully placed on top of the deposit. Clearly, contrasts exist between Chaco and Hohokam with regard to which animals were appropriate to place in caches – the paws and claws of carnivorous animals at Chaco and the horns and antlers of wild game for the Hohokam.

The cache from Kiva Q at Pueblo Bonito more resembles a Plains medicine bundle (Zedeño 2008) than any of the other caches at Chaco – as in the Plains, this bundling of objects may have been a metaphor for the widespread network of relations experienced by those who used the structure. The contents of this cache provide a glimpse into the relational ontologies at Chaco – including the importance of turquoise (Plog 2003) in raw and modified form. Among the other few whole artifacts in this cache was a sandstone palette (used for grinding pigments), bone awls, and a "cloud blower," which based on analogy to historic and modern Pueblos, was used to blow smoke to form rain clouds that would bring rain. Two large bifaces are forms that were more common in the Paleoindian rather than agricultural periods, although bifaces are known to have been carried by religious personages during Puebloan ceremonies and the knowledge of how to make them continued into the historic period (Kaldahl 2000).

By contrast, one of the most important qualities of the Hohokam caches is that they resemble cremation burials. All of the cached objects at Snaketown show evidence of having been burned or broken. The burning or breaking of objects is usually associated with the "killing" of objects, and accounts for 65 per cent of the Snaketown cremation offerings (McGuire 1992:22). The massing and burning of the cache contents was so similar to cremation features that early excavators classi-fied caches as cremations (Gladwin et al. 1937), even when there was no evidence of human bone or ash. In the case of the Preclassic Hohokam, the objects were burned and broken and then placed in pits on abandoned house floors, but it is not clear that they were objects owned by only one person.

The breaking and burning of cache contents, like the burning and subsequent fragmentation of the body during cremation, was a practice that tied caches to mortuary ritual. The practice of fragmenting objects reproduced some of the practices that marked the death of individuals. Another linkage is through the physical partitioning of objects and people. Beck (2005), and more recently Cerezo-Román (2012), noticed that the weights of Hohokam cremations are too small to represent the product of a single individual. They were apparently dug up, subdivided, and then secondarily reinterred in subsequent memorializing rituals. Excavators of Hohokam caches, too, have noted that there are incomplete stone bowls, censers, and other objects that occur in caches – removed from other contexts and then redeposited. This process resembles the discussion of Bronze Age fragmentation presented by Chapman (2000), in which pieces of objects create chains between people in disparate places.

That the Hohokam caches are metaphors for the cremation of bodies is under-scored by the form and use of the objects themselves. Although there are dozens and sometimes hundreds of objects in these caches, the minimum set comprises censers, which make up about one-quarter of all cache artifacts. Made of stone early on, then of ceramic during the Sedentary period, these objects were used to burn substances during the cremation ritual. Palettes, often thought to be closely associated with censers, are less common in the earlier Colonial period, but they are associated with the later ceramic censers. In at least one case, they have burn marks that appear to match the size and shape of the ceramic censers. Effigies of people, including ceramic jars and figurines also are frequently found in Hohokam caches, especially during the Sedentary period. Although many figurines in the Hohokam area are found in trash middens, and have been argued to be part of women's ritual practice (Stinson 2004), some sets are also found in caches (Fish and Fish 2007:Figure 5.1; Thomas and King 1985). Some of the latter include figurines and other objects in tableaus resembling West Mexican ceramic groupings.

Discussion

So what do these metaphors tell us about identity communities? In the Hohokam area, one of the strongest social networks was brought together in mortuary ritual. The accoutrements of funerary rites were themselves considered to be so alive that they, too, had to be disposed of in a highly controlled manner. Treated like the body, censers, in particular, were burned, broken, and deposited, with their fragments later re-excavated, dispersed, and re-accumulated. During their re-accumulation, they were buried with the symbols of Hohokam identity: *Glycymeris* bracelets and decorated ceramic vessels. Dozens of vessels were placed in some caches. In fact, one Snaketown cache yielded more whole vessels than were found on all house floors dating to the Sedentary period (Lamotta and Schiffer 1999).

Some cremation burials in the Hohokam area are similarly rich. However, like Brück's (2004) interpretation of the Early Bronze Age burials in Europe, we doubt that these objects were owned exclusively by the individual interred. Similarly, we think that the many objects placed in Hohokam caches were the result of networks of people, tied by their associations with the place where the caches appear – the remains of past structures – and who contributed the products of multiple cremation rituals. The placing of objects reinforced associations of people to things, moments, and places, and represented their common participation in what appears to be a highly homogenous community of practices centered on memorialization and mortuary ritual.

The Hohokam caches therefore contrast with those from the Chaco area in that the latter appear to show more variety. Mills' (2008) analysis of Chacoan caches reveals the existence of multiple identity communities. Different scales of cross-cutting sodalities are represented by the placement of objects in small kivas, court kivas, and great kivas, while the communities that shared in the deposition of objects in pueblo rooms are evidence for the participation of different families in these networks. At least two family clusters have been identified at Pueblo Bonito, in burial clusters that contain the remains of what appear to be genetically distinct lineages (Akins 2003), which have been interpreted as the founding families of Pueblo Bonito. This site is unique in the Chaco World, and these families held positions of leadership with responsibilities for the care of objects that eventually were deposited in rooms adjacent to the long-term burial chambers of their ancestors. Both primary and secondary burials are present in these rooms, and as some archaeologists have recently suggested, they are like family crypts used over long periods of time (Heitman and Plog 2005; Mills 2008). Many of these ritually retired objects are staffs of office and altarpieces, but they underscore the importance of participation in ritual sodalities in the Chaco area. Even the objects cached in ritual storerooms at Chaco were used in sodality rituals, such as staffs of office. Their final deposition near the clusters of burials at Pueblo Bonito shows how people were part of multiple identity communities in Chaco society. The placement of sodality-associated objects in the areas of long-term family burial chambers reinforced their prominence at the same time as they reproduced the practices of crosscutting groups.

Conclusion

By comparing the spatiality, temporality, and content of ritual caches from two contemporaneous yet distinct cultural areas in the prehispanic Southwest (Table 7.1), we have demonstrated that patterns in depositional practices shed light on associative networks of people, things, animals, and places. Indigenous taxonomies of being or relational logics guided the placement, organization, and treatment of cached objects. Prioritizing the discernment of these logics over the intrinsic or physical properties of objects represents an important analytical shift in the study of identity in the past – from the actor as an isolated entity, alienable from the surrounding world, to the actor whose identity is constituted by his/her/its participation in any number of interaction networks. In this case, identity is not restricted to human actors, but extends to a physical world imbued with animacy, power, and personhood. The relational ontologies that guide the behavior of these human communities of practice are embedded in transactions with a subjective material world.

One of the most important observations to emerge from our comparison of Chacoan and Hohokam cache deposits is the vastly different relational ontologies of these groups, despite the fact that they had access to the same range of materials during the same period of time. Both areas used shell, stone, minerals, ceramics, fossils, and animals in their caches, but our study demonstrates that these materials were used in entirely distinctive ways. Fowler (2010:376) has noted that "different cultures appreciate the properties of substances in distinctive ways, so that we might talk of distinct 'materialities,' but in each case there are underlying relationships by which materials share properties." Shell trumpets, for example, have the property of being able to create sounds – yet they were used in very different contexts and associated with different materials in the Chaco and Hohokam worlds.

Despite these differences, a significant and overarching commonality between the two regions emerged from our research – caching behavior in both societies often communicated the personhood of places or things. For example, ornaments used to adorn a ritually charged space were one of the dominant artifact classes cached in Chaco religious structures. In the Hohokam area, caches were treated like

TABLE 7.1 Comparison of Chaco and Hohokam caches.

Cache Attributes	Chaco	Hohokam
Size of assemblage	Variable–some with thousands of objects (e.g., ritual storerooms), others very small (e.g., kiva pilaster offerings)	Highly varied, some with hundreds of objects, others singular
Locations of discard	Intramural	In rooms, but since these were abandoned and filled pit structures, they were unroofed spaces
Cache container preparation	High–architectural cavities	Low–pits only
Figurines/effigies	Rare	Many, especially in Sedentary period when there is a transition from middens to cache contexts for figurines
Diversity of materials	High in some places (e.g., the bundle from the Great Kiva at Bonito), but low in others–common denominator turquoise	High in some places, very little turquoise
Intentional fragmentation	Low; most caches contain whole objects or were whole when deposited without obvious intentional breakage	High, especially for censers
Visibility of discard	Low for most areas, such as small kivas and placement in ritual storerooms, potentially higher for some great kivas	In dismantled rooms that had already been filled so moderately visible
Distances material acquired	Shell from Sea of Cortez and Pacific Coast, turquoise from throughout Southwest, cacao from Mesoamerica (residues associated with cached vessels), other materials from Greater Chaco area	Some from West Mexico (mirrors), many forms emulating Mesoamerican styles (e.g., footed vessels), shell from the Sea of Cortez and Pacific Coast, other sources from greater Hohokam area
Labor investment	Variable depending on context, some highly worked (e.g., inlaid scapulae, mosaic covered baskets) but in small kivas many unfinished objects	Variable, higher in earliest caches, e.g., stone censers early, replaced by ceramic censers; some caches with hundreds of items, others more limited
Associated birds and animals	Macaws, parrots, dogs, mountain lions, bears	Big horn sheep, deer, and dogs. Macaws and parrots rare

cremation burials. The patterned breakage of cached objects is consistent with the physical treatment of the dead. An analytical focus on individual objects would not have made these associations apparent – it is only by viewing them as sets or assemblages that the centrality of object personhood in caching practices becomes obvious. In the Chacoan case, caching appears to be a means of animating buildings, while among the Hohokam, caching is a means of de-animating objects. The Hohokam and Chaco case studies illustrate how identities were differentially materialized, and how shared perceptions of the social and material worlds were manifested in patterns of object association, placement, and treatment in ritual caches. They also underscore the importance of context, scale, and the relational logics that guided deposition for interpretations of identity in the past. As discrete embodiments of object/person/space networks, caches are in a sense, materialized ontologies of the identity communities that created them. The patterns evident in caching behavior at Chaco and Hohokam sites suggest that the individuals we study were defined not by their social status or individual attributes, but by the web of social relations that continuously defined them.

Theoretical frameworks that emphasize the relationality of human and non-human subjects in the constitution of identity force us to confront a host of oversimplified assumptions about the role of the material in the lived experiences of the communities we study. An unfounded reliance on the *categorical* significance of objects obscures the *relational* qualities that lent those objects meaning in the eyes of the people who interacted with them (see Murray 2011; Zedeño 2009). In this chapter, we have demonstrated that this human-material engagement exhibits patterns through space and time. These patterns, in turn, lend insight into the identities of the people who created them. By embodying social networks of peoples, places, and things, caches are ideal units of analysis for accessing not only the identities of participating actors – human and non-human – but also bring into focus the network topologies within which they reside.[1]

Note

1 Several individuals provided access to notes and collections used in this chapter. We thank Art Vokes, Suzanne Fish, and Paul Fish and the staff of the Arizona State Museum for access to the Snaketown notes and Hohokam collections. David Hurst Thomas and Anibal Rodriguez provided invaluable help with the Chaco collections at the American Museum of Natural History. Earlier versions of this paper were presented in symposia at the Theoretical Archaeology Group meeting at Stanford and the World Archaeological Congress in Dublin. We thank Serena Love and Rosemary Joyce for organizing these symposia, respectively. Zedeño and T. J. Ferguson provided valuable insights on relational significance and object animacy. Finally, we thank Christopher Watts for his vision of this volume and for his careful editing of our chapter.

Bibliography

Akins, Nancy J. 2003. The Burials of Pueblo Bonito. In *Pueblo Bonito: Center of the Chacoan World*, edited by Jill E. Nietzel, pp. 94–106. Smithsonian Institution Press, Washington, D.C.

Beck, Lane A. 2005. Secondary Burial Practices in Hohokam Cremations. In *Interacting with the Dead: Perspectives on Mortuary Archaeology for the New Millennium*, edited by Gordon F. M. Rakita, Jane E. Buikstra, Lane A. Beck, and Sloan R. Williams, pp. 150–54. University Press of Florida, Gainesville.

Bell, Catherine 1992. *Ritual Theory, Ritual Practice*. Oxford University Press, New York.

Bernardini, Wesley 2005. *Hopi Oral Tradition and the Archaeology of Identity*. University of Arizona Press, Tucson.

Bradley, Richard 2000. *An Archaeology of Natural Places*. Routledge, London.

Brück, Joanna 2004. Material Metaphors: The Relational Structure of Identity in Early Bronze Age Burials in Ireland and Britain. *Journal of Social Archaeology* 4(3):307–33.

——(2006). Fragmentation, Personhood and the Social Construction of Technology in Middle and Late Bronze Age Britain. *Cambridge Archaeological Journal* 16(3):297–315.

Casella, Eleanor, and Chris Fowler 2005. Beyond Identification: An Introduction. In *The Archaeology of Plural and Changing Identities*, edited by Eleanor Casella and Chris Fowler, pp. 1–8. Kluwer Academic/Plenum Press, New York.

Cerezo-Román, Jessica I. 2012. Pathways to Personhood: Cremation as a Social Practice among the Tucson Basin Hohokam. In *Fire and the Body: Cremation as a Social Context*, edited by Gabriel Cooney, Ian Kuijt, and Colin Quinn. University of Arizona Press, Tucson (forthcoming).

Cerezo-Román, Jessica I., and Henry D. Wallace 2008. "Mortuary Practices at Honey Bee Village." Paper presented at the 73rd Annual Meeting of the Society of American Archaeology, Vancouver, British Columbia.

Chapman, John 2000. *Fragmentation in Archaeology: People, Places and Broken Objects in the Prehistory of South Eastern Europe*. Routledge, New York.

Craig, Douglas B. 2007. Courtyard Groups and the Emergence of House Estates in Early Hohokam Society. In *The Durable House: House Society Models in Archaeology*, edited by Robin A. Beck, Jr., pp. 446–63. Occasional Paper No. 35. Center for Archaeological Investigations, Southern Illinois University, Carbondale.

Crown, Patricia L., and W. Jeffrey Hurst 2009. Evidence of Cacao Use in the Prehispanic American Southwest. *Proceedings of the National Academy of Sciences* 106:2110–13.

Ferguson, T. J., and Chip Colwell-Chanthaphonh 2006. *History Is in the Land: Multivocal Tribal Traditions in Arizona's San Pedro Valley*. University of Arizona Press, Tucson.

Fish, Paul R., and Suzanne K. Fish 2007. Community, Territory, Polity. In *The Hohokam Millennium*, edited by Suzanne K. Fish and Paul R. Fish, pp. 39–48. School for Advanced Research Press, Santa Fe, New Mexico.

Fowler, Chris 2001. Personhood and Social Relations in the British Neolithic with a Study from the Isle of Man. *Journal of Material Culture* 6(2):137–63.

——(2004). *The Archaeology of Personhood: An Anthropological Approach*. Routledge, London.

——(2010). From Identity and Material Culture to Personhood and Materiality. In *The Oxford Handbook of Material Culture Studies*, edited by Dan Hicks and Mary C. Beaudry, pp. 352–85. Oxford University Press, New York.

Gillespie, Susan D. 2001. Personhood, Agency, and Mortuary Ritual: A Case Study from the Ancient Maya. *Journal of Anthropological Archaeology* 20:73–112.

——(2008). History in Practice: Ritual Deposition at La Venta Complex A. In *Memory Work: Archaeologies of Material Practices*, edited by Barbara J. Mills and William H. Walker, pp. 109–36. School for Advanced Research Press, Santa Fe, New Mexico.

Gladwin, Harold S., Emil W. Haury, Edwin B. Sayles, and Nora Gladwin 1937. *Excavations at Snaketown: Material Culture*. Medallion Papers No. 25. Gila Pueblo, Globe, Arizona.

Groleau, Amy B. 2009. Special Finds: Locating Animism in the Archaeological Record. *Cambridge Archaeological Journal* 19(3):399–406.

Haury, Emil W. 1976. *The Hohokam: Desert Farmers and Craftsmen*. University of Arizona Press, Tucson.

Heitman, Carrie, and Stephen Plog 2005. Kinship and the Dynamics of the House: Rediscovering Dualism in the Pueblo Past. In *A Catalyst for Ideas: Anthropological Archaeology and the Legacy of Douglas W. Schwartz*, edited by Vernon L. Scarborough, pp. 69–100. School of American Research Press, Santa Fe, New Mexico.

Hewett, Edgar L. 1936. *The Chaco Canyon and Its Monuments*. University of New Mexico Press, Albuquerque.

Helms, Mary 1988. *Ulysses' Sail: An Ethnographic Odyssey of Power, Knowledge, and Geographical Distance*. Princeton University Press, Princeton, New Jersey.

Hill, Erica 2000. The Contextual Analysis of Animal Interments and Ritual Practice in Southwestern North America. *Kiva* 65(4):361–98.

Hillier, Bill, and Julienne Hanson 1984. *The Social Logic of Space*. Cambridge University Press, Cambridge.

Hoskins, Janet 1998. *Biographical Objects: How Things Tell the Stories of People's Lives*. Routledge. London.

Ingold, Tim 2006. Rethinking the Animate, Re-Animating Thought. *Ethnos* 71(1):9–20.

——(2007). Materials against Materiality. *Archaeological Dialogues* 14(1):1–16.

Jackson, Gary, and Claire Smith 2005. Living and Learning on Aboriginal Lands: Decolonizing Archaeology in Practice. In *Indigenous Archaeologies: Decolonizing Theory and Practice*, edited by Claire Smith and H. Martin Wobst, pp. 328–51. Routledge, New York.

Joyce, Rosemary A. 2008. Practice in and as Deposition. In *Memory Work: Archaeologies of Material Practices*, edited by Barbara J. Mills and William H. Walker, pp. 25–39. School for Advanced Research Press, Santa Fe, New Mexico.

Judd, Neil M. 1954. *The Material Culture of Pueblo Bonito*. Smithsonian Miscellaneous Collections No. 124. Washington, D.C.

——(1964). *The Architecture of Pueblo Bonito*. Smithsonian Miscellaneous Collections Vol. 147, No. 1. Washington, D.C.

Kaldahl, Eric J. 2000. "Late Prehistoric Technological and Social Reorganization along the Mogollon Rim, Arizona." Unpublished Ph.D. dissertation, Department of Anthropology, University of Arizona, Tucson.

Keane, Webb 2010. Marked, Absent, Habitual: Approaches to Neolithic Religion at Çatalhöyük. In *Religion in the Emergence of Civilization: Çatalhöyük as a Case Study*, edited by Ian Hodder, pp. 187–219. Cambridge University Press, Cambridge.

Lamotta, Vincent L., and Michael B. Schiffer 1999. Formation Processes of House Floor Assemblages. In *The Archaeology of Household Activities*, edited by Penelope M. Allison, pp. 19–29. Routledge, London.

Latour, Bruno 2005. *Reassembling the Social: An Introduction to Actor-Network Theory*. Oxford University Press, Oxford.

Lave, Jean, and Etienne Wenger 1991. *Situated Learning: Legitimate Peripheral Participation*. Cambridge University Press, Cambridge.

Lucero, Lisa 2003. The Politics of Ritual: The Emergence of Classic Maya Rulers. *Current Anthropology* 44(4):523–58.

Maxwell, David Bruce Saxon 1996. "An Analysis of Caches from Four Sites in the Maya Lowlands." Unpublished Ph.D. dissertation, Department of Anthropology, University of Arizona, Tucson.

McGuire, Randall H. 1992. *Death, Society, and Ideology in a Hohokam Community*. Westview, Boulder, Colorado.

McGuire, Randall H., and Elisa C. Villalpando 2007. The Hohokam and Mesoamerica. In *The Hohokam Millennium*, edited by Suzanne K. Fish and Paul R. Fish, pp. 57–74. School for Advanced Research Press, Santa Fe, New Mexico.

Mills, Barbara J. 2004. The Establishment and Defeat of Hierarchy: Inalienable Possessions and the History of Collective Prestige Structures in the Puebloan Southwest. *American Anthropologist* 106(2):238–51.

——(2008). Remembering while Forgetting: Depositional Practices and Social Memory at Chaco. In *Memory Work: Archaeologies of Material Practices*, edited by Barbara J. Mills and William H. Walker, pp. 81–108. School for Advanced Research Press, Santa Fe, New Mexico.

Mills, Barbara J., Mark Elson, Paul Fish, Glen Rice, and Henry Wallace (forthcoming). Ritual Practice and Hohokam Trajectories. In *Hohokam Trajectories in Worldwide Perspective*, edited by Paul R. Fish and Suzanne K. Fish. Amerind Foundation and University of Arizona Press, Tucson.

Mills, Barbara J., and T. J. Ferguson 2008. Animate Objects: Shell Trumpets and Ritual Networks in the Greater Southwest. *Journal of Archaeological Method and Theory* 15:338–361.

Mills, Barbara J., and William H. Walker 2008. Introduction: Memory, Materiality, and Depositional Practice. In *Memory Work: Archaeologies of Material Practices*, edited by Barbara J. Mills and William H. Walker, pp. 3–23. School for Advanced Research Press, Santa Fe, New Mexico.

Murray, Wendi Field 2011. Feathers, Fasting, and the Eagle Complex: A Contemporary Analysis of the Eagle as a Cultural Resource in the Northern Plains. *Plains Anthropologist* 56(218):143–53.

Nelson, Ben A. 2006. Mesoamerican Objects and Symbols in Chaco. In *The Archaeology of Chaco Canyon: An Eleventh-Century Pueblo Regional Center*, edited by Stephen H. Lekson, pp. 339–71. School of American Research Press, Santa Fe, New Mexico.

Olsen, Bjørnar 2003. Material Culture after Text: Re-membering Things. *Norwegian Archaeological Review* 36(2):87–104.

——(2010). *In Defense of Things: Archaeology and the Ontology of Objects*. AltaMira, Lanham, Massachusetts.

Owoc, Mary Ann 2005. From the Ground Up: Agency, Practice, and Community in the Southwestern British Bronze Age. *Journal of Archaeological Method and Theory* 12(4):257–81.

Pepper, George H. 1920. Pueblo Bonito. *Anthropological Papers of the American Museum of Natural History* 27. New York.

Plog, Stephen 2003. Exploring the Ubiquitous through the Unusual: Color Symbolism in Pueblo Black-on-White Pottery. *American Antiquity* 68(4):665–95.

Pollard, Joshua 2001. The Aesthetics of Depositional Practices. *World Archeology* 33(2):315–33.

——(2008). Deposition and Material Agency in the Early Neolithic of Southern Britain. In *Memory Work: Archaeologies of Material Practices*, edited by Barbara J. Mills and William H. Walker, pp. 41–59. School for Advanced Research Press, Santa Fe, New Mexico.

Preucel, Robert W., and Lynn Meskell (editors) 2004. Knowledges. In *A Companion to Social Archaeology*, edited by Lynn Meskell and Robert W. Preucel, pp. 3–22. Blackwell, Malden, Massachusetts.

Richards, Colin, and Julian Thomas 1984. Ritual Activity and Structured Deposition in Later Neolithic Wessex. In *Neolithic Studies: A Review of Some Current Research*, edited by Richard Bradley and Julie Gardiner, pp. 189–218. BAR British Series 133. British Archaeological Reports, Oxford.

Salmón, Enrique 2000. Kincentric Ecology: Indigenous Perceptions of the Human-Nature Relationship. *Ecological Applications* 10(5):1327–32.

Stahl, Ann B. 2008. Dogs, Pythons, Pots, and Beads: The Dynamics of Shrines and Sacrificial Practices in Banda, Ghana, 1400–1900 CE. In *Memory Work: Archaeologies of Material Practices*, edited by Barbara J. Mills and William H. Walker, pp. 159–86. School for Advanced Research Press, Santa Fe, New Mexico.

Strathern, Marilyn 1988. *The Gender of the Gift*. University of California Press, Berkeley.

——(1993). Making Incomplete. In *Carved Flesh/Cast Selves: Gendered Symbols and Social Practices*, edited by Vigdis Broch-Due, Ingrid Rudie, and Tony Bleie, pp. 41–51. Berg, Oxford.

Stinson, Susan L. 2004. "Household Ritual, Gender, and Figurines in the Hohokam Regional System". Unpublished Ph.D. dissertation, Department of Anthropology, University of Arizona, Tucson.

Thomas, Charles Matthew, and Jeffrey Howard King 1985. Hohokam Figurine Assemblages: A Suggested Ritual Context. In *Proceedings of the 1983 Hohokam Symposium, Part II*, edited by Alfred E. Dittert, Jr., and Donald E. Dove, pp. 687–732. Occasional Paper No. 2. Arizona Archaeological Society, Phoenix.

Van Dyke, Ruth M. 2007. *The Chaco Experience: Landscape and Ideology at the Center Place*. School of American Research Press, Santa Fe, New Mexico.

Vargas, Victoria D. 1995. Copper Bell Trade Patterns in the Prehispanic U.S. Southwest and Northwest Mexico. *Archaeological Series No. 187*. Arizona State Museum, University of Arizona, Tucson.

Viveiros de Castro, Eduardo 2004. Exchanging Perspectives: The Transformation of Objects into Subjects in Amerindian Ontologies. *Common Knowledge* 10(3):463–84.

Vivian, R. Gwinn, Dulce N. Dodgen, and Gayle H. Hartman 1978. *Wooden Ritual Artifacts from Chaco Canyon, New Mexico*. Anthropological Papers of the University of Arizona No. 32. University of Arizona Press, Tucson.

Walker, William H. 1995. Ceremonial Trash? In *Expanding Archaeology*, edited by James M. Skibo, William H. Walker, and Axel E. Nielsen, pp 67–79. University of Utah Press, Salt Lake City.

Weiner, Annette B. 1992. *Inalienable Possessions: The Paradox of Keeping while Giving*. University of California Press, Berkeley.

Wenger, Etienne 1998. *Communities of Practice: Learning, Meaning, and Identity*. Cambridge University Press, Cambridge.

Woodward, Arthur 1931. *The Grewe Site*. Occasional Paper 1. Los Angeles Museum of History, Science, and Art, Los Angeles.

Yaeger, Jason 2000. The Social Construction of Communities in the Classic Maya Countryside: Strategies of Affiliation in Western Belize. In *The Archaeology of Communities: A New World Perspective*, edited by Marcello-Andrea Canuto and Jason Yaeger, pp. 123–42. Routledge, London.

Zedeño, María Nieves 2008. Bundled Worlds: The Roles and Interactions of Complex Objects from the North American Plains. *Journal of Archaeological Method and Theory* 15 (4):362–78.

——(2009). Animating by Association: Index Objects and Relational Taxonomies. *Cambridge Archaeological Journal* 19(3):411–21.

8

INTIMATE CONNECTION: BODIES AND SUBSTANCES IN FLUX IN THE EARLY NEOLITHIC OF CENTRAL EUROPE

Daniela Hofmann

The Neolithic as a set of categories

In central Europe, the Neolithic is defined as the point when an economy largely based on agriculture and animal husbandry replaces hunting and gathering. This shift is also associated with a greater degree of sedentism and is largely contemporary with the introduction of pottery. As such, the beginning of the Neolithic is a watershed in terms of categorization – both by researchers, and regarding the emic categories we impute to people in the past.

The Neolithic is a time of new technologies, most notably pottery production and stone polishing, but also woodland clearance, the keeping of domestic plants and animals, and the creation of buildings. Regardless of whether we see the Neolithic as introduced by colonists, adapted by indigenous hunter-gatherers, or a mixture of the two (for discussion, see, e.g., Kienlin 2006; Scharl 2004:57–84; Zvelebil 2004), in central Europe the change is generally characterized as both rapid and profound. However, for this area, worldviews and ontologies are not often explicitly problematized (but see, e.g., Whittle 2003, 2009). One well-known attempt is Hodder's (1990) statement that this new material culture and economy was not just about new ways of production, but also about a new way of defining humanity itself in relation to nature, or taming the 'wild.' Although rarely formulated with such clarity elsewhere, this categorization between human and animal, culture and nature, and self and other is part and parcel of many more recent narratives. These stress how the new Neolithic communities variously struggled against foragers, bad harvests, climatic fluctuations, and population pressure, ultimately unsuccessfully (e.g., Farruggia 2002; Golitko and Keeley 2006; Gronenborn 2006, 2010; Schade 2004). In all these models, Neolithic farmers act on the world from the outside, battling against its adverse conditions.

This contribution focuses on a smaller scale of social interaction, taking the treatments of individual human bodies as its starting point. I suggest that new material practices were also used to negotiate the continuous connections, equivalences, and transformations which embedded people in their worlds. This does not mean that the Neolithic world was one without categories, but that these had to be defined and maintained against a world in constant flux and were therefore temporary and open to change.

In central Europe, the Neolithic begins with the *Linearbandkeramik* culture or LBK (ca. 5600–4900 cal BC), which eventually covers an area from Hungary to the Paris Basin and Ukraine, and from south of the Danube into the northern European plain (Figure 8.1). The modalities of its appearance and spread remain debated, with some arguing that the speed at which it becomes established could only have been achieved by an influx of colonists (e.g., Ammerman and Cavalli-Sforza 1984; Lüning 1988; Svoboda 2008; for an overview, see Scharl 2004:57–89), a position recently strengthened by aDNA analysis (Haak et al. 2010). In addition, the archaeological record for the preceding Mesolithic is scanty in many parts of central Europe and suggests small-scale, highly mobile populations. This stands in stark contrast to the LBK way of life, which is centered on wooden longhouses up to 30m long or more (e.g., Coudart 1998) and the intensive farming of cereals, probably in small, carefully maintained garden-style plots (Bogaard 2004, 2012). Although hunting remains important at some sites, domesticated animals – cattle, pig, and sheep/goat – are now exploited. The fast spread of the LBK culture has a distinct aura of imposition, of stamping a new way of life onto a yielding environment, in spite of the risks that may be associated with such an undertaking (e.g., Bogucki 1988).

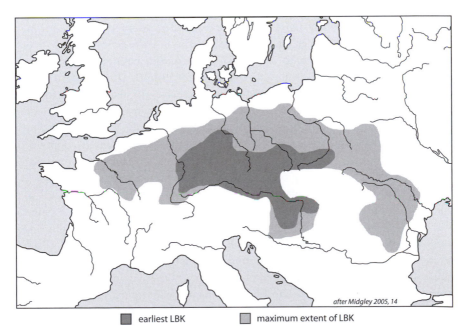

after Midgley 2005, 14

■ earliest LBK   ■ maximum extent of LBK

FIGURE 8.1 Map of LBK distribution. After Midgley (2005:14).

Others have argued that the process of forager-farmer interaction is regionally varied and complex, potentially involving several ethnic groups at least on the fringes of the Bandkeramik world (Gronenborn 1999; Whittle 1996). A certain economic diversity within LBK communities has also been revealed, with possibly distinct herder or hunter identities suggested on the basis of isotopic analyses of mobility patterns and animal bone assemblages (Bentley et al. 2003; Hachem 2000; Price and Bentley 2005; Price et al. 2001). Yet an element of categorization remains in these accounts. For example, 'herders' or 'hunters' were initially assumed to be singled out by specific grave goods or burial treatments (Price and Bentley 2005), an interpretation that has been considerably nuanced recently (Bickle and Whittle 2013; Bickle et al. 2011). Similarly, items of material culture, behaviors, and even animal species are treated as straightforward indicators of people's identities. For instance, continued mobility is seen as being a 'Mesolithic' trait (e.g., Whittle 2001), although the rhythms and social interactions afforded by herding would be very different from the kinds of mobility experienced in hunting and gathering (Bogaard 2004:161–65). Given the importance of hunted animals in farming societies across the globe (Hachem 2011:263–70; Kent 1989), these need not simply be the trace of a residual, partly acculturated hunter-gatherer population.

Overall, then, whether we see the LBK as internally unified or internally diverse, we are still thinking in terms of fixed identity categories. In the former instance, the Neolithic is more or less explicitly characterized as a managerial undertaking, the creation of a tamed landscape opposed to the natural world. Domestic animals, for instance, are part of a rational economic strategy involving calculations about their needs for grazing land and costs for winter fodder, resources extracted from a passive environment (see e.g., Bakels 1982; Ebersbach 2006; Schade 2004). Here, humans impose their will onto nature from the outside, using a range of new technologies (see, e.g., discussion in Ingold 2000:89–110). In Hodder's (1990) influential model, humans also domesticate themselves in the process: in their attempts to forge a distinctiveness from 'nature,' they create increasingly fixed divisions between categories of people (see also Russell 2002).

This parallels the arguments of those who advocate the indigenous adoption of agriculture. For them, the LBK may be internally diverse, but it is composed of people belonging to distinct groups with their own characteristics. Any incoming 'farmers,' for example, are often seen as sedentary, potentially hierarchical and rigidly traditionalist, as opposed to the mobile, egalitarian, and flexible 'foragers' who freely chose to join LBK communities (for critiques, see, e.g., Kienlin 2006; Robb and Miracle 2007). If Bandkeramik sites therefore exhibit signs of change, creativity, or adaptation – such as hunting – this must be due to the large role of hunter-gatherers in re-inventing and re-molding an otherwise rigid system of cultural rules. People would presumably also interact with animals and the natural environment in predictable ways, with foragers bringing their more egalitarian ethic and an attitude of a giving or nurturing environment to the equation (as described e.g., in Barnard 2007; Bird-David 1990).

In this paper, I briefly discuss how recent ideas of the world as a meshwork of relations have helped to break down unhelpful distinctions between people and the world around them. This has opened up new ways in which researchers can approach past lifeworlds as dynamic and transformative. Practices of categorization and boundary-making were still present, but existed in conjunction with those centered on transformation. Particularly in the developed phases of the LBK culture, from about 5300 cal BC onwards, there is the potential for artifacts and practices being used to define categories of person. However, the materials in which these categories were framed – the human body, pottery, and architecture – were not durable, and exhibit a strong parallel concern with transformation and fluidity. LBK bodies may have been seen as transient, with several practices necessary for their temporary congealment. New technologies are involved in both creation/congealment and deconstruction/transformation over the long-term, and they challenge our predicted divisions, such as 'hunter-gatherer' or 'farmer.'

Transformative ontologies

In a series of contributions, Ingold (2000, 2011) has spoken out against the idea of a detached mind acting on a separate material world from the outside, and many others have reached similar conclusions by drawing on various sources of inspiration (e.g., Barrett and Ko 2009; Gosden 2005; Hodder 2011; Olsen 2007; Webmoor and Whitmore 2008). Instead, it is argued that people and things co-constitute one another, and that objects are so central to orienting, framing, and carrying forward people's actions that social life would not exist without them. In a more sinister twist, Hodder (2011:162) describes this process as 'entrapment' – once objects, animals, or plants exist in a certain form, they demand specific kinds of interaction, tending, repair, and disposal. Through this mutual accommodation, people come to be entangled in the world in a particular way.

In this view, processes of making and transformation are granted interpretive priority over final products, which are in themselves unstable entities prone to decompose or to bind with other substances in new ways (Ingold 2011:210). The primary metaphor is of flow, of a world in constant formation in which actors are not discrete bundles with defined boundaries, but instead extend outwards as threads within a meshwork of connections. In this way, all kinds of beings continuously bring each other into existence. This state of 'animacy' is ontologically prior to the differentiation of entities such as people or things, and any such congealment of form is in any case temporary (Ingold 2011:26–30, 68–70).

This experience is borne of practical engagement within the world (Ingold 2011:30). For instance, the human body is inherently volatile (e.g., Grosz 1994), changing over a lifetime as we grow, mature, pick up new skills, scar, or lose our eyesight and mobility. As malleable entities, bodies change in response to repeated task patterns and injuries, as well as through aging (Sofaer 2006) and eventually death and decay (Duday 2009). Similarly, new Neolithic technologies of shaping and making, such as house construction or potting, offered new paths into the affordances of the world (e.g., Barrett 2006). These technologies are inherently transformative, bringing together different substances and materials. Clay, as a particularly malleable material, lends itself to explorations of plasticity and shape-shifting, and alongside wood and other substances was brought into people's daily existence in new ways as part of houses, containers, ovens, fences, and so on. The sociality of the animal herds that were now tended offered yet new paths of entanglement (see e.g., Bickle 2009; Whittle 2003:78–106), while the substances of which animals were composed and which they produced – meat, hide, bone, blood, milk, or excrement – found their ways into the material universe as food and sustenance, building materials and fertilizer, clothing, and tools. In short, the Neolithic world was rife with transformations.

However, moving away from a human-centered perspective has implications for understanding directed, planned human action and people's attempts to draw boundaries. With a dominant metaphor of meshworks and flows, these aspects are in danger of becoming sidelined. While processes of making are inevitably exercises of compromise and improvization, once people are characterized as simply 'swept up' in sequences of action or as beginning their tasks merely 'in anticipation of what might emerge' (Ingold 2011:212–14), it is hard to interpret human action as directed, and to recognize constraints, motivations, and goals. Even in a world in constant flow, people reflect on and try to manage this process, although this may be more akin to a journey than to the imposition of a design. While it is appreciated that goals and motivations also emerged from interaction and can be integrated into the model of the meshwork (e.g., Ingold 2011:251, n.7), in practice they often remain sidelined. Yet within the same society, we may find ways of understanding which explicitly rely on categorization, definition, and separation (albeit not necessarily employing distinctions familiar in the modern West) alongside those which stress flow, entanglement, and impermanence. We must reckon with both to capture the full complexity of past ways of being.

In sum, in the Neolithic potentialities of flux may have existed side by side with new drives towards categorization. Both would have been grounded in new bodily experiences and sedimented through new ways of interaction with materials, and in this way would have been experienced as real at an ontological level. New things and practices had the capacity to entrap people in novel ways, but this does not mean that there would have been one coherent outcome. Instead, the same new objects and practices could have created contradictions, tensions, and alternative paths, crucial for understanding processes of change (see also Hofmann 2013a). In what follows, I argue that the Neolithic, as a new way of participating in the flows of existence, was not entirely devoid of attempts to create categories, and that there was a concern with boundaries, surfaces, and skins. However, these were also experienced as precarious and fleeting. I will particularly focus on the human body, its categorization through burial and architecture, and its entanglements with animal bodies and objects.

Bandkeramik categories

For the LBK, efforts at categorization can be suggested, amongst others, for architecture, pottery, and cemetery burial. Monumental wooden longhouses are a key innovation and feature relatively standardized interiors (e.g., Barrett 2006; Coudart 1998; Hofmann 2014; Modderman 1970). Rows of three posts separate spaces into narrow segments (Figure 8.2). The distances and constellations of these posts, as well as details of wall construction, have been used to suggest a typology for Bandkeramik buildings and to identify recurrent combinations of house parts or modules, often believed to be associated with specific functions: one end of the house for storage, the central part for day-to-day life, and the other end as anything from a cattle byre to an ancestral shrine (Bradley 2001; Coudart 1998; Lüning 2009; Modderman 1970:110). In any case, LBK architecture, at least from the middle phases onwards, offered great potential for categorizing people and activities by splitting house interiors into small and regularly arranged spaces. As living surfaces are rarely preserved, we cannot actually assign a specific activity to a specific place. Yet, by creating powerful visual barriers, LBK architecture could define roles, tasks, and the people carrying them out by juxtaposing them in specific, recurrent spatial arrangements.

Similarly, pottery decoration can be used to identify social boundaries at various scales. At one level, pottery with incised linear bands is distinctive enough to lend its name to what we now call the 'Linear Pottery Culture,' setting it apart both from other pottery-using groups and from aceramic hunter-gatherer societies. Within the LBK, regional groups can be identified through preferred motifs or ways of executing bands – through continuous or dotted lines, for example, or using single- or multi-pointed tools. Frontiers between styles can be sharp (e.g., Kerig 2010; Lefranc 2007:26–30). At a smaller scale, preferred motifs can differ within a site. At Vaihingen in southwest Germany, two pottery styles were in use simultaneously, but produced in discrete areas of the village (Bogaard et al. 2011). At an even smaller scale, secondary motifs below the rim – so-called *Zwickel* – are often said to represent potters' marks. *Zwickel* move between house clusters in successive generations and may hence track the movement of female potters upon marriage in a patrilocal system (Krahn 2003; for discussion, see Hofmann 2014). In sum, the intricate vessel surfaces could be made to carry a range of meanings about users and producers, locating them in genealogical sequences of potters with distinctive motifs, as well as in contemporary networks of affinity and boundary marking played out in space.

Finally, burial can be an elaborate system of categorization. In most accounts, cemetery burial is seen as the standard practice, with the dead interred in single graves, crouched on their left, and oriented in a dominant direction. Many have grave goods such as pottery, polished stone tools, or beads, armrings, and belt buckles made from Spondylus, a shell imported from the Mediterranean (Jeunesse 1997; see also Figure 8.3, below). The extent to which interments on any given site actually follow these standard practices has been used to infer social groupings

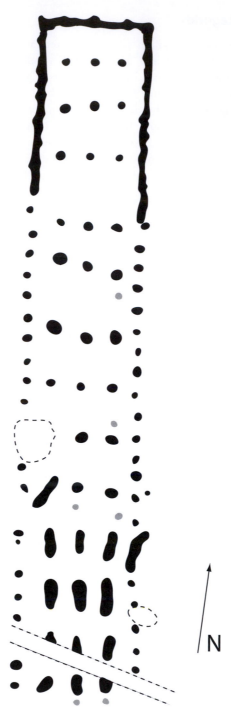

FIGURE 8.2 Plan of an LBK building from Lerchenhaid, Lower Bavaria. After Brink-Kloke (1992:58).

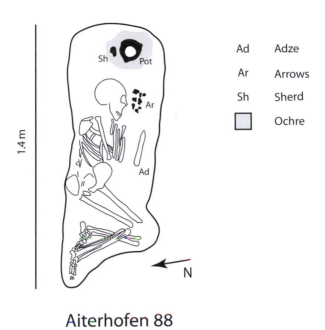

Ad   Adze

Ar   Arrows

Sh   Sherd

☐   Ochre

Aiterhofen 88

FIGURE 8.3 Grave 88 from the Aiterhofen cemetery, Lower Bavaria (after Nieszery 1995:Plate 35).

who expressed their identities by conforming to or deviating from this norm. For example, at the Alsatian site of Vendenheim, burials in an extended, rather than a crouched, position are suggested to be of indigenous hunter-gatherer stock (Boës et al. 2007; Jeunesse 2002:203), and similar arguments regarding orientation have been made elsewhere (e.g., Price and Bentley 2005). It has also been suggested that grave goods may reflect male or female identity, wealth and social status, or hunter-gatherer/herder/farmer divisions (e.g., Jeunesse 1997; Price and Bentley 2005). According to some interpretations, the importance of the cemetery as a space to express distinctions in wealth increases over time (Jeunesse 1997:111–27). Much as with houses, then, the bodies of those buried in cemeteries are seen as reflecting newly created categories of identity. The corpse in the grave, surrounded by goods, can be classified according to a set of oppositions, such as male/female, rich/poor, or farmer/hunter.

On closer examination, however, neither of these devices for categorization is as stable as they at first appear. The interior of Bandkeramik houses, for example, may be used flexibly. Where phosphate analysis has been carried out – admittedly on a small minority of sites (e.g., Hofmann et al. 2012; Stäuble and Lüning 1999) – concentrations do not routinely occur in the same parts of buildings, so some leeway in use existed. In addition, Bandkeramik houses probably stood for only about 20–25 years (see Claßen 2009; Stehli 1989), with a new house constructed in every generation. This, too, provided opportunities for changing the layouts of internal spaces, as well as the size and sturdiness of the building compared to others past and present (Hofmann 2013a). Overall, the house emerges as a site of negotiation – between its inhabitants, between them and other contemporary households, and between current practice, established ways of doing things, and future potentialities. Physically, the imposing Bandkeramik structures were not particularly permanent. It is still debated how long an oak-built house would have lasted (Schmidt et al. 2005), or what happened to houses once they were abandoned. Possibilities include being left to decay (e.g., at Štúrovo, Slovakia; Pavúk 1994:223), being burnt down deliberately (e.g., at Bylany, Bohemia; see Hofmann 2014, chapter 3) or accidentally (e.g., at Frankfurt-Praunheim, Hesse; Veit 1996:120), or having some or most posts removed, perhaps to be re-used in other structures (e.g., at Weisweiler 17, Rhineland; Krahn 2006:23–27). At any particular point, an LBK site would hence comprise houses in various states of construction, repair, and decay. The house emerges as a key composite of diverse materials – wood, reeds, clay, water, twigs, and so on – only ever temporarily congealed.

Pottery, too, does not simply encode static meanings. Although the surfaces of excavated LBK sherds are often very weathered, it is clear that some at least were painted (e.g., Baumann 1965; Novotný 1958:12–14), their red, white, and black decoration echoing the possible painted motifs on house walls (e.g., Marton 2004; Schade-Lindig 2002:177) and the human body in the grave with its red ochre, white shells, and sometimes black colorants (Bickle 2008:194; Pechtl 2011). Color highlights pottery motifs, but the incised lines could be smoothed over again before firing (e.g., Bánffy 2004:258; Kloos 1997:167) or the design could be radically altered by painted motifs which run across the incised lines (Pechtl 2014). Perhaps most striking are the pots which had been entirely coated in birch tar before applying a new motif made of light bark strips, entirely obscuring any original decoration (e.g., Landesamt für Archäologie Sachsen 2010). These complex biographies suggest that the process of continued beautification itself may have been an important aspect, with much of the significance of motifs lying in their application.

The body in the grave, too, is more than an idealized picture of the deceased. Recent work on burial as performance has stressed that key items of material culture, notably ornaments, could be passed on, rather than being deposited. On the one hand, Spondylus armrings may have been a relatively fixed ornament that could not be removed from the upper arm without breakage (Nieszery 1995:185f), the body literally molding around the ring as the individual grew. In contrast, beads and belt buckles of the same material were passed on and many exhibit signs of repairs and re-shaping (e.g., Bonnardin 2009:283–86). Ornaments were recombined and split up as a way to entangle their owners in a range of relationships. Similarly, pottery and other goods could be smashed at the grave side, and sometimes only parts are deposited with the body, the remainder apparently taken away or left on the surface. Most tellingly, the physical body of the deceased was occasionally interfered with, with the grave re-opened and parts of the body reburied higher up in the grave fill (e.g., Sondershausen, Thuringia; Kahlke 2004:55), in separate pits (e.g., Mezőkövesd, Hungary; Kalicz and Koós 2002), or entirely removed from the cemetery (e.g., Gerling 2009:105). LBK people were familiar with and managed the transformations brought on by decay. The work of composing and decomposing the self was a drawn-out process.[1]

Transforming bodies

Actions such as interfering with the decay of the body show an interest with managing flows of substances, rather than exclusively with fixing identity categories in the grave. This is also evident in the alternative burial rites current in the LBK. Cemetery burial was not present in all phases and regions, and in any case seems to have applied to only a proportion of the dead from adjacent settlements. The treatments described in this section, which by their nature are less likely to be preserved, may accordingly have been more widespread.

First among these is the interest in the corpse sometimes exhibited for settlement burials. Here, instances of reburied heads and other bones (e.g., Pariat 2007; Rienäcker 1978) could be the result of either directed intervention or of more accidental disturbances. Researchers in the Paris Basin have recently identified changes in the architecture of the grave pit itself, which allowed the body to decay in an empty space free from sediment, probably under an organic covering. Occasionally, the survivors deliberately interfered with the decaying corpse, moving bones out of anatomical connection (Boës 2000; Thevenet 2004).

More explicitly, processes of decay and re-admixture are also foregrounded in cremation, a rite attested on several LBK cemeteries and probably more frequent in later phases. In the course of a cremation, the body of the deceased and associated grave goods are broken down by the action of fire, a rapid process of managed decay which transforms the body into smoke, calcinated bone, charred tissue, and broken objects (e.g., Oestigaard 1999). Afterwards, the remains are collected up, forming a new, composite substance – burnt-bone-and-things – which is eventually deposited.

Dissolution and admixture also come to the fore in burial rites centered on defleshing. There are now several Bandkeramik sites which have yielded the frag-mented remains of multiple individuals (e.g., Hofmann 2013b). Many come from enclosure ditches such as Menneville in the Paris Basin (Farruggia et al. 1996), Eilsleben in Saxony-Anhalt (Kaufmann 1989), and Ittenheim in Alsace (Lefranc and Boës 2009). The best known and most intensively discussed is Herxheim in the Palatinate, western Germany (Figure 8.4), where this practice has taken on an unprecedented scale (Zeeb-Lanz et al. 2007, 2009). Here, the remains of well over 450 people of all ages and both sexes were unearthed, mostly broken into very small fragments. They were admixed with various materials, some equally frag-mented, and tipped into open sections of a 'pit enclosure,' a circuit of longitudinal pits which were not all open simultaneously, and thus did not form a continuous ditch (Schmidt 2004). Compared to the adjacent settlement, the animal bones from the enclosure, some intensively fragmented, show elevated percentages of cattle, dogs, and fur-bearing animals, while the pottery comprises items imported from over a hundred kilometers away alongside local wares. Grinding stones, flint, and

FIGURE 8.4 Complex 9 from the pit enclosure at Herxheim, Rhineland-Palatinate. Reproduced with permission of Andrea Zeeb-Lanz, Generaldirektion Kulturelles Erbe Rheinland-Pfalz, Direktion Archäologie Speyer.

bone tools are also routinely deposited, and can be broken (Arbogast 2009; Zeeb–Lanz et al. 2009). The resulting assemblages are not carefully arranged, but thoroughly admixed before disposal.

Herxheim is certainly unique in the scale of activity, particularly if, as the excavators suggest, all these depositional events took place in the space of just one or two generations. The site has also been meticulously excavated, allowing for additional observations. For example, human heads were often selected for extended treatment, showing cut marks indicative of scalping and defleshing. The face and lower parts of the skull were then expertly removed, leaving just the calotte (Orschiedt and Haidle 2009). Deliberate defleshing may also have extended to other parts of the body, and cannibalism has been suggested for some of the remains (Boulestin et al. 2009). Most of the bones are so intensively fragmented, however, that marrow extraction is unlikely to have been the goal, while the attention lavished on the meat–poor head suggests other concerns (Orschiedt and Haidle 2009). The debate at Herxheim has therefore perhaps unhelpfully oscillated between those supporting a crisis scenario of mass killings and cannibalism in the face of economic collapse (e.g., Gronenborn 2006) and the reconstruction of a 'cultural crisis,' resulting in the subversion of accepted burial norms (e.g., Zeeb-Lanz 2009; for discussion see Hofmann 2013b). In either case, the human body was seen and experienced as composed of various substances which could be dissolved, transformed and recombined, and these processes could be at least partly controlled. The outcome was a new, composite substance for burial.

Overall, the LBK body was on occasion deliberately broken down. Most of these instances are thought to date relatively late in the LBK sequence, and one could therefore argue that there is a general and possibly increasing trend towards dissolution. Through practices of defleshing, fragmentation, and consumption, which could be more or less controlled and carried out either directly by people, or by a mediator such as fire or earth, the constant flux of materials became an experienced reality. These engagements did not concern human bodies in isolation, but also comprised animals and objects. At this level at least, then, the latter were not ontologically separate and clearly bound off from human beings, but capable of being disentangled and recombined in the same way.[2]

Outlook

With their focus on the assembly, exchange, and dissolution of substances, these practices act as a strong counterpoint to categorization. With this background, categories can only ever be temporary. This does not mean that they had no salience in people's lives, but that they were unstable and had to be constantly enacted and renewed. In the LBK, considerable effort went into these enactments. House construction, routine inhabitation, and decorating the surfaces of bodies and pottery are all relevant here and are subject to constant re-fashioning.

There are hence two aspects we should no longer take for granted. One is the permanence of categorizations. In many of our social models, we tend to see entities such as individuals, households, age or gender groups, lineages, or regional networks as unproblematic and easily reproduced over time. Both social groupings and the identity of individuals – as hunters versus farmers, for example – are often debated in terms of what the 'correct' social scale of analysis is, or of whether a certain practice or item should be connected with one or the other group (discussed e.g., in Bickle and Hofmann 2009). The continued relevance of the categories themselves is rarely questioned. These static boundaries can cause problems for interpreting change and transformation. By focusing on the inherent need to re-fashion these categories through practice, we can appreciate how they may change or even disappear over time (see e.g., Hofmann 2013a).

Secondly, new technologies, such as building houses or making pottery, were not straightforwardly about taming the land or domesticating people. Rather, they offered the potential to become entangled in the world in contrasting and contradictory ways. As such, we can no longer classify some practices as fluid, transformative, and therefore 'Mesolithic,' and others as static, categorizing and 'Neolithic' (see also Robb and Miracle 2007). What may have mattered was their relative capacity for transformation and/or congealment of forms.

At a more general level, the constitution of the human body mirrors the way social relations were organized at other scales, too. Based on suggested building sequences in settlement sites and on continuous, long-term investment in specific fields, it is likely that building plots and agricultural land in the LBK were ideally passed down over the generations (e.g., Bogaard 2004; Claßen 2009; Strien 2010). However, to maintain the social groups associated with these places, individuals and substances also had to move 'sideways,' between contemporaries. For example, it seems that women may often have moved to new communities upon marriage, as suggested by isotopic work (e.g., Bickle and Whittle 2013; Bickle et. al. 2011; Price and Bentley 2005), thus maintaining the fertility and viability of their new social groups. Cattle, too, may occasionally have been exchanged between communities (Knipper 2010:25), as were a whole host of other materials crucial for everyday tasks and for cementing identities and affiliations, amongst others cherts, stone for adzes, and Spondylus shells (see Hofmann 2014, chapter 5). Maintaining possession of land and key substances, while ensuring the continuity of social life through the necessary inflow of outsiders and against the pressures of giving in exchange, was a crucial balancing act. As a consequence, managing flow and change was an inherent part of maintaining groups. Continuity at one level had to be matched by flexibility at another. In such a context, when and how to stress either connection or categorization would have been a matter of negotiation and of balancing out expectations at various social levels.

In this context, the differences between LBK bodies could be either heightened through categorization – by displaying different kinds of bodies with different kinds of artifacts, or by managing routine movements and locations for bodies – or negated, e.g., through dismemberment and admixture. In the latter case, this could take place in the interest of stressing larger-scale groupings, and it seems no accident that in the long run the disappearance of carefully orchestrated individual burial goes hand-in-hand with a rise in collective monuments such as enclosures.

Focusing on the relational aspects of past ontologies has questioned many of our deeply held assumptions about the kinds of categorizations that may have been relevant to Neolithic people, such as culture/nature, farmer/hunter, and human/non-human. Nevertheless, in our search for transformations and meshworks, we should not underestimate the work that went into at least temporarily congealing boundaries, as well as into carefully guiding and managing the processes of their further transformation. Only by recognizing these efforts, and by appreciating that these actions may be contested and open to multiple readings, can we eventually come to understand how shifts in associations, alternative ways of categorizing, and, crucially, different kinds of entanglements may have come into being.[3]

Notes

1 There are interesting parallels between treatments of the human body in death (cremation, deliberate dismemberment, or decay in the grave) and the treatment of abandoned houses (burning, dismantling, or leaving to decay) (see Hofmann 2014, chapter 3). Whittle (2012) also suggests further ways in which LBK houses may have been seen in ways analogous to human bodies.
2 This point can also be made on the basis of clay figurines (Hofmann 2012).
3 I would like to thank Christopher Watts for inviting me to his SAA session and for the opportunity to publish this paper. Gratitude is also due to the Leverhulme Trust for funding the research on which this paper is based as part of an Early Careers Research Fellowship.

Bibliography

Ammerman, Albert, and Luigi Cavalli-Sforza 1984. *The Neolithic Transition and the Genetics of Populations in Europe*. Princeton University Press, Princeton, New Jersey.

Arbogast, Rose-Marie 2009. Les vestiges de faune associés au site et structures d'enceinte du site rubanée de Herxheim (Rhénanie-Palatinat, Allemagne). In *Krisen-Kulturwandel-Kontinuitäten. Zum Ende der Bandkeramik in Mitteleuropa. Beiträge der internationalen Tagung in Herxheim bei Landau (Pfalz) vom 14.-17.06.2007*, edited by Andrea Zeeb-Lanz, pp. 53–60. Marie Leidorf, Rahden.

Bakels, Corrie 1982. The Settlement System of the Dutch Linearbandkeramik. *Analecta Praehistorica Leidensia* 15:31–44.

Bánffy, Eszter 2004. *The 6th Millennium BC Boundary in Western Transdanubia and its Role in the Central European Neolithic Transition (The Szentgyörgyvölgy-Pityerdomb Settlement)*. Archaeological Institute of the Hungarian Academy of Sciences, Budapest.

Barnard, Alan 2007. From Mesolithic to Neolithic Modes of Thought. In *Going Over: The Mesolithic-Neolithic Transition in North-west Europe*, edited by Alasdair Whittle and Vicky Cummings, pp. 5–19. Oxford University Press, Oxford.

Barrett, John 2006. A Perspective on the Early Architecture of Western Europe. In *Constructing Power – Architecture, Ideology and Social Practice*, edited by Joseph Maran, Carsten Juwig, Hermann Schwengel, and Ulrich Thaler, pp. 15–30. Lit, Hamburg.

Barrett, John, and Ilong Ko 2009. A Phenomenology of Landscape. A Crisis in British Landscape Archaeology? *Journal of Social Archaeology* 9:275–94.

Baumann, Wilfried 1965. Bemalte Gefäßscherben der Bandkeramik aus Dresden-Nickern. *Ausgrabunden und Funde* 10:65–66.

Bentley, R. Alexander, Rüdiger Krause, T. Douglas Price, and Bruno Kaufmann 2003. Human Mobility at the Early Neolithic Settlement of Vaihingen, Germany: Evidence from Strontium Isotope Analysis. *Archaeometry* 45:481–96.

Bickle, Penny 2008. "The Life and Death of the Longhouse: Daily Life during and after the early Neolithic in the River Valleys of the Paris Basin." Unpublished Ph.D. dissertation, Department of Archaeology, Cardiff University.

——(2009). Scene by the Brook: Early Neolithic Landscape Perspectives in the Paris Basin. In *Creating Communities: New Advances in Central European Neolithic Research*, edited by Daniela Hofmann and Penny Bickle, pp. 132–41. Oxbow, Oxford.

Bickle, Penny, and Daniela Hofmann 2009. Introduction: Researching across Borders. In *Creating Communities: New Advances in Central European Neolithic Research*, edited by Daniela Hofmann and Penny Bickle, pp. 1–10. Oxbow, Oxford.

Bickle, Penny, Daniela Hofmann, R. Alexander Bentley, Robert Hedges, Julie Hamilton, Fernando Laiginhas, Geoff Nowell, D. Graham Pearson, Gisela Grupe, and Alasdair Whittle 2011. Community Heterogeneity in the Linearbandkeramik: Isotope Evidence in its Archaeological Context at Aiterhofen (Bavaria, Germany). *Antiquity* 85:1243–58.

Bickle, Penny, and Alasdair Whittle (editors) 2013. *The First Farmers of Central Europe: Diversity in LBK Lifeways*. Oxbow, Oxford (in press).

Bird-David, Nurit 1990. The Giving Environment: Another Perspective on the Economic System of Gatherer-Hunters. *Current Anthropology* 31:189–96.

Boës, Eric 2000. Evolution des comportements funéraires entre les 6e et 5e millénaires avant J.-C. en Alsace. *Cahiers Alsaciens d'Archéologie, d'Art et d'Histoire* 43:5–18.

Boës, Eric, Christian Jeunesse, Rose-Marie Arbogast, Philippe Lefranc, Michel Mauvilly, François Schneikert, and Isabelle Sidéra 2007. Vendenheim 'Le Haut du Coteau' (Bas-Rhin): remarques sur l'organisation interne d'une nécropole du Néolithique ancien danubien. In *Sociétés néolithiques. Des faits archéologiques aux fonctionnements socio-économiques. Actes du 27e colloque interrégional sur le Néolithique (Neuchâtel, 1 et 2 octobre 2005)*, edited by Marie Besse, pp. 279–83. Cahiers d'Archéologie Romande, Lausanne.

Bogaard, Amy 2004. *Neolithic Farming in Central Europe. An Archaeobotanical Study of Crop Husbandry Practices*. Routledge, London.

——(2012). *Plant Use and Crop Husbandry in an Early Neolithic Village: Vaihingen an der Enz, Baden-Württemberg*. Habelt, Bonn.

Bogaard, Amy, Rüdiger Krause, and Hans-Christoph Strien 2011. Towards a Social Geography of Cultivation and Plant Use in an Early Farming Community: Vaihingen an der Enz, South-west Germany. *Antiquity* 85:395–416.

Bogucki, Peter 1988. *Forest Farmers and Stockherders: Early Agriculture and its Consequences in North-central Europe*. Cambridge University Press, Cambridge.

Bonnardin, Sandrine 2009. *La parure funéraire du Néolithique ancien dans les Bassins parisien et rhénan. Rubané, Hinkelstein et Villeneuve-Saint-Germain*. Société Préhistorique Française, Paris.

Boulestin, Bruno, Andrea Zeeb-Lanz, Christian Jeunesse, Fabian Haack, Rose-Marie Arbogast, and Anthony Denaire 2009. Mass Cannibalism in the Linear Pottery Culture at Herxheim (Palatinate, Germany). *Antiquity* 83:968–82.

Bradley, Richard 2001. Orientations and Origins: A Symbolic Dimension to the Longhouse in Neolithic Europe. *Antiquity* 75:50–56.

Brink-Kloke, Henriette 1992. *Drei Siedlungen der Linienbandkeramik in Niederbayern. Studien zu den Befunden und zur Keramik von Alteglofsheim-Köfering, Landshut-Sallmannsberg und Straubing-Lerchenhaid*. Marie Leidorf, Buch am Erlbach.

Claßen, Erich 2009. Settlement History, Land Use and Social Networks of Early Neolithic Communities in Western Germany. In *Creating Communities: New Advances in Central European Neolithic Research*, edited by Daniela Hofmann and Penny Bickle, pp. 95–110. Oxbow, Oxford.

Coudart, Anick 1998. *Architecture et société néolithique. L'unité et la variance de la maison danubienne*. Editions de la Maison des Sciences de l'Homme, Paris.

Duday, Henry 2009. *The Archaeology of the Dead: Lectures in Archaeothanatology*. Oxbow, Oxford.

Ebersbach, Renate 2006. 17 Generationen bandkeramische Bauern in der Mörlener Bucht. GIS-gestützte Modelle der Landnutzung. *Berichte der Kommission für Archäologische Landesforschung in Hessen* 8:11–22.

Farruggia, Jean-Paul 2002. Une crise majeure de la civilisation du Néolithique danubien des années 5100 avant notre ère. *Archeologické Rozhledy* 54:44–98.

Farruggia, Jean-Paul, Yves Guichard, and Lamys Hachem 1996. Les ensembles funéraires rubanés de Menneville 'derrière le village' (Aisne). In *La Bourgogne entre les Bassins rhénan, rhodanien et parisien: carrefour ou frontière? Actes du 18e Colloque interrégional sur le Néolithique, Dijon 25–27 octobre 1991*, edited by Pascal Duhamel, pp. 119–74. Ministère de la Culture, Dijon.

Gerling, Claudia 2009. Schwetzingen, ein 'reguläres' Gräberfeld der jüngeren Linearbandkeramik. In *Krisen-Kulturwandel-Kontinuitäten. Zum Ende der Bandkeramik in Mitteleuropa. Beiträge der internationalen Tagung in Herxheim bei Landau (Pfalz) vom 14.-17.06.2007*, edited by Andrea Zeeb-Lanz, pp. 103–10. Marie Leidorf, Rahden.

Golitko, Mark, and Lawrence Keeley 2006. Beating Ploughshares Back into Swords: Warfare in the Linearbandkeramik. *Antiquity* 81:332–42.

Gosden, Chris 2005. What Do Objects Want? *Journal of Archaeological Method and Theory* 12:193–211.

Gronenborn, Detlef 1999. A Variation on a Basic Theme: The Transition to Farming in Southern Central Europe. *Journal of World Prehistory* 13:123–210.

——(2006). Climate Change and Socio-political Crises: Some Cases from Neolithic Central Europe. *Journal of Conflict Archaeology* 2:13–32.

——(2010). Climate, Crises, and the 'Neolithisation' of Central Europe between IRD-Events 6 and 4. In *Die Neolithisierung Mitteleuropas. Internationale Tagung Mainz, 24.-26. Juni 2005*, edited by Detlef Gronenborn and Jörg Petrasch, pp. 61–80. Verlag des RGZM, Mainz.

Grosz, Elizabeth 1994. *Volatile Bodies: Toward a Corporeal Feminism.* Indiana University Press, Bloomington.

Haak, Wolfgang, Oleg Balanovsky, Juan Sanchez, Sergey Koshel, Valery Zaporozhchenko, Christina Adler, Clio Der Sarkissian, Guido Brandt, Carolin Schwarz, Nicole Nicklisch, Veit Dreseley, Barbara Fritsch, Elena Balanovska, Richard Villems, Harald Meller, Kurt Alt, Alan Cooper, and the Genographic Consortium 2010. Ancient DNA from European Early Neolithic Farmers Reveals their Near Eastern Affinities. *Public Library of Science Biology* 8:e1000536.

Hachem, Lamys 2000. New Observations on the Bandkeramik House and Social Organisation. *Antiquity* 74:308–12.

——(2011). *Le site néolithique de Cuiry-lès-Chaudardes I: De l'analyse de la faune à la structuration sociale.* Marie Leidorf, Rahden.

Hodder, Ian 1990. *The Domestication of Europe: Structure and Contingency in Neolithic Societies.* Blackwell, Oxford.

——(2011). Human-Thing Entanglement: Towards an Integrated Archaeological Perspective. *Journal of the Royal Anthropological Institute* 17:154–77.

Hofmann, Daniela 2012. The Life and Death of Linearbandkeramik Figurines. In *Visualising the Neolithic: Abstraction, Figuration, Performance, Representation*, edited by Andrew Cochrane and Andrew Jones, pp. 226–42. Oxbow, Oxford.

——(2013a). Narrating the House: The Transformation of Longhouses in Early Neolithic Europe. In *Memories Can't Wait: Memory, Myth and Long-term Landscape Inhabitation*, edited by Adrian Chadwick and Catriona Gibson. Oxbow, Oxford (forthcoming).

——(2013b). The Burnt, the Whole and the Broken: Funerary Variability in the Linearbandkeramik. In *Death Embodied: Archaeological Approaches to the Treatment of the Corpse*, edited by Zoe Devlin and Emma-Jayne Graham. Oxbow, Oxford (forthcoming).

——(2014). *Longhouse People: Life, Death and Transformation in the Early Neolithic Linearbandkeramik Culture of Central Europe.* Oxford University Press, Oxford (forthcoming).

Hofmann, Daniela, R. Alexander Bentley, Penny Bickle, Amy Bogaard, John Crowther, Philippa Cullen, Linda Fibiger, Gisela Grupe, Julie Hamilton, Robert Hedges, Richard

Macphail, Geoff Nowell, Joachim Pechtl, Melanie Salque, Michael Schultz, and Alasdair Whittle 2012. Kinds of Diversity and Scales of Analysis in the LBK. In *Siedlungsstruktur und Kulturwandel in der Bandkeramik. Beiträge der internationalen Tagung 'Neue Fragen zur Bandkeramik oder alles beim Alten?!'*, edited by Sabine Wolfram, Harald Stäuble, Maria Cladders, and Thomas Tischendorf, pp. 103–13. Arbeits-und Forschungsberichte zur Sächsischen Bodendenkmalpflege, Dresden.

Ingold, Tim 2000. *The Perception of the Environment: Essays in Livelihood, Dwelling and Skill.* Routledge, London.

——(2011). *Being Alive: Essays on Movement, Knowledge and Description.* Routledge, London.

Jeunesse, Christian 1997. *Pratiques funéraires au Néolithique ancien. Sépultures et nécropoles danubiennes 5500–4900 av. J.-C.* Editions Errance, Paris.

——(2002). Synthèse. In *Vendenheim 'le Haut du Coteau'. Une nécropole du Néolithique ancien. Document final de synthèse. Tome 1: texte*, pp. 191–210. Unpublished document, Service Régional de l'Archéologie d'Alsace, Strasbourg.

Kahlke, Hans-Dietrich 2004. *Sondershausen und Bruchstedt. Zwei Gräberfelder mit älterer Linienbandkeramik in Thüringen.* Thüringisches Landesamt für Archäologische Denkmalpflege, Weimar.

Kalicz, Nándor, and Judit Koós 2002. Eine Siedlung mit ältestneolithischen Gräbern in Nordostungarn. *Preistoria Alpina* 37:45–79.

Kaufmann, Dieter 1989. Kultische Äußerungen im Frühneolithikum des Elbe-Saale Gebietes. In *Religion und Kult in ur-und frühgeschichtlicher Zeit*, edited by Friedrich Schlette and Dieter Kaufmann, pp. 111–39. Akademie-Verlag, Berlin.

Kent, Susan 1989. Cross-cultural Perceptions of Farmers as Hunters and the Value of Meat. In *Farmers as Hunters: The Implications of Sedentism*, edited by Susan Kent, pp. 1–17. Cambridge University Press, Cambridge.

Kerig, Tim 2010. Grenzen ziehen: zur Chronologie regionaler und sozialer Unterschiede im hessischen Altneolithikum. In *Die Neolithisierung Mitteleuropas. Internationale Tagung Mainz, 24.-26. Juni 2005*, edited by Detlef Gronenborn and Jörg Petrasch, pp. 475–86. Verlag des RGZM, Mainz.

Kienlin, Tobias 2006. Von Jägern und Bauern, Theorie(n) und Daten: Anmerkungen zur Neolithisierungsdebatte. *Prähsitorische Zeitschrift* 81:135–52.

Kloos, Ulrich 1997. Die Tonware. In *Ein Siedlungsplatz der Ältesten Bandkeramik in Bruchenbrücken, Stadt Friedberg/Hessen*, edited by Jens Lüning, pp. 151–255. Habelt, Bonn.

Knipper, Corina 2010. Die räumliche Organisation der linearbandkeramischen Tierhaltung. Beiträge von Isotopenanalysen. In *Isotopie und DNA – biografische Annäherung an namenlose vorgeschichtliche Skelette?*, edited by Harald Meller and Kurt Alt, pp. 77–86. Landesmuseum für Vorgeschichte, Halle.

Krahn, Christiane 2003. Überlegungen zum Interaktionssystem der bandkeramischen Siedlungen auf der Aldenhovener Platte. In *Archäologische Perspektiven. Analysen und Interpretationen im Wandel. Festschrift für Jens Lüning zum 65. Geburtstag*, edited by Jörg Eckert, Ursula Eisenhauer, and Andreas Zimmermann, pp. 515–44. Marie Leidorf, Rahden.

——(2006). *Die bandkeramischen Siedlungen im oberen Schlangengrabental.* Philipp von Zabern, Mainz.

Landesamt für Archäologie Sachsen 2010. *Funde, die es nicht geben dürfte. Brunnen der Jungsteinzeit in Sachsen. Eine Sonderausstellung des Landesamtes für Archäologie im Stadtgeschichtlichen Museum Leipzig.* Landesamt für Archäologie Sachsen, Leipzig.

Lefranc, Philippe 2007. *La céramique du Rubané en Alsace: Contribution à l'étude des groupes régionaux du Néolithique ancien dans la pleine du Rhin supérieur.* Université Marc Bloch, Strasbourg.

Lefranc, Philippe, and Eric Boës 2009. Les restes humains manipulés du site rubané d'Ittenheim 'Complex Sportif' (Bas-Rhin). In *Krisen-Kulturwandel-Kontinuitäten. Zum Ende der Bandkeramik in Mitteleuropa. Beiträge der internationalen Tagung in Herxheim bei Landau (Pfalz) vom 14.-17.06.2007*, edited by Andrea Zeeb-Lanz, pp. 197–211. Marie Leidorf, Rahden.

Lüning, Jens 1988. Frühe Bauern in Mitteleuropa im 6. und 5. Jahrtausend v. Chr. *Jahrbuch des Römisch-Germanischen Zentralmuseums Mainz* 35:27–93.

———(2009). Bandkeramische Kultanlagen. In *Krisen-Kulturwandel-Kontinuitäten. Zum Ende der Bandkeramik in Mitteleuropa. Beiträge der internationalen Tagung in Herxheim bei Landau (Pfalz) vom 14.-17.06.2007*, edited by Andrea Zeeb-Lanz, pp. 129–90. Marie Leidorf, Rahden.

Marton, Tibor 2004. Material Finds from Balatonszárszó, Neolithic Settlement: Connections within and without the TLPC Territory. *Antaeus* 27:81–86.

Midgley, Magdalena 2005. *The Monumental Cemeteries of Prehistoric Europe*. Tempus, Stroud.

Modderman, Pieter 1970. Linearbandkeramik aus Elsloo und Stein. *Analecta Praehistorica Leidensia* 3:1–217.

Nieszery, Norbert 1995. *Linearbandkeramische Gräberfelder in Bayern*. Marie Leidorf, Espelkamp.

Novotný, Bohuslav 1958. *Die Slowakei in der jüngeren Steinzeit (Textteil, Übersetzung L. Kramerová)*. Archeologický ústav Slovenskej akadémie vied v Nitre, Bratislava.

Oestigaard, Terje 1999. Cremations as Transformations: When the Dual Cultural Hypothesis Was Cremated and Carried Away in Urns. *European Journal of Archaeology* 2:345–64.

Olsen, Bjørnar 2007. Keeping Things at Arm's Length: A Genealogy of Asymmetry. *World Archaeology* 39:579–88.

Orschiedt, Jörg, and Miriam Haidle 2009. Hinweise auf eine Krise? Die menschlichen Skelettreste von Herxheim. In *Krisen-Kulturwandel-Kontinuitäten. Zum Ende der Bandkeramik in Mitteleuropa. Beiträge der internationalen Tagung in Herxheim bei Landau (Pfalz) vom 14.-17.06.2007*, edited by Andrea Zeeb-Lanz, pp. 41–52. Marie Leidorf, Rahden.

Pariat, Jean-Gabriel 2007. *Des morts sans tombe? Le cas des ossements humains en contexte non sépulcral en Europe tempéré entre les 6e et 3e millénnaires av. J.-C.* Archaeopress, Oxford.

Pavúk, Juraj 1994. *Štúrovo. Ein Siedlungsplatz der Kultur mit Linearkeramik und der Želiezovce-Gruppe*. Archäologisches Institut der Slowakischen Akademie der Wissenschaften, Nitra.

Pechtl, Joachim 2011. Die neolithische Graphitnutzung in Südbayern. Mit einem Beitrag von Florian Eibl. In *Vorträge des 29. Niederbayerischen Archäologentages*, edited by Karl Schmotz, pp. 349–432. Marie Leidorf, Rahden.

———(2014). Linearbandkeramik Pottery and Society. In *The Oxford Handbook of Neolithic Europe*, edited by Chris Fowler, Jan Harding, and Daniela Hofmann. Oxford University Press, Oxford (forthcoming).

Price, T. Douglas, and R. Alexander Bentley 2005. Human Mobility in the Linearbandkeramik: An Archaeometric Approach. In *Die Bandkeramik im 21. Jahrhundert. Symposium in der Abtei Brauweiler bei Köln vom 16.9.-19.9.2002*, edited by Jens Lüning, Christiane Frirdich, and Andreas Zimmermann, pp. 203–15. Marie Leidorf, Rahden.

Price, T. Douglas, R. Alexander Bentley, Jens Lüning, Detlef Gronenborn, and Joachim Wahl 2001. Prehistoric Human Migration in the Linearbandkeramik of Central Europe. *Antiquity* 75:593–603.

Rienäcker, Christa 1978. Die neolithische Besiedlung Quedlinburgs. *Jahresschrift für Mitteldeutsche Vorgeschichte* 62:109–33.

Robb, John, and Preston Miracle 2007. Beyond 'Migration' Versus 'Acculturation': New Models for the Spread of Agriculture. In *Going Over: The Mesolithic-Neolithic Transition in North-west Europe*, edited by Alasdair Whittle and Vicky Cummings, pp. 99–115. Oxford University Press, Oxford.

Russell, Nerissa 2002. The Wild Side of Animal Domestication. *Society & Animals* 10:285–302.

Schade, Christoph 2004. *Die Besiedlungsgeschichte der Bandkeramik in der Mörlener Bucht/Wetterau. Zentralität und Peripherie, Haupt-und Nebenorte, Siedlungsverbände*. Habelt, Bonn.

Schade-Lindig, Sabine 2002. *Das Früh-und Mittelneolithikum im Neckarmündungsgebiet*. Habelt, Bonn.

Scharl, Silviane 2004. *Die Neolithisierung Europas. Ausgewählte Modelle und Hypothesen*. Marie Leidorf, Rahden.

Schmidt, Burghart, Wolfgang Gruhle, Oliver Rück, and Klaus Freckmann 2005. Zur Dauerhaftigkeit bandkeramischer Häuser im Rheinland (5300–4950 v. Chr.) – eine Interpretation dendrochronologischer und bauhistorischer Befunde. In *Klimaveränderung und Kulturwandel in neolithischen Gesellschaften Mitteleuropas, 6700–2200 v. Chr.*, edited by Detlef Gronenborn, pp. 151–70. Verlag des RGZM, Mainz.

Schmidt, Katja 2004. Das bandkeramische Erdwerk von Herxheim bei Landau, Kreis Südliche Weinstraße. Untersuchung der Erdwerksgräben. *Germania* 82:333–49.

Sofaer, Joanna 2006. *The Body as Material Culture: A Theoretical Osteoarchaeology*. Cambridge University Press, Cambridge.

Stäuble, Harald, and Jens Lüning 1999. Phosphatanalysen in bandkeramischen Häusern. *Archäologisches Korrespondenzblatt* 29:165–87.

Stehli, Petar 1989. Zur relativen und absoluten Chronologie der Bandkeramik in Mitteleuropa. In *Bylany Seminar 1987: Collected Papers*, edited by Jan Rulf, pp. 69–78. Archeologický Ústav CSAV, Prague.

Strien, Hans-Christoph 2010. Demographische und erbrechtliche Überlegungen zur bandkeramischen Familienstruktur. In *Familie – Verwandtschaft – Sozialstrukturen: Sozialarchäologische Forschungen zu neolithischen Befunden*, edited by Erich Claßen, Thomas Doppler, and Britta Ramminger, pp. 71–80. Welt und Erde, Kerpen-Loogh.

Svoboda, Jiří 2008. The Mesolithic of the Middle Danube and Upper Elbe Rivers. In *Mesolithic Europe*, edited by Geoff Bailey and Penny Spikins, pp. 221–37. Cambridge University Press, Cambridge.

Thevenet, Corinne 2004. Une relecture des pratiques funéraires du Rubané récent et final du Bassin parisien: l'exemple des fosses sépulcrales dans la vallée de l'Aisne. *Bulletin de la Société Préhistorique Française* 101:815–26.

Veit, Ulrich 1996. *Studien zum Problem der Siedlungsbestattung im europäischen Neolithikum. Tübinger Schriften zur ur-und frühgeschichtlichen Archäologie*. Waxmann, Münster.

Webmoor, Timothy, and Christopher Whitmore 2008. Things Are Us! A Commentary on Human/Thing Relations under the Banner of a 'Social' Archaeology. *Norwegian Archaeological Review* 41:53–70.

Whittle, Alasdair 1996. *Europe in the Neolithic: The Creation of New Worlds*. Cambridge University Press, Cambridge.

——(2001). From Mobility to Sedentism: Change by Degrees. In *From the Mesolithic to the Neolithic. Proceedings of the International Archaeological Conference Held in the Damjanich Museum of Szolnok, Sept. 22–27 1996*, edited by Robert Kertész and Janos Makkay, pp. 447–51. Archaeolingua, Budapest.

——(2003). *The Archaeology of People: Dimensions of Neolithic Life*. Routledge, London.

——(2009). The People Who Lived in Longhouses: What's the Big Idea? In *Creating Communities: New Advances in Central European Neolithic Research*, edited by Daniela Hofmann and Penny Bickle, pp. 249–63. Oxbow, Oxford.

——(2012). Being Alive and Being Dead: House and Grave in the LBK. In *Image, Memory and Monumentality: Archaeological Engagements with the Material World (Papers in Honour of Richard Bradley)*, edited by Andrew Jones, Joshua Pollard, Mike Allen, and Julie Gardiner, pp. 194–206. Oxbow, Oxford.

Zeeb-Lanz, Andrea 2009. Gewaltszenarien oder Sinnkrise? Die Grubenanlage von Herxheim und das Ende der Bandkeramik. In *Krisen-Kulturwandel-Kontinuitäten. Zum Ende der Bandkeramik in Mitteleuropa. Beiträge der internationalen Tagung in Herxheim bei Landau (Pfalz) vom 14.-17.06.2007*, edited by Andrea Zeeb-Lanz, pp. 87–101. Marie Leidorf, Rahden.

Zeeb-Lanz, Andrea, Fabian Haack, Rose-Marie Arbogast, Miriam Haidle, Christian Jeunesse, Jörg Orschiedt, and Dirk Schimmelpfennig 2007. Außergewöhnliche Deponierungen der Bandkeramik – die Grubenanlage von Herxheim. Vorstellung einer Auswahl von Komplexen mit menschlichen Skelettresten. Keramik und andere Artefaktgruppen. *Germania* 85:199–274.

Zeeb-Lanz, Andrea, Rose-Marie Arbogast, Fabian Haack, Miriam Haidle, Christian Jeunesse, Jörg Orschiedt, Dirk Schimmelpfennig, and Samuel van Willigen 2009. The LBK Settlement with Pit Enclosure at Herxheim near Landau (Palatinate): First Results. In *Creating Communities: New Advances in Central European Neolithic Research*, edited by Daniela Hofmann and Penny Bickle, pp. 202–19. Oxbow, Oxford.

Zvelebil, Marek 2004. The Many Origins of the LBK. In *LBK Dialogues: Studies in the Formation of the Linear Pottery Culture*, edited by Alena Lukes and Marek Zvelebil, pp. 183–205. Archaeopress, Oxford.

9

RELATIONAL COMMUNITIES IN PREHISTORIC BRITAIN

Oliver J. T. Harris

Introduction

How should we approach communities in the past? Should we consider them the natural result of people living together, perhaps, or the specific outcomes of people's practices? Should we be concerned with our etic attempts to define communities in the past, or should it be a search for the more emic dimensions of community that matter to us? All of these questions have been manifest in the extensive discussions of community that have taken place in archaeology over the last decade and more. What has underlain almost all of them (Pauketat 2008 is a notable exception) is the view that communities are solely collections of human beings. In contrast, and in keeping with the theme of this volume, this chapter examines community as a relational concept. This means focusing not simply on what human beings do, but rather on the interweaving relations between people, things, places, landscapes, animals, and plants. In doing so, it becomes apparent that communities are made up of all of these different constituents, rather than just people alone.

Taking a community-scale perspective in archaeology is useful, I suggest, as it allows us to begin to tackle wide-ranging, long-term, and manifest differences between different groups and different time periods, in a way that concentrating on personal identity does not always allow. People, things, animals, and communities are always in a state of becoming, and depending on the scale of analysis selected, we can choose to focus on the becoming of communities, or on the becoming of their constituent parts; here I choose communities.

In this chapter, I aim to explore some of the ways in which a relational approach can help us to better understand the communities that formed the pasts we excavate as archaeologists. In particular, I intend to demonstrate the usefulness of this approach through a series of thumbnail examples from Neolithic and Bronze Age Britain.

I am deliberately taking a large-scale view here, in order to look at historical differences in how communities manifested themselves relationally through time. In so doing, I will tack between specific small-scale examples and general themes. Of course, this will mean that much variation within the different periods will be put to one side, and will need to be explored elsewhere. This sacrifice is necessary for breadth of coverage in a short paper.

Communities in archaeology

Before we move to examining in more detail the relational approach I want to take, it is worth saying something about the ways in which archaeologists have approached the notion of community. I will not attempt a full-scale review of the literature here, as I have done this elsewhere (see Harris 2012), but it is worth pulling out a few key themes that have emerged in studies of past communities. The first is the emphasis, in the Americas particularly, on the way communities emerge through people's active practices (e.g., papers in Canuto and Yaeger [eds.] 2000; Varian and Potter [eds.] 2008). This approach strongly contrasts with some older characterizations of community that saw it as the natural outcome of people living together (e.g., Kolb and Snead 1997). Community, for this generation of scholars, is a much more dynamic concept, incorporating both real and imagined aspects and often operating at multiple scales (e.g., Yaeger 2000). In Europe meanwhile, interesting approaches to community have focused on the ways in which different kinds of community draw on landscape features (e.g., Moore 2007) or particular kinds of architecture (e.g., Whittle 2003). The term 'community' on both sides of the Atlantic has been expanded to include the notion of 'communities of practice,' drawn from the work of Lave and Wenger (1991; see also Wenger 1998). In particular, this has been applied to aspects of pottery production to examine how shared practices link people across other kinds of group boundaries (e.g., Kohring 2011; Sassaman and Rudolphi 2001).

There is much to applaud in this work, including its recognition of the contingent nature of community, the acknowledgement that communities are produced through action, rather than being the passive outcomes of other practices, and the complex and multi-scaled nature of community. There are also a number of difficulties, however, with how the term has been used, and in each case I suggest this difficulty emerges precisely because the approaches taken to community have not been explicitly relational. Although there are others that are fully worthy of discussion there are two specific difficulties that I want to concentrate on here. First, there has not been sufficient attention paid to the political uses of the term 'community' in the present. As Gerald Creed (2006) has noted, there has been almost an obsession with community in certain circles, and the term is regularly used by politicians to evoke a somehow timeless, yet absent, form of sociable sociality. The 'failure' of communities and the lack of community 'spirit' are constantly hailed as playing crucial roles in the social ills of our day. If only we had communities with 'oomph,' as the Prime Minister of Great Britain, David Cameron, called for in a speech in July 2010, then everything (allegedly) would be okay. As archaeologists have long realized (e.g., Shanks and Tilley 1987), our work has political implications in the present. If we do not take a critical stance on community, we risk legitimating this modern obsession by providing a historical foothold for this image of timeless sociality. In talking and writing about community, therefore, it is incumbent upon archaeologists to consider not only the positive aspects of community, but also the negative ones.

Second, if we are to recognize the complexity of past communities, their differences from those in the present, and thus challenge the ways in which politicians use the term to evoke an absent and happy past, we have to give non-humans their due. This is essential because it automatically begins the job of historicizing the communities we study, and demonstrating their differences from the human-centric, timeless, versions of the present, which in themselves are always more apparent than real. Enacting a relational approach forces us to take seriously the role of non-humans (of all kinds) within these communities. This is because the relations themselves are what constitute both human and non-human, and thus community becomes distributed across a range of different constituents rather than being a purely human preserve.

Both these challenges to studying communities in archaeology call for a relational approach. However, such an approach obviously covers all manner of potential perspectives from Latourian networks, via Strathernian dividuals, to Deleuzian assemblages. How should we plot our way through this tangled set of perspectives, and how will they help us improve our understanding of community?

A relational approach to community

As already noted, there are a number of different ways that archaeologists have chosen to approach archaeology from a relational perspective. Amongst the earliest attempts to do so were accounts of personhood (e.g., Brück 2001; Chapman 2000; Fowler 2000, 2001; Thomas 2002; Whittle 2003) that drew on Marilyn Strathern's (1988) work in Melanesia (alongside other anthropological accounts, e.g., Busby 1997) to problematize our most basic understandings of identity. Eschewing notions of the bounded individual in non-Modern, non-Western contexts, these approaches have provided an outstanding resource for critiquing views of identity. When approaching the concept of community, however, they are more problematic (cf. Harris 2012). Because of the emphasis on personhood, the active role for material things (as well as animals and plants) is clearest when the object in question is incorporated within, or stands as a metaphor for, people's bodies and identities. As I will suggest below, it is not necessary for this to be the case for an object or an animal to play an active part in the relations that constitute community.

A second line of relational thought has drawn extensively on the work of Bruno Latour (1993, 1999, 2005; for archaeological applications, see e.g., Jones 2002; various papers in Knappett and Malafouris [eds.] 2008; Whitridge 2004). Perhaps the most internally coherent of these approaches is the emerging symmetrical school, which includes amongst others Michael Shanks (e.g., 2007), Tim Webmoor (e.g., 2007) and Chris Witmore (e.g., 2007; see also Webmoor and Witmore 2008). These archaeologists have argued for a symmetrical relationship between people and things, and that we should not automatically presume that action, intentionality, and agency are the sole preserve of humans in whatever society (or "collective," in Latourian terms) we are studying. Instead, agency here is an emergent feature of relationships between humans and non-humans, and both can be agents (or "actants," to be Latourian again). This separation is a reaction against the "modern constitution," as Latour (1993) calls it – the tendency for people in modernity to artificially separate people and things, culture and nature, and mind and body, into two opposed camps. Archaeologies of community that have emphasised the role of humans exclusively, are thus implicitly relying upon these oppositions. In contrast, a move towards this relational approach fundamentally disrupts assumptions about the centrality of humans to the communities we study. Having accepted the Latourian point that we need to start from a position that does not oppose people and things, it is difficult to avoid the conclusion that our concept of community needs to be widened.

The Latourian position has been critiqued by Tim Ingold (e.g., 2008, 2011, 2012), however, both for its opaque language and for a central conceptual difficulty. Ingold argues that Latour and his followers hold that relations always exist between pre-existing entities (whether human or non-human). So, in Latour's (1999) famous example, the rifle and the person, which together produce a network capable of acting in a particular way (shooting), pre-exist their encounter. They are not produced through relations, in other words, but simply altered by them. This reading of Latour's work is shared with other writers (e.g., Alberti and Marshall 2009), but not, interestingly, by symmetrical archaeologists. For example, Witmore (2007:549) remarks that "archaeology begins with mixtures," drawing attention to how relations precede the emergence of either humans or non-humans for Latour. Similarly, philosopher Graham Harman (2009) has identified Latour as a philosopher of relations "all the way down." Indeed, this is his principal critique of Latour. That said, Harman (in Latour et al. 2011:29) does recognize that two different readings of Latour are possible, describing them as a paradox, if a potentially productive one.

A more significant problem, I suggest, lies in the way in which Latour conceives of his networks as static. Taking the Harman reading of Latour literally means that any change in a network does not merely alter the existing structures, but rather produces a new network all together (Harman 2009:129; cf. De Landa 2006). This is clearly problematic when studying past communities as it would mean that any change in the community (e.g., the death of an individual or, in my terms, a single pot being smashed) would result in a whole new community. This is demonstrably not the case; indeed, as I have suggested elsewhere, one of the key things about non-humans is their ability to allow communities to persist through time (Harris 2012). What Latour lacks, therefore, is a sense of flow or change through time, and inspirational as his accounts are, like those of symmetrical archaeologists, they will not let us address communities relationally as fully as is required. Of course this approach to networks, and indeed this reading of Latour, is only one of several that are possible. There are multiple alternative approaches that raise their own issues (for a good summary see Knappett 2011). I will not detail these here for reasons of space, and I will concentrate instead upon the particular perspective I want to develop in response to the Latourian position.

From networks to assemblages

In response to Latour, I suggest, therefore, that we require turning to another mode of relationality. Rather than networks, I suggest that we concentrate on assemblages. The term 'assemblage' emerges from the work of Deleuze and Guattari (e.g., 2004) and has been used by a range of thinkers to imagine a world of relations in flux and in flow (in archaeology, see, e.g., Conneller 2011). Assemblages are clusters of affective bodies, whether human, non-human, animal, plant, or whatever, capable of changing those around them (Bennett 2010:24). Each of these is in process, moving through time and space, and is also itself an assemblage, a gathering of other things. Each is gathered together with a history and a finite lifespan (Bennett 2010: 24). The assemblage cannot, however, be reduced to the sum of its parts, as it emerges in a specific context and can itself act in particular ways (De Landa 2006:37). Because each of the affective bodies is in process, Deleuze and Guattari (2004) refer to them as lines of flight, or lines of becoming. It is here that we can see the close relationship between the concept of the assemblage and Ingold's (2011) notion of the meshwork. For Ingold (2011), the world is best thought of as a meshwork, a tangle of lines of becoming as they relate to one another, with particular gatherings of these lines – knots – emerging as people, things, or animals at particular moments. Thus, although I disagree with Ingold's (2008) reading of Latour, I certainly prefer his concept of the meshwork to Latour's network, although for different reasons. It is the notion of process – of life – that is at the heart of both the assemblage and the meshwork. My personal preference for the term 'assemblage' comes both from the active recognition of material things proposed by scholars who use the term, such as Bennett (2010), and also because the work of Manuel De Landa (2002, 2006) allows us to use it to begin to be more specific about the kinds of relations involved, and the roles that they play. I return to this point below.

What does it mean therefore, to see a community as an assemblage? Taking communities as assemblages means approaching them as the outcome of relations between humans, animals, places, landscapes, monuments, materials, things, and so on (De Landa 2006:12). Ingold (2012:431) is precisely right when he argues we need to broaden our considerations of non-humans well beyond material things. It means recognizing that all relations within this mixture are crucial to the emergence of the assemblage, whether friendly, violent, intentional, or unintentional. It requires us to recognize the historical specificity of the relations (De Landa 2006:12), but also that these can endure through time; because the assemblage itself is in a state of flow, it is always in process (De Landa 2006:28). By focusing on the ongoing production of the assemblage/community, we can also thus avoid reifying community into an ideal type (De Landa 2006:38), helping to avoid associations with the appeals of modern politicians. It also emphasizes the need to consider affect and therefore *emotion* as crucial vectors in how different parts of the assemblage impact and impress on one another, and therefore produce the assemblage as a whole (Bennett 2010). Each of the parts of the assemblage, each line of becoming (which itself is an amalgam of other lines), has the capacity to register affectively on others. Of course, this does not happen in the same way between all the different constituents. Human beings affect, and are affected by, others in a very different manner than axes, pots, or cows (cf. Bennett 2010). Taking this approach does not mean ontologically equating humans with everything else. Certain kinds of affective relations, for example, can generate feelings or emotions in human beings (e.g., homesickness) that other members of the assemblage do not experience. This does not mean the emotion is solely located within the human being, however; rather, it is part of the way in which other members of the community (including plants and objects, but also places, animals, and other people) affect that person (cf. Harris and Sørensen 2010). The notion of the assemblage thus both recognizes difference, but also recognizes how these differences in themselves are relational. Dogs will be able to smell things that people cannot; stone axes can endure for millennia in ways unavailable to either people or animals; and all three were part of past communities, and each brought to those assemblages their own capabilities to affect and be affected by the others.

But while it may be argued that all communities are assemblages, not all assemblages are communities. Take the human body, for example. It is certainly an assemblage of materials, actions, practices, beliefs, bacteria, potentially other parasites, cancers, and so on. Similarly, a collection of planets and a star that together form a solar system could also be seen as an assemblage. Neither of these would normally be thought of by archaeologists as a community. The question of community is thus in part a question of scale. Communities are heterogeneous assemblages containing multiple human beings, along with material things and other elements. And while archaeological communities are not present at all scales of analysis, they exist – at least those that involve human beings – in all times and places at more than one scale. As other scholars have noted (Thomas 1996; Yaeger 2000), communities are in effect multi-scalar, and I will give examples of this below. This acknowledgement of the importance of multiple scales is essential if we are to avoid reductionism at either the micro- or macro-scales (De Landa 2006:5; cf. Robb and Harris 2013).

This turn to assemblages means that archaeological communities are neither defined solely by the people who created them in the past, nor by archaeologists in the present. Rather, the identification of community emerges in the engagement of the archaeologist with the material remains – it too is relational. This definition of community thus bypasses another modernist dichotomy, that between emic and etic, and recognizes that, in archaeology at least, such a distinction is extremely problematic. In a famous paper, Strathern (1996) poses the question: Where do we cut the network? A similar concern can be identified here: Where do we define the edges of the assemblage? The answer can only ever be found in practice.

Describing assemblages

A final strength of taking an approach that treats communities as assemblages, I suggest, is that it gives us a new set of tools for describing the relations that comprise these communities. It is all very well describing things as 'relational' – indeed it is a crucial first step – but this surely leaves us a lot more to say. How do relations vary between things? How do relations change through time? Do new technologies facilitate new kinds of relations? Here in the final theoretical section of the paper, I want to draw on a specific reading of assemblage theory, that developed by Manuel De Landa (2006), to offer axes of analysis that I suggest can help develop this further.

Heterogeneity

One of the key elements of any assemblage is that it is made up of multiple elements (De Landa 2006:11), much as I have described above. A crucial element of De Landa's argument, however, is that we need to go beyond merely acknowledging assemblages as heterogeneous. Instead of taking "heterogeneity as a constant property of assemblages," we should instead treat it as a "variable that may take different values" (De Landa, 2006:12). Thus, in treating communities as assemblages, describing the form and variation in heterogeneity will be important.

Territorialization and deterritorialization

De Landa draws on Deleuze and Guattari to discuss the manner in which different processes can act to sharpen the boundaries around an assemblage, or help to break them down. He refers to these as processes of "territorialization" and "deterritorialization." The former can be understood literally, De Landa argues (2006:12), as processes that define the spatial boundaries of an assemblage. It also works to increase the homogeneity of an assemblage, by excluding particular elements or making boundaries increasingly clear between those things (human and non-human) within or outside the assemblage. Territorialization can thus help to stabilize an assemblage and extend its existence through time. Deterritorialization works in the opposite direction by blurring boundaries and extending hetero-geneity. In one sense, territorialization helps to stabilize and secure the boundaries of an assemblage, whilst deterritorialization breaks them down. However, it would be misleading to suggest this automatically destabilizes an assemblage. Processes of deterritorialization can allow assemblages to exist outside of the intimate spatial scales at which they might have been formed – for example, in the way commu-nication technologies allow partners to maintain a relationship over long distances in a manner that would previously have been impossible. Both practices and material things can play a crucial role as full members of the assemblage in both territorialization and its counterpart (De Landa 2006:54, 64). Indeed, as we will see, the same practices can work in both directions simultaneously.

Extensive and intensive

De Landa uses the terms 'extensive' and 'intensive' to discuss different elements of scale. Whilst the former might sound like it refers to a geographical dimension, De Landa (2006:6) uses it to discuss the number of relations in a particular assemblage. So a family of four and their various material things spread over several thousand miles is less extensive, in these terms, than a tight knit village of a hundred people and their various houses and possessions, even if the latter only occupies a square mile or so. The measurement of intensiveness, by comparison, examines the density of the relations or interconnections in an assemblage (De Landa 2006:7).

These terms help us to think not only about the way in which communities are fundamentally relational, I suggest, but also give us tools for describing the strength, stability, density, and variability of assemblages and the relations they encompass. This is obviously a personal reading of De Landa's rich and complex reworking of Deleuze's ideas, not all of which are discussed here in the interests of brevity. Taking an approach rooted in assemblages, and using De Landa's (admittedly abstruse) vocabulary can provide us with a new way of describing past communities. It is to this that I turn now.

Communities through time

The aim of the following case studies is clearly not to set out in detail a different understanding of each of the different periods I will discuss. Although I believe this is a project that this approach can contribute to, it would do deep disservice to the complexity of each of them (and the scholarship that goes with it) if I pretended this was achievable in a single short paper. Instead, what I want to do here is outline some of the ways in which this vocabulary can usefully be employed to generate relational understandings of communities between the Neolithic and Early Bronze Age in Britain. Also, by examining a series of communities through time (rather than a more detailed study of a single period), I aim to demonstrate that a focus on assemblages also allows us to access historical differences between periods as well.

Early Neolithic communities

There are a number of similarities between the Early Neolithic period and the preceding Mesolithic, not least in the ongoing importance of gathering practices and mobility (see Cummings and Harris 2011). However, there is little point in denying the wide-ranging changes as well; this period marks the beginnings of agriculture in Britain after all. The Neolithic begins in different parts of Britain in the century or so around 4000 cal BC (see Whittle et al. 2011 for details). It is characterized from the beginning by the presence of domesticated plants and animals and the first use of pottery. On one level, we can clearly detect an increased level of heterogeneity compared to their hunter gatherer forebears. There are more material members of the community (not only pots, but the first widespread appearance of polished stone axes). In turn, the landscape members of the assemblage become more heterogeneous as well: clay sources, stone axe sources, and the deep recesses plumbed by the new flint mines all indicate that Neolithic communities were more heterogeneous than their predecessors.

The new practices acted to deterritorialize in one sense. Pottery, for example, opened up a new range of places to engage with, materials to be bound into the assemblage, and practices (like the storage of milk and blood) that could flow from that. Simultaneously, of course, pottery also acts as a territorializing practice, allowing the definition of particular clay sources (and not others) as members of the community, or allowing particular kinds of pottery to be established as parts of one assemblage but not another. This should not be surprising. De Landa comments explicitly that particular practices can act in both of these ways at the same time by "enacting different capacities" (De Landa 2006:12). Wild animals continued to be important members of the community in certain contexts where hunting took place. One example is that of the Coneybury Anomaly in Wiltshire, a large pit dug and filled with a rich assemblage of finds early in the fourth millennium cal BC (Richards 1990). Even in this unusual case, however, where a significant number of fallow deer were deposited, there remains a greater reliance on cattle, demonstrating that relationships with wild animals became increasingly less intensive in the Early Neolithic as their places were taken by domesticated counterparts (Cummings and Harris 2011; Pollard 2006). Human-animal relations in general became more intensive, however, through domestication, and most likely increasingly territorialized (in De Landa's senses of the terms).

One of the most famous elements of the Early Neolithic is the construction of monuments, with long barrows and chambered tombs appearing patchily from 3800 cal BC (with a couple of possible earlier ones, for example Coldrum in Kent) and causewayed enclosures – circuits of interrupted ditches – largely from 3700 cal BC (Whittle et al. 2011). The recent re-dating of these monuments suggests that neither set emerge regularly, but rather appear in concentrated periods of building (Whittle et al. 2011). These point to the regular emergence and decay of communities constructed at different scales, and they can be read as a clear process of territorialization followed by deterritorialization, as monuments brought people together to form extensive, and for a short period intensive, larger-scale communities. On occasion, in the building and use of smaller monuments, these assemblages might be constructed from only a few of the different groups of people, animals, and materials that normally lived together on a daily basis. At others, however, like the construction of the larger causewayed enclosures such as Hambledon Hill in Dorset, many different communities would have assembled together to construct something on a much larger scale, with clear experiential and emotional consequences for their human members (Harris 2010). Monuments here are not merely the embodiment or the symbol of these larger-scale communities – they are a process, member, and outcome of their construction. The end of their use lives thus suggests a process of destabilization and deterritorialization of the larger community.

Yet at the same time, there are more complex narratives of relational territorialization and deterritorialization at play. Many monuments have a clear relationship to moments of interpersonal violence. People buried at many long barrows and chambered tombs show evidence of having died through violent means (Fowler 2010; Schulting and Wysocki 2005). Similarly, causewayed enclosures like Hambledon Hill and Crickley Hill show clear evidence of having been attacked. Amongst other evidence for violence, the former saw a hastily constructed palisade burnt down on one occasion, and on another two people died after being shot with arrows (Mercer and Healy 2008). At Crickley, there is significant evidence for a full-blown assault, with hundreds of leaf-shaped arrowheads having been fired at the entrance (Dixon 1988). At one scale, these processes can clearly be read as territorializing, as De Landa (2006:57–58) suggests, with different communities defining their boundaries through the use of weapons and fire. Yet how we understand these processes is also affected by the scale at which we analyze them. For example, if we conceptualize these as moments of conflict and dispute within the larger-scale communities that had constructed these monuments, they can also be seen as moments of deterritorialization, in which the boundaries defining the larger-scale community broke down. The fact that many, in fact most, monuments were short-lived affairs that were in use for only a generation or two, suggests that larger-scale communities were fragile, constantly capable of collapsing, sometimes violently. On other occasions – say, at chambered tombs like Wayland's Smithy I, where the construction of the monument follows a moment of violence (Whittle et al. 2007) – these may have been means of (re)territorializing a larger community threatened by that aggression. The communities of the Early Neolithic would have been highly dependent on one another, and members (including pots, plants, animals, and people) would have regularly changed their membership between different assemblages. This process would have been threatened by violence, and so relations had to be actively worked on through the construction of monuments, which assembled and territorialized the community together again.

Late Neolithic communities

Taking the Late Neolithic to date to between 3000 and 2500 cal BC, this period represents another significant change in the assemblages we can term "communities." At one level, communities in this period become – once again – increasingly heterogeneous. Assemblages reveal significant growth in a range of what has been termed 'prestige goods' (Thorpe and Richards 1984), including boar tusks, jet belt sliders, maceheads of stone and antler, chalk phalli and balls, polished discoidal flint knives, and complex arrowheads (Thomas 1996). These material things forged a new scale of community which helped construct new forms of relational identity for its members (Thomas 1996). This scale of community, associated with a relationally constructed sense of prestige, was territorialized through these material things; only they, and people in relation to them, were members. The evidence for increasing levels of hunting in this period also suggests arenas in which this community/assemblage was increasingly exercising itself (Pollard 2006:142–43). These communities were neither intensive nor extensive, and were not highly territorialized – part of the reason they did not take on a dominant role at this point.

This represents only one of the scales of community present in Late Neolithic Britain, however, which, as Thomas (1996:180) has noted, becomes increasingly multi-scalar in this period. Processes of farming continued in daily life, perhaps now associated on occasions with an increasing number of houses, which helped to maintain assemblages at the local level in the face of increasingly potent wider-scale communities (cf. Thomas 2010). These are manifest at two separate scales. At the largest scale, we see the construction of monuments indicating the emergence of long-lasting macro-assemblages (cf. De Landa 2006:17) unparalleled even in comparison with the large Early Neolithic causewayed enclosures. Termed henges, these include the enormous monuments of Mount Pleasant, Marden and Durrington Walls. They are defined by the presence of a bank set outside a ditch, defining a central area, and often contain timber or stone circles inside them. At least some of these henges were sustained through ongoing processes of territorialization, remaining in use for significant periods of time, and apparently without the violence that sometimes ensued at comparative sites from earlier periods. Durrington Walls, for example, was a site where large numbers of people repeatedly gathered for large-scale ceremonies, living in houses there for part of the year, killing and feasting on pigs, and conducting ceremonies (Parker Pearson 2007). It has been convincingly argued that people gathered there from across many parts of southern Britain (Viner et al. 2010). These assemblages were extensive in the extreme, not due to their geographical origins, but instead to the numbers of relations that must have been involved. Between the smaller communities of daily life and the large-scale gatherings at the big henge monuments, other scales also emerge. Mid-level monuments proliferate in this period, including small henges and so called 'hengiforms.' These suggest the territorialization of mid-scale assem-blages between the micro-gatherings of daily life and the macro-scales instantiated at larger monuments (Harris 2006).

As Thomas (2010) has argued, a crucial technology for sustaining these communities was a new form of pottery: Grooved Ware. Decorated with spirals and lozenges, this form of pottery was used at all levels. Often larger than previous forms (and the Beakers that would follow) it was clearly a part of a community that had the capacity to extend the sharing of different substances collectively (cf. Hamilton and Whittle 1999:45). The decoration is widespread as well, limited not only to this pottery but also found on chalk plaques, maceheads, passage graves, and in rock art (Thomas 2010). Grooved Ware, as a member of assemblages operating at different scales simultaneously (De Landa 2006:45), formed both a deterritorializing technology and a territorializing one. In the former case, it allowed the large-scale communities to maintain their existence even when people themselves were not gathered together. It allowed a sense of the large-scale community to be made affectively manifest at multiple scales of practice. As a territorializing material, it permitted specific places to become associated with these practices through its role in deliberate acts of deposition both in small pits and at large-scale monuments such as Mount Pleasant in Dorset, as Thomas (1996) has demonstrated. The ability of Grooved Ware to strengthen the relations forming the large-scale community through both territorializing and deterritorializing processes ensured that this scale of community remained important through the Late Neolithic in a way which was not the case in the Early Neolithic, when larger-scale communities could not be sustained. As Thomas has so rightly argued, these materials were "the means by which new forms of collective affinity were brought into being" (2010:1; cf. Jones 2002:166–67). Grooved Ware both gained its importance through its relations to the macro-communities at henge monuments, and allowed these communities to be sustained in the absence of co-presence (cf. De Landa 2006:33), ensuring these communities were both extensive and intensive. Grooved Ware here is what Deleuze and Guattari (2004:358) call an assemblage "converter" or an "operator": something centrally placed between assemblages, linking them and playing crucial driving roles in both (cf. Bennett 2010:42).

The pits at Fir Tree Field in Cranborne Chase in Dorset, Southern England, are an example of the territorialization of different scales of community. One group of pits here, to the north, seem to contain the general remains of sociality, mixtures of pottery sherds, flint debitage, and animal bone. In a second group to the south, specific deposits are located, such as in Pit 7, which featured a Group VIII axe from Graig Llwyd in North Wales, next to a boar's tusk and a large scraper (Green 2000:70). The same pit also featured another boar's tusk (Barrett et al. 1991:77). Other pits close by contained remarkable deposits, such as Pit 11a. This pit featured a complete ox skull on top of an antler pick. Above this in the fill was a roe deer antler, a fragment of polished stone axe, and the bone of a brown bear (Green 2000:70). In neither group of pits should we assume the acts of deposition were merely the functional disposal of rubbish. Rather, in the northern group we see general repeated affirmations of community, assembled from the materials that had sustained the people, connected them to clay sources and pastures, and remains of the flints they had worked. These assemblages helped to territorialize the communities of daily life; repeated intensive relations were marked here in the moment of deposition. In the other group of pits, more specific objects were linked to communities of prestige. These communities were territorialized through the way important identifiable objects, from the axe to the boar's tusk, brought specific assemblages into being, forging alliances between their histories, creating connections, and mediating the links between people and place. The bear bone, a rare find indeed in Neolithic contexts, linked people to the world outside their communities and brought particular qualities and connotations with it into the assemblages ter-ritorialized in the pits at Fir Tree Fields. Grooved Ware, notably, was present in both sets of pits (Barrett et al. 1991:80), though it is more common in the northern group.

Coda: early Bronze Age communities

The arrival of metal around 2500 cal BC was connected to a series of transformations in the relational assemblages I have termed 'communities.' At one level, much remained the same, with stone tools still important and farming still the dominant form of securing food. At the same time, however, heterogeneity increased once again, with the introduction of metal work, including weapons and personal decoration in copper, bronze, and gold. These new material things were incorporated within the exchange communities that had been established in the Late Neolithic and formed parts of the ways in which these came to dominate others. The careful relationships with people and places needed to access metals increased the importance of prestige and increasingly territorialized this scale of community, associating it with particular people, things, and places. It is from here that this community became visible not only in life, but in death, as its members (both human and non-human) were increasingly buried under round barrows. This need not be seen as either the rise of individual burial (cf. Gibson 2004), or the appearance of the individual as a mode of personhood (cf. Brück 2006), but was rather the emerging importance of one scale of relational community. These burials helped further territorialize these communities in particular barrows and cemeteries across the landscape, allowing, as Barrett (1994) argued so brilliantly almost 20 years ago, new relations of descent to be traced.

The skills of metalworking were themselves elements of these new assemblages, and whilst these acted to territorialize this scale of community, they simultaneously acted to undermine the macro-communities so important in the Late Neolithic. Although this transition was not immediate (Mount Pleasant, the enormous henge in Dorset was important throughout this period), the collective nature of these monuments could not be sustained in the new world of the Bronze Age. Part of this resulted not from the emergence of metal work but rather from the decline of Grooved Ware, and its replacement by smaller, more personal, forms of pottery in the form of Beakers. These drinking vessels could not sustain collective community in the manner Grooved Ware could, and so they were incorporated instead into the world of exchange communities, forming another member of these prestige-assemblages. Thus, when metal work was introduced, it was not something that transformed the communities in an unprecedented way – rather it was incorporated into particular forms of assemblage that were already on the rise. These assemblages became more intensive as they became more important, and perhaps more extensive too, though by neither measure would they reach the levels achieved by the macro-communities of the previous period.

Conclusion

These case studies are obviously thumbnail examples from these complex periods, and there is much, especially in both regional and temporal variation, that I have ignored. Yet it is always important to recognize that history can be told at multiple scales and the privileging of any scale – micro, meso, or macro – is always reductionist (De Landa 2006; cf. Robb and Harris 2013). To appreciate the sweep of transformations that took place over the millennia covered here, I have mainly operated at a large scale. This perspective has allowed certain macro-patterns to emerge, such as an increase in the heterogeneity of communities, even as other elements, such as the broader scale of assemblages, waxed and waned. In each case, I have argued that by treating communities as relational assemblages, we can appreciate the processes that brought them into being, defined their boundaries, maintained them, and in the end undermined them. These processes necessarily included human beings, but also all manner of animals, plants, places, monuments, and material things – only some of which have been touched on here. The terms defined by De Landa allow us to begin to specify some of the ways in which these relational communities emerged, and some of the axes along which they can be analyzed. By attending to the practices of territorialization and deterritorialization, and by defining levels of heterogeneity, intensiveness, and extensiveness we can recognize the parts of an assemblage that play crucial roles in bringing communities together and breaking them apart. Through this we can attest to the gatherings that link affective bodies through a process of becoming (Bennett 2010).

Communities are important for archaeologists because they are multi-scalar, operating through and across processes of history. Only by approaching them relationally can we reveal them as more-than-human-sociality. Only by approaching them relationally can we capture their complexity and variation. And only by approaching them relationally can we use them to show that the kinds of timeless-yet-absent sociality so beloved of politicians are modern constructs, much like the bifurcations that keep people and things on either side of an unbridgeable divide.

Bibliography

Alberti, Benjamin, and Yvonne Marshall 2009. Animating Archaeology: Local Theories and Conceptually Open-Ended Methodologies. *Cambridge Archaeological Journal* 19:344–56.

Barrett, John C. 1994. *Fragments from Antiquity: An Archaeology of Social Life in Britain, 2900–1200 BC*. Blackwell, Oxford.

Barrett, John C., Richard Bradley, and Martin Green 1991. *Landscape, Monuments and Society: The Prehistory of Cranborne Chase*. Cambridge University Press, Cambridge.

Bennett, Jane 2010. *Vibrant Matter: A Political Ecology of Things*. Duke University Press, London.

Busby, Cecilia 1997. Permeable and Partible Persons: A Comparative Analysis of Gender and Body in South India and Melanesia. *Journal of the Royal Anthropological Institute* 3:261–78.

Brück, Joanna 2001. Monuments, Power and Personhood in the British Neolithic. *Journal of the Royal Anthropological Institute* 7:649–67.

——(2006). Death, Exchange and Reproduction in the British Bronze Age. *European Journal of Archaeology* 9(1):73–101.

Canuto, Marcello-Andrea, and Jason Yaeger (editors) 2000. *The Archaeology of Communities: A New World Perspective*. Routledge, London.

Chapman, John 2000. *Fragmentation in Archaeology: People, Places and Broken Objects in the Prehistory of South-Eastern Europe*. Routledge, London.

Conneller, Chantal 2011. *An Archaeology of Materials: Substantial Transformations in Early Prehistoric Europe*. Routledge, London.

Creed, Gerald W. 2006. *Reconsidering Community*. In *The Seductions of Community: Emancipations, Oppressions, Quandaries*, edited by Gerald W. Creed, pp. 3–22. School of American Research Press, Santa Fe, New Mexico.

Cummings, Vicki, and Oliver J. T. Harris 2011. Animals, People and Places: The Continuity of Hunting and Gathering Practices across the Mesolithic-Neolithic Transition in Britain. *European Journal of Archaeology* 14(3):361–82.

De Landa, Manuel 2002. *Intensive Science and Virtual Philosophy*. Continuum, London.

——(2006). *A New Philosophy of Society: Assemblage Theory and Social Complexity*. Continuum, London.

Deleuze, Gilles, and Felix Guattari 2004. *A Thousand Plateaus: Capitalism and Schizophrenia*. Continuum, London.

Dixon, Philip. 1988. *The Neolithic Settlements at Crickley Hill*. In *Enclosures and Defences in the Neolithic of Western Europe*, edited by Colin Burgess, Peter Topping, Claude Mordant, and Margaret Maddison, pp. 75–88. BAR International Series 403. British Archaeological Reports, Oxford.

Fowler, Chris 2000. The Individual, the Subject, and Archaeological Interpretation. Reading Luce Irigaray and Judith Butler. In *Philosophy and Archaeological Practice: Perspectives for the 21st Century*, edited by Cornelius Holtorf and Hakan Karlsson, pp. 107–33. Bricoleur, Götborg.

——(2001). Personhood and Social Relations in the British Neolithic with a Case Study from the Isle of Man. *Journal of Material Culture* 6:137–63.

——(2010). Pattern and Diversity in the Early Neolithic Mortuary Practice of Britain and Ireland: Contextualising the Treatment of the Dead. *Documenta Praehistorica* 37:1–22.

Gibson, Alex 2004. Burials and Beakers: Seeing beneath the Veneer in Late Neolithic Britain. In *Similar but Different: Bell Beakers in Europe*, edited by Janus Czebreszuk, pp. 173–92. Adam Mickiewicz University, Poznañ.

Green, Martin 2000. *A Landscape Revealed: 10,000 Years on a Chalkland Farm*. Stroud, Tempus.

Hamilton, Michael, and Alasdair Whittle 1999. Grooved Ware of the Avebury Region: Styles, Contexts and Meaning. In *Grooved Ware in Britain and Ireland*, edited by Ros Cleal and Ann MacSween, pp. 36–47. Oxbow, Oxford.

Harman, Graham 2009. *Prince of Networks: Bruno Latour and Metaphysics*. Re.Press, Melbourne.

Harris, Oliver J. T. 2006. "Identity, Emotion and Memory in Neolithic Dorset." Unpublished Ph.D. dissertation, School of History, Archaeology and Religion, Cardiff University.

——(2010). Emotional and Mnemonic Geographies at Hambledon Hill: Texturing Neolithic Places with Bodies and Bones. *Cambridge Archaeological Journal* 20(3):357–71.

——(2012). (Re)assembling Communities. *Journal of Archaeological Method and Theory* Online first publication, DOI 10.1007/s10816-012-9138-3.

Harris, Oliver J. T., and Tim Flohr Sørensen 2010. Rethinking Emotion and Material Culture. *Archaeological Dialogues* 17(2):145–63.

Ingold, Tim 2008. When ANT Meets SPIDER: Social Theory for Arthropods. In *Material Agency: Towards a Non-Anthropocentric Approach*, edited by Carl Knappett and Lambros Malafouris, pp. 209–15. Springer, New York.

——(2011). *Being Alive: Essays in Movement, Knowledge and Description*. Routledge, London.

——(2012). Toward an Ecology of Materials. *Annual Review of Anthropology* 41:427-42.

Jones, Andrew 2002. *Archaeological Theory and Scientific Practice*. Cambridge University Press, Cambridge.

Knappett, Carl 2011. *An Archaeology of Interaction: Network Perspectives on Material Culture and Society*. Oxford University Press, Oxford.

Knappett, Carl, and Lambros Malafouris (editors) 2008. *Material Agency: Towards a Non-Anthropocentric Approach*. Springer, New York.

Kohring, Shelia 2011. Social Complexity as a Multi-Scalar Concept: Pottery Technologies, 'Communities of Practice' and the Bell Beaker Phenomenon. *Norwegian Archaeological Review* 44(2):145–63.

Kolb, Michael J., and James E. Snead 1997. It's a Small World after All: Comparative Analyses of Community Organization in Archaeology. *American Antiquity* 62(4):609–28.

Latour, Bruno 1993. *We Have Never Been Modern*. Translated by C. Porter. Harvard University Press, Cambridge, Massachusetts.

——(1999). *Pandora's Hope: Essays on the Reality of Science Studies*. Harvard University Press, Cambridge, Massachusetts.

——(2005). *Reassembling the Social: An Introduction to Actor Network Theory*. Oxford University Press, Oxford.

Latour, Bruno, Graham Harman, and Peter Erdélyi 2011. *The Prince and the Wolf: Latour and Harman at the LSE*. Zone, London.

Lave, Jean, and Etienne Wenger 1991. *Situated Learning: Legitimate Peripheral Participation*. Cambridge University Press, Cambridge.

Mercer, Roger, and Francis Healy 2008. *Hambledon Hill, Dorset, England: Excavations and Survey of a Neolithic Monument Complex and its Surrounding Landscape*. English Heritage Archaeological Report, London.

Moore, Tom 2007. Perceiving Communities: Exchange, Landscapes and Social Networks in the Later Iron Age of Western Britain. *Oxford Journal of Archaeology* 26(1):79–102.

Parker Pearson, Mike 2007. The Stonehenge Riverside Project: Excavations at the East Entrance of Durrington Walls. In *From Stonehenge to the Baltic: Living with Cultural Diversity in the Third Millennium BC*, edited by Mats Larson and Mike Parker Pearson, pp. 125–44. BAR International Series 1692. British Archaeological Reports, Oxford.

Pauketat, Timothy 2008. The Grounds for Agency in Southwest Archaeology. In *The Social Construction of Communities: Agency, Structure, and Identity in the Prehispanic Southwest*, edited by Mark D. Varien and James M. Potter, pp. 233–49. AltaMira, Lanham, Maryland.

Pollard, Joshua 2006. A Community of Beings: Animals and People in the Neolithic of Southern Britain. In *Animals in the Neolithic of Britain and Europe*, edited by Dale Serjeantson and David Field, pp. 135–48. Oxbow, Oxford.

Richards, Julian 1990. *The Stonehenge Environs Project*. English Heritage Report Number 16, London.

Robb, John E., and Oliver J. T. Harris 2013. *The Body in History*. Cambridge University Press, Cambridge (forthcoming).

Sassaman, Kenneth E., and Wictoria Rudolphi 2001. Communities of Practice in the Early Pottery Traditions of the American Southeast. *Journal of Anthropological Research* 57 (4):407–25.

Schulting, Rick, and Michael Wysocki 2005. "In this Chambered Tumulus were found Cleft Skulls … ": An Assessment of the Evidence for Cranial Trauma in the British Neolithic. *Proceedings of the Prehistoric Society*, 71:107–38.

Shanks, Michael 2007. Symmetrical Archaeology. *World Archaeology* 39(4):589–96.

Shanks, Michael, and Christopher Tilley 1987. *Social Theory and Archaeology*. Polity, Cambridge.

Strathern, Marilyn 1988. *The Gender of the Gift*. Cambridge University Press, Cambridge.

——(1996). Cutting the Network. *Journal of the Royal Anthropological Institute* 2:517–35.

Thomas, Julian 1996. *Time, Culture and Identity: An Interpretive Archaeology*. Routledge, London.

——(2002). Archaeology's Humanism and the Materiality of the Body. In *Thinking Through the Body: Archaeologies of Corporeality*, edited by Yannis Hamilakis, Mark Pluciennik, and Sarah Tarlow, pp. 29–45. Kluwer Academic/Plenum Publishers, London.

——(2010). The Return of the Rinyo-Clacton Folk? The Cultural Significance of the Grooved Ware Complex in Later Neolithic Britain. *Cambridge Archaeological Journal* 20(1):1–15.

Thorpe, I. J. Nick, and Colin Richards 1984. The Decline of Ritual Authority and the Introduction of Beakers into Britain. In *Neolithic Studies: A Review of Some Current Research*, edited by Richard Bradley and Julie Gardiner, pp. 67–84. BAR British Series 133. British Archaeological Reports, Oxford.

Varien, Mark D., and James M. Potter (editors) 2008. *The Social Construction of Communities: Agency, Structure, and Identity in the Prehispanic Southwest*. AltaMira, Lanham, Maryland.

Viner, Sarah, Jane Evans, Umberto Albarella, and Mike Parker Pearson 2010. Cattle Mobility in Prehistoric Britain: Strontium Isotope Analysis of Cattle Teeth from Durrington Walls (Wiltshire, Britain). *Journal of Archaeological Science* 37:2812–20.

Webmoor, Timothy 2007. What About 'One More Turn After the Social' in Archaeological Reasoning? Taking Things Seriously. *World Archaeology* 39(4):563–78.

Webmoor, Timothy, and Christopher L. Witmore 2008. Things Are Us! A Commentary on Human/Things Relations under the Banner of a 'Social Archaeology'. *Norwegian Archaeological Review* 41(1):1–18.

Wenger, Etienne 1998. *Communities of Practice: Learning, Meaning and Identity*. Cambridge University Press, Cambridge.

Whitridge, Peter 2004. Whales, Harpoons, and Other Actors: Actor-Network Theory and Hunter-Gatherer Archaeology. In *Hunters and Gatherers in Theory and Archaeology*, edited by George Crothers, pp. 445–74. Occasional Paper No. 31. Center for Archaeological Investigations, Southern Illinois University, Carbondale.

Whittle, Alasdair 2003. *The Archaeology of People: Dimensions of Neolithic Life*. Routledge, London.

Whittle, Alasdair, Alex Bayliss, and Michael Wysocki 2007. Once in a Lifetime: The Date of the Wayland's Smithy Long Barrow. *Cambridge Archaeological Journal* 17(S1):103–21.

Whittle, Alasdair, Frances Healy, and Alex Bayliss 2011. *Gathering Time: Dating the Early Neolithic Enclosures of Southern Britain and Ireland*. Oxbow, Oxford.

Witmore, Christopher L. 2007. Symmetrical Archaeology: Excerpts of a Manifesto. *World Archaeology* 39(4):546–62.

Yaeger, Jason 2000. The Social Construction of Communities in the Classic Maya Countryside: Strategies of Affiliation in Western Belize. In *The Archaeology of Communities: A New World Perspective*, edited by Marcello-Andrea Canuto and Jason Yaeger, pp. 123–42. Routledge, London.

10

SHIFTING HORIZONS AND EMERGING ONTOLOGIES IN THE BRONZE AGE AEGEAN

Andrew Shapland

Introduction

Like a Homeric stock phrase, the Shaft Graves of Grave Circle A at Mycenae have come to be associated with the words of a famous telegram: "I have gazed upon the face of Agamemnon." That this apocryphal quote has come to stand for the discoveries at Mycenae is problematic for a number of reasons. The first is that Heinrich Schliemann did not quite use those words in his telegram announcing the discovery of a well-preserved body during the course of his excavations in 1876 (nor was it associated with what is now called 'The Mask of Agamemnon') (Traill 1995:163). The second is that archaeologists no longer believe that he had discovered the burial of Agamemnon, leader of the Greek forces in the Trojan War, although the Shaft Graves remain perhaps the single most important Aegean Bronze Age discovery. The third is the ontological problem which is central to this chapter: namely, that the grave goods have been metaphorically stripped away so that Schliemann's discovery becomes essentially interpersonal. Indeed, the extraordinary assemblage of objects was something of an obstacle to Schliemann's identification of the accompanying bodies with those of Agamemnon and his followers, murdered on their return from Troy. Although copiously illustrated in his publication, the objects had to be explained away: "it would therefore appear that, in burying the fifteen royal personages with immense treasures, the murderers merely acted according to an ancient custom, and consequently only fulfilled a sacred duty" (Schliemann 1878:345). The idea that these treasures were simply expressions of the royal or princely identity of those buried has proved more enduring than the more literal aspects of Schliemann's interpretation. This paper will instead seek to place these acts of burial in the context of the network of people and objects, or humans and non-humans, which expanded over the course of the Bronze Age in the Aegean.

Like Sir Arthur Evans' later discoveries at Knossos, Heinrich Schliemann's excavations did more than recover the lost remains of the Aegean Bronze Age. Schliemann and Evans can be credited as the inventors of the Mycenaean and Minoan civilizations: their poetic evocations of the societies centered on Mycenae and Knossos were also impositions of a modern ontology. Their excavations, however, remain of fundamental importance for the understanding of these past societies and their ontologies. In order to understand these ontologies, it is necessary to focus more closely on the artifacts found in assemblages such as the Shaft Graves; recasting them as non-human constituents of past collectives opens the way to an account of the relations of people, animals, and things in the Bronze Age Aegean. The Shaft Grave phenomenon will be seen as one of a number of practices which emerged as the result of the circulation of bodies and things in the Bronze Age.

The Shaft Graves offer a useful starting point for considering the question of ontologies because they establish a contextual association between a variety of entities. Shaft Grave V, associated by Schliemann with Agamemnon, offers a useful snapshot. As well as gold masks and pectorals, it contained a variety of other objects, including swords and daggers, some decorated with griffins or lilies. Another dagger was inlaid with a scene of a cat chasing birds. There were vessels of different materials, including gold, silver, copper, alabaster, and rock crystal. One of the more remarkable vessels was an ostrich egg which had been modified with a spout and faience dolphin appliqués. Other materials represented include amber and glass beads and boar's tusk plaques for a helmet (Karo 1930:121–55). It has been suggested that some of these objects were produced in Crete, and certainly the lily iconography, for example, is characteristically Cretan; its association with weapons is less so (Burns 2010). Explaining this mix of local and foreign materials and iconography is central to this chapter: it will be suggested that the Shaft Grave assemblages and palaces on Crete and the Mainland can be understood in terms of the emergence of elite collectives founded on an ontology of difference.

Ontologies

> Now a system of relations cannot be understood independently from the elements it connects, provided these elements are taken not as interchangeable individuals, or already institutionalised into social units, but as entities which are endowed *ab initio* with specific properties that render them able or not to establish certain links between them.
>
> *(Descola 2006:139)*

The work of Philippe Descola offers a challenging approach to ontologies which will be explored in this paper in relation to the Bronze Age Aegean. Its usefulness lies in the broad applicability indicated in the above quote: by starting with the relationships between entities, without losing sight of their properties, Descola's approach is sufficiently open-ended to apply to a range of different contexts. This is significant because critiques of a modernist ontology, whether from within (Latour

1993) or from an Amerindian point of view (Viveiros de Castro 1998), have tended towards a binary view of modern/non-modern ontologies. Modernism is characterized as a Cartesian ontology of binary contrasts between culture and nature, subject and object, mind and body, and so on. In Viveiros de Castro's influential account, this is a Western multiculturalism which contrasts with an Amazonian multinaturalism in which human culture is the universal backdrop for a range of different perspectives derived from non-human bodies. As Viveiros de Castro (2010) has acknowledged, this "perspectivist" ontology is more applicable to the small-scale societies he has derived it from; the intention is more to undermine the dominant Western ontology often applied in the other direction, in which nature is taken as a universal standpoint from which to understand human interactions with a variety of non-humans in the Amazon.

Descola's work also emerged from his experiences as an ethnographer among Amazonian societies, particularly the Achuar; like a number of other anthropologists, his experiences resulted in a realization that the nature-culture division was not relevant in many non-Western societies (Descola and Pálsson 1996). Indeed, his early work provided the model for Latour's characterization of premodern hybridized nature-cultures which had been purified by the modern world (Latour 1993:14, 91). Descola and Viveiros de Castro's approaches converge on the animist ontologies of the Amazonian societies they have studied, but archaeologists have also been influenced by Ingold's (2000:89–131) outline of a similar ontology of reciprocity in the circumpolar North, and its implications for the study of material culture (Borić this volume). An animist ontology has been identified in an even wider range of case studies, primarily as a means to go beyond a Western understanding of the relation between people and things (Alberti and Marshall 2009; Bird-David 1999; Brown and Walker 2008). As Holbraad (2009) points out, this runs the risk of an anachronistic application of ethnographic analogy to ambiguous archaeological evidence. As he suggests, however, the attempt to apply an animistic ontology can have a useful disruptive effect on archaeologists' own anachronistic understandings; in this way Viveiros de Castro's multinaturalism becomes allied to the internal critique of modernist thinking in archaeology (Thomas 2004).

In contrast to Viveiros de Castro, Descola (2005, 2006) has developed a pluralist, rather than antagonist, approach to reconciling the different ontologies of Western and non-Western societies (Latour 2009). Of central importance was the broadening of his framework of ontologies so that it became applicable to all societies. This is founded upon the assumed universality of a human recognition of what he calls interiority and exteriority. Although associated with a mind-body split in the Western "naturalist" ontology, he argues that it results from a basic phenomenological experience of the human body (Descola 2005:168). This results in a fourfold ontological scheme based on whether non-humans are understood as sharing human interiority and exteriority (totemism), shared interiority among a diversity of bodies (animism), shared exteriority but unique human mind (naturalism), or neither (analogism). Analogism "is predicated on the idea that all the entities in the world are fragmented into a multiplicity of essences, forms and substances separated by minute intervals, often ordered along a graded scale" (Descola 2006:145). These are the four "modes of identification" in which non-human and human others in the world are understood in terms of similarity and difference from the human self. These define ontologies, which are themselves the "systems of distribution of properties among existing objects in the world" (Descola 2006:141). Ontologies are activated through "modes of relation," namely exchange, predation, and reciprocity between similar entities, and protection, production, and transmission where difference is perceived (Descola 2005:423–58). Naturalism is the ontology of the modern West, and animism and totemism are largely found among small-scale societies, but analogism emerges as the ontology which applies to a large number of premodern and non-Western internally differentiated societies. Although Descola does not link ontologies to particular social formations, also preferring the term "collective," he notes that analogism results in a hierarchical ordering of the world: these unequal relations are more often found in stratified societies.

These definitions of different ontologies will be accepted here as different ways of understanding the same world, rather than worldviews which are fundamentally incommensurable with a modern ontology. Animism and totemism have been variously defined as oppositions to a Western mode of thinking, but also recognized within it (Bird-David 1999; Gell 1998; Lévi-Strauss 1963, 1966; Willis 1990). Animism, in the form of Merleau-Ponty's phenomenology, has also been advocated as a form of archaeological practice (Tilley 2004:19–22). Similarly, approaches to the "embodied mind" in cognitive science have sought to replace a body-mind dichotomy with an awareness of the interaction of brain, body, and world in cognition (Clark 2008; Lakoff and Johnson 1999). Malafouris (2008) usefully explores this perspective in terms of the relation between bodies and swords in Mycenaean Greece, as a challenge to prevailing views that swords are symbols of power, based on a Cartesian separation of body and object. There is a distinction to be made, however, between the way in which all humans interact with the world, and the ways in which different people and cultures understand these interactions. For Descola, we all live in the same interrelated world of humans and non-humans, but we understand it differently: "There can be no multiple worlds because it is highly probable that the potential qualities and relations afforded to human cognition and enactment are the same everywhere until some have been detected and actualized, others ignored" (Descola 2010:339).

The alternative is to accept the paradox that anthropologists seek to understand the ontologies of societies which are utterly incommensurable with their own. The middle way is provided by Lloyd who has applied Descola's scheme to his longstanding comparative study of Ancient Greek and Chinese culture. Lloyd (2007, 2010) argues that the comparison of societies, whether historically or ethnographically, requires an acceptance of two principles which he terms the "psychic unity of mankind" and "the multidimensionality of the phenomena." In other words, Descola's starting point of interiority vs. exteriority is only a restatement of the mind-body dichotomy to the extent that it can be considered a universal feature of human cognition to differentiate oneself from the world beyond. At the same time, the paradox of incommensurable ontologies is dissolved by allowing for different facets of any particular phenomenon. Lloyd (2007:147) suggests that Viveiros de Castro's (1998:470) frequently cited observation that, from an animist perspective, jaguars regard blood as manioc beer is not invalidated or rendered less objective by the simultaneous recognition that blood is not manioc beer from a Western point of view. Similarly, the existence of basic universal schemes for classifying animals and plants does not undermine the perspectivist understanding of jaguars' humanity, because these are different aspects of the same phenomenon (Atran 1990; Boyer 2010).

In Descola's scheme, both Ancient Greek and Chinese societies, or collectives, are analogist, and this will be extended here to the Aegean Bronze Age. As Lloyd (2007, 2011) points out, however, there are significant differences between Greek and Chinese understandings of the world, and, perhaps more importantly, considerable diversity within each. If Greek philosophers could not agree on their outlook on the world, it seems reductive to group together the ontologies of a variety of different societies. As Descola (2010) stresses, however, his scheme is a heuristic device, rather than a societal classification, and he argues only that one type of ontology will be dominant among a given group of people. What matters is how the basic inferences about interiority and exteriority guide the way in which the properties of other bodies and things are actualized. In this, his scheme has affinities with the affordance concept, in which properties emerge in the course of interaction (Gibson 1979).

Analogism takes as its starting point an understanding that all the entities in the world are different from one another, necessitating an ontology which establishes order out of chaos. "This disposition allows for a recombination of the initial contrasts into a dense network of analogies linking the intrinsic properties of each autonomous entity present in the world" (Descola 2006:145). The modes of relation of production, protection, and transmission are ways to bring these separate entities into relationship along different axes: genetic, spatial, and temporal. These are non-reversible, and so hierarchical, types of relationships (Descola 2005:439).

This raises the problem of applying this scheme to a prehistoric setting such as the Bronze Age Aegean: it is possible to compare and contrast Classical Greek and Chinese science because they are literate societies which recorded their observations of the world (only a small number of documents recording economic transactions survive from the Bronze Age Aegean). The reason for attempting to extend Descola's scheme to prehistory is that Bronze Age Crete has long been accommodated within a modern naturalist scheme, particularly influenced by the excavator of Knossos, Sir Arthur Evans (Shapland 2010). One of the few to consider the material culture of the "Minoans" (a label also inherited from Evans) outside a naturalist ontology has been Herva (2005, 2006a, 2006b). He suggested that depictions of humans interacting with rocks and trees should be understood in terms of an animist conception of the world. Given the evidence for social differentiation, Bronze Age Aegean collectives can better be understood as predominantly analogist within Descola's scheme; this does not exclude animist beliefs, but it is not clear from the available evidence whether rocks and trees were seen as persons. It is important to note, however, that even if relations between humans and non-human elements of the landscape were understood in terms of reciprocity, their depiction on gold rings suggests a form of social exclusivity for these activities. The role of depictions will be considered further below, but first it is important to address another critique of Descola's scheme.

The other problem leveled at Descola's scheme is that of a change in ontology (Lloyd 2010:209). It is widely agreed that the Enlightenment resulted in the conceptual splitting up of the world, which resulted in our own naturalist mode of identification, but it is harder to explain why such an ontology should emerge where and when it did. The emergence of naturalism will be addressed briefly below, but it is worth pointing out that archaeology is well-placed to describe and explain long-term change. For instance, relations with things multiplied as a result of farming and urbanism delegating tasks to non-humans (Olsen 2010:10). The emergence of craft specialization meant that relations with things were increasingly unevenly distributed among the collective. These shifts in scale had particular implications for the relations between humans and things, resulting in the segmentation that characterizes analogist collectives. As Descola (2005:525–31) stresses, technological changes did not automatically result in a change in ontology, but made this possible by changing the way the properties of non-humans were perceived by changing the relations between them.

The domestication of animals and plants has fundamental implications for the relations between humans and non-humans (Russell 2012; Serpell 1986; Tapper 1988). For instance, whereas from an animist point of view non-human animals give themselves to human hunters based on a shared understanding of reciprocity, domestication results in a shift in both human-animal relations and the way these are understood. Although Ingold's (1994) characterization of domestication as a shift from trust to domination has been questioned on the grounds that relations between humans and domesticated animals can also be seen in terms of trust and reciprocity (Knight 2005; Oma 2010), the point stands that there is a fundamental shift in the terms of relations. At the same time, a distinction emerged between domesticated and wild, farming and hunting (Cassidy and Mullin 2007:11). It is important to see each agricultural society in its historical and environmental context: as Morris (1998:125) argues for Malawi, agriculture results in a domestic-wild split, but without the "promethean ethic" of domination over nature. In general, hunted animals are to some extent encountered at the periphery of an agricultural collective, and so the animist relation of reciprocity is replaced by an analogist relation of difference, even antagonism. One indication of the understanding of this relationship in Bronze Age Mycenae is a gold seal found in one of the Shaft Graves (Figure 10.1). This finely crafted seal cannot be understood, however, solely in terms of human-animal relations: it is also necessary to understand the place of depictions in Aegean Bronze Age collectives.

FIGURE 10.1 Gold seal from Mycenae Shaft Grave III showing man and lion in conflict, 1600–1500 BC. © CMS Archive.

Art

Given that Aegean Bronze Age texts are few in number, and those that have been deciphered deal with economic transactions, images provide an important source of evidence for exploring the question of ontology. In order to address this question, however, it is important to look at what is shown and how, rather than focusing on symbolic meanings (Gell 1998). Nor should the materiality of art objects be forgotten: an object such as the seal shown in Figure 10.1 has both pragmatic aspects, relating to how it was worn and the possibility of making an impression in clay, as well as significative aspects (Knappett 2005:137). As Knappett stresses, things often signify indexically rather than symbolically, that is through their connections with other things found in the same context or made of the same material: in both cases there is a part-whole relationship, termed "factorality" (Sonesson 1994:275). Seals are a prime example of another type of indexicality since they are used to leave a trace in wet clay. This is an example of contiguity. Here indexicality will be seen as a prime way of establishing connections between different objects.

The style of depictions provides another aspect which need not be addressed symbolically. Recently, Descola has applied his scheme of ontologies to different types of images, resulting in what he terms "modes of figuration." He links naturalism to perspective drawing, in which the world is reduced to mathematical space and rendered as if from a single distanced viewpoint (Descola [ed.] 2010:87). By contrast, the X-ray style of some aboriginal Australian collectives simultaneously shows the inside and outside of ancestral beings; their bodies and the totemic collective are one and the same. In analogism, the world is split up and recombined, resulting in images such as composite beings. Descola also suggests that analogist images play the role of connectors, showing the relationships between different entities (Descola [ed.] 2010:14, 165). The objects of the Shaft Graves demonstrate this sort of fractal effect, with images of lion hunting repeated on media including seals, daggers, and grave stele; the famous Lion Hunt Dagger shows lions hunting deer on one side and men hunting lions with spears on the other side. Not only does this establish an analogy between lions and hunters as predators, the wider analogy is between hunting and warfare; it is notable that the man attacks the lion with a sword in Figure 10.1, a weapon for close combat in contrast with the hunters' spears shown on the Lion Hunt Dagger. Although Aegean Bronze Age images are often called "naturalist" because of their lifelike depiction of humans and animals, this relates more to the sense of movement and close observation in the absence of perspective rendering (Groenewegen-Frankfort 1951). It is the absence of perspective drawing that allows these images to play the role of connectors rather than distancing the viewing subject from depicted object as in Descola's naturalist mode of figuration.

The content of the images themselves also has the potential to provide insights into past ontologies: images of tree-shaking and rock-hugging led Herva (2006b) to identify animism on Minoan Crete. By contrast, in Figure 10.1, man and lion appear to be opposed. It can be argued that these depictions illustrate the different worldviews of 'peaceful' Minoan Crete and 'warlike' Mycenaean Greece, but this is to fall back upon stereotypes: a large number of Cretan sealstones show depictions of hunting. In both cases, images illustrate practices involving the interaction of humans and non-humans, but, it can be argued, these are the exclusive practices of an elite sector of society, differentiated by their clothing and reinforced by the gold medium of the depiction. It will be suggested here that depictions such as these emerged to associate an elite group with restricted practices such as lion-hunting or rock-hugging. This fits with Descola's observation that:

> the analogic collective is always divided into interdependent constitutive units which are structured according to a logic of segmentary nesting: lineages, moieties, castes, descent groups prevail here and expand the connections of humans with other beings from the infraworld to the heavens. Although the exterior of the collective is not entirely ignored, it remains an 'out-world' where disorder reigns, a periphery that may be feared, despised or predestined to join the central core as a new segment that will fit in the slot that has been allocated to it long before.
>
> *(Descola 2006:152)*

The material culture of the Bronze Age Aegean includes practices involving the 'out-world' but also its incorporation into the elite segment of the collective. These developments will now be traced, at the risk of grossly over-simplifying a far more complex history. It will be suggested that the diversity of the Shaft Grave assemblage can be seen as part of a process of incorporation of different bodies and things into an elite collective. This elite collective was a segment of a wider analogist collective whose development can be traced particularly on Crete. Here the increasing number of different non-humans resulted in the segmentation of the collective and the emergence of palaces.

Neolithic (7000–3200 BC)

The Neolithic package of domestic plants and animals can be seen as the founding collective into which other entities were incorporated over time. Unlike mainland Greece, there were no wild predators on Crete at the time of the introduction of domestic animals and so it was more the topography and insularity of Crete which defined the periphery of these collectives. Settlements such as Knossos were sited in fertile valleys suitable for domestic crops and animals. Non-human elements of the collective came to include pots, figurines, and stone tools. The earliest pottery at Knossos included skeuomorphs of baskets and wooden containers, showing analogical relations between materials (Tomkins 2007).

Although Neolithic communities are regarded as largely egalitarian until the end of the period, there are indications of an analogic mode of identification. The introduction of domestic plants and animals to Crete and the establishment of permanent settlements provided the ontological foundations for a collective with clearly defined boundaries. Those within these settlements were part of relations of production (both breeding and manufacture), protection (different entities were brought together within the household), and transmission (between generations). The overlap between patterns on pots and figurines potentially indicates a wider metaphorical connection between human bodies and non-human containers (Knappett et al. 2010:599). These analogies between different materials and different bodies were played out repeatedly over the course of the Bronze Age, but collectives grew larger and more differentiated as more humans and non-humans were incorporated.

Early Bronze Age (3200–2000 BC)

More entities were absorbed into the collective in the Early Bronze Age: Renfrew's (1972) account of an "international spirit" in the Aegean, as a result of the introduction of bronze, points the way to an increased set of interconnections. Relations between Crete and the Cyclades resulted in an influx of Cycladic material culture to the north of the island (Broodbank 2000:300–304). The diversity of burial traditions suggests that, although off-island imports were a common feature of Early Bronze Age mortuary assemblages, different communities were adopting these imports in different ways (Legarra Herrero 2009).

The tombs of South Central Crete at the end of this period provide an important example of the response to new things and materials. The appearance of Egyptian and Near Eastern objects, including stone vessels and amulets, suggests that communities had become part of the wider Eastern Mediterranean trading circuit (Bevan 2007; Phillips 2008). Circular tombs were the locations for collective burials in which the bones of different members of the local community were mingled together. Within this collective, however, there was differentiation in the form of objects such as seals. One group of seals termed "white pieces" was an adaptation of Egyptian faience technology, and the seals were frequently in the shape of scarabs (Pini 1990). The designs on their faces, however, were of a local geometric style, rather than imitations of Egyptian designs. This illustrates how different non-humans were incorporated into the collective by establishing analogies with existing aspects of the collective.

As has often been stressed, rather than a wholesale adoption of Cycladic and wider Eastern Mediterranean objects, the Early Bronze Age shows local selection and adaptation of materials and technologies. There are signs that the reception of these imports was linked to social differentiation: objects such as seals were used to mark property and are too few in number for each person in these collective burials to have been associated with one. From an ontological point of view, it is significant that these things were incorporated in such a way that they became part of the local collective, but maintained their capacity for difference. New materials also resulted in social differentiation because only certain members of society would have developed the skills to work with these materials requiring control of high temperatures, intricate carving, or both, as in the case of "white pieces." Early Bronze Age communal burials can be seen as important forums for the negotiation of the expansion of local collectives and for maintaining order among these diverse bodies and things by containing them within single contexts.

Middle Bronze Age (2000–1600 BC)

Over the course of the Middle Bronze Age, clear material hierarchies emerged on Crete centered around building complexes conventionally termed "palaces." The exact nature of the social hierarchies is the subject of debate: terms such as "heterarchy" have been used to express a sense of social fluidity and competition (Schoep and Knappett 2004). Of interest here is how an increase in trade with the Eastern Mediterranean resulted in the influx of new bodies and things. Of particular interest are the new bodies which entered Crete: depictions of cats suggest that they were imported to Crete at this time, although cat bones from this period have yet to be identified (Phillips 2008). Other bodies depicted on seals include griffins, sphinxes, and the so-called "Minoan genius," a transformation of the Egyptian goddess Tawaret. Wengrow (2011:144) links the appearance of these traveling monsters with emergent elites across the Eastern Mediterranean, who demonstrated "the ability to engage with and encompass the foreign." As before, these acts of incorporation show adaptations to local practices, with Tawaret acquiring a jug, for example, but it is apparent that these bodies are closely associated with a distinct palatial collective, rather than a broader local collective.

Imported technologies also transformed the material culture associated with the emergent elites. The bow drill allowed the use of hard stones, often imported, for sealstones. At the same time, a script known as Cretan Hieroglyphic was developed, which was both carved on hard stone sealstones and used for administrative documents. Writing epitomizes an analogist logic, separating the things of the world

FIGURE 10.2 Four-sided seal bearing Cretan Hieroglyphic Script, 1850–1600 BC. GR 1934, 1120.1. © Trustees of the British Museum.

into discrete objects and recombining them to produce new meanings. Sealstones used to produce inscriptions combined these new technologies and materials in single objects (Figure 10.2).

Across Crete, the combination of sealing practices and writing was used by an elite collective to establish a redistributive system centered on the palaces. The palaces were not just buildings, but focal points for combining foreign bodies and technologies, and practices such as communal eating and drinking. It is notable that unlike Egypt and the Near East, there was no clear iconography of individual leadership: rather than power being focused on a single person, it is likely to have been a property of this network of different bodies and things, accumulated and transformed in these key places. Rather than reflections of absent leaders or social systems, the palaces can be seen as the centers of elite collectives comprised of a diverse range of bodies and things brought together in new material configurations.

Late Bronze Age (1600–1100 BC)

Established at the start of the Neolithic, Knossos was long an important place on Crete, but it came to particular prominence at the start of the Late Bronze Age. Other Middle Bronze Age palaces developed distinct configurations of the new technologies, materials, and bodies, with two different writing systems in use, for instance, but, following a series of destructions towards the end of the Middle Bronze Age, the collective centered on Knossos can increasingly be recognized across Crete. A deposit from the palace at Knossos dating to the period immediately following these destructions shows how marine animals were incorporated into this elite collective. Although skeuomorphs of shells were known from the Middle Bronze Age, the adoption of faience-making at Knossos allowed the creation of marine animals, including flying fish and argonauts, which were inhabitants of the

FIGURE 10.3 Faience sea creatures from the Knossos Temple Repositories, ca. 1600 BC. Ashmolean Museum, University of Oxford.

open sea (Figure 10.3). The so-called Temple Repositories assemblage with which they were found included other faience objects, including the well-known snake goddesses, as well as painted shells and seal impressions showing shells and other marine animals (Evans 1921:495–523; Panagiotaki 1999). The use of faience to create these diverse bodies establishes an indexical link between them, bringing animals from the sea into the collective centered on the palace.

Another artistic development at Knossos is the use of a realistic style of depiction to capture certain practices, including the tree-shaking mentioned above, but also humans leaping over bulls. Such depictions of bulls, also including relief frescoes and three-dimensional models in materials such as bronze and ivory, act to demonstrate the practices of the elite collective. Bull-leaping in particular is differentiated from the animal practices of the everyday which are not depicted (Shapland 2010). The realistic style captures the moment of these relationships between humans and non-humans. Over time, this developed into a more abbreviated form, resulting in condensed depictions of human–animal relations conventionally termed "minotaurs," although composed of a variety of animal bodies with human legs (Krzyszkowska 2005:207–8). These epitomize the chimeras of Descola's ([ed.] 2010:165–72) analogist mode of figuration (Figure 10.4).

The Shaft Grave assemblages cannot be understood without considering Knossos: the ostrich egg with faience dolphin appliqués is one of many foreign objects which had first passed through Crete and been modified there. As Burns (2010:76) points out, however, "even if they did not arrive directly from Egypt, the objects denote foreign places, creatures and people." Although debates have centered on the possible presence of 'Minoans' in the Shaft Graves with the arrival of 'Mycenaeans,'

FIGURE 10.4 Sealstone showing a human-animal hybrid, or 'minotaur', 1450–1375 BC. GR 1877, 0728.3. © Trustees of the British Museum.

one important difference is that contemporary burial assemblages from Crete are virtually unknown. The assembling of this collective at the moment of death is a departure from Cretan practices, but shows the same identification with the world beyond. It is the indexical links established by burial that capture the ontology most clearly.

Over the course of the Late Bronze Age, these elite collectives become more difficult to distinguish. After a second set of destructions in Crete in 1450 BC, Knossos was the only remaining palace, showing increasing 'Mycenaean' influence. Around the same time, palaces emerged on the Greek Mainland at Mycenae and elsewhere. The Linear B tablets found at these palaces record vast flocks of sheep and the industrial production of textiles and perfumed oil. Although dyed textiles do not survive, characteristic Mycenaean stirrup jars, into which the perfumed oil was packaged for export, are found across the Eastern Mediterranean. Other materials flowed in return: the Uluburun shipwreck dating to 1300 BC is an isolated snapshot of a much wider circulation of goods. Along with approximately 11 tons of copper and tin ingots (in the proportion needed to make bronze), a ton of glass ingots represents another new material (Pulak 1998). Glass beads found across the Aegean were the result of melting down this new imported material and pouring it into molds to produce local forms, making sense of a different material (Figure 10.5). Although the quantity of bronze circulating was larger than in the Early Bronze Age, and new materials such as glass had appeared, the same process of incorporating difference into the collective by analogy with local forms is apparent.

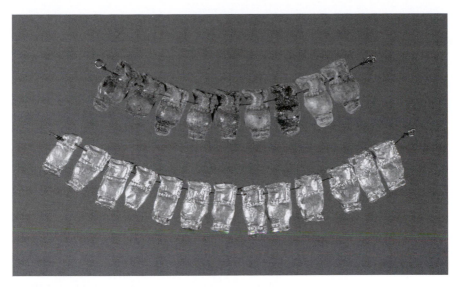

FIGURE 10.5 Mycenaean glass beads and gold covers from Ialysos, 1350–1250 BC. GR 1870, 1008.50. © Trustees of the British Museum.

This brief and incomplete account of the material culture of the Bronze Age Aegean has sought to trace the continuity of an analogist logic in which different humans and non-humans were brought together in coherent collectives. Earlier collectives showed local responses to the influx of new things and bodies, before the emergence of elite collectives in the Middle to Late Bronze Age, which successfully incorporated a wide range of new materials, things, monsters, and animals as a means of differentiation. This can be seen as a process of segmentation in response to the increasing contact with the world beyond the Aegean: an overarching analogy between the elite and the outside provided the basis for the formation of an elite collective centered on palaces. This analogy can be seen most clearly at the point when a new elite collective emerged centered on Mycenae whose members, human and non-human, were brought together in the Shaft Graves. The change seen over the course of the Late Bronze Age as the circulation of materials increased in scale was an increased industrialization, involving the mass production of export goods. As trade networks shifted at the end of the Bronze Age, the palaces were destroyed and these elite collectives disappeared.

From analogism to naturalism

There are instructive similarities between the Bronze Age Aegean and Medieval Europe. Descola (2005:282–88) identifies the latter as an example of an analogist collective which divided the world into differentiated entities linked by the Great Chain of Being. In Medieval Europe, an elite identified with the hunt and sought to control this practice (Cartmill 1993). Medieval maps show monsters at the periphery of the world (Friedman 2000). Aegean Late Bronze Age depictions, such as the Shaft Grave imagery of lions, associate the hunting of certain animals with an elite. Griffins were not hunted, but were brought from the extreme periphery to sit in frescoes either side of the throne at the palace of Knossos. In both periods there was extensive trade with this periphery, but whereas Bronze Age trading systems ultimately broke down, those of Medieval Europe grew until they reached across the globe. It can be suggested that it is in this growth that the origins of naturalism lie (Latour 1993:117; 1999:195).

The influx of plants, animals, and things from the 'New World' ultimately caused a crisis in European classification systems. Rather than each plant species being recognized as separate, and categorized by their different medicinal uses, new levels of classification such as 'genus' and 'family' developed to show evolutionary relationships between species from different places in the globe (Atran 1990). Genus and species tend to be equivalent in a given area because each genus is usually represented by a single local species, and so it is only when species from different areas were systematically compared in post-Medieval Europe that the concept of genus emerged (Atran and Medin 2008: 25–28). In other words, the only way the collective could cope with the vast number of new species was to recognize the essential continuity between them.

The same process of comparison occurred between humans. Viveiros de Castro returns to Lévi-Strauss's observation that the Amerindian equivalent of the Spanish Inquisition was to see whether European bodies rotted in the same way as theirs: "For the Europeans, the issue was to decide whether the others possessed a soul; for the Indians, the aim was to find out what kind of body the others had" (Viveiros de Castro 1998:475). The result for the Europeans was a conception of humanity as distinct, a Cartesian split between humans and animals. The separation of the human mind from a body shared with the rest of the animal kingdom characterizes Descola's naturalistic ontology. The point to be made is that an increase in the number of entities within the collective can be seen as resulting in the emergence of a new ontology.

Although contact increased between regions of the Eastern Mediterranean over the course of the Bronze Age, it is hard to see the same ontological crisis which arguably resulted in the development of 'naturalism' in modernity. The Neolithic had seen the gradual expansion of a collective of humans and non-humans from the Fertile Crescent whose relations were already defined by the domestication of animals and plants by humans. The circulation of bodies and things around the Mediterranean only started in earnest at the end of the Early Bronze Age, but this did not result in connections between such radically different collectives as did the later encounter between Europe and the Americas. The arrival of new bodies such as cats, and new technologies such as writing, did result in changes in the organization of collectives, but this has been seen here in terms of segmentation rather than an ontological shift. Cats and ostrich shells provided an analogy with the outside to be incorporated within an elite collective, rather than a fundamental challenge to the collective's understanding of the world.

Conclusion

The Bronze Age Aegean offers a challenge to thinking about the ontologies of hierarchical societies. Archaeologists have more frequently considered the ontologies of small-scale societies in terms of renewed anthropological debates about animism. Where the ontology of a Bronze Age state has been considered, written records have helped to reveal certain aspects of human engagement with objects (Meskell 2004). In the absence of clear ethnographic parallels or illuminating texts, archaeologists have tended to extend the ontology of the modern world to render the 'Minoans' and 'Mycenaeans' a familiar reflection of our own society (Hamilakis 2002). The ontological scheme proposed by Descola, however, provides a convincing alternative to the animism or totemism largely found in small-scale societies, and to the naturalism of our own projected onto accounts of the Bronze Age. Analogism offers a framework for understanding how humans make sense of their increasingly variegated interactions with other humans, in the form of social hierarchy, and with a variety of non-human animals and things circulating around an ever more connected world.

It has been suggested that assemblages such as the Shaft Graves or the Temple Repositories are constituents of a collective of humans and non-humans which demonstrated the successful incorporation of ontologically different bodies and things. The human members of these collectives were the elites of these societies, differentiated by their relationships with unfamiliar non-humans, whether animals, things, or perhaps even deities. Whereas an elite collective incorporated a wide variety of non-humans, other more locally based groups were composed of a range of familiar non-humans, and experienced the unfamiliar largely at second-hand. Imported materials, for instance, passed through the elite collectives, whose craftspeople acted as agents of transformation. The Temple Repositories or Shaft Grave assemblage shows how new bodies and things could be put together to create material analogies with the world beyond.

The art of these societies has often been seen as the reflection of an interest in the natural world, religious beliefs, or a warlike spirit. Following an analogist logic, such depictions can instead be seen as a form of negotiation between humans and non-humans, ordering these different entities into a coherent whole. From the Neolithic period onwards, skeuomorphs established a set of indexical connections between things made from different materials. Even marine animals were reproduced in other materials to bring them into contexts such as the palace at Knossos or the Shaft Graves at Mycenae. The realistic depictions of animal practices, such as hunting or bull-leaping of the early Late Bronze Age, also demonstrated relationships between different bodies. Despite Schliemann's first impressions, it has become clear that the Bronze Age Aegean lacked any clear imagery of rulers. Instead, an elite collective emerged at the center of a dense network of relationships between an ever-increasing diversity of bodies and things. That, however, would not have made for a very exciting telegram.[1]

Note

1 With thanks to Chris Watts for putting together this volume and a stimulating SAA conference session, and to Lesley Fitton and the British Museum for making my attendance in Memphis possible. Carl Knappett, David Wengrow and Todd Whitelaw all made helpful comments on a draft of this paper.

Bibliography

Alberti, Benjamin, and Yvonne Marshall 2009. Animating Archaeology: Local Theories and Conceptually Open-Ended Methodologies. *Cambridge Archaeological Journal* 19(3):344–56.

Atran, Scott 1990. *Cognitive Foundations of Natural History: Towards an Anthropology of Science.* Cambridge University Press, Cambridge.

Atran, Scott, and Douglas Medin 2008. *The Native Mind and the Cultural Construction of Nature.* MIT Press, Cambridge, Massachusetts.

Bevan, Andrew 2007. *Stone Vessels and Value in the Bronze Age Mediterranean.* Cambridge University Press, Cambridge.

Bird-David, Nurit 1999. "Animism" Revisited: Personhood, Environment and Relational Epistemology. *Current Anthropology* 40(S):567–91.

Boyer, Pascal 2010. Why Evolved Cognition Matters to Understanding Cultural Cognitive Variations. *Interdisciplinary Science Reviews* 35(3–4):376–86.

Broodbank, Cyprian 2000. *An Island Archaeology of the Early Cyclades.* Cambridge University Press, Cambridge.

Brown, Linda A., and William H. Walker 2008. Prologue: Archaeology, Animism and Non-Human Agents. *Journal of Archaeological Method and Theory* 15:297–99.

Burns, Bryan E. 2010. *Mycenaean Greece, Mediterranean Commerce, and the Formation of Identity.* Cambridge University Press, Cambridge.

Cartmill, Matt 1993. *A View to a Death in the Morning: Hunting and Nature through History.* Harvard University Press, Cambridge, Massachusetts.

Cassidy, Rebecca, and Molly Mullin 2007. *Where the Wild Things Are Now: Domestication Reconsidered.* Berg, Oxford.

Clark, Andy 2008. *Supersizing the Mind: Embodiment, Action and Cognitive Extension.* Oxford University Press, Oxford.

Descola, Philippe 2005. *Par-delà nature et culture.* Gallimard, Paris.

——(2006). Beyond Nature and Culture. *Proceedings of the British Academy* 139:137–55.

——(2010). Cognition, Perception and Worlding. *Interdisciplinary Science Reviews* 35(3–4):334–40.

Descola, Philippe (editor) 2010. *La Fabrique des images.* Musée du quai Branly and Somogy, Paris.

Descola, Philippe, and Gísli Pálsson 1996. Introduction. In *Nature and Society: Anthropological Perspectives*, edited by Philippe Descola and Gísli Pálsson, pp. 1–21. Routledge, London.

Evans, Arthur J. 1921. *The Palace of Minos at Knossos*, vol. I. Macmillan, London.

Friedman, John B. 2000. *The Monstrous Races in Medieval Art and Thought.* Syracuse University Press, Syracuse, New York.

Gell, Alfred 1998. *Art and Agency.* Clarendon Press, Oxford.

Gibson, James J. 1979. *The Ecological Approach to Visual Perception.* Houghton Mifflin, Boston.

Groenewegen-Frankfort, Henrietta 1951. *Arrest and Movement.* Faber and Faber, London.

Hamilakis, Yannis 2002. What Future for the 'Minoan' Past? Rethinking Minoan Archaeology. In *Labyrinth Revisited: Rethinking 'Minoan' Archaeology*, edited by Yannis Hamilakis, pp. 2–28. Oxbow, Oxford.

Herva, Vesa-Pekka 2005. The Life of Buildings: Minoan Building Deposits in an Ecological Perspective. *Oxford Journal of Archaeology* 24(3):215–27.

——(2006a). Flower Lovers, After All? Rethinking Religion and Human-Environment Relations in Minoan Crete. *World Archaeology* 38(4):586–98.

——(2006b). Marvels of the System. Art, Perception and Engagement with the Environment in Minoan Crete. *Archaeological Dialogues* 13(2):221–40.

Holbraad, Martin 2009. Ontology, Ethnography, Archaeology: An Afterword on the Ontography of Things. *Cambridge Archaeological Journal* 19(3):431–41.

Ingold, Tim 1994. From Trust to Domination: An Alternative History of Human-Animal Relations. In *Animals and Human Society: Changing Perspectives*, edited by Aubrey Manning and James Serpell, pp. 1–22. Routledge, London.

——(2000). *The Perception of the Environment: Essays in Livelihood, Dwelling and Skill*. Routledge, London.

Karo, Georg 1930. *Die Schachtgräber von Mykenai*. Bruckmann, Munich.

Knappett, Carl 2005. *Thinking Through Material Culture*. University of Pennsylvania Press, Philadelphia.

Knappett, Carl, Lambros Malafouris, and Peter Tomkins 2010. Ceramics (as Containers). In *The Oxford Handbook of Material Culture Studies*, edited by Dan Hicks and Mary Beaudry, pp. 588–612. Oxford University Press, Oxford.

Knight, John 2005. Introduction. In *Animals in Person: Cultural Perspectives on Human-Animal Intimacies*, edited by John Knight, pp. 1–13. Berg, Oxford.

Krzyszkowska, Olga 2005. *Aegean Seals: An Introduction*. Bulletin of the Institute of Classical Studies, Supplement 85. Institute of Classical Studies, London.

Lakoff, George, and Mark Johnson 1999. *Philosophy in the Flesh: The Embodied Mind and its Challenge to Western Thought*. Basic Books, New York.

Latour, Bruno 1993. *We Have Never Been Modern*. Harvester Wheatsheaf, London.

——(1999). *Pandora's Hope: An Essay on the Reality of Science Studies.* Harvard University Press, Cambridge, Massachusetts.

——(2009). Perspectivism: 'Type' or 'Bomb'? *Anthropology Today* 25(2):1–2.

Legarra Herrero, Borja 2009. The Minoan Fallacy: Cultural Diversity and Mortuary Behaviour on Crete at the Beginning of the Bronze Age. *Oxford Journal of Archaeology* 28(1):29–57.

Lévi-Strauss, Claude 1963. *Totemism*. Beacon, Boston.

——(1966). *The Savage Mind*. Weidenfeld and Nicolson, London.

Lloyd, G. E. R. 2007. *Cognitive Variations: Reflections on the Unity and Diversity of the Human Mind*. Oxford University Press, Oxford.

——(2010). History and Human Nature: Cross-cultural Universals and Cultural Relativities. *Interdisciplinary Science Reviews* 35(3–4):201–14.

——(2011). Humanity between Gods and Beasts? Ontologies in Question. *Journal of the Royal Anthropological Institute (N.S.)* 17:829–45.

Malafouris, Lambros 2008. Is it 'Me' or Is it 'Mine'? The Mycenaean Sword as a Body–part. In *Past Bodies*, edited by John Robb and Dušan Borić, pp. 115–23. Oxbow, Oxford.

Meskell, Lynn 2004. *Object Worlds in Ancient Egypt*. Berg, Oxford.

Morris, Brian 1998. *The Power of Animals: An Ethnography*. Berg, Oxford.

Olsen, Bjørnar 2010. *In Defense of Things: Archaeology and the Ontology of Objects*. AltaMira, Lanham, Maryland.

Oma, Kristin Armstrong 2010. Between Trust and Domination: Social Contracts between Humans and Animals. *World Archaeology* 42(2):175–87.

Panagiotaki, Marina 1999. *The Central Palace Sanctuary at Knossos*. Supplementary Volume 31. British School at Athens, London.

Phillips, Jacqueline 2008. *Aegyptiaca on the Island of Crete in their Chronological Context: A Critical Review*, Vol. I. Verlag der Österreichischen Akademie der Wissenschaften, Vienna.

Pini, Ingo 1990. Eine Frühkretische Siegelwerkstatt? In *Pepragmena tou Diethnous Kritologikou Synedriou, A2*, pp. 115–27. Philologikos Sillogos "O Chrisostomos," Chania.

Pulak, Cemal 1998. The Uluburun Shipwreck: An Overview. *International Journal of Nautical Archaeology* 27(3):188–224.

Renfrew, Colin 1972. *The Emergence of Civilisation*. Methuen, London.

Russell, Nerissa 2012. *Social Zooarchaeology: Humans and Animals in Prehistory*. Cambridge University Press, Cambridge.

Schliemann, Heinrich 1878. *Mycenae: A Narrative of Researches and Discoveries at Mycenae and Tiryns*. Murray, London.

Schoep, Ilse, and Carl Knappett 2004. Dual Emergence: Evolving Heterarchy, Exploding Hierarchy. In *The Emergence of Civilisation Revisited*, edited by John C. Barrett and Paul Halstead, pp. 21–37. Oxbow, Oxford.

Serpell, James 1986. *In the Company of Animals: A Study of Human-Animal Relationships*. Basil Blackwell, Oxford.

Shapland, Andrew 2010. Wild Nature? Human-Animal Relations in Neopalatial Crete. *Cambridge Archaeological Journal* 20(1):109–27.

Sonesson, Göran 1994. Prolegomena to the Semiotic Analysis of Prehistoric Visual Displays. *Semiotica* 100:267–331.

Tapper, Richard 1988. Animality, Humanity, Morality, Society. In *What Is an Animal?*, edited by Tim Ingold, pp. 47–62. Unwin Hyman, London.

Thomas, Julian 2004. *Archaeology and Modernity*. Routledge, London.

Tilley, Christopher 2004. *The Materiality of Stone: Explorations in Landscape Phenomenology*. Berg, Oxford.

Tomkins, Peter 2007. Communality and Competition: The Social Life of Food and Containers at Aceramic and Early Neolithic Knossos, Crete. In *Cooking Up the Past: Food and Culinary Practices in the Neolithic and Bronze Age Aegean*, edited by Christopher Mee and Josette Renard, pp. 174–99. Oxbow, Oxford.

Traill, David 1995. *Schliemann of Troy: Treasure and Deceit*. Murray, London.

Viveiros de Castro, Eduardo 1998. Cosmological Deixis and Amerindian Perspectivism. *Journal of the Royal Anthropological Institute* 4(3):469–88.

——(2010). In Some Sense. *Interdisciplinary Science Reviews* 35(3–4):318–33.

Wengrow, David 2011. Cognition, Materiality and Monsters: The Cultural Transmission of Counter-intuitive Forms in Bronze Age Societies. *Journal of Material Culture* 16(2):131–49.

Willis, Roy 1990. Introduction. In *Signifying Animals: Human Meanings in the Natural World*, edited by Roy Willis, pp. 1–24. Unwin Hyman, London.

11

CLASSICISM AND KNOWING THE WORLD IN EARLY MODERN SWEDEN

Vesa-Pekka Herva and Jonas M. Nordin

Introduction

The foundations of Western culture and society are commonly traced back to the ancient Greco-Roman world, and classical antiquity has been appropriated in myriad ways in the literal and figurative building of the post-medieval modern world. The complex process of modernization involved, among other things, the development of new economic systems, large-scale urbanization, European colonization of the world, multiculturalism, and ultimately the birth of an industrialized consumer society. Modernization also involved a gradual secularization of Western society and the emergence of a scientific understanding of the world. Our aim in this chapter is to consider the material and intellectual appropriation of the classical and ancient worlds in early modern Sweden, and in particular to discuss how the uses of the past were embedded in – and came to manipulate – people's perception and understanding of the world.

"Classicism" is a term which can mean different things in different contexts, but we use it in an inclusive sense to denote any form of appropriating real or imagined classical antiquity. Fascination with classical antiquity started in Renaissance Italy and spread elsewhere in Europe, including regions like Sweden which historically had very little, if any, direct contact with the classical world. Classicism influenced both the European intellectual environment and its architecture and other types of material culture. In addition to classicism, the early modern period saw the birth of a broader antiquarian interest in the ancient past, which in Sweden developed into the curious ideology of Gothicism (see Eriksson 2002).

Classicism and the broader appropriation of ancient worlds in early modern Sweden are considered in this chapter from a material culture perspective informed by the recent discussion of relational ontologies and epistemologies in anthropology and archaeology. While the views discussed below are relevant to and have implications for the study of excavated materials (e.g., Herva 2009, 2010a), the approach taken in this chapter is archaeological in the sense that it revolves around the more general issue of how people related with material culture and the material world in the early modern period. Classicism and other forms of appropriating the past in seventeenth-century Sweden provide a useful perspective on that broader issue.

This chapter will consider relational thinking in the context of early modern Sweden from two perspectives, or on two levels. First, it seeks to appreciate the relational dimension of the perception and understanding of the world in the Renaissance and Baroque period. A key idea in this respect is that magic and magical thinking were more important and integral to everyday engagement with the world than has previously been recognized in post-medieval archaeology. Relational thinking, we propose, provides tools for reassessing the nature and significance of magical thinking, which rationalism has dismissed and misrepresented since the later seventeenth century. Second, this chapter will address the role of dynamic two-way relationships between people and the material world on a more general level. In particular, we will discuss how knowledge about the world has been constituted in relation to material culture in the post-medieval period, and how material culture contributed to historical processes by shaping people's thought and behavior, albeit perhaps unconsciously.

Knowing and engaging with the world

The rise of scientific thinking has conventionally been represented as a triumph of rationalism over religious and superstitious delusions, which supposedly results in better knowledge about the world and how it works. There is some truth to this view, of course, but rationalism has also come to monopolize true knowledge, which in turn has obfuscated the fact that there are other ways of knowing the world (Ingold and Kurttila 2000). Recent discussions of relational ontologies and epistemologies propose not only that there are alternative modes of knowing the world, but also that reality itself may be quite different from how it is portrayed by science. Very briefly put, the established scientific view holds that the real world is composed of bounded and autonomous physical entities which have a fixed identity and properties, whereas relational thinking proposes that relationships between things determine what things are; the identities and properties of all things are generated through their involvement in the world (e.g., Ingold 2000, 2011; Järvilehto 1998).

The significance of relational thinking for archaeological research is two-fold. First, it provides new tools for understanding cultures where the world and its workings were understood in other than mechanistic and dualistic terms (see also Brück 1999). Relational thinking can therefore help to avoid modernist biases. Second, a relational approach allows for an exploration of the dynamics of human-thing relationships beyond subject-object and related dualisms. If, as relational thinking proposes, there is a deeply dynamic and reciprocal relationship between people and material things, any proper understanding of historical processes requires appreciating the more or less active contribution of things to the unfolding of human life.

Relational thinking, with its proposal that the world can be known and manipulated in various ways, also provides new perspectives on magic and magical thinking which will be referred to frequently below. A thorough discussion of the famously difficult concept of magic is beyond the scope of this chapter, but a few general remarks will suffice for our present purposes. It must be recognized, first, that Enlightenment rationalism has resulted in the misrepresentation of the nature and significance of magic and magical thinking in the pre-Enlightenment world. Magic is commonly associated with the supernatural and superstitious, but in pre-Enlightenment Europe (natural) magic was about studying the properties of things and the relationships between them, and it was not separable from the 'rational' or 'scientific' pursuits of the time (e.g., Goodrick-Clarke 2008:40–41; Henry 2008:8–9).

Indeed, magic can be understood – and not only in the context of the pre-Enlightenment world, but more generally – as a mode of connecting and engaging with a rich, relationally constituted reality. "Magic," as Glucklich (1997:12) puts it, is "based on a unique type of consciousness: the awareness of the interrelatedness of all things in the world by means of a simple but refined sense of perception." Magic thus conceived can help to assess from a fresh perspective aspects of people-thing relationships in early modern Sweden and beyond. In what follows, we will discuss modes of knowing and engaging with the world, where all kinds of material things could have special properties and causation was not limited to mechanical cause-effect relations.

Gothicism and classicism in early modern Sweden

Runestones and other ancient relics were of much interest in seventeenth-century Sweden. This interest stemmed from a longer-term project of building the Swedish state and identity after Sweden separated from a Danish-led union of Nordic Kingdoms in the 1520s. Sweden had identified itself with the historical Goths since the late Middle Ages, and Gothicism became an important element in the construction of the Swedish identity in the sixteenth century and especially during the seventeenth century, when Sweden established itself as a European great power (e.g., Ekman 1962; Neville 2009). Gothicism, then, served the purpose of finding or inventing historical roots for the Swedish nation and glorifying the past of the short-lived Swedish empire. In addition to the study of classical and other historical sources, the project of building history and identity for the Swedish nation involved the documentation and study of material remains, such as runestones, which testified to its great past.

Ancient relics, however, had a deeper meaning than illustrating real and fabricated histories. In seventeenth-century Sweden, runestones were more than just stones etched with old writing; they were thought to be causally linked to the world through their magical properties (Karlsson 2009:71–72, 213; see also below).

Runestones may be a particularly clear example of the special powers invested in material things, but the entire pre-Enlightenment world was loaded with similar magical potency and special powers in both the popular and learned view (as will be discussed below), and the appropriation of classical and ancient pasts must also be considered against that wider background.

Swedish Gothicism is one of the most striking examples of the early modern interest in alternative pasts and of identifying with ancient people, but similar interests emerged also elsewhere in Europe (Burke 2003:282–83). "In the Renaissance as in the Middle Ages," Burke (1992:16) explains, "'legitimation by descent' was one of the most common and persuasive means of justifying claims of different kinds, including claims to nationhood." In addition to a Gothic past, classical heritage was also appropriated in early modern Sweden, and elements of barbarian and classical identities were combined in an apparently unproblematic manner (Neville 2009:215).

Renaissance culture developed late in Sweden. It was not until the second half of the sixteenth century that Renaissance ideas started to shape the Swedish cultural climate, though they became stronger during the reign of Gustav II Adolf and his successors in the seventeenth century (McKeown 2009). Renaissance ideals of urban planning were increasingly adopted towards the mid-seventeenth century, and classical architecture began to appear in Sweden roughly at the same time. The capital, Stockholm, for instance, was modeled after Rome, and it was transformed into a Baroque city during and after the reign of Queen Christina (Laitinen and Lindström 2008:275–77; McKeown 2009:145). The Dutch played a key role in the transmission of classical planning and building in Sweden and elsewhere in Northern Europe (e.g., Ottenheym 2003), but the Swedish intervention in the Thirty Years' War also contributed to the adoption of classical architecture and Renaissance and Baroque culture in general (see e.g., Revera 1988).

The adoption of classical ideals of planning and building in the seventeenth century was associated with the spread of new styles or aesthetic ideals within Europe. In order to truly appreciate the significance of appropriating the classical world, however, it is necessary, first, to consider classicism as embedded in the early modern understanding of the world more generally. Secondly, given the deeply dynamic two-way relationship between people and built environments (or the material world in general), there is also a need to consider how classically-inspired changes in built environments would have been linked to broader changes in patterns of life and thought. It will be suggested below that the uses and appropriation of the past in early modern Sweden were not related solely to matters of, for instance, memory, ideology, and legitimacy. Rather, in a relational world, the past was recognized as 'magically' potent or alive and considered to affect human life more actively or directly than dualistic and mechanistic views would allow.

A world of correspondences

Classicism, of course, involved much more than adopting new artistic and architectural styles. Ideas derived from the real and imagined classical world have shaped modern Western culture, society, and thought in innumerable ways from the Italian Renaissance up to the present day. Yet there is an important aspect to classical heritage and its appropriation that has been effectively marginalized since the Enlightenment: the significance of what might be called "magical thinking." It is well known in principle that forms of magic and magical thinking were part of Renaissance culture, and historians of ideas have recently addressed and scrutinized popular and scholarly misconceptions about magic and its significance in early modern Europe (e.g., Henry 2008).

It may, however, be impossible to truly appreciate the nature and role of magic in early modern Europe within the modernist framework of thinking that has naturalized a host of problematic conceptual divisions, such as culture/nature, subject/object, and mind/world. A part of the problem lies in the fact that such divisions may be of little use for analyzing the Renaissance and Baroque world where, for instance, the division between the natural and the supernatural was drawn differently from today (e.g., Henry 2008). Another problem is that, as noted above, such divisions may be faulty and misleading to begin with.

The Renaissance revival of the classical world involved the discovery of ancient magical traditions, especially Hermeticism, which was initially thought to represent ancient Egyptian wisdom. Rather than some marginal or deviant phenomenon, magical thinking was integral to the Renaissance and Baroque understanding of the world. This is reflected in the thought of early humanist philosophers like Marsilio Ficino and Giovanni Pico della Mirandola, as well as pioneering scientists from Paracelsus, to Tycho Brahe and Isaac Newton (for further examples, see e.g., Goodrick-Clarke 2008; Henry 2008). While a variety of natural philosophies and cosmological ideas flourished at the time, the Renaissance and Baroque understanding of the world generally revolved around an idea of an animate cosmos which was bound together by all kinds of correspondences, analogies, and sympathies, and where all kinds of spiritual beings and forces operated (e.g., Livingstone 1988:277; Thomas 1971:337–38; see also Herva 2010b; Herva et al. 2010). A world like that could be manipulated by various means beyond mechanical causation, and the theory of correspondences was also the basis of Renaissance magic (Karlsson 2009:212–13).

Tycho Brahe's manor and observatory on the Danish island of Ven is illustrative of how cosmological notions could be embodied in built environments (Figure 11.1). Both buildings were oriented to the compass directions and the four elements of the world (Artursson 1992). The compass directions were combined with towers, turrets, and lanternines, making Brahe's palace a panoptic edifice which was elevated so as to provide Brahe with an excellent position to look at the world, scientifically as well as socially.

Although Sweden was a cultural backwater of Europe, classical learning and Renaissance ideas about the world were not unfamiliar in the country in the seventeenth century. Scholars like Johannes Bureus – who served as a tutor to Prince Gustav Adolf and Princess Christina, and as the state antiquarian – were deeply immersed in the Renaissance-Baroque magical universe (Karlsson 2009).

FIGURE 11.1 Tycho Brahe's Uraniborg, as represented in his book *Tychonis Brahe Astronomiae instauratae mechanica* (1598).

While the likes of Bureus may have been special cases, Paracelcian and Rosicrucian ideas, for instance, were also more widely known in Sweden (e.g., Åkerman 1991, 1998; Lindroth 1943). Concepts of magical correspondences or related notions were not limited to the learned Renaissance views of the cosmos either, but broadly similar ideas were central to the folk perception and understanding of the world on the northern fringe of Europe (Herva 2009; Herva and Ylimaunu 2009). Forms of Renaissance and Baroque magical thinking are of interest here because they can be understood not simply as fallacious ideas about the world and its workings, but as reflecting a wider awareness of the relational nature of reality and the significance of 'animistic' modes of knowing the environment in the early modern world (Herva 2010a; 2010b; Herva et al. 2010).

Materiality and the construction of knowledge

An idea central to relational thinking is that the boundary between humans and their environment, or mind and world, is a modernist illusion. The relationship between people and the world, in other words, is more deeply dynamic and reciprocal than what the conceptual division between subjects and objects allows. This means, among other things, that knowledge about the world is also constituted in dialogue between people and the things around them. Knowing "is an *extension* of perceiving" (Gibson 1986:258 [1979], emphasis in original), and material culture rather obviously structures people's perceptions, thus contributing to a knowing of the world.

Cabinets of curiosities provide an illustrative example of how the display and arrangement of natural and cultural things was linked to knowledge about the world in general in the Renaissance and Baroque periods. Cabinets of curiosities "were structured as a microcosm of creation, ordered by sympathy, allegory and correspondence" (Thomas 2004:15). The ordering of things in cabinets of curiosities suggests that the world was perceived very differently in Renaissance and Baroque times from today. In Snickare's view:

> Most striking for a beholder of today is the apparent lack of order and categorization: natural objects are juxtaposed with cultural artifacts; objects made for practical use are placed next to exquisite art works; European objects are mixed with objects from the most distant parts of the world. This is suggestive of a time before what might be called the dichotomization of the world, that is, before the strict distinction between nature and culture, art and science, art works and ethnographic objects, etc.
>
> *(Snickare 2011:129)*

A further important point is that "display can be a powerful rhetorical tool by which one perspective, one way of viewing the world, is emphasized at the expense of another" (Snickare 2011:128). This rhetorical power, however, is not limited to purposefully constructed displays or "theaters of the world" but is rather an aspect of all built environments in general. The castle of Skokloster (Figure 11.2) provides an example of the "microcosmic" aspect of buildings in early modern Sweden. In other words, the case of Skokloster exemplifies some aspects of how

FIGURE 11.2 The Skokloster castle today. Photo: J. Nordin.

knowledge about the world was constituted and ordered in relation to material culture.

Skokloster Castle was erected by the Admiral, Marshal, and Count Carl Gustaf Wrangel in 1654–76. One of the most famous Baroque castles in Sweden, Skokloster manifests Palladian ideals, which were widespread during the period (Hidemark 2004:69–72). The plan of the castle is square-shaped, with a tower at each corner and an open courtyard with loggias and a well. On the western side, a geometrically strict Baroque garden was constructed. Building materials for the castle were brought from all over the Swedish-Baltic realm, while the roof tiles were made in Delft and the marble quarried in Carrera (Hidemark 2004:74). The towers were crowned by armillary spheres – which were paralleled by terrestrial globes and various instruments in the collection of the castle (Kylsberg 2006:77–85; Losman and Sigurdsson 1975) – and many rooms were given names of places and cities of the world, whereas several paintings depicted conceptual global landscapes. The harmonic layout of the castle is aligned to the compass points and the four elements, resembling Tycho Brahe's Uraniborg in that respect. While the latter manifestly expresses a geocentric worldview, the former emphasized a Eurocentric ideology. Brahe was an astronomer and astrologist concerned with cosmic matters, whereas Wrangel – a warrior and politician – was more concerned with places on earth.

The stucco ceilings of Skokloster show an abundant world of motives: Roman arms and armor are blended with seventeenth-century guns and artillery, coats of arms and cartouches, and everywhere are depictions of animals and flowers from all over the world. Only the great dining hall of the castle was decorated with painted stucco which still survives in its original condition. The motifs are emblematic, representing the four continents known to Europeans at the time. The symbol of Europe – Europa – is provided with a pair of compasses, musical instruments, a vaulted and ruined stone house, and a varied set of arms – all symbols of the noble arts of architecture, music, and warfare. Africa is depicted as a woman riding a rhinoceros, wearing a parasol, and seeking shelter from the merciless African sun. Asia is identified by a woman wearing a turban alongside a resting camel. America, diagonally opposite Europe, is depicted as a wreathed and partially nude woman alongside an armadillo carrying a packet, probably consisting of tobacco, and on top of it a parrot (cf. Losman 1988:88). On one level, this imagery is not difficult to decode. Europe is depicted as culture, whilst the other three continents to varying extents are shown as nature: the animals are as important as the humans and are displayed as their equals. Europe is presented with a classical vaulted building, with ruins of past greatness as its companion; Europe is history.

The combination of classical and colonial imagery was common in early modern Europe (Gosden 2004:112–13). The mixing of ancient and indigenous peoples suggests that it was the similarities, rather than the differences, between the two that intrigued early modern Europeans (Ryan 1981:529). This is understandable, of course, in the view that ancient and indigenous peoples had a decisive element of exoticism to them. Ringmar argues that:

If we simplify a very complex development, we can explain the breakdown of medieval culture as a result of Europe's confrontation with the radically different, with otherness: most importantly, perhaps, otherness in the form of a Greek and Roman heritage. As classical texts on science, philosophy and the arts became widely known and widely diffused, educated Europeans were suddenly confronted with a discursive universe which was simultaneously a part of their own tradition, yet also curiously foreign and of course completely non-Christian.

(Ringmar 1996:146)

Ryan (1981:532) proposes that "genealogy was powerful medicine against the confusions introduced by novelties, and it served as an effective prophylaxis against the impact of the new worlds." The discovery of classical and ancient pasts on the one hand, and new regions of the globe on the other, marked an expansion and enriching of the world known to Europeans, which in turn necessitated coming to terms with that world.

Theaters of the world – whether in the form of cabinets of curiosities or places like Skokloster and Uraniborg – can be understood as tools or instruments for coming to know a larger and richer universe. Collecting, displaying, and representing objects enabled ordering the world and negotiating relationships, as well as discovering and determining the position of European people and culture within it. Collections and displays provided people with kinds of maps – and like all maps, they did not simply reflect what was already known, or what the world was 'really' like. Rather, they contributed to the generation of a particular kind of world by rendering some things, relationships, categories, and boundaries more real than others (see also Herva 2010b; Schwartz 1985; Snickare 2011:127).

Collections and displays may also be thought of as contributing to the objectification of the world. That is, they would have promoted a sense that the world, large and rich as it was turning out to be, could nonetheless be subjected to human control (cf. Mrozowski 1999). Like Renaissance map galleries (Herva 2010b), theaters of the world brought the globe – even otherwise unknown and distant lands – within human reach in a psychological sense at least. Furthermore, the recognition that there were lands that existed, and had existed, without European knowledge of them might have proposed that the world in general existed somehow separately from people, just like the association of the 'New World' with the 'non-cultural' in a European sense – as illustrated in the emblematic paintings of the continents in Skokloster – contributed to the emerging dualism with nature and culture.

Classicism and the material appropriation of the past as magic

Olof Verelius, a seventeenth-century Swedish antiquarian who followed Johannes Bureus in the study of runes, argued that those initiated in the secrets of runes could use them to summon the dead and call spirits (Andersson 1997:102; Karlsson

2009:71–72). Whatever exactly Verelius may have meant by that, his argument provides a useful cue for rethinking the significance of appropriating the past and its material remains in Baroque Sweden more generally. The ancient past, it will be proposed below, was not separate from the present, but elements of the past remained alive and could (be used to) make a causal difference in the early modern 'magical reality.' A proper knowledge of the world required, among other things, appreciating the agency or active role of the past in the present.

When he was crowned in 1617, Gustav II Adolf was dressed as and played the role of Berik, a fictitious ancient king of the Goths (Neville 2009:215; Ringmar 1996:108–9, 160). King Carl X Gustav, who in turn ascended the throne in 1654, wore white silk and silver clothing in his coronation, as well as at his wedding, which would have made him resemble Roman statues that had become increasingly popular in royal courts at that time. The king and the queen appeared as if made of marble, and they thus emphasized their association with the legacy of ancient Rome in a manner typical of the late Renaissance.

Rather than just symbolic statements, such references to the Gothic and Roman past can be understood as a form of image magic: "by performing a role in the world of symbolic forms, the ruler could make the symbols real" (Ringmar 1996:108). Image-making was an ontological act in the Renaissance world (Cosgrove 1990:350), a form of sympathetic magic which established a causal link between a representation and the object of representation. This image magic, in turn, was embedded in the broader understanding of the cosmos as deeply interconnected by sympathies, analogies, and resemblances (Gombrich 1948:176). The praxis of image making and its cultural role also helps to explain the rather confusing Renaissance habit of blending different types of imagery. The juxtaposing of imagery on the stucco ceiling of Skokloster has already been discussed, but curious forms of blending and mimicry occurred also in very different contexts (Nordin 2012:147–48).

Classical planning and building, like dressing as Goths, could similarly be conceived as a means of establishing a magical correspondence with a past world – that is, in Gell's (1998) terms, "abducting" qualities or virtues from the classical world. The imitation of classical forms in planning and building, in this view, would not have been simply an aesthetic matter of prettifying towns – which Gustav II Adolf himself described as "rotten and broken down" (Lilja 1995:50) – but charging the urban fabric with 'spiritual' qualities and virtues channeled from the classical world. Likewise, the naming of house blocks in Stockholm after Roman deities, such as Diana and Juno, served to embody a classical cosmology into the very fabric of the city.

As far-fetched as the proposed forging of a magical relationship between seventeenth-century Swedish urban space and classical antiquity might appear at first, it should be kept in mind that correspondences and harmonies were of considerable interest to Renaissance urban planning and architecture, and spatial and built forms were actually designed and constructed so as to channel cosmic powers and take on talismanic properties (e.g., Akkerman 2001; Sack 1976). In folk culture, likewise, planning and building had to account for 'spiritual' properties and beings of the ordinary everyday world, as indicated in folklore (Korhonen 2009), while so-called ritual deposits associated with buildings can be understood as infusing houses with special properties (Herva 2010a), which compares – albeit on a very general level – to the idea of investing towns with special virtues through image magic.

The uses of material remains from the past can, of course, also be considered in similar terms as an imitation of the classical world – that is, a form of magical communion or bonding with the past. At Skokloster, for instance, Wrangel had in his possession a Renaissance stone manor in the center of the estate, but he also had the remains of a medieval monastery, including a church and a ruined parish church, all well situated on small hilltops by the waterways of Lake Mälaren (Figure 11.3). Instead of tearing down the medieval buildings, which was a rather common practice after the Reformation (Howard 2003), and recycling them as building materials for the castle, Wrangel decided to keep the old buildings in use. It is difficult to understand this decision in purely practical terms, and Wrangel apparently found it important to incorporate history in the landscape of Skokloster. Old buildings were not just memorials; the medieval churches on the Sko peninsula continued to be used as religious sanctuaries, in addition to serving as nodes of historic meaning in the landscape.

The incorporation of old buildings or their remains in the landscape of Skokloster may be understood as manifesting ownership and control over the land, but it can also be considered as a form of magical or spiritual connection with past worlds. Buildings, and houses in particular, are intimately linked to their inhabitants – they are, indeed, extensions of the people who build and inhabit

FIGURE 11.3 The Skokloster castle and its surroundings in 1666. From Erik Dahlberg's *Svecia Antiqua et Hodierna* (1716).

them (Carsten and Hugh-Jones 1995:2–3; cf. Turner 2000). Houses are deeply immersed in social relations and accumulate relationally constituted "life forces" as the result of their involvement in people's daily practices (Carsten and Hugh-Jones 1995:37; Gell 1998:226, 252–53; Herva 2010a). The old buildings and ruins at Skokloster would similarly have been charged with a life and power that they had abducted from history, thus bringing the past to life in a very tangible way.

The recycling of building materials, which is commonly attested in early modern Sweden, can also be understood in similar terms. Recycling was not just a cost-efficient practice, but also a form of spatially and temporally distributing the lives of buildings and the people associated with them – it passed on something of the identity and properties of the original buildings and transplanted them into new ones (see Gell 1998:222, 225–26; Hicks and Horning 2006:287–92). Intriguingly, Finnish folklore suggests that the recycling of timber could result in the trans-planting of household spirits, although this theme is more common in the case of ship spirits (Haavio 1942:171–77). What the above discussion indicates, in short, is that material things had, and were recognized to have, special properties which enabled 'animistic' two-way relations between people and things.

The rise of the classical town in Sweden: reasons and consequences

Like all practices, planning and building are necessarily embedded in a particular understanding of what the world is like and how it works. This does not mean that early modern urban plans, for instance, were designed so as to intentionally express metaphysical concepts, but it does mean that the logic of planning is not necessarily self-evident or reducible to transparent practical-rational principles that are readily obvious to us today. Lilley (2009), for example, has made the case that ordinary urban forms in medieval cities were imbued with cosmological meaning; even basic geometric forms, such as the square and circle, were symbolically charged and established connections to dimensions of reality beyond the readily accessible physical world. The point here, quite obviously, is that occasionally 'odd' or apparently non-rational elements in urban landscapes not only call for symbolic readings, but planning and building in general must be considered against broader ideas about the world. While medieval urban forms would have reflected, in Lilley's (2009) view, Christian cosmological concepts, early modern planning and building in Sweden – including the classicizing of urban landscapes – will have to be con-sidered in a similar manner, albeit in somewhat different terms. In this final section, we consider some possible motives for the classicizing of built environments in Sweden from a relational view and discuss how classically inspired changes would have restructured people's experience and knowledge of the world.

The Swedish crown promoted the regulation of urban spaces rather intensively from around 1640 onwards. This was associated with the wider influence of classicism and Renaissance culture in northern Europe, but there is more to the adoption and promotion of a grid plan than just new aesthetic preferences, and the crown's preoccupation with regulation must be seen against broader developments in seventeenth-century Sweden. As Grant's (2001) survey shows, the grid plan has been favored in different social and cultural contexts for over 3000 years, but there is a recurrent association between the grid plan and colonialism, and this association is certainly clear in the context of the early modern world (see also Kostof 1991:100–103). The seventeenth-century Swedish fascination with the grid plan must also be considered against that background. The strict geometrical plans implemented at the Dutch-funded and -influenced iron-works in central Sweden around the mid-seventeenth century had a clear colonial undertone, which has parallels in the town planning and foundation of plantations in the overseas colonies (cf. Nordin 2012:156–59).

Sweden was a colonial power in the seventeenth century – a small-time agent in comparison to major European colonial powers, but it nonetheless acquired (rather unsuccessfully) overseas colonies, such as New Sweden in the Delaware valley in 1638–55 and coastal possessions on the Gold Coast in 1649–63 (Fur 2006; Weiss 2010). The capital of New Sweden, Christinehamn, was provided with a geometrical town plan which was designed on-site in 1654, and which was not at all adapted to the geographical realities of the marshy area at the mouth of River Christina (see e.g., Dahlgren and Norman 1988:168). More importantly, perhaps, Sweden also exercised colonial power in Sápmi (Lapland), where an association between Renaissance planning and Sweden's colonial pursuits is evident in the spatial organization of silver-works established in the 1630s. The crown was also planning to found a colonial town in Arjeplog, which was never realized, but which would have been built on a geometrically regular grid plan and divided between Sámi and Swedish inhabitants (see Nordin 2012:150–59).

The association between colonial pursuits and the geometric organization of built environments is rather clear in the Swedish overseas colonies and Sápmi. Somewhat less obviously, however, the regulation of organically organized urban spaces on the geometric plan in other parts of the realm can also be understood as the crown's attempt to 'conquer' its own towns. Sweden was a geographically enormous, but sparsely populated, country in the sixteenth century, and it grew even larger during the seventeenth century. The crown had struggled for a long time to tighten control over trade in the vast kingdom and the seventeenth-century urbanization boom, like the colonization of Lapland, was associated with the implementation of a strict mercantilist policy (cf. Fur 2006). It has been argued elsewhere that the extensive mapping campaign launched by King Gustav II Adolf in 1628 reflects an attempt to bind the expanding realm together in a new manner, and is not reducible to straightforward practical concerns of collecting geographical or other information (Herva and Ylimaunu 2010). The regulation project, we would suggest, can also be considered in similar terms.

The regulation of towns changed or restructured the relationship between the crown and its territories and subjects. Rather than simply asserting its power and presence by means of churches, town halls, or other symbols associated with it, the crown now embedded its agency in the very fabric of towns. The crown, in other

FIGURE 11.4 A streetscape of a 'classical' wooden town (Rauma, Southwest Finland). Photo: V.-P. Herva.

words, came to control, or affect, the patterns of everyday life and the experience of urban environments in new ways (Figure 11.4). As Grant (2001:237) puts it, "the grid clearly signifies that planners were at work. It denies spontaneity and indigenous landscape traditions. It imposes a rational conceptual order that transcends time and space and proclaims the control and power of central authorities." The geometrization of urban space would have manipulated the townsfolk and their perception and understanding of the world in various ways and on several levels.

To begin with, the geometric organization of urban space, just like that of the iron- and silver-works in central and northern Sweden, implied a division between cultural environments and nature. Geometrically organized towns with straight streets made people perceive places differently and move between them in manners quite distinct from places with more organic spatial organization. The very experience of, or living in, geometrically ordered environments would also have proposed, subtly and subconsciously, a difference between distinctively cultural spaces and what was being constructed as the natural world (cf. Ingold 2007:153; Kostof 1991:95). The construction of the nature-culture divide is, of course, but one example of how the change from the organic to geometric spatial organization of lived environments affected people. By way of comparison, Akkerman (2001) has made an interesting case for how urban environments affected the thought of Kepler and Descartes and thereby contributed to the birth of rationalism. Changes in early modern Swedish towns, and their impact on common concepts of what the world is like, can be considered in similar terms.

An issue of particular interest here is how organic and geometric ordering of urban space may have linked to different ways of knowing the world. Organic towns would have emphasized a relational and contextual mode of knowing, due to their more or less labyrinthine organization and the diversity of locales connected with each other in a variety of ways. Towns organized on a geometric plan, by contrast, presented much more predictable and standardized spatial arrangements which could be reduced to certain basic principles, and be therefore known in a more abstract and generalized way. Although specific locales differed from each other in geometrically oriented towns, they nonetheless promoted a new sense of continuity, order, and homogeneity on a fundamental structural level, which was further underlined by the Renaissance and especially the eighteenth-century, neo-classical desire to construct unified street facades. All this implied a predictable world and downplayed the sense of wonder and the richness of the lived world.

The experience of organic towns can perhaps be compared to the world as it appeared in cabinets of curiosities – that is, "the exuberant and labyrinthine displays of the armories and *Wunderkammern* evoke an image of a world much more enigmatic, unfixed, and open than in the centuries to come" (Snickare 2011:129). In brief, then, the transformation of organic towns into geometric towns "conditioned" people to a mechanistic understanding of the world at the expense of relational knowing, though this did not happen all of the sudden. It can be argued that 'animistic' social relationships with the material world persisted not only in rural areas, but also in seventeenth-century urban settings, at least in the more peripheral regions of Sweden (Herva 2010a). Yet relational knowing did ultimately lose its authority as modernization progressed (Ingold in Bird-David 1999:81), and social relations with the environment became trivialized and misrepresented as folk beliefs and superstitious magical thinking (see Herva and Ylimaunu 2009).

A variety of smaller-scale changes in built environments, such as modifications to building materials and techniques, can similarly be considered as resonating with broader concepts about the world and people's relationship with it. The construction of proper stone foundations for wooden houses (which generally dominated Swedish built environments in the early modern period) could be seen as a means of separating buildings from their surroundings. In the mid-seventeenth century, the plan of the so-called "double house" (Sw. *parstuga*) spread rapidly all over Sweden, implementing a new regularity in vernacular architecture (Nordin 2012:152). The painting of previously gray houses with red ochre paint – a practice which was adopted among the elite beginning in the eighteenth century – and the later practice of boarding houses with planks, served a similar purpose. Thus, the boundaries of houses became more emphasized – a shell, in essence, was created around buildings to separate the inside from the outside (cf. Glassie 2000:59–61). This enclosing of houses would have naturalized, through everyday experience of the world, the modernist "logic of inversion" through which, as Ingold (2006:11) puts it, "beings originally open to the world are closed in upon themselves, sealed by an outer boundary or shell that protects their inner constitution from the traffic of interactions with their surroundings."

Conclusions

The ancient and classical worlds were not only appropriated in various ways and contexts in early modern Sweden, but they were also mixed with each other and the "New World" in a manner that seems curious in the modern view. The appropriation of the past and the mixing of apparently unrelated things have often been understood in ideological terms, or as reflecting somehow tenuous or erroneous understandings of the world. While not entirely wrong, such views are too narrow and fail to appreciate that the Renaissance and Baroque worlds – and the modes of knowing and manipulating those worlds – were very different from the world, and how it is understood, today. The rise of antiquarian interests in seventeenth-century Sweden in general had a political and ideological background, but the fascination with runestones and other ancient objects must also be considered against, and as embedded in, the magical (or relational) understanding of reality.

While the Swedish adherence to the ancient Goths appears exotic from a modern point of view – and thus something that calls for a 'special' explanation – classicism by contrast has become such a naturalized aspect of modern European culture and identity that the appropriation of the classical world in early modern Europe is easily just taken as given. We propose, however, that like the Swedish cult of the Goths, classicism in seventeenth-century Sweden had magical under-pinnings. Classical planning and building, for instance, can be thought of as a means of establishing a magical connection with, or channel to, the ancient classical world. Yet even though the classicizing of built environments was originally embedded in a magical understanding of reality, classical planning and building came to alter people's experience of the world in a manner that facilitated the emergence of a rationalist and mechanical understanding of the world.

Relational ontologies and epistemologies have usually been explored in distinctively pre-modern or non-Western contexts, but relational thinking provides useful tools for reconsidering various aspects of the post-medieval European past as well. Relational thinking affords, among other things, a consideration of the dynamics between people and material culture, or the material world in general, quite different from the standard dualistic and mechanistic frameworks of thought. In this chapter, we have discussed how diverse kinds of material culture and material practices – from runestones to cabinets of curiosities, and from dressing up as Goths to the classicizing of urban built environments – were linked and contributed to the knowing and understanding of the world in seventeenth-century Sweden.

Bibliography

Åkerman, Susanna 1991. *Queen Christina of Sweden and Her Circle: The Transformation of a Seventeenth-Century Philosophical Libertine*. Brill, Leiden.
——(1998) *Rose Cross over the Baltic: The Spread of Rosicrucianism in Northern Europe*. Brill, Leiden.
Akkerman, Abraham 2001. Urban Planning in the Founding of Cartesian Thought. *Philosophy and Geography* 4(2):143–69.
Andersson, Björn 1997. *Runor, magi, ideologi: en idéhistorisk studie*. Umeå University, Umeå.

Artursson, Magnus 1992. Uraniborg i bild och verklighet. *Ale: Historisk tidksirift för Skåneland* 1992(2):13–25.

Bird-David, Nurit 1999. "Animism" Revisited: Personhood, Environment, and Relational Epistemology (with comments). *Current Anthropology* 40(S):67–91.

Brahe, Tycho 1598. *Astronomiae instauratae mechanica.* Peter de Ohr, Wandesburg.

Brück, Joanna 1999. Ritual and Rationality: Some Problems of Interpretation in European Archaeology. *European Journal of Archaeology* 2(3):313–44.

Burke, Peter 1992. The Uses of Italy. In *The Renaissance in National Context*, edited by Roy Porter and Mikuláš Teich, pp. 6–20. Cambridge University Press, Cambridge.

——(2003). Images as Evidence in Seventeenth-Century Europe. *Journal of the History of Ideas* 64(2):273–96.

Carsten, Janet, and Stephen Hugh-Jones 1995. Introduction: About the House – Lévi-Strauss and Beyond. In *About the House: Lévi-Strauss and Beyond*, edited by Janet Carsten and Stephen Hugh-Jones, pp. 1–46. Cambridge University Press, Cambridge.

Cosgrove, Denis 1990. Environmental Thought and Action: Pre-Modern and Post-Modern. *Transactions of the Institute of British Geographers* NS 15(3):344–58.

Dahlberg, Erik 1716. *Svecia Antiqua et Hodierna.* s.n, Stockholm.

Dahlgren, Stellan, and Hans Norman 1988. *The Rise and Fall of New Sweden: Governor Risingh's Journal 1654–1655 in Its Historical Context.* Almqvist and Wiksell International, Uppsala.

Ekman, Ernst 1962. Gothic Patriotism and Olof Rudbeck. *Journal of Modern History* 34(1):52–63.

Eriksson, Gunnar 2002. *Rudbeck 1630–1702: liv, lärdom, dröm i barockens Sverige.* Atlantis, Stockholm.

Fur, Gunlög 2006. *Colonialism in the Margins: Cultural Encounters in New Sweden and Lapland.* Brill, Leiden.

Gell, Alfred 1998. *Art and Agency: An Anthropological Theory.* Clarendon Press, Oxford.

Gibson, James J. 1986 [1979]. *The Ecological Approach to Visual Perception.* Lawrence Erlbaum, Hillsdale, New Jersey.

Glassie, Henry 2000. *Vernacular Architecture.* Indiana University Press, Indianapolis.

Glucklich, Ariel 1997. *The End of Magic.* Oxford University Press, New York.

Gombrich, Ernst 1948. Icones Symbolicae: The Visual Image in Neo-Platonic Thought. *Journal of the Warburg and Courtauld Institutes* 11:163–92.

Goodrick-Clarke, Nicholas 2008. *The Western Esoteric Traditions: A Historical Introduction.* Oxford University Press, New York.

Gosden, Chris 2004. *Archaeology and Colonialism: Cultural Contact from 5000 BC to the Present.* Cambridge University Press, Cambridge.

Grant, Jill 2001. The Dark Side of the Grid: Power and Urban Design. *Planning Perspectives* 16:219–41.

Haavio, Martti 1942. *Suomalaiset kodinhaltiat.* Werner Söderström, Helsinki.

Henry, John 2008. The Fragmentation of Renaissance Occultism and the Decline of Magic. *History of Science* 46(1):1–48.

Herva, Vesa-Pekka 2009. Living (with) Things: Relational Ontology and Material Culture in Early Modern Northern Finland. *Cambridge Archaeological Journal* 19(3):388–97.

——(2010a). Buildings as Persons: Relationality and the Life of Buildings in a Northern Periphery of Early Modern Sweden. *Antiquity* 84:440–52.

——(2010b). Maps and Magic in Renaissance Europe. *Journal of Material Culture* 15(3):323–43.

Herva, Vesa-Pekka, and Timo Ylimaunu 2009. Folk Beliefs, Special Deposits, and Engagement with the Environment in Early Modern Northern Finland. *Journal of Anthropological Archaeology* 28(2):234–43.

——(2010). What's on the Map? Re-Assessing the First Urban Map of Torneå and Early Map-Making in Sweden. *Scandinavian Journal of History* 35(1):86–107.

Herva, Vesa-Pekka, Kerkko Nordqvist, Anu Herva, and Janne Ikäheimo 2010. Daughters of Magic: Esoteric Traditions, Relational Ontology and the Archaeology of the Post-Medieval Past. *World Archaeology* 42(4):609–21.

Hicks, Dan, and Audrey Horning 2006. Historical Archaeology and Buildings. In *The Cambridge Companion to Historical Archaeology*, edited by Dan Hicks and Mary Beaudry, pp. 272–92. Cambridge University Press, Cambridge.

Hidemark, Ove 2004. Slottsbyggnaden berättar. In *Skoklosters slott under 350 år*, edited by Carin Bergström, pp. 62–95. Byggförlaget, Stockholm.

Howard, Maurice 2003. Recycling the Monastic Fabric: Beyond the Act of Dissolution. In *The Archaeology of the Reformation 1480–1580*, edited by David Gaimster and Roberta Gilchrist, pp. 221–34. Maney, Leeds.

Ingold, Tim 2000. *The Perception of the Environment: Essays in Livelihood, Dwelling and Skill*. Routledge, London.

——(2006). Rethinking the Animate, Re-Animating Thought. *Ethnos* 71(1):9–20.

——(2007). *Lines: A Brief History*. Routledge, London.

——(2011). *Being Alive: Essays on Movement, Knowledge and Description*. Routledge, London.

Ingold, Tim, and Terhi Kurttila 2000. Perceiving the Environment in Finnish Lapland. *Body and Society* 6(3–4):183–96.

Järvilehto, Timo 1998. The Theory of the Organism – Environment System: I. Description of the Theory. *Integrative Physiological and Behavioral Science* 33(4):321–34.

Karlsson, Thomas 2009. *Götisk kabbala och runisk alkemi: Johannes Bureus och den götiska esoterismen*. University of Stockholm, Stockholm.

Korhonen, Teppo 2009. Rakennuspaikan valinta ja valtaus sekä kodin turvaaminen. In *Maasta, kivestä ja hengestä: Markus Hiekkanen festschrift*, edited by Hanna-Maria Pellinen, pp. 262–71. University of Turku, Turku.

Kostof, Spiro 1991. *The City Shaped: Urban Patterns and Meanings through History*. Thames and Hudson, London.

Kylsberg, Bengt 2006. *A Glimpse of the World: Non-European in Skokloster Castle*. Skoklosterstudier, Linköping.

Laitinen, Riitta, and Dag Lindström 2008. Urban Order and Street Regulation in Seventeenth-Century Sweden. *Journal of Early Modern History* 12(3–4):257–87.

Lilja, Sven 1995. Small Towns in the Periphery: Population and Economy of Small Towns in Sweden during the Early Modern Period. In *Small Towns in Early Modern Europe*, edited by Peter Clark, pp. 50–76. Cambridge University Press, Cambridge.

Lilley, Keith D. 2009. *City and Cosmos: The Medieval World in Urban Form*. Reaktion Books, London.

Lindroth, Sten 1943. *Paracelsismen i Sverige till 1600-talets mitt*. Almqvist and Wiksell, Uppsala.

Livingstone, David N. 1988. Science, Magic and Religion: A Contextual Reassessment of Geography in the Sixteenth and Seventeenth Centuries. *History of Science* 26(3):269–94.

Losman, Arne 1988. Skokloster – Europe and the World in a Swedish Castle. In *The Age of New Sweden*, edited by Arne Losman, Agneta Lundström, and Margareta Revera, pp. 85–101. Livrustkammaren, Stockholm.

Losman, Arne, and Ingrid Sigurdsson 1975. *Äldre vetenskapliga instrument på Skokloster*. Skoklosterstudier, Uppsala.

McKeown, Simon 2009. Reading and Writing the Swedish Renaissance. *Renaissance Studies* 23(2):141–50.

Mrozowski, Stephen 1999. Colonization and the Commodification of Nature. *International Journal of Historical Archaeology* 3(3):153–66.

Neville, Kristoffer 2009. Gothicism and Early Modern Historical Ethnography. *Journal of the History of Ideas* 70(2):213–34.

Nordin, Jonas M. 2012. Embodied Colonialism: The Cultural Meaning of Silver in a Swedish Colonial Context in the 17th Century. *Post-Medieval Archaeology* 46(1):143–65.

Ottenheym, Konrad A. 2003. Dutch Contributions to the Classicist Tradition in Northern Europe in the Seventeenth Century. *Scandinavian Journal of History* 28(3–4):227–42.

Revera, Margareta 1988. The Making of a Civilized Nation: Nation-Building, Aristocratic Culture and Social Change. In *The Age of New Sweden*, edited by Arne Losman, Agneta Lundström, and Margareta Revera, pp. 103–31. Livrustkammaren, Stockholm.

Ringmar, Erik 1996. *Identity, Interest and Action: A Cultural Explanation of Sweden's Intervention in the Thirty Years War*. Cambridge University Press, Cambridge.

Ryan, Michael T. 1981. Assimilating New Worlds in the Sixteenth and Seventeenth Centuries. *Comparative Studies in Society and History* 23(4):519–38.

Sack, Robert D. 1976. Magic and Space. *Annals of the Association of American Geographers* 66 (2):309–22.

Schwartz, Robert 1985. The Power of Pictures. *The Journal of Philosophy* 82(12):711–20.

Snickare, Mårtin 2011. The King's Tomahawk: On the Display of the Other in Seventeenth-Century Sweden, and after. *Konsthistorisk tidskrift* 80(2):124–35.

Thomas, Julian 2004. *Archaeology and Modernity*. Routledge, London.

Thomas, Keith 1971. *Religion and the Decline of Magic*. Penguin, London.

Turner, J. Scott 2000. *The Extended Organism: The Physiology of Animal-Built Structures*. Harvard University Press, Cambridge, Massachusetts.

Weiss, Holger 2010. Danskar och svenskar i den atlantiska slavhandeln, 1650–1850. In *Global historia från periferin: Norden 1600–1850*, edited by Leos Müller, Göran Rydén, and Holger Weiss Holger, pp. 39–73. Studentlitteratur, Lund.

12

THE IMBRICATION OF HUMAN AND ANIMAL PATHS: AN ARCTIC CASE STUDY

Peter Whitridge

Introduction

Humans endlessly make and follow trails. Laetoli – the oldest hominin trackway – is striking evidence of the character of an emerging bipedal adaptation, but also of path making and path following; the site is interpreted as the prints produced by a few *Australopithecus afarensis* walking in fresh volcanic ash, at least one of whom likely stepped in the prints made by another (Leakey and Hay 1979). The site also preserves trackways left by numerous other animals – from elephants to birds – which reminds us that the fossil record of tracks actually extends back half a billion years, to the impressions left by Ediacaran fauna on the floors of Precambrian seas (Liu et al. 2010). Although the contemporary world, dissected and built over with tens of millions of miles of human roads and paths, might represent a sensible perspective from which to view the archaeological record of route making, and is the one usually adopted by archaeologists equipped with contemporary geomatic technologies (hence a focus in the literature on *roads* rather than *trails*), the animal world provides another, equally appropriate, point of view. We are, after all, animals.

Adopting an animal-oriented perspective, the novelty of human pathmaking immediately becomes suspect. Many animals produce trails, and deliberately utilize trails produced by other species, and although animal trail blazing may not, typically, be a self-conscious activity, neither is much traditional human trail making. Humans choose the most efficient paths through a landscape, subject to our spatial goals, which means that, like other animals, we readily follow preexisting trails. Since humans typically only enter landscapes that are already inhabited by the game we pursue, we are trail followers before we are trail blazers. A zoocentric archaeology of paths thus seems worth exploring, and particularly apt in the Arctic. For its enormous size, the North American Arctic has few developed paths and fewer roads, but is nonetheless thoroughly dissected by animal travel routes, some deeply incised by millennia of use, and many also travelled by human hunters. Human spatial practices are still caught up in the larger and more ancient web of animal spatial practices from which they emerged over five million years ago. Following brief discussions of human and animal travel, the overlapping trail networks of precontact northern Labrador are considered more closely. Ultimately, the traces of animal and human use in the Nunatsiavut landscape prove impossible to disentangle. Not only that, but the material and the immaterial also seem to be knotted together. Travel routes are sung, dreamt, cited, imagined, and remembered as much as they are trod.

Archaeological paths and roads

Paths and roads have traditionally received limited archaeological attention. Objects, buildings, and settlements are visible, tangible, and analytically tractable, but the routes that enmesh them are harder to envision. They are often difficult to discern on the ground, and are inevitably less productive of archaeologically interesting things. The most formally engineered roadways are relatively well studied, such as the widespread traces of the vast imperial road networks of Tawantinsuyu (Jenkins 2001) and Rome (van Tilburg 2007). The latter illustrates how transportation networks are optimal only with respect to a given set of spatial practices; although at the northwestern frontier of the empire, the Roman road network in Britain was well-constructed, vast, and rational, connecting settlements in radiating straight-line arrays. Nevertheless, much of it was quickly abandoned when Rome withdrew (Reynolds 1995:24); the logic of regional economies and relatively small polities made pointless an infrastructure designed to meet the idiosyncratic needs of an empire.

The roads produced by repetitive human traffic rather than deliberate design and construction efforts, such as the Anglo-Saxon routes that replaced the Roman ones, may be equally spectacular, especially where surviving holloways record the centuries or millennia of traffic required to incise a trail seven meters deep into the landscape. The Sweet Track of southwest England, a two-kilometer-long section of wooden boardwalk built over a marsh almost 6,000 years ago, illustrates a different situation, where a deliberately constructed variety of trail has survived under unusual taphonomic circumstances (Brunning et al. 2000; Coles and Coles 1986). Paths are not necessarily ephemeral, but such distinctive traces have not often been recognized and discussed archaeologically. In recent decades, however, satellite imagery revealing road and trail networks that are hard to detect on the ground has become widely available, and Geographic Information Systems (GIS) have come to provide the global mapping environment in which the spatial connections amongst settlements have become increasingly sensible (e.g., Dore and McElroy 2011). Field recording technologies have become more sophisticated in concert with GIS, and community-oriented archaeologies have drawn out local knowledges of trails and travel practices (Snead et al. [eds.] 2009). Traditional knowledge of the places connected by trails is the focus of the ethnogeographic inventories of place names that have gained renewed attention from ethnographers and archaeologists (e.g., Müller-Wille [ed.] 1987).

Even in the absence of a Gaussian spatial logic, places are always nested in landscapes through the connections enacted by trails and roads. Heidegger (1977:330) used the example of a bridge to talk about the way in which things act to assemble the world around them: "it brings stream and bank and land into each other's neighbourhood. The bridge *gathers* the earth as landscape around the stream." The landscape comes into existence through the effects that trails produce, channeling human movements in meaningful and redundant ways. These effects are fractal. Regions are knit together by the long distance circulation of people and things along roads and trails, and communities by the paths that link neighborhoods to each other. Dwellings in turn articulate with their neighborhoods by way of well-trodden lanes of movement that pass through doorways, encircle buildings, and connect with other features, both nearby and far out across the landscape. Within houses, habitual paths of movement and rest link entrance, tunnel, halls, rooms, furniture, and so on (Figure 12.1; see also Dawson [2002] on the intricate networks of loci constituted by Inuit dwellings). Even bodies, both human and animal, and inert things have topological structures that can be thought of in terms

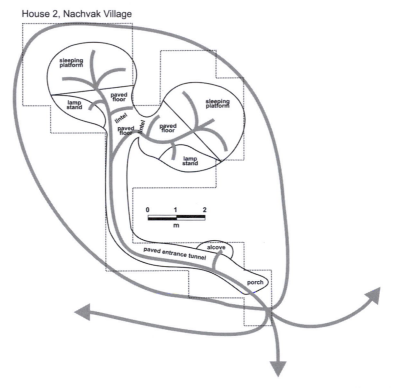

FIGURE 12.1 Paths of movement in and around a precontact and protohistoric Inuit winter house (House 2 at Nachvak Village [IgCx-3], northern Labrador).

of places and paths, whether for the eye or the hand or the mind (Whitridge 2004a). Archaeologically, some of these routes are accessible as constructed roads and accretional trails, and the less tangible networks can be explored using spatial analytic techniques (Menze and Ur 2012).

Animal tracks and trails

Animals, of course, generate and use patterned networks of paths themselves; Lefebvre (1991:118) noted that the "reticular patterns" of wild and domestic fauna resemble human paths of movement. These consist of both the visible traces of redundant movement through the landscape – tracks, trails, markings, spoor – and less humanly tangible features, such as the pheromonal scent trails by which many animals deliberately mark and negotiate their place within a larger faunal community. While some animal movement takes advantage of natural travel corridors, such as stream beds or beaches, animals frequently create paths by their own redundant route following. Muskoxen provide an extreme example of this; to conserve energy, bands will travel across the snow-covered winter landscape in single file, each animal carefully stepping in the prints left by the one ahead of it, like the Laetoli hominids. Game trails leading to water sources, or paths through rough or steep terrain, are characteristic features of many landscapes, and are often created and entrenched by multiple species. Just as animals pursue, or lie in wait for, each other along such paths, human hunters pursue game along them, and set snares, traps, and ambushes (see Gell [1996] for a marvelous discussion of the setups entailed in trapping animals along game trails, and Latour [1988] on the notion of the "setup"). The human relation to trails is thus dually animalistic. Like non-human animals, we produce durable trails in moving through and using the landscape in purposive, repetitive ways; but, like other carnivores, we often employ animals' own trails in doing so, both tactically and out of convenience.

Animal trails are thus a logical starting point for an archaeology of paths and roads, and the Arctic a suitable place to begin. In many parts of the north, large numbers of a variety of trail-making and trail-using species still traverse the landscape along well-worn paths that have been (and continue to be) used by humans. Although it would be difficult to trace these very far back into the past for any great spatial extent, the persistence of such jointly utilized routes can sometimes be inferred. For example, near the site of Onion Portage in northwestern Alaska, the seasonal movements of the Western Arctic caribou herd bring thousands of animals to an area of shallow water crossings on the Kobuk River every fall. The enduring importance of this locale for caribou travel routes has resulted in a nearly 10,000-year-long cultural sequence of human settlement and harvesting (Anderson 1988). Here, as at game ambush sites in many times and places, humans took advantage of habitual and topographically constrained animal movements. Such movements are archetypally embodied in the paw or hoof print, perhaps because, with our attenuated sense of smell and hyper-developed sense of sight, such visual traces are particularly apt for prey monitoring. It is not surprising then that animal prints have frequently been taken up symbolically (e.g., the bear paw print petroglyphs of the Columbia Plateau; Keyser 1992). The print is a kind of fundamental symbol, a miniature, static and stylized, but essentially unambiguous, token of a living thing. These signs are part of the sensory wake that animals produce as they move through the world, and that cumulatively manifests itself as a trail. Inuit existed in a world that was perpetually overwritten with the tracks of animals.

Inuit and animal movements

Like all hunter-fisher-gatherers, Inuit organized themselves spatially in coordination with the anticipated movements of animals (and maturing of plants) at different times of year. The traditional processualist notion of a subsistence-settlement system reflects precisely this tactical orchestration of human-resource co-presence at locations suitable for human harvesting. Game was acquired in a variety of landscape settings and using a variety of more or less distinct strategies, including chance encounter, deliberate stalking, passive trapping, and active driving. Most involved the intersection of human and animal paths along game trails.

Any animal might be killed if it strayed into a person's path, whether purely by accident or while a hunter was on a more deliberate tramp or paddle across land, ice, or water seeking such encounters. In many cases, this occurred along visible game trails, but the hunter might follow tracks, spoor, and other visual cues wherever they might lead. The use of dogs to detect animal scents was not only important for tracking on land but for locating seal breathing holes on the winter sea ice that would then be watched by a hunter (Boas 1964 [1888]; Jenness 1922; Rasmussen 1931). Traps could be bulky, such as the baited stone beehive constructions used to capture arctic fox, or spare, such as the fine baleen snares laid along the trails used by small mammals. Both of these are static, and dependent on the hunter's having identified an active trail or frequent travel route. One of the most cunning involved the insertion of a bent, sharpened segment of baleen in a chunk of frozen blubber; when it warmed inside a wolf's stomach it sprang straight, killing the animal at the end of its tracks (Mathiassen 1927). Animal trails, tracks, and breathing hole networks constituted the dispersed sites for the extraction of food and fuel using a massive inventory of harvesting equipment and learned skills.

Breathing hole sealing, in particular, depended on an exceedingly complex, Rube Goldberg-like setup of humans, non-human animals, and things: the hunter, dressed in multiple animal skin garments; a dog, sometimes harnessed in teams to a wood-and-whale-bone sled; an array of specialized gear, including a slender bone probe for detecting the location, size, and lie of a breathing hole, a muskox horn scoop for clearing the hole, a down indicator to warn of a seal exhaling in the hole, a composite toggling harpoon for securing a line to the prey, a stand on which to rest the harpoon, a stool for the waiting hunter; and sometimes multiple hunters so equipped to monitor several holes; and of course the seal itself, and its network of breathing holes painstakingly scratched out from beneath and then diligently maintained as the sea ice thickens over the course of the winter. The resulting paths of humans and animals include the coordinated movements of hunter and dog between camp and breathing hole, and the submarine rounds of the seal in its mirrored world. The hunter's elaborate technological arsenal was necessary to fix the surface and subsurface worlds long enough that game could be extracted from the latter.

The notion that hunter, equipment, game, and path represented a particularly meaningful array is borne out by the figurative art produced by precontact Inuit, in which this arrangement figures repeatedly. The most common examples are simple stick figure scenes incised on everyday equipment (typically drill bows and the handles of men's knives) that depict boatloads of hunters pursuing and harpooning bowhead whales, sometimes in concert with kayakers (e.g., Maxwell 1983; McCartney 1980). These whaling scenes represent a duly obsessive interest in a principal harvesting activity (at least in much of the precontact Central Arctic; McCartney [ed.] 1979; Savelle and McCartney 1994; Whitridge 2002), and a particular concern with the moment at which the paths of all participants intersected (Whitridge 2004b). Although a path is not explicitly indicated, a line frequently demarcates the surface of the water, which represents both the plane across which the hunter travels and the hinge between the human and cetacean worlds. More complex marine trails can be envisaged, however, such as the oceanic currents and blooms travelled by plankton, fish, and their mammalian predators, or the leads that predictably open between landfast ice and floe edge in spring, providing passage for marine mammals. Indeed, it was precisely the latter that recurrently brought bowheads to the principal whaling zones of the Central Arctic.

Rather than merely making passive use of recurrent trails (whether with ambushes or traps) hunters may also strategically interfere with animal travel routes through the deployment of fences, static decoys, deliberately set fires, and human drivers in concert with natural topographic features. Prey can be encouraged to shift its program of action, so as to better align it with human intentions. The bison drive systems and jumps used by Plains First Nations for millennia are the best known North American examples (e.g., Brink 2008), but analogous setups were used for other game (white-tailed deer, pronghorn, hare, etc.) in different regions. Inuit constructed elaborate features to channel the movements of various kinds of prey, especially stone weirs (saputiit) spanning streams to pen anadromous char, and substantial stone-and-turf drive systems for harvesting migrating caribou (e.g., for the Eastern Arctic: Brink 2005; Grønnow et al. 1983; McGhee 1972; Stewart et al. 2004; Taylor 1972). The latter were typically composed of stacked boulders, or inuksuit (sing. inuksuk, literally 'acting in the capacity of a person'; Hallendy 1994), arranged in long converging lines, and sometimes fences constructed of stakes, brush, or stone (Brink 2005:20–24; Burch 1998:40–43). They were used in concert with drivers on land and hunters, the latter both in kayaks and stationed on land where the lines of cairns narrowed.

Inuksuit systems deployed hunters' understandings of general caribou behavior and local movement patterns, and strategically intervened to align the animals' trails with humanly-devised ones. The nexus of hunters, trail, and caribou is depicted on

FIGURE 12.2 End-slotted antler knife handle from the precontact Inuit site of Qariaraqyuk (PaJs-2), Nunavut. The incised design depicts a kayaker, caribou, archer, and inuksuk.

an end-slotted knife handle (Figure 12.2) from the site of Qariaraqyuk (PaJs-2) in the central Canadian Arctic (ca. 1200–1450 AD; Whitridge 1999). One side shows kayakers hunting what appear to be swimming caribou, and the other a kayaker, caribou, hunter with bow and arrow, and what appears to be an inuksuk (although actual precontact inuksuit exist throughout the Eastern Arctic [e.g., Brink 2005; Hallendy 2000; Savelle 1987], this seems to be the only reported depiction of its kind). The implied scenario is one that was repeated seasonally for centuries all across the Eastern Arctic: in concert with armed kayakers, caribou (perhaps guided first into a lake) have been channeled along the shore by inuksuit, to be dispatched by waiting archers. Inuksuit assumed a wide variety of functions (Hallendy 1994, 2000) but were principally a wayfinding technology, marking locations and travel routes in a way that could be read at a distance. The inuksuit tuktunnutiit (Hallendy 2000:48) that figured in caribou drive systems evoke an artificially managed itinerary, like that of the char funneled into the saputit's central pen, that guaranteed the intersection of human and animal paths.

A final example of archaeologically discernible trails is the complex network of surviving footpaths that connected late summer-fall dwellings (qarmat) with a communal ceremonial structure (qargi) at the site of PaJs-4 on southeast Somerset Island, not far from Qariaraqyuk (Savelle and Wenzel 2003; these paths are presently visible at 72° 05' 48" N, 94° 01' 45" W on Google Maps and Google Earth). Long term traffic to and from the qargi, likely by members of whaling crews, tamped down regular footpaths and produced durable, clearly visible ruts that crosscut the sparsely vegetated gravel beach ridges, connecting houses and house clusters to the community's focal structure. Animals of all kinds move redundantly across the landscape, whether out of necessity, convenience, familiarity, or safety.

Human and animal paths in Labrador

It has become a conventional ethnographic trope to depict the movements of humans on a landscape two-dimensionally, as a series of superimposed loops and squiggles and patches on a topographic map. *Inuit Land Use and Occupancy Project* (Freeman [ed.] 1976), *Our Footprints Are Everywhere* (Brice-Bennett [ed.] 1977), and other traditional use studies of hunter's recalled paths, and more recently GPS-based logs of electronically monitored paths, have fixed this image in the Arctic anthropologist's imagination. This sort of depiction is homologous with the conventional, and similarly two-dimensional, representations of animal territories and paths, whether a summary distribution map or, like the GPS track, a precise record of radio- or satellite-tagged movements (Fancy et al. 1989). While this constitutes an improvement over the static geometric modeling of earlier generations of spatial analysis, the perspective has hardly changed: it is still remote, satellitic, two-dimensional, that of a voyeur-god for de Certeau (1984:93), or the eye that "fucks the world" in Haraway's (1991:189) memorable phrase. While this style of spatial representation is not ineffective – indeed, it seems archaeologically inescapable, given the collapsed, compressed, and nearly two-dimensional character of many archaeological traces – we do need to recognize that it embodies a distinctively situated perspective – that of the lofty outsider. Other perspectives, including those of animals (grounded insiders) are also interesting, and might even be analytically rewarding. This demands that we descend to ground level and look outwards, adopting the sort of democratic perspective represented on the Qariaraqyuk knife handle, where caribou, hunter, and inuksuk (animal, human, and thing) are adjacent and similarly scaled. Recent cooperative research addressing Inuit, Iñupiat, and Yupik traditional knowledge (Aporta 2009; Gearheard et al. 2011; Krupnik et al. [eds.] 2010) is similarly grounded, adopting the perspectives of hunters as they travel over the land and sea ice.

Conducting fieldwork in the Arctic, the movements of animals in the land-, sea-, and ice-scapes are readily apparent. Not only are wild taxa abundant that are missing from many humanly modified ecosystems – cervids, wild canids, ursids – but the lack of trees and buildings makes their movements visible at a distance. A herd of harp seals swimming up the fjord or a polar bear walking alone along the shore can sometimes be observed from kilometers away, distinguished by their spatial setting and pattern of movement even when their bodies cannot be clearly discerned. Moreover, in the virtual absence of humans, beyond the odd hunter or scientist, the paths that animals utilize are frequently visible and distinct. What one might assume to be a trackless waste is in fact threaded with tracks and trails. Some of these are tiny. The trails produced by microtine rodents represent microcosms of the networks used by larger mammals (Figure 12.3a). Although these tiny trackways seem quaint, almost recreational, lemmings use them effectively to move incredibly quickly over uneven, boggy, or thickly vegetated terrain. They often lead to tunnels or other cover, to allow quick escape from raptors and mustelids. The latter produce tracks, but like the larger carnivores do not carve out their own rutted pathways.

FIGURE 12.3 Game trails in northern Labrador: a) lemming trail running through Inuit tent ring; b) polar bear paw prints; c) caribou trail crossing Dorset site; d) caribou trail reused by archaeologists.

Arctic carnivores seem to prefer to utilize their prey's existing trails, or none at all (Figure 12.3b), whereas herbivores are the great trail makers. In some cases, this seems to be a mere byproduct of huge numbers of animals traversing the landscape. The George River caribou herd of northern Quebec and Labrador numbered around 800,000 in the late 1980s (Boudreau et al. 2003; Couturier et al. 1990), although now it is substantially smaller. In areas with a large summer population, the movements of such a vast number of animals easily result in dense networks of crisscrossing paths (Boudreau and Payette 2004). At the coastal margins of their distribution, however, smaller numbers of animals move across the landscape more selectively and redundantly, resulting in simple, if somewhat sporadic, trails. These trails are valuable archaeologically, since they may expose buried site deposits (Figure 12.3c; see also Thomson 1985). They also represent the easiest paths of movement across a landscape that is sometimes boggy and often covered with a nearly continuous layer of knee-high willow. Out of pure convenience, we regularly employed these trails in commutes from our field camp to the site of Nachvak Village (IgCx-3), a precontact Inuit winter settlement in northern Labrador (Fig 12.3d), while conducting archaeological research there in the mid-2000s. Other animals sometimes used these trails as well. Polar bears and wolves were occasionally seen on them, and black bear and arctic fox occur in the area and almost certainly use them. Caribou, bears, wolves, and humans are sufficiently close in body size that a 20cm wide path broken through dense vegetation can present an equally attractive travel route to all, at least for a time.

Like Inuit elsewhere, northern Labrador groups traditionally utilized an array of sophisticated travel technologies where appropriate: crampon-like "ice creepers" for walking on ice, dogs to carry packs and pull sleds on land and ice, multi-person skin boats for ocean travel, and single-person kayaks for both freshwater and saltwater use. Most of these produce some durable trace (e.g., the ubiquitous sled shoes and dog trace buckles or the occasional kayak paddle tips). They also systematically utilized trails pioneered by game for a variety of purposes. These included pursuing the very game that produced the trails, and traveling tens of kilometers to specialized harvesting sites in the interior during the warm season. Trails, both short and long, were employed to avoid stormy headlands while traveling by kayak, and as shortcuts across a tortuous, deeply indented coastline. Indeed, a common style of rapid summer travel involved alternately paddling and portaging a light kayak (weighing as little as 15kg; Arima 1994:195). Maps of the Labrador coast produced by Moravian missionaries in the late eighteenth and nineteenth centuries are interesting collations of Inuit knowledge (mainly in the form of place names that indexed a mass of cultural information) and European style cartography, and often include dashed lines that represent the overland portions of extended travel routes.

Place names and itineraries that were discussed, taught, performed, visited, and travelled constituted the primary archive of geographical knowledge (Wheeler 1953), but Inuit produced physical maps where the situation demanded it. These were typically incised in snow or sand for the benefit of an Inuk traveler, but solid versions carved out of wood or ivory or drawn with pen and paper were collected by Euro–American explorers (Spencer 1959; Spink and Moodie 1972; Whitridge 2004a). Another genre of geographical discourse was the depiction of a location in figurative art. Only the inuksuk in the knife handle harvesting setup in Figure 12.2 is a durable landscape feature, and bowhead whaling scenes from the Canadian Arctic do not include shoreline. Occasionally, however, more concrete spatial information is provided, such as the tents, qariyit, and ground surface depicted in some precontact engravings (e.g., Maxwell 1983), or the base of a miniature soapstone pot from Nachvak Village incised with a representation of what appears to be a mountainous coastline (Figure 12.4; Whitridge 2012). The mountains resemble those visible from the site where the miniature was recovered, and evoke the seasonal round of movement between coastal villages and caribou hunting camps in the mountainous interior. Indeed, this object encapsulates a characteristic landscape setting in northern Labrador.

FIGURE 12.4 Base of miniature soapstone pot from Nachvak Village with likely depiction of mountainous coastline.

Immaterial paths

If the paths of humans and animals are to be considered symmetrically, it also seems appropriate to consider the movements of other things in the world. Clouds, wind, snow, rain, and changing light animate the atmosphere, while water flows and breaks in waves, rivulets, streams, rivers, and ocean currents, and freezes into sheets or vast sea ice platforms. Rock, sediment, and soil creep and boil imperceptibly, or collapse catastrophically. In the Inuit world, many of these phenomena were recognized as quasi-sentient agents in their own right. The site of Nachvak Village, for example, looks out across Nachvak Fjord to the sheer north face of Kutyaupak, a peak in the Torngat Mountains that marks the juncture of Tallek and Tasiuyak Arms with the main body of the fjord. The churning of ocean currents in winter gives rise to perpetually fractured and refrozen sea ice, and the early appearance of open water. The polynya is a magnet for seals, and accounts for the siting of a major winter village here. During fieldwork, the strong winds that funnel along the fjord arms and meet here were frequently observed to give rise to whirlwinds that became visible as they picked up spray and travelled for hundreds of meters up the fjord. The sun heating the rock face precipitated frequent massive rock falls, which sent dusty clouds of debris crashing 750 meters to the water below. The unusually animated quality of the atmosphere, land, and water here was likely a distinctive quality of the place for its occupants, and helped give rise to its reputation as a "big" place that was home to the dangerous deity Torngâsok (Whitridge 2012).

Torngâsok and other agentic entities – spirits or torngait – took weird, unnatural forms, and some creatures shifted between forms, like the shaman or angagok who might become a bear or fly through the air, or both. A man from Clyde River (Kanngiqtugaapik) who showed me winter caribou hunting on Baffin Island in March 1991 recounted having seen a set of bear tracks that simply ended in the middle of the fjord ice, as if the creature had taken flight. Paths passed from one dimension to another and traversed enormous distances, as in the world-encompassing wanderings of the Inupiat culture hero Qayak (Oman 1995). The fundamental kinship of a wide array of sentient beings – caribou, wolf, bear, fox, human, torngak – is figured in their movement along the same trails. They take different forms, have different powers, pursue different interests but, for one reason or another, all need to make their way through the world, from place to place (Ingold 2009).

Tangible representations of otherworldly or immaterial paths occasionally occur in the Inuit record. A spectacular example from Alaska is illustrated by Hoffman (1895:923–24). An anagagok, together with a helper playing a drum, conducts a shamanic séance inside a structure; a line issues from the anagagok to a flying figure – probably the same person – who visits a bowhead whale. This appears to depict one of the customary roles of the anagagok, who was hired to visit the whale ahead of the hunt and ensure its cooperation (Rainey 1947; Spencer 1959). The notion of immaterial power lines linking various agentic entities is widespread cross-culturally, and evokes networks of supernatural paths analogous to the trails

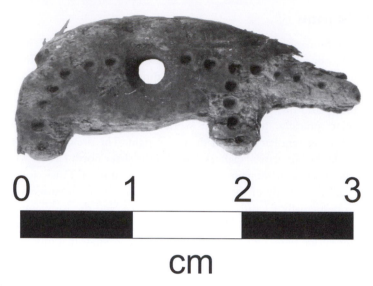

FIGURE 12.5 Tooth or walrus ivory pendant from Nachvak Village depicting stylized polar bear.

connecting humans and animals in the everyday world (like the dreamt trails along which Dene realize future hunting success; Ridington 1990).

Less explicit than the anagagok's ethereal tether are the abstract patterns of lines and dots that are often incised on Inuit tools, ornaments, and amulets. These constitute pathways of sight and touch that emphasize an object's beauty, its length or girth, or the energy immanent within it, and, like the lines of text on this page, guide the mind of the viewer toward a comprehension of the thing. A miniature bear from Nachvak (Figure 12.5), centrally pierced for suspension, has lines of dots issuing from the legs and following the curve of the body to the snout. The dots ambiguously evoke various things: the stylized bones depicted on pre-Inuit (Dorset) "X-ray" carvings of bears (LeMoine et al. 1995); purely decorative flourishes (though these are absent on the larger wooden bear figurines that are likely toys); the power points sometimes shown at the joints of Inupiat carvings and marked on Inuit bodies through tattooing; and the footprints left by actual bears in snow or earth, like those in Figure 12.3b. The animal's body is here a canvas onto which any number of esoteric and sensual understandings may be projected, fossilizing a visual track imagined by the carver. Trails can be meaningful and powerful without necessarily being walkable.

Discussion and conclusion

Animals gravitate toward trails. They often represent the most direct or convenient routes through a landscape – along a ridge free of mosquitoes, around a mountain, toward a water source – but inevitably, and perhaps most importantly, they are the routes most frequently travelled by other animals, whether conspecifics or prey.

Humans in turn map onto game trails, so human spatial practices are inseparable from those of non-human animals. In the roadless terrain of precontact northern Labrador, overland travel routes used by people were used initially, and simultaneously, by animals. The human-animal co-production of the landscape was a discursive hinge of much Inuit representational art, but this was less the case for subsequent Euro-Canadian occupants of the north. The spatial imagery employed by the political regimes of the last few centuries is diverse and expressive, but aims at an ever more precise and encompassing inorganic control of the landscape whose present culmination seems to be the GIS layered over satellite imagery. Even at its most technologically complex, in the form of an enormous cybernetic web of strategically situated cairns, Inuit negotiation of their relationship to the landscape represented a collaboration with animals: the inuksuk is simultaneously a wayfinding device and a technology for directing the movement of game.

The manufactured roadway is only one materialization of human route following. It leaves the most durable trace, and has acquired an archetypal inevitability, but other categories of path were more important to people in the past and continue to organize many aspects of our spatial existence. These include ephemeral traces (prints), durable tracks (both humanly created ones and co-opted game trails), sensory traces (visual, auditory, olfactory), conceptual routes (imagined, remembered, dreamt), and the representations (maps, models, illustrations) that guide the latter. All of these were important to Inuit in the past, and all were shared with animals in some fashion.

Archaeologically, the Arctic perhaps represents a peculiar case of human and animal paths, one in which the animal trails take clear precedence over the human ones. In other times and places, human road networks have been far more visible and more important to their users, and many places fall somewhere in between. Nevertheless, the homology between human and non-human trail use in the Arctic seems important. It reminds us of the underlying continuity between humans' and other animals' path-making and -using, and the ultimate priority of the latter. It suggests a useful approach to the archaeological and ethnographic records, focusing not only on the spatial distribution of sites, but also on the material representations of places, paths, and animals. It suggests a practical research tack on hunter-fisher-gatherer trail networks. In an area such as northern Labrador that has been progressively abandoned by Inuit hunters over the past century, there is enormous potential to explore the articulation of game trails and archaeological traces of Inuit use of the interior, particularly for late summer caribou hunting. It also encourages us to attend to the role of domestic animals – horses, yaks, llamas, dogs – in contributing to path production and maintenance in settings of denser human settlement. Non-human paths have been an integral part of human path use for ages, indeed since a time when we were non-human animals ourselves.[1]

Note

1 Many thanks to Christopher Watts for the invitation to expand on these thoughts and for suggestions that improved the text, and to James Flexner for inviting me to participate in the session "Archaeological Cartographies" at the 2011 Society for American

Archaeology meeting in Sacramento, where the ideas first took shape. Fieldwork in northern Labrador was supported by the Social Sciences and Humanities Research Council of Canada, Canadian Foundation for Innovation, Wenner-Gren Foundation for Anthropological Research, J. R. Smallwood Foundation and Institute for Social and Economic Research at Memorial University, and the Newfoundland and Labrador Provincial Archaeology Office (PAO). The Torngâsok Cultural Centre, PAO, and Parks Canada provided permission to conduct this research, and field assistants from Nain and Memorial University were instrumental in its success.

Bibliography

Anderson, Douglas D., 1988. *Onion Portage: The Archaeology of a Stratified Site from the Kobuk River, Northwest Alaska*. Anthropological Papers No. 22. University of Alaska, Fairbanks.

Aporta, Claudio, 2009. The Trail as Home: Inuit and Their Pan-Arctic Network of Routes. *Human Ecology* 37:131–46.

Arima, Eugene, 1994. Caribou and Iglulik Inuit Kayaks. *Arctic* 47(2):193–95.

Boas, Franz, 1964 [1888]. *The Central Eskimo*. University of Nebraska Press, Lincoln.

Boudreau, Stéphane, Serge Payette, Claude Morneau, and Serge Couturier, 2003. Recent Decline of the George River Caribou Herd as Revealed by Tree-Ring Analysis. *Arctic, Antarctic, and Alpine Research* 35(2):187–95.

Boudreau, Stéphane, and Serge Payette, 2004. Caribou-Induced Changes in Species Dominance of Lichen Woodlands: An Analysis of Plant Remains. *American Journal of Botany* 91(3):422–29.

Brice Bennett, Carol (editor), 1977. *Our Footprints Are Everywhere: Inuit Land Use and Occupancy in Labrador*. Labrador Inuit Association, Nain.

Brink, Jack, 2005. *Inukshuk:* Caribou Drive Lanes on Southern Victoria Island, Nunavut, Canada. *Arctic Anthropology* 42(1):1–28.

——(2008). *Imagining Head-Smashed-In*. Athabasca University Press, Edmonton.

Brunning, Richard, David Hogan, Julie Jones, Mark Jones, Ed Maltby, Mark Robinson, and Vanessa Straker, 2000. Saving the Sweet Track: The *In Situ* Preservation of a Neolithic Wooden Trackway, Somerset, UK. *Conservation and Management of Archaeological Sites* 4:3–20.

Burch, Ernest S., Jr., 1998. *The Iñupiaq Eskimo Nations of Northwest Alaska*. University of Alaska Press, Fairbanks.

Coles, Bryony, and John M. Coles, 1986. *Sweet Track to Glastonbury*. Thames and Hudson, New York.

Couturier, Serge, Josée Brunelle, Denis Vandal, and Guy St-Martin, 1990. Changes in the Population Dynamics of the George River Caribou Herd, 1976–87. *Arctic* 43(1):9–20.

Dawson, Peter C., 2002. Space Syntax Analysis of Central Inuit Snow Houses. *Journal of Anthropological Archaeology* 21(4):464–80.

de Certeau, Michel, 1984. *The Practice of Everyday Life*. University of California Press, Berkeley.

Dore, Christopher, and Stephen McElroy, 2011. Automated Trail Identification and Mapping: An Experiment in Archaeological Spectral-Image Analysis Using Commercial High-Resolution Satellite Remote-Sensing Data. *Archaeological Practice*, January 2011, pp. 12–18.

Fancy, S., L. Pank, K. Whitten, and W. Regelin, 1989. Seasonal Movements of Caribou in Arctic Alaska as Determined by Satellite. *Canadian Journal of Zoology* 67:644–50.

Freeman, Milton M. R. (editor), 1976. *Inuit Land Use and Occupancy Project, Volume One: Land Use and Occupancy*. Department of Indian and Northern Affairs, Ottawa.

Gearheard, Shari, Claudio Aporta, Gary Aipilee, and Clyde O'Keefe, 2011. The Igliniit Project: Inuit Hunters Document Life on the Trail to Map and Monitor Arctic Change. *The Canadian Geographer* 55(1):42–55.

Gell, Alfred, 1996. Vogel's Net: Traps as Artworks and Artworks as Traps. *Journal of Material Culture* 1:15–38.

Grønnow, Bjarne, Morten Meldgaard, and Jørn Berglund Nielsen, 1983. *Aasivissuit – The Great Summer Camp: Archaeological, Ethnographical and Zoo-Archaeological Studies of a Caribou-Hunting Site in West Greenland*. Meddelelser om Grønland – Man and Society No. 5, Copenhagen.

Hallendy, Norman, 1994. *Inuksuit*: Semalithic Figures Constructed by Inuit in the Canadian Arctic. In *Threads of Arctic Prehistory: Papers in Honour of William E. Taylor, Jr.*, edited by David Morrison and Jean-Luc Pilon, pp. 385–408. Mercury Series Paper No. 149. Archaeological Survey of Canada, Canadian Museum of Civilization, Hull, Québec.

——(2000). Inuksuit: *Silent Messengers of the Arctic*. British Museum Press, London.

Haraway, Donna, 1991. *Simians, Cyborgs, and Women: The Reinvention of Nature*. Routledge, New York.

Heidegger, Martin, 1977. Building, Dwelling, Thinking. In *Basic Writings / Martin Heidegger*, edited by David Farrell Krell, pp. 319–39. Harper, San Francisco.

Hoffman, Walter James, 1895. *The Graphic Art of the Eskimos, Based Upon the Collections in the National Museum*. Report of the United States National Museum for 1895, Washington, D.C.

Ingold, Tim, 2009. Against Space: Place, Movement, Knowledge. In *Boundless Worlds: An Anthropological Approach to Movement*, edited by Peter Wynn Kirby, pp. 29–43. Berghahn Books, New York.

Jenkins, David, 2001. A Network Analysis of Inka Roads, Administrative Centers, and Storage Facilities. *Ethnohistory* 48(4):655–87.

Jenness, Diamond, 1922. *Life of the Copper Eskimos*. Report of the Canadian Arctic Expedition 1913–18, Vol. XII, Part A, Ottawa.

Keyser, James D., 1992. *Indian Rock Art of the Columbia Plateau*. University of Washington Press, Seattle.

Krupnik, Igor, Claudio Aporta, Shari Gearhead, Gita Laidler, and Lene Kielsen Holm (editors), 2010. *SIKU: Knowing Our Ice: Documenting Inuit Sea-Ice Knowledge and Use*. Springer, New York.

Latour, Bruno, 1988. Mixing Humans and Nonhumans Together: The Sociology of a Door-closer. *Social Problems* 35:298–310.

Leakey, M. D., and R. L. Hay, 1979. Pliocene Footprints in the Laetoli Beds at Laetoli, Northern Tanzania. *Nature* 278:317–23.

Lefebvre, Henri, 1991. *The Production of Space*. Blackwell, Oxford.

LeMoine, Genevieve, James Helmer, and Donald Hanna, 1995. Altered States: Human–Animal Transformational Images in Dorset Art. In *The Symbolic Role of Animals in Archaeology*, edited by Kathleen Ryan and Pam J. Crabtree, pp. 38–49. MASCA Research Papers in Science and Archaeology, Vol. 12. The University Museum of Archaeology and Anthropology, University of Pennsylvania, Philadelphia.

Liu, Alexander, Duncan McIlroy, and Martin Braisier, 2010. First Evidence for Locomotion in the Ediacaran Biota from the 565 Ma Mistaken Point Formation, Newfoundland. *Geology* 38(2):123–26.

Mathiassen, Therkel, 1927. *Archaeology of the Central Eskimo*. Report of the Fifth Thule Expedition 1921–24, Vol. 4(1–2). Gyldendalske Boghandel, Copenhagen.

Maxwell, Moreau S., 1983. A Contemporary Ethnography from the Thule Period. *Arctic Anthropology* 20(1):79–87.

McCartney, Allen P. (editor), 1979. *Archaeological Whalebone: A Northern Resource*. Archaeological Papers No. 1. University of Arkansas, Fayetteville.

McCartney, Allen P., 1980. The Nature of Thule Eskimo Whale Use. *Arctic* 33:517–41.

McGhee, Robert, 1972. *Copper Eskimo Prehistory*. Publications in Archaeology No. 2. National Museum of Man, Ottawa.

Menze, Bjoern H., and Jason A. Ur, 2012. Mapping Patterns of Long-Term Settlement in Northern Mesopotamia at a Large Scale. *Proceedings of the National Academy of Sciences of the United States*, early edition, March 19, 2012.

Müller-Wille, Ludger (editor), 1987. *Gazetteer of Inuit Place Names in Nunavik (Quebec, Canada)*. Avataq Cultural Institute, Inukjuak.

Oman, Leila Kiana, 1995. *The Epic of Qayak: The Longest Story Ever Told by My People*. McGill-Queen's University Press, Montreal.

Rainey, Froelich G., 1947. *The Whale Hunters of Tigara*. Anthropological Papers of the American Museum of Natural History, Vol. 41(2), New York.

Rasmussen, Knud, 1931. *The Netsilik Eskimos: Social Life and Spiritual Culture.* Report of the Fifth Thule Expedition 1921–24, vol. 8(1/2), Gyldendalske Boghandel, Nordisk Forlag, Copenhagen.

Reynolds, Andrew, 1995. Avebury, Yatesbury and the Archaeology of Communications. *Papers from the Institute of Archaeology* 6:21–30.

Ridington, Robin, 1990. *Little Bit Know Something: Stories in a Language of Anthropology.* Douglas and McIntyre, Vancouver.

Savelle, James M., 1987. *Collectors and Foragers: Subsistence-Settlement Systems in the Central Canadian Arctic, AD 1000–1960.* BAR International Series 358. British Archaeological Reports, Oxford.

Savelle, James M., and Allen P. McCartney, 1994. Thule Inuit Bowhead Whaling: A Biometrical Analysis. In *Threads of Arctic Prehistory: Papers in Honour of William E. Taylor, Jr.,* edited by David Morrison and Jean-Luc Pilon, pp. 281–310. Mercury Series Paper No. 149. Canadian Museum of Civilization, Hull, Québec.

Savelle, James M., and George W. Wenzel, 2003. Out of Alaska: Reconstructing the Social Structure of Prehistoric Canadian Thule Culture. In *Hunter-Gatherers of the North Pacific Rim,* edited by Junko Habu, James Savelle, Shuzo Koyama, and Hitomi Hongo, pp. 103–21. Senri Ethnological Studies No. 63. National Museum of Ethnology, Osaka.

Snead, James, Clark Erickson, and Andrew Darling (editors), 2009. *Landscapes of Movement: Trails, Paths, and Roads in Anthropological Perspective.* University of Pennsylvania Museum of Archaeology and Anthropology, Philadelphia.

Spencer, Robert F., 1959. *The North Alaskan Eskimo: A Study in Ecology and Society.* Bulletin No. 171. Bureau of American Ethnology, Smithsonian Institution, Washington, D.C.

Spink, J., and D. W. Moodie, 1972. *Eskimo Maps from the Canadian Eastern Arctic.* Cartographica Monograph No. 5. Department of Geography, York University, Toronto.

Stewart, Andrew, Darren Keith, and Joan Scottie, 2004. Caribou Crossings and Cultural Meanings: Placing Traditional Knowledge and Archaeology in Context in an Inuit Landscape. *Journal of Archaeological Method and Theory* 11(3):183–211.

Taylor, William E., Jr., 1972. *An Archaeological Survey between Cape Parry and Cambridge Bay, N.W.T., Canada in 1963.* Mercury Series Paper No. 1. Archaeological Survey of Canada, National Museum of Man, Ottawa.

Thomson, Callum, 1985. Caribou Trail Archaeology: 1985 Investigation of Saglek Bay and Inner Saglek Fjord. In *Archaeology in Newfoundland and Labrador 1985,* edited by Jane Sproull Thomson and Callum Thomson, pp. 9–53. Annual Report No. 6. Newfoundland Museum Historic Resources Division, Government of Newfoundland and Labrador.

van Tilburg, Cornelis, 2007. *Traffic and Congestion in the Roman Empire.* Routledge, London.

Wheeler, E. P., 1953. *List of Labrador Eskimo Place Names.* Bulletin No. 131, Anthropological Series No. 34, National Museum of Canada, Ottawa.

Whitridge, Peter, 1999. "The Construction of Social Difference in a Prehistoric Inuit Whaling Community". Unpublished Ph.D. dissertation, Department of Anthropology, Arizona State University, Tempe.

——(2002). Social and Ritual Determinants of Whale Bone Transport at a Classic Thule Winter Site in the Canadian Arctic. *International Journal of Osteoarchaeology* 12:65–75.

——(2004a). Landscapes, Houses, Bodies, Things: "Place" and the Archaeology of Inuit Imaginaries. *Journal of Archaeological Method and Theory* 11(2):213–50.

——(2004b). Whales, Harpoons, and Other Actors: Actor-Network Theory and Hunter-Gatherer Archaeology. In *Hunters and Gatherers in Theory and Archaeology,* edited by George Crothers, pp. 445–74. Occasional Paper No. 31. Center for Archaeological Investigations, Southern Illinois University, Carbondale.

——(2012). Invented Places: Environmental Imaginaries and the Inuit Colonization of Labrador. In *Settlement, Subsistence, and Change among the Labrador Inuit: The Nunatsiavummiut Experience,* edited by David Natcher, Larry Felt, and Andrea Procter, pp. 43–60. University of Manitoba Press, Winnipeg.

13

THE MAZE AND THE LABYRINTH: REFLECTIONS OF A FELLOW-TRAVELLER

Tim Ingold

Are we cast, in life, into the corridors of a maze, or are we destined to follow the threads of a labyrinth? Perhaps you will think that the difference between the maze and the labyrinth is of minor semantic import, or that it hinges on a technicality, namely that the labyrinth – regardless of how convoluted it might be – prescribes only one path, whereas the maze offers multiple choices, the majority of which lead to dead ends. I believe, however, that the difference is profound, and that it gives us as good a starting point as any to enter the tangle of issues surrounding the question of what it might mean to adopt a relational approach to understanding the world and human ways of living in it.

In many respects, the maze epitomizes the predicament of modern metropolitan life. Whether over- or underground, whether navigating the streets or the metro, the city dweller has to find his way through a maze of passages flanked by walls or high buildings. Any particular passage, once selected, is impossible *not* to follow, since it is walled in on either side. These walls, however, are not usually bare. Rather, they are replete with advertisements, window displays, and the like, which continually remind the traveller of possible side-tracks he might choose to take, as and when the opportunity arises, to satisfy his desires. Every time there is a fork in the way, a decision has to be taken: to go to the left, to the right, or possibly straight ahead. A journey through the maze may thus be represented as a stochastic sequence of moves punctuated by decision-points, such that every move is predicated upon the preceding decision. That is to say, it is an essentially game-like, strategic enterprise. This is not to deny, of course, the tactical manoeuvring that goes on as pedestrians and even drivers jostle with one another in making their ways through the throng of a busy street or subway. But negotiating a passage through the throng is one thing; finding a way through the maze quite another.

In the labyrinth, by contrast, the problem is to follow the path. Here, choice is not an issue. The labyrinth commands you to follow. You cannot just decide to read it differently or to adopt a different perspective. However the path is not always easy to see, and you have continually to keep your wits about you so as not to lose the thread. Like the hunter tracking an animal or a hiker on the trail, it is important to remain alert to the subtle signs – footprints, piles of stones, nicks cut in the trunks of trees – that indicate the way ahead. Thus signs keep you on the path; they do not, like advertisements, tempt you away from it. The danger lies not in coming to a dead end, but in wandering off the track. Death is a deviation, not the end of the line. At no point in the labyrinth do you come to an abrupt stop. No buffers, or walls, block your onward movement. You are rather fated to carry on, nevertheless along a path that, if you are not careful, may take you ever further from the living, to whose community you may never make it back. In the labyrinth you may indeed take the wrong turn, but not by choice. For at the time, you did not notice that the path divided. You were sleep-walking, or dreaming. Indigenous hunters often tell of those who, lured on by the prey they are following, drift into the prey's world, in which the animals appear to them as human. There they carry on their lives while lost, presumed dead, to their own people.

The maze puts all the emphasis on the navigator's intentions. He has an aim in mind, a destination, and is determined to reach it. This may, of course, be broken down into a number of subsidiary objectives. And it may also be complicated by all the other competing aims that assail him from all sides. Choices are never clear-cut, and they are rarely taken with sufficient information as not to leave a considerable margin of uncertainty. In the maze, however, the outward cast of action follows the inward cast of thought. When we say that action is intentional, we mean that a mind is at work, operating from within the actor and lending the action a purpose and direction beyond what the physical laws of motion would alone dictate. Intentions distinguish the travellers in a maze from the balls in a game of bagatelle which – we suppose – have no idea of where they are heading and are quite incapable of deliberating whether to go in one way or another. In the labyrinth, by contrast, path-following is *attentional*. The follower has no objective save to carry on, to keep on going. But to do so, his action must be closely and continually coupled with his perception – that is, by an ever-vigilant monitoring of the path as it unfolds. Simply put, you have to watch where you are going, and to listen and feel as well. Of course there is a mind at work in the attentional wayfaring of the labyrinth, just as there is in the intentional navigation of the maze. But this is a mind immanent in the movement itself rather than an originating source to which such movement may be attributed as an effect.

It was in reference to such an originating source that the notion of agency first entered the literature. Everyone agreed that all human beings were agents. Indeed, this seemed almost a truism. Being human ourselves, do we not know from experience that we have the power to initiate actions, and that these actions have effects? That all humans are agents is one thing, however; that all agents are human quite another. And on this there has been sharp and still continuing disagreement. There are those who would still insist that agency is conditional upon such properties of intentionality and self-awareness as define the state of the human, with the corollary that were any creatures of other-than-human ancestry found to possess such properties, then they would be human, too. Chimpanzees, dolphins, elephants, maybe even rats (which, as psychologists have shown, do very well in mazes), might turn out to be honorary humans! Others would allow that human beings may offload some of their agency onto the things around them, which can then act at a distance – as it were by proxy – on their behalf. These things thus become 'secondary agents' to the 'primary agency' that empowers them. This book, for example, in which you are now reading my words, is serving as a secondary agent for me, as it is for my fellow contributors. Yet others, however, go the whole hog and insist that assorted 'non-humans' have as much of a right to be credited with agency as any human. But who or what are these non-humans, and why – when their agency is at stake – are humans invariably in the frame as well?

When you look at the kinds of things that in the writings of theorists of agency, the word 'non-human' is commonly invoked to cover, they bear an uncanny resemblance to what were once known – in the days before we had woken up to the structuring force of the modern constitution on our habits of thought – as *objects*. And when you look at what the word 'human' covers, it looks suspiciously congruent to what we used to know collectively as *subjects*. Thus the old world of subjects and objects has become a new world of humans and non-humans. Has anything, apart from the nomenclature, actually changed? Has the traditional hierarchy of subjects and objects been replaced by a field in which humans and non-humans play on level terms? I am inclined to think not. For the attribution of agency to what were formerly known as objects rests on, and upholds, the assumption that humans enroll such objects into their lives in a way that no other creature does. It is, in other words, underpinned by the very claim to human uniqueness that drives classical evolutionary narratives of the rise of human civilization. That is why philosophers who still carry the intellectual baggage of the nineteenth century are content to speak of 'collectives of humans and non-humans,' yet would balk at the idea, for example, of 'collectives of rats and non-rats.'

We are, in effect, still in the maze. The non-humans are the objects and images that line the walls and that assail us with their temptations and demands. We can argue *ad nauseam*, as theorists do, about whether objects and images can have wants or desires of their own – about whether, like the effigies of that fairground ride known as the 'ghost train,' they can come out from the walls and threaten to strike passers-by – or whether such agency as they are deemed to possess is but a ventriloquistic projection of those who stalk the corridors. The outcome of this argument, however, does nothing to alter the fact that the division between humans and non-humans, in its current formulation, leaves no room for animate life – for growth and becoming, and for the contrapuntal flows of attentive awareness and vital materials that compose it. Consider, for example, our experimental rat. Are we to regard it as a quasi-human or as a non-human? If the former, then we would have to conclude that it navigates the maze, acting on its intentions, just as humans are supposed to do. If the latter, then it is no better than an effigy stuck to the wall. It might as well be an inanimate object. Either way, its actual life – its vitality and attentiveness – has fallen through the cracks.

Real rats, outside the psychologists' experiments with their artificial and constraining set-up, do not live in mazes. Nor are real human beings passengers in a ghost train. It is not that rats are agents, just as humans are. It is that in the real world, the language of agency is no more appropriate for humans than it is for rats. Both rats and humans, along with all other living beings, inhabit the labyrinth. Just as with intention and attention, it seems, agency and animacy pull in opposite directions. The more theorists speak about agency, the less they have to say about life. Indeed the language of agency remains as tied to cognitivism as the language of animacy to vitalism. And the way of animate life, I would contend, is not the maze but the labyrinth, or what I have elsewhere called the *meshwork*. The plant in its growth, in sending out roots, shoots, or tendrils, and the animal as it lays its trails on or in the ground, continually weaves its way into the meshwork, adding to its strands as it does so. In what sense, then, can life in the labyrinth be described as 'relational'? And when we speak of persons or things as 'bundles of relations,' what can we mean?

This idea is not new. As a student of social anthropology in the late 1960s, schooled in classical structural-functionalism, I was taught that the social person, as opposed to the biophysical individual, is *by definition* a bundle of relations. A man, for example, may be a husband, a father, an employee in a business, a patient on the register of a doctor, a worshipper in a particular congregation, and many other things besides. Each of these statuses implies a specific relation, with spouse, children, employer, doctor, church. Yet in this classical view, every relation was one link or joint in an assembly, the 'social structure,' into which the individual was to be inserted like a key in a lock. What is new in the kind of relational thinking that claims to have surpassed the structuralism of old is the idea that the constituents of the bundle are not abstract statuses, divorced from the flesh-and-blood human beings that fill them, but pathways of lived experience from which people craft themselves and one another. But if that is so, then the 'relation' has to be understood rather differently. Once again, the difference comes down to that between the maze and the labyrinth. We could, without too much distortion, re-describe the maze as a network, the lines of which are corridors and the points where they converge or divide. In the network, relations are between points. But the lines of the labyrinth or meshwork do not connect points. They simply carry on, as life itself carries on. Thus in the labyrinth, relations run not *between* but *along*. And so the 'bundle of relations' is literally that: a collection of life-lines wrapped up together like corn-stalks in a sheaf.

A relational approach, then, could take two forms. Either we stay with the maze, and speak the language of intention, agency, humans, and non-humans, or we enter the labyrinth, and speak the quite different language of attention, animacy, growth, and becoming. Most archaeologists and anthropologists, I suspect, are either torn between the two or trying to have it both ways. It is all too easy to treat key theoretical concepts as flags of convenience under which almost anything can sail. But the flag I would fly from my mast bears the insignia of life. I see a world not of embodied agents but of living, breathing beings. Life depends on respiration – that is, on the constant interchange of materials across the convoluted and permeable surfaces of what we call 'the body.' Bodies are poor containers; they continually leak, indeed their life depends on it. Through this leakage, they grow into the world as the world grows in them. But breathing in and breathing out are not exactly the reverse of one another. The first is a movement of gathering; the second is a movement of propulsion. In any process of life, there is a rhythmic alternation between the two. And this brings in an element that I have not so far considered, and that is indeed conspicuous by its absence from most theoretical accounts of being-in-the-world. This element is the atmosphere, taken in its broadest sense to include the mixtures, fluctuations, and illuminations of the aerial medium in which all terrestrial life is lived, and which make movement and perception possible.

It is easy to say that the living being is of the same flesh as the world that envelops it. Every being, in its movement, stitches itself into the fabric of this world, along the pathways of the labyrinth. This stitching, we could say, is haptic. Regardless of the sensory modality or combination of modalities involved, the being has continually to feel its way forward, following whatever clues it can pick up. But every living being, too, is necessarily immersed in an atmosphere. Is the flesh, then, meshwork or atmosphere? Is its perception haptic or atmospheric? The answer is that it is, alternately, both. It is atmospheric on the inhalation, and haptic on the exhalation. Meshwork and atmosphere are, if you will, two sides of the flesh, corresponding to the alternation of breathing out and in. And the living, respiring being is the site where atmospheric immersion is transformed into the growth of the meshwork along its proliferating lines. It is where the weather is turned into the furrows of the ploughman, the wind into the wake of the sailboat, and sunlight into the stems and roots of the plant. It is a transformation, indeed, that is fundamental to all animate life. And it is perhaps from this transformation – not in the interactions of embodied agents with images and objects, but in the polyphony of material flows and bodily kinaesthesia, performed under the arch of the sky – that a relational archaeology should take its point of departure.

INDEX

Page numbers in italics refer to figures and tables. Page numbers followed by an *n* refer to notes.